Φ

PHAIDON DESIGN CLASSICS VOLUME ONE

The 999 design classics included in this book have been chosen in consultation with a wide range of international design-world insiders. Academics, critics, historians, curators, journalists, designers and architects were asked to select industrially-manufactured objects that conform to our definition of a Phaidon Design Classic, as specified on the cover. Every object selected meets at least one of the criteria within our overall definition and many of them meet more than one.

The final choice of objects illustrated in this three-volume set is the result of a rigorous selection process and meticulous research. The collection includes a huge variety of consumer products, ranging from chairs to aeroplanes, which date from the Industrial Revolution to the present day. Garments, fashion accessories and objects that have been designed for highly specialist use, are not included.

Most of the objects are still in production and the majority of them are available to buy. When something is no longer manufactured, it is not usually because the design itself has become obsolete, but rather because the technology it was designed for has since become outdated.

To make the book as contemporary as possible we have also included objects created more recently. It is, of course, more difficult to judge which of the products created in more recent decades will eventually be regarded as classics, but we have included those we consider to be the 'classics of tomorrow' according, once again, to our definition.

001

Household Scissors (1663)
Zhang Xiaoquan (c.1643–83)
Hangzhou Zhang Xiaoquan 1663 to present

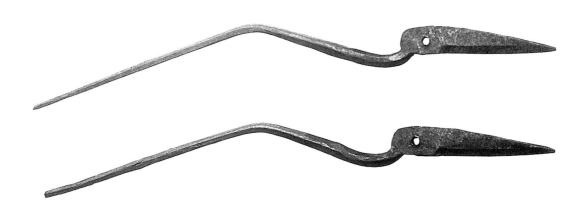

In China the Zhang Xiaoquan brand represents not only a pair of scissors but also a part of Chinese culture. It is said that every household in the country owns a pair. The Hangzhou Zhang Xiaoquan scissors factory has been in operation for over 300 years and now sells 120 types of scissors in 360 specifications, including sewing, garden, office, hairdressing and kitchen scissors. Their largest, 'King's Scissors', which are 115 cm (45 in) long and weigh 56 kilos (123 lb), are recorded in *The Guinness Book of Records*, while the smallest scissors are only 3 cm (1.2 in) long and weigh only a few grams. The original scissors are a beautiful example of simple, functional design. A copper rivet fixes two identical steel halves, each consisting of one blade and one hooped handle. The perfectly symmetrical design works for both right- and left-handed users. The scissors are lightweight, comfortable in the hand and extremely hard-wearing. In 1663 when the Zhang Dalong scissors factory in Hangzhou, Zhejiang province, was taken over by the son of its founder, it also took on its inheritor's name, Zhang Xiaoquan. From then until now the company has grown enormously and has enjoyed the patronage of China's emperors. A huge milestone in the history of the company came in 1956 when Chairman Mao, in his writings focussing on the socialist reconstruction of the handicraft industry, cited Zhang Xiaoquan scissors for their contribution to the nation and advised that the industry be developed. With substantial government backing, the new enterprise began to build larger premises and in 1958 the state-run factory was founded. The company is now continually ranked first in national quality evaluations and since 2000 has transformed from a state-run concern to a limited company. As a result of continued mechanization and technological advancement, the factory now produces a phenomenal 45 million pairs annually. Zhang Xiaoquan Household Scissors can be bought in 90 per cent of China and its sales make up 40 per cent of the Chinese scissors market.

Arare Teapot (1700s)
Designer Unknown
Various 1700s to present
Iwachu 1914 to present

It is not necessary to have visited Japan to be familiar with the Arare Teapot. Despite the fact that only Japanese nationals are likely to recognize the design by name, the ubiquitous presence of the teapot throughout Japan as an everyday piece of kitchen equipment has elevated this purposeful design into an international standard. Made from cast iron, Arare, which means 'hail' in Japanese, takes its name from the traditional hobnail design that covers the top two-thirds of the pot's black body and that also appears as a band encircling the outer edges of the lid. The short, purposeful spout is almost lost beneath the well-defined arc of the handle, which attaches to hinges on either side of the pot. Arare's rise to prominence has its roots in eighteenth-century Japan, when the social significance of the tea ceremony became more wide-spread. At that time the Japanese literati adopted the Sencha tea ceremony method as a symbolic revolt against the more gilded Chanoya ceremony favoured by the ruling classes. The Sencha method, which uses tea leaves instead of powder, offered a far less formal alternative to the Chanoya, dispensing with the intricate practices and decorative utensils as it did so. As Sencha encouraged more to take up the pleasure of the tea ceremony, so, too, a market opened up for a less expensive Japanese teapot that could be produced in large quantities. The Arare design is an adaptation of earlier *Tetsubin*, or teapot designs, that arose during this period and it emerged in its contemporary form in 1914. The Arare's most popular manufacturer, the Iwachu Company of Morioko, is now Japan's largest and foremost producer of cast iron kitchenware, with a history that is over 100 years old. The Arare Teapot, with the design adopted by Iwachu, remains in production today and is exported in vast quantities all over the world.

The history of design can sometimes be traced by following the path of more humble objects, those whose shape and function have been left untouched by the evolution of technology and are unlikely to feature in the most famous museums, but are undoubtedly part of everyday life. Sheep Shears form part of this anonymous crowd of neglected master-pieces of design and have been around in the same basic shape for thousands of years. They are known to have existed from 300 BC in Egypt and there are also records of their existence from Roman times, in more or less their current form. Over the generations, there have been numerous patents and attempts to improve the basic design. The introduction of electric shearing at the end of the 1800s did not jeopardize the spread of the old manual shears, which further developed in a variety of sizes and patterns suitable for different kinds of breed and fleece, and in this way met the specific needs of sheep farmers around the world. These models contributed to the persistence of sheep

shears throughout the centuries. The reason for this enduring success lies in the perfection of the design, which ensures the maximum performance in the simplest shape. The mechanism of the shears – two pieces of steel riveted together in the centre of the handle – allows the user to put the hand right over the blades, concentrating all the energy into the cut. 'Maximum possible cutting control, plus maximum energy efficiency', say Burgon & Ball of Sheffield, established in 1730 and one of the largest sheep shears manufacturers in the world. Today the company produces over sixty different patterns, but its bestseller remains the Red Drummer Boy, which is noticeable for its peculiar double-bow pattern and red painted handles. Those sceptics who do not equate classic design with flocks of sheep will have to reconsider: the longevity and simple perfection of the Sheep Shears means that they need no prestigious acknowledgements to merit the title of an elegant and effective design.

Sheep Shears (1730)
Designer Unknown
Burgon & Ball 1730 to present
Various 1700s to present

A.D. 1902. Aug. 22. N°. 18,512.
POMEROY'S Complete Specification.

(1 SHEET)

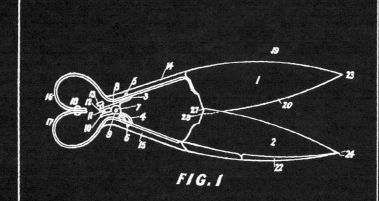

FIG. 1

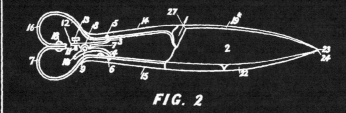

FIG. 2

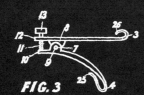

FIG. 3

[This Drawing is a reproduction of the Original on a reduced scale.]

Maiby & Sons, Photo-Litho.

Early versions of Windsors-like chairs date back to the Gothic period but the true development of the Windsor began during the 1700s and continued to evolve as a handmade form until the beginnings of the Industrial Revolution. Since then the Windsor has continued in popularity to the present day in both handmade and manufactured versions. Initially developed in Britain as a rural chair, developed perhaps first by wheelwrights, the Windsor was used in farms, taverns and gardens. The chair's name may have derived from the fact that, that early on, many makers originated in Windsor, England, peddling their chairs in farm wagons throughout the countryside from Windsor to London. In America, the form of the chair evolved into a leaner, more sophisticated, and graceful version, with a steeper leg cant and more definition in the shaped and tapered spindles. The American version quickly became popular with the affluent and American Windsors from 1730–1870 were made in greater volume and variety than any other chair type. The Sack-Back Windsor is a superior example of the form, which incorporates the refinements of the Federal period. The comfortable, lightweight back uses the structural innovation of the horizontal crest, working together with the broad oval seat to compose a beautiful whole. The name 'sack-back' is thought to have originated from the shape and height of the back, suited to allow a 'sack' to be pulled over the back to deflect winter drafts. The enduring nature of the design is evidenced in the wide-ranging use and popularity of the Windsor in contemporary times. A distinct Windsor structural characteristic is that all parts emanate from the central platform of the seat. Another innovation is the use of a range of woods, each for their best attributes. Seats were usually formed from stable, easy-to-carve planks of pine or chestnut, which resist warping and shaped readily with adze, gouges and cutting tools. Seats were thick enough to allow strong joinery and the ample comfort of a carved 'saddle' form. Stretchers and legs were often maple, a tight-grained wood with inherent strength, responsive to tools and shaping. Bent parts were hickory, white oak or ash, which resist fracture when steamed and bent. The overall result was a durable structure that took advantage of the unique attributes of different wood species. Chairs were unified visually, with the application of painted finishes. The Windsor Chair exemplifies principles of good design: its form and structure embody centuries of craftsmanship, material ingenuity, simple yet sophisticated engineering and aesthetic beauty, while fulfilling the complex requirements of comfort and durable construction.

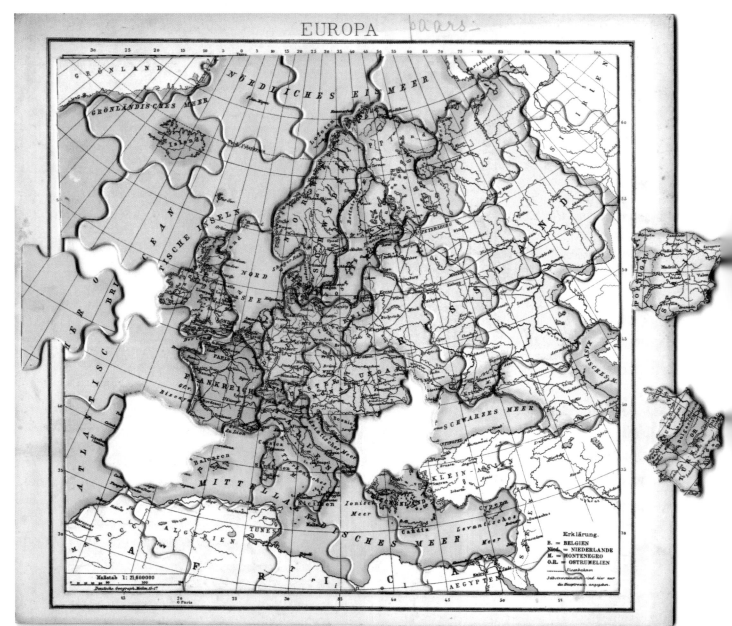

Early example of a die-cut Jigsaw Puzzle, c.1900

Today, we would never guess that the Jigsaw Puzzle began life in 1766 as an educational tool. John Spilsbury, a London-based engraver and map maker, decided to mount one of his maps onto hardwood and then to cut around the country's borders using a fine marquetry saw. Known as the Dissected Map, it would be used for decades to come as a way of teaching children geography. Adult puzzles in a wooden format were not introduced until the 1900s and at first were highly expensive to produce because they were cut one piece at a time and were not cut to lock together. They were only sold in limited numbers to the well-heeled, who quickly adopted this new mode of entertainment at weekend house parties. The ensuing craze brought innovation to puzzle manufacturing, and the name 'puzzle' was coined in 1908, referring to the inter-locking pieces. By 1909, jigsaw puzzles had become so lucrative that the Parker Brothers games company switched its attention entirely to mass-produced jigsaw puzzles. Surprisingly, it was not until the onset of the Depression in 1929 that jigsaw puzzles were cemented as a national pastime enjoyed by the masses, regardless of social position. By producing jigsaws depicting both nostalgic scenes and the optimism of new rail and shipping technology, companies like Chad Valley and Victory in the UK and Einson-Freeman and Viking in the USA offered an innocent diversion to the sober reality of the day. Plus, the intro-duction of die-cut cardboard sets for adults, which were far less expensive to produce in comparison to wood, sent sales sky high. In 1932–3 the great jigsaw rush took place in the United States. By 1933, jigsaws sales had reached 10 million per week by offering a cheap home-based entertainment alternative to the nightclubs, restaurants and bars so prohibitively expen-sive to those on reduced wages. It was at this point that the exploitation of jigsaw puzzles as marketing tools further raised their profile, as small sets were given away with hundreds of domestic products. Perhaps the most important link in the jigsaw story was the intro-duction of the weekly puzzle in September 1932, in the midst of the darkest depths of the Depression. On the back of an initial printing of 12,000, their ensuing success meant pro-duction quickly rose to 100,000 and then 200,000 – sales statistics of an impressive scale. The Jigsaw Puzzle has since been adopted by the majority of the Westernized world as a civilized form of entertainment, which endures despite competition from the tide of technological achievement.

005

Jigsaw Puzzle (1766)
John Spilsbury (1739–69)
Various 1766 to present

Machine Aérostatique de 70 Pieds de hauteur sur 46 de Diamétre, qui s'est élevée à Paris, avec deux homme à la hauteur de 324 Pieds le 19. Oct, 1783.

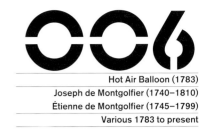

006

Hot Air Balloon (1783)
Joseph de Montgolfier (1740–1810)
Étienne de Montgolfier (1745–1799)
Various 1783 to present

While working for their father's prestigious paper manufacturing company in Paris, Joseph and Étienne de Montgolfier developed a product somewhat outside the company's usual remit. They constructed a hot air balloon from elaborately decorated paper. Beneath the balloon, which had a capacity of 2,235 m (79,000 ft), the brothers attached a fire pit that burnt straw, manure and sheep's wool.

They wrongly believed that the smoke, rather than the hot air, produced by this concoction elevated the balloon. The short, but historic inaugural flight was carried out in front of an august audience including King Louis XVI, and the passengers were a sheep, a duck and a chicken. The balloon rose 1,830 m (6,000 ft) and travelled a little over 1 mile (1.6 km). Louis was reassured by the survival of the animals that human beings would be able to breathe the atmosphere at higher levels. Two months later the Marquis François d'Arlandes (an infantry major) and Pilatre de Rozier (a physics professor) became the first humans to ride in the Montgolfier balloon. Just eleven days after that, another Frenchman, Professor Jacques Charles, demonstrated an alternative balloon design that used hydrogen gas as its lifting medium. Charles had noted that a lighter-than-air medium was essential to make the balloon rise efficiently. By creating a rubberized and airtight silk balloon with a passenger basket suspended beneath, he created something close to the gas balloons in use today. By 1800 the Montgolfier brothers' hot air balloon had been overtaken by gas balloons. Their design lost popularity when Pilatre de Rozier's balloon burst into flames as he was attempting to cross the English Channel and he was killed. The superiority of the gas models with their longer flying times and greater manoeuvrability soon made them unassailable.

The initial development of bone china, a form of porcelain, made from china clay, feldspathic rock, flint and calcined animal bone, is attributed to Josiah Spode, who introduced it in around 1800. Adding calcined animal bone to the original china clay compound was found to give the ceramic body both its strength and durability and contributed to the translucency of the material, creating an ivory-white appearance. Wedgwood, founded in 1759, first put bone china into production in 1812, at its factory near Stoke-on-Trent in the United Kingdom. Although bone china production was discontinued between 1828 and 1875 due to the company's dire economic situation, from around 1876 bone china was much sought after and became an important part of Wedgwood production with a wide range of patterns to suit all tastes. Traditional White was an undecorated range in bone china and earthenware that grew alongside the Queen's ware, a fine cream-coloured earthenware that earned Wedgwood a royal appointment from Queen Charlotte in 1762. Traditional White was not specifically a range of its own until the 1930s, although many of the pieces of the Traditional White range actually date back to c.1770 as far as the shape is concerned. At the beginning of the 1800s the fashion was for highly decorated wares, brilliantly coloured and lavishly gilded, often with Oriental motifs, and Traditional White was used as a basis for these highly decorative pieces. It is worth noting that a precursor of the White ware can be traced in a range of white bone china (although with a different design) that had gilded handles and finials, and was in production between c.1812 and the 1920s. Without a specific date of design and records of the history of its development, the White range seems to have evolved from being made in earthenware to bone china, and was progressively stripped down of its decoration to feature a simple, extremely refined, white. Today, the Traditional White minimal elegance has achieved its own status, because of its simplicity and sophistication. The Wedgwood factory has continued to use this most traditional of ceramic materials, introducing innovative new shapes, and evolving designs with the help of the in-house Design Studio. But the strength, durability, whiteness and translucency of Traditional White have ensured its enduring quality and lasting appeal.

Traditional White China (1796)
Josiah Wedgwood & Sons
Josiah Wedgwood & Sons 1796 to 1830,
c.1930 to 2004, 2005 to present

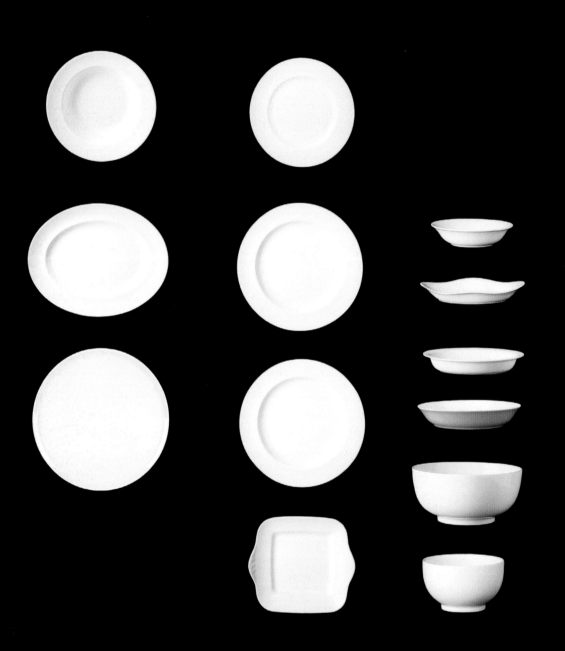

Garden Chair and Bench for Potsdam (1825)
Karl Friedrich Schinkel (1781–1841)
Royal cast-iron works Saynerhütte 1825
to 1900
Tecta 1982 to present

Although the origins of mass-produced seating are most commonly associated with the mid-nineteenth-century bentwood innovations of the Thonet brothers, volume production in cast iron was already underway in Germany decades earlier. In fact, a former weapons factory founded by Peter the Great had been producing considerable quantities of cast-iron furniture there as early as 1736. Schinkel is best known as Germany's foremost Neo-Classical architect, but he was also recognized as a furniture maker. His role as a member of Prussia's technical buildings inspectorate enabled his designs to be frequently featured in *Vorbilder für Fabrikanten und Handwerker*, an influential publication that laid down standards for manufacturers and craftsmen. This Garden Chair comprised two identical, separately cast side pieces, providing maximum stability but requiring minimum materials. Both sections could be made with the same casting mould. Also, because the wrought-iron rods forming the seat and spanning the legs were set into drilled holes in the sides and riveted from the outside, the same mould could also be used to produce a larger bench; the only change required was longer rods. The decorative elements, featuring typical classical motifs such as lyre, lion heads and foliage, were moulded while still hot so as to fit the curve of the backrest. Schinkel worked regularly for Prussian royalty and his cast-iron furniture was used in the royal gardens of Berlin and Potsdam. In its outline form and proportions this design is remarkably similar to the foldable metal and slatted wood garden chair design that would later become ubiquitous. Schinkel's chair also resembles the benches still found in public places such as parks and stations today.

Fig.1

These jars are an example of those utilitarian objects that have quietly become a fixture in the domestic landscape, rising from the ranks of anonymous canning and preserving jars to become something like the equivalent of the café chair by Thonet, the Chair No.14, now a universal standard. Early examples of this type of clip-top preserving jar have been made since at least the beginning of the nineteenth century, and used for storage of conserves, fruits, terrines and, of course, *foie gras*. Modern French-made Le Parfait Preserve Jars are constructed in pressed glass to form a perfect seal. The jars are available in a variety of sizes, from 50 ml to 3 litres (0.1 to 5.25 pt) and each has a glass lid that flips closed using a wire bail and is sealed by the distinctive orange rubber gasket. When the jar is heated a vacuum forms inside, making the seal airtight. The flat lid with slight recess is designed for easy stacking, and the wide mouth for easy filling. The openings vary in size from 7 to 10 cm (2.75 to 4 in), with the standard 8.75 cm (3.4 in) gasket. The 'Le Parfait' logo is embossed on the exterior of one side of the jar, making it immediately recognizable and emphasizing its iconic position among household goods. Now that few of us have time to can or preserve foods at home, we still buy jams and terrines charmingly packaged in Le Parfait Jars, and the distinctive glass pot has become associated with high-quality artisanal foods. It has survived this subtle shift because it serves a multitude of purposes with apt and economic means. The jars have been repeatedly patented, imitated and distributed, but none quite equals the distinctive orange sealed jar that can be found in most kitchens.

Le Parfait Jars (c.1825)
Designer Unknown
Various c.1825 to present

The origins of the Galvanized Metal Dustbin have faded in the memory of long-standing manufacturers such as Garrods of Barking in East London. The company has been manufacturing dustbins for more than 200 years and is the oldest bin manufacturer in the country. Originally, the steel rubbish bin was handmade for the gentry of London. In the 1700s rubbish, which was previously stored within house walls, was moved to external containers and the need arose for a vessel that could withstand weathering. In 1851 Garrods' management saw the first examples of industrial machinery that could be used to manufacture metal dustbins at the 1851 Great Exhibition in London and shortly afterwards, the company invested capital in order to start industrial production. Today, half of the company's production still runs off the same Victorian machinery. Production is divided in to two main families of machinery: corrugators and rimming tools. Thin sheets of galvanized steel, appropriate for its resistance to corrosion and rust due to its zinc coating, are passed through the corrugating machine in a procedure known familiarly as a 'granny's' process, as the corrugators resemble the old-fashioned clothes mangles last seen in prewar homes. Corrugating the steel gives rigidity and allows a considerable efficiency of material use. Next, the dustbin is finished in all its details with the aid of the rimming machines. Garrods is one of the last remaining manufacturers of a mass-produced, low-cost product to have resisted relocating its facilities to countries with cheap labour. The company's unique heritage is beginning to be recognized and discussions are underway for the creation of a museum displaying the machinery and processes of dust-bin manufacture. But the story of the steel dustbin is not all down to rubbish. The Galvanized Metal Dustbin, with its fluted lid, drop handles and corrugated sides, has a permanent place in the Smithsonian Institution's Museum of American History in Washington, DC, as the home of Oscar the Grouch, the Muppet character from the TV programme *Sesame Street*.

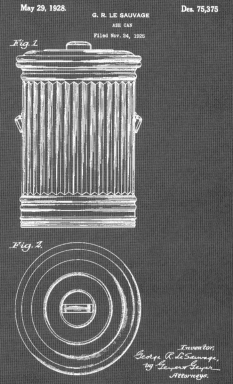

May 29, 1928.   Des. 75,375

G. R. LE SAUVAGE
ASH CAN
Filed Nov. 24, 1926

Fig. 1

Fig. 2

Inventor,
George R. Le Sauvage,
by Geyer Geyer
Attorneys.

From 1813 to 1837 Froebel devoted himself to education, publishing his first book, *The Education of Man,* in 1826. He invented the concept of kindergarten in 1837, conceiving it as a place where children could develop their own potential. He believed that children learn about the world through structured play, and it was in creating objects for this structured play that Froebel was led to design a series of wooden construction toys. Froebel called his specially designed toys 'Gifts', each a treasured plaything kept in its own box. By playing with the Gifts children could explore the world around them, expressing their thoughts and ideas creatively. The Gifts are divided into five categories: solids, surfaces, lines, points and lines-and-points. The scale of the toys is very important as it allows children to manipulate and to explore the world in miniature. The geometry, colours and components of the toys allow the child to learn about science, mathematics, fractions, and history by reconfiguring and manipulating them. For example, a wooden cube that divides into eight smaller cubes or eight rectangular prisms can at once be a castle and a lesson in fractions or science. And by returning the toys to their proper boxes the children learn both respect and insight into the workings of the toys. Today, building blocks and other educational toys are taken for granted, but in 1837 few, if any, existed. Froebel's Gifts have given rise to incredible numbers of playthings that have educational value, but it is still difficult to find simple, unpretentious educational toys. Perhaps that is the reason why Froebel's have survived so long. They are willing collaborators with the child's mind in the construction of the child's fantasy. They do little to impose themselves or impress themselves on the child's play, as many of today's toys do. The Gifts endure, perhaps, because they are abstractly treasured items that support, with little pretence, the joy of being a child.

O11

Gifts (1837)
Friedrich Froebel (1782–1852)
Milton Bradley 1869 to c.1930
Uncle Goose Toys 1997 to present

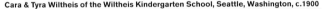

Cara & Tyra Wiltheis of the Wiltheis Kindergarten School, Seattle, Washington, c.1900

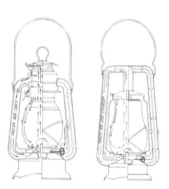

Hurricane Lanterns, or Storm Lanterns as they are also known, were named after their ability to remain lit with a steady flame, even in high winds. But, although a generic term, the title 'Hurricane' normally refers to a tubular lantern; that is, a lantern whose flame is generated by air supplied into a semi-enclosed system via metal side-tubes. The air feeds into the kerosene-based burning mixture to create a bright and well-regulated flame that burns steadily, even in adverse conditions. The main types of tubular lanterns are named after the two principles which govern them: Hot- and Cold-Blast systems, both of which were invented by John Irwin – the former in 1868, the latter in 1874. Hot-Blast allows fresh air to enter the main body of the lantern – the glass 'globe' – at its base. The mixture of heated air and spent gases that is produced then rises up into the lantern canopy, set above the globe, from where a significant percentage descends back through the side tubes to the base in order to re-supply the flame. The Cold-Blast principle, as the name implies, does not allow the heated by-products of combustion to re-enter the system. Instead, these escape via a chimney-like opening in the canopy; meanwhile, an air chamber surrounding the 'chimney' brings unsullied fresh air into the tubes and straight to the flame. For this reason, although less fuel-efficient, Cold-Blast lanterns produce by far the strongest light in the form of a tall white flame, twice as high as that produced by their Hot-Blast cousins. The American lamp and lantern manufacturer, R E Dietz Company, had been selling utility lanterns since the 1840s and produced the first Hot-Blast lantern in 1868 and the first Cold-Blast in 1880; however, as common practical items, tubular lamps have been produced by many different manufacturers over the years. The Hurricane Lantern shown here is a Dietz Hot-Blast Lantern, originally intended for use on streets and highways to demarcate barricades or road hazards. Despite the lanterns' practical functionality remaining undiminished, Hurricane Lanterns today are mostly used as part anachronistic ornament, part pleasing light source for patios or cosy domestic interiors, rather than in the dangerous conditions or situations for which they were initially intended.

Hurricane Lantern (1840)
Designer Unknown
R E Dietz Company 1840 to present
Various 1840s to present

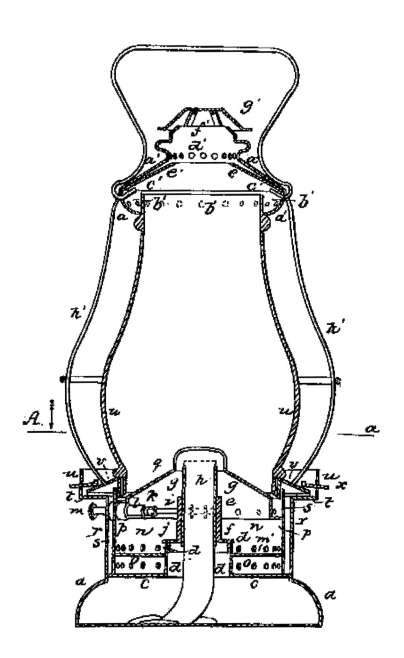

Pocket Measuring Tape (1842)
James Chesterman (1795–1867)
Various 1842 to present
Stabila 1930 to present

When it comes to measuring devices, precision is crucial, but practicality and easy manageability are also qualities that help a great innovation become a classic. In 1821 James Chesterman was awarded a patent for an innovative way to rewind a measuring tape automatically using a spring mechanism. The previous year, the twenty-five-year-old Chesterman had moved from London to Chesterfield, and with his patent granted, he founded the Chesterman Steel Company in Sheffield. In the following decades the Chesterman Steel Company established itself as a synonym for high-quality measuring instruments, especially tapes, callipers and squares, and exported its products to the USA. It released its pocket measuring tape in 1842. Initially the tape was made from cloth reinforced with wire, but later, by heating and riveting long strips of steel used for crinoline skirts, Chesterman was able to create a steel tape that could coil inside a leather case. When pulled out from its case the tape kept straight and, best of all, it didn't stretch or shrink for a guaranteed length of time. The tape is jointed every 6 m (20 ft) or so, and a handle folds into the leather case. In 1869 it gained favourable comments from *Scientific American* magazine on the uniqueness of the patent steel tape's exact measuring capability, neatness and portability. In 1954, Stabila, another longstanding manufacturer of measurement tools, brought a fibreglass measuring tape onto the market, with a strengthening zigzag thread; steel measuring tapes suffer from more significant changes in length over time but require less traction force than fibreglass ones. Today, tape ends are available with folding hooks, plumb lines, eyes or rings. Pocket measuring tapes are one of the most common tools found in every household, as ubiquitous as they are essential.

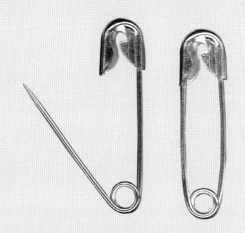

W. Hunt.
Pin.

N.º 6281.   Patented Apr. 10. 1849.

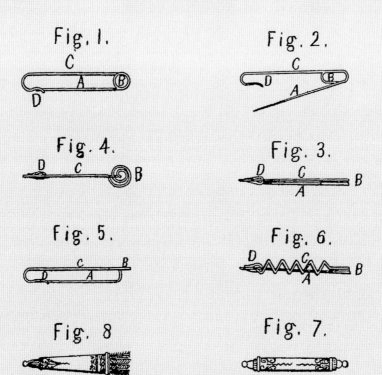

Fig. 1.
C
A   B
D

Fig. 2.
C
D   B
A

Fig. 4.
D   C   B

Fig. 3.
D   C   B
A

Fig. 5.
c   B
D   A

Fig. 6.
D   C   B
A

Fig. 8.

Fig. 7.

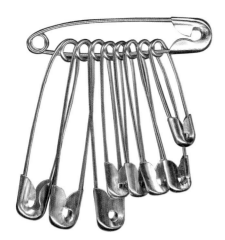

Sometimes a design is so commonplace that it seems as if it has always been in existence. Such is the case with the Safety Pin, the ubiquitous household helpmate that was designed by Walter Hunt, a New Yorker who was also responsible for such creations as hob nails and the fountain pen. Hunt, it seems, was frustrated by the flimsiness of straight pins that seemed to bend when inserted into thick cloth, as well as by their pernicious pricking. Working with a 20 cm (8 in) piece of brass wire, Hunt conceived a simple solution to these problems by fashioning a coil at one end to provide spring action, and a simple catch at the other end that would hold the pin in place and protect users from punctures. Hunt's 1849 patent application included drawings of variations on the 'Dress-Pin', which included simple round, elliptical and flat spiral coils, as well as three illustrations that showed how well suited his design was to fashionable intervention. Hunt's Dress-Pin, he wrote in the patent application, 'is equally ornamental, and at the same time more secure and durable than any other plan of a clasp pin heretofore in use, there being no joint to break or pivot to wear or get loose as in other plans. Hunt was a prototypical absent-minded inventor who was brilliantly creative but a disaster at making money. Fifteen years earlier he had invented the first reasonably functioning sewing machine, but had decided against patenting it for fear that he would put factory hand-sewers out of work. Similarly, Hunt received all the historical kudos for designing the Safety Pin, but none of the money. Legend has it that Hunt designed the Safety Pin in order to pay off a $15 debt that had accrued with a friend. After receiving the patent for his creation on 10 April 1849, he proceeded to sell the idea to his friend for a paltry $400.

For anyone who spent a childhood kneeling on hard surfaces playing jacks, it might come as a surprise that this seemingly modern game has ancient origins. The metal jacks themselves, with their sharp points and knobbly ends, are a modern, sanitized version of *tali*, or the knucklebones, of sheep that were used as far back as Ancient Egypt in games of skill, chance, and soothsaying. Indeed, it was only in the twentieth century that the term "jacks" started replacing earlier descriptors such as 'knucklebones', 'skittlebones' and 'jackstones'. The game's challenge is one of dexterity and reaction and the rules are very simple. The jacks are thrown on to the ground; the player then bounces the ball and must pick up one jack and catch the ball in the same hand before it bounces back on the ground for a second time. The player continues with this process until all the jacks have been gathered. The number of jacks to be picked up, and therefore the difficulty, increases until the player is unable to go on. After several rounds, the winner is whoever manages to pick up the most number of jacks simultaneously. As with most games, Jacks is played in many slightly different ways with individual groups often customising the game with their own new rules and challenges. Art history has many visual references to the game's endless incarnations. Egyptian tombs of adults and children alike offer up evidence of gaming knucklebones; Venus challenges Pan to a game of Greek *astragaloi* on decorative mirrors from 350 BC; Roman girls huddle to play *pentelitha* in a marble painting from Herculaneum; and the Flemish master Pieter Brueghel depicts two women engaged in a heated match of skittlebones in the bottom left corner of his 1560 tribute to youthful pastimes, *Children's Games*.

C. C. Johnson,

Clothes Pin,

N.º 63,393.   Patented Apr. 2, 1867.

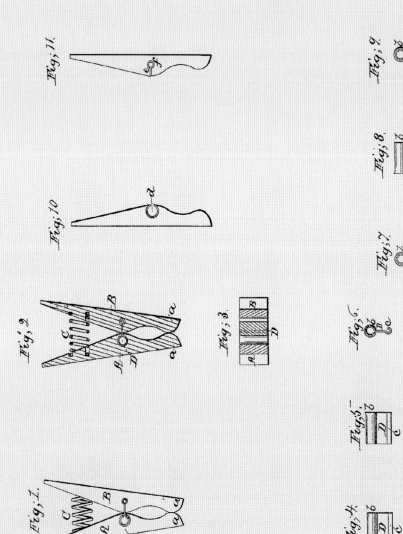

Fig. 11.

Fig. 10.

Fig. 2.

Fig. 3.

Fig. 1.

Fig. 9.

Fig. 8.

Fig. 7.

Fig. 6.

Fig. 5.

Fig. 4.

Witnesses;
Geo. H. Andrews
Samuel N. Piper

Inventor,
Chas. C. Johnson.
by his attorney.
R. H. Eddy

In the fashion for what has become known as 'lifestyle', we like to be able to attribute every product to an individual genius. Some of our most useful products have developed rather more organically. The credit for the original Clothes Peg is often ascribed to the Shakers, the religious sect founded in the US in 1772 by Ann Lee. While they were notable for their espousal of celibacy, they also left a legacy of furniture design, believing it to be a three-dimensional expression of their faith. To this end, the products they crafted were completely pared down. All that was left were the essentials, with any form of ornamentation being severely frowned upon. In true style their peg was simply a piece of wood with a split in it to fasten the clothes to the line. But no one can really claim credit for designing the Clothes Peg. Indeed between 1852 and 1887, the US Patent Office granted patents to 146 different pegs, although it seems likely that most of them were based on the same premise as the Shaker two-prong clothespin. The classic peg, of course, consists of two wooden pins fastened by a steel spring that clamps them firmly together, created by D M Smith of Springfield, Vermont, in 1853. The contemporary peg as we know it was created in 1944 when Mario Maccaferri produced a hard-wearing plastic version. The Clothes Peg was firmly fixed as an icon in 1976 by the artist Claes Oldenburg, who installed a giant model bluntly titled *Clothespin* in Center Square Plaza, Philadelphia, measuring an enormous 13.7 m (45 ft) in height.

Moleskine Notebooks are oilcloth-covered notebooks based on a legendary two-hundred-year-old product. The last manufacturer was a small family-run firm in Tours, France, which closed in 1985, and the notebook went out of production. Reissued by the Italian company Modo & Modo in 1998, the design has been the beneficiary of a strong advertising campaign, which builds on the original's literary and artistic mystique. The small, pocket-sized notebook has developed a remarkable following among budding writers and trend-setting creatives, due to Modo & Modo's claim that the product is 'the legendary notebook of Hemingway, Picasso and Chatwin'. By citing such iconic users, the product has developed a strong and lucrative brand identity. While it is arguably true that these individuals used similar archetypal notebooks, they did not, of course, use the actual Modo & Modo product; the Milan-based company, however, claims that it is adhering to the spirit of the original product and maintaining its undoubted status as a creative tool. The standard Moleskine Notebook measures 14 × 9 cm (5.5 × 3.5 in) and contains lightweight, acid-free paper within its covers. The design features a foldable pocket in the back cover, a cloth ribbon attached to the spine that acts as a bookmark, and a woven elastic band stitched to the back cover that keeps the notebook securely closed when not in use. The product's name derives from the French spelling of 'moleskin', which the notebook's oilcloth covering resembles. By the time the original French notebooks were phased out, the term 'moleskine' had become something of a generic brand name. That familiarity made it a 'brand of fact', according to the Italian government, allowing Modo & Modo to resurrect the product legally, raise its status to an uppercase M and inherit its legacy. The famous name is now to be found on over three million upmarket notebooks and related stationery sold every year.

017

Moleskine Notebook (c.1850)
Designer Unknown
Anonymous firm (Tours) c.1850 to 1985
Modo & Modo 1998 to present

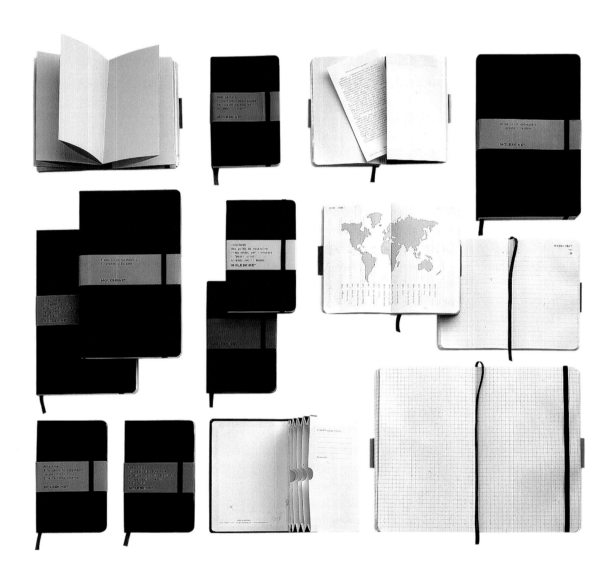

In France, these notebooks are known as carnets moleskins: 'moleskine', in this case, being its black oilcloth binding. Each time I went to Paris, I would buy a fresh supply from a *papeterie* in the Rue de l'Ancienne Comédie. The pages were squared and the end-papers held in place with an elastic band. I had numbered them in series. I wrote my name and address on the front page, offering a reward to the finder. To lose a passport was the least of one's worries: to lose a notebook was a catastrophe. In twenty odd years of travel, I lost only two. One vanished on an Afghan bus. The other was filched by the Brazilian secret police, who, with a certain clairvoyance, imagined that some lines I had written – about the wounds of a Baroque Christ – were a description, in code, of their own work on political prisoners.

Bruce Chatwin, *The Songlines*, 1987

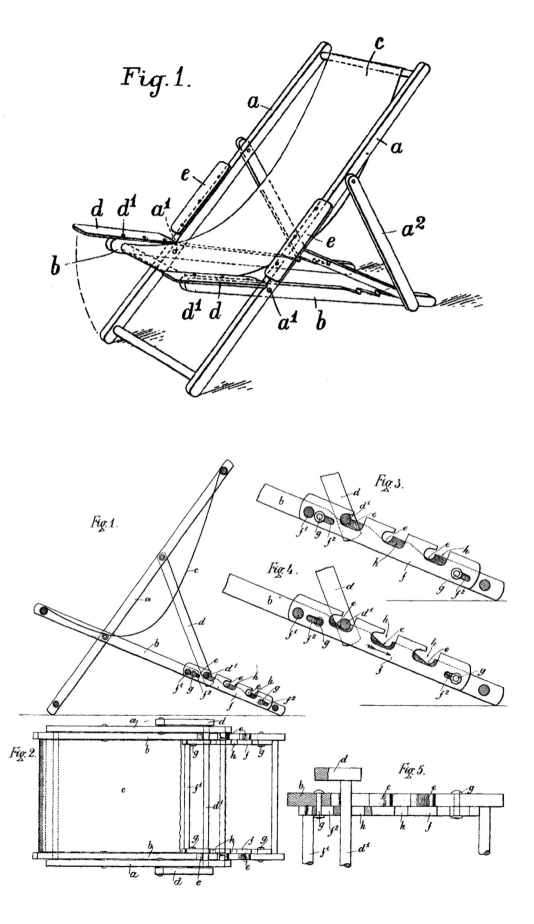

Fig. 1.

Fig. 1.

Fig. 2.

Fig. 3.

Fig. 4.

Fig. 5.

There is no mistaking

the nautical origins of the Textile Garden Folding Chair, first used on the decks of cruise ships. Its debt to the hammock, the traditional space-saving berth for sailors, is clear, and its fabric, often canvas, seat, commonly printed in bold-coloured stripes, takes its visual cue from sails; ranks of unfolded but unoccupied deck chairs, their seats blown out by the breeze, can resemble a flotilla on the move. As well as strong pointers to the sea and seaside, the design is informed by maritime practicality. As an outdoors item, the chair is seasonal and not needed in bad weather or the colder months when it can be folded flat and stored without taking up a great deal of space, a premium commodity both below deck on a ship and in the garden shed. The seasonal and recreational uses of the Textile Chair have vested in it a great deal of charm and make it as much a part of the image of the bank holiday weekend or seaside excursion as the ice-cream or knotted handkerchief. By happy accident, it

seems ideally designed for enforced relaxation. Being impossible to sit up straight in a Textile Chair, the occupant has to recline and few useful tasks, other than reading or dozing, can be accomplished from it. Once in, you may be there for a while as it is quite difficult to get out of. For all its no-nonsense roots and practicality, the Textile Chair is the ultimate labour-saving device – a machine for maximizing idleness.

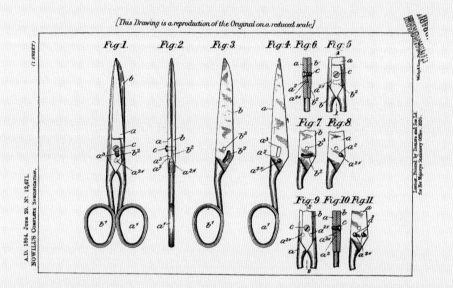

Fig.1. Fig.2. Fig.3. Fig.4. Fig.6. Fig.5.

Fig.7 Fig.8.

Fig.9 Fig.10 Fig.11.

As scissors are thought to have been around since the fourteenth century BC in the form of shears and since the first century AD as scissors, it is not surprising that variations in scissor design are nearly endless. From the points to the sharpness, thickness, curvature, length and width of the blades, from the shanks – straight, cranked or offset – to the bows, and in the overall finish, there are scissors tailored to every possible function, improved and refined over the centuries. Household scissors are the most common form and are called the sharp blunt, which refers to the form of the points. When closed, the blunt part protects the sharp part, making them safer; when open, the sharp point can get under the material more easily to start the cut. Bright steel or nickel plate finishes, rather than chrome plate, are the preferred materials for a non-corrosive environment; they are usually hot-dropped forged, machine grounded and finished by hand. The road to the industrial production of scissors began with the invention of steel in mid-eighteenth-century England. Sheffield had been an important centre for the cutlery trade since the thirteenth century and Chaucer (c.1340–1400) mentions a Sheffield 'thwyttle' or general purpose knife in his *Canterbury Tales*. Industry was certainly helped by the natural resources of this area, including waterpower from the rivers in a pre-steam era along with extensive woodland and limestone research. Cutlery and therefore scissor production was massively increased with the invention of the Bessemer converter by Henry Bessemer in 1856, a large crucible that could convert thirty tonnes of steel in half an hour; Sheffield could now respond to the formidable demand for steel from the increasing populations of America. Even though the Bessemer converter was used worldwide until the 1970s, only three known examples remain, one of which can be still seen at the Kelham Island Museum in Sheffield. Today, Sheffield is still one of the best-known manufacturing centres. Companies like William Whiteley & Sons have been manufacturing scissors here since 1760, with the business passing through at least eleven generations of the same family.

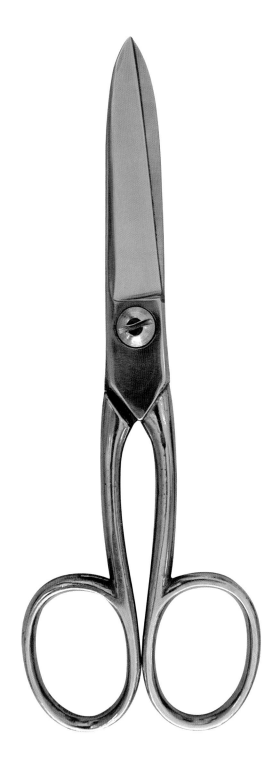

The archaeologist Alfred Percival Maudsley, working in Chichen Itza, Colombia, 1880

An icon in the world of folding chairs, the original version was devised by Joseph Beverly Fenby in England around 1855 for use by officers during British Army campaigns. Fenby later went on to patent the chair in 1877. Like most 'campaign' furniture, it is slightly unusual for its time, in that its utilitarian appearance and lack of any extraneous decoration give it a sense of modernity not usually found in nineteenth-century furniture intended for the upper classes. This 'modern spirit' was most likely born out of a requirement for lightness and robustness, to allow it to function on the battlefield, and was what made it a fitting chair to put into production approximately sixty years later. A slightly developed version, using leather instead of canvas, was manufactured throughout the 1930s in Italy under the name Tripolina, and was presumably intended for domestic peacetime use. Essentially the chair is an attempt to make a more comfortable, and more collapsible, version of the ubiquitous and famously unsupportive X-framed deck chair seen dotted around seaside resorts and parks. The ergonomic problems of the X-framed chair arise from the configuration of wooden poles and a canvas sling. The sling is supported only at the top of the back and the front of the seat by the poles, and the front pole pushes uncomfortably under the back of the thighs. The Tripolina uses a much more complex, three-dimensional folding structure to get round this problem, with the canvas or leather sling supported from four points. However, it is still lacking in good lumber support, a problem associated with many slung seats. And yet, its presence is a reminder of another time and usage, while its style survives its origins and it continues to stand out in any given environment.

Tripolina (c.1855)
Joseph Beverly Fenby (nd)
Various 1930s
Gavina 1955 to present
Citterio 1960s to present

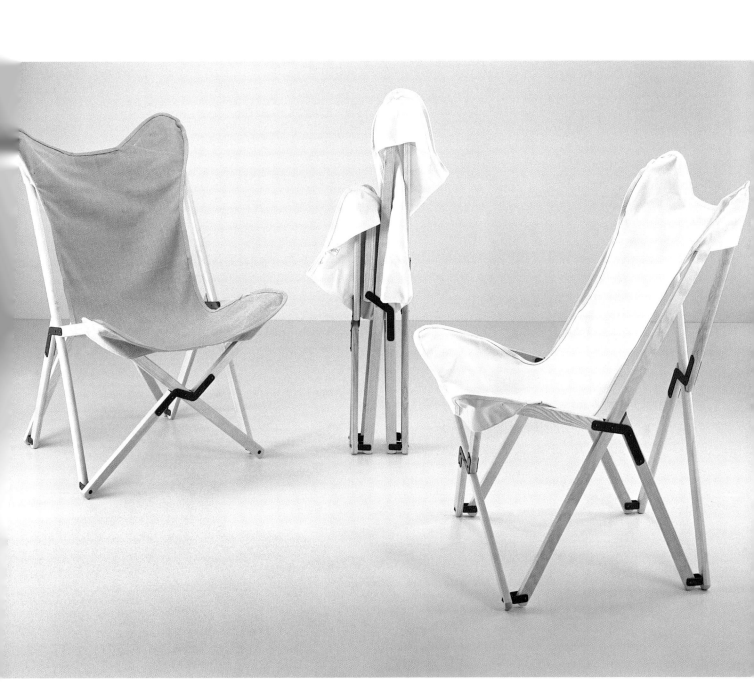

Mustard is yellow, and Colman's products are yellow. That might sound like an absurd simplification, but that single quality has given the brand an unsurpassable association with its flagship product. Few other brands can claim such a deep connection in the mind of the consumer. Colman's Mustard was founded by Jeremiah Colman in 1814, but the distinctive packaging only started to appear in 1855 with the addition of the renowned bull's head, a good device to evoke associations not only of strength, but also of reliability. This notion of consistency was developed in 1864 when the red and yellow colours were introduced across the range. Reliability was important to Colman's. Everything about the brand was tuned to sell the company's products as consistent and trustworthy to often wary Victorian consumers. Its effectiveness is clearly shown by the fact the design has altered so little in 150 years, and even the earliest cans are easily recognizable. Of course, the product itself, and by extension the company, has to live up to its presentation. Colman's as a company was extremely conscious of this and took a close interest in the welfare of its workforce: it was among the first firm to offer its workers hot meals and access to a staff nurse. The Royal Warrant was awarded to the company, and added to its packaging, in 1866. A planned effort to build a coherent brand was just part of Colman's marketing strategy, which has through the years demonstrated continued astuteness. For example, the first tins bearing the bull's-head logo were also square, rather than round, which both made them distinctive and saved shelf-space in shops. There were also repeated promotions to keep the product in the public eye: a 'Mustard Club' for consumers, sponsorship of Norwich Football Club and frequent appeals to patriotism and national pride, including special pictorial tins to mark royal occasions.

O21

Colman's Mustard Tin (1855)
Colman's of Norwich Design Team
Colman's of Norwich
(Unilever Bestfoods UK) 1855 to present

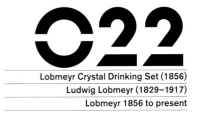

Ludwig Lobmeyr was part of a family firm of Austrian glassware sellers, and added his own design legacy by creating an innovative and highly sought after range of crystal glasses. His father Josef opened a glassware shop in Vienna in the 1820s, after an apprenticeship with an uncle. This was originally just a dealership; the designs were produced by a factory in Bohemia. While his brother, also called Josef, took care of the commercial side of the business, Ludwig had a passion and understanding of glass design. Inspired by the eastern, Greek, Roman and Venetian glass he saw at the Great Exhibition of 1851 in London, he began experimenting with enamelling and painting glass. By 1856 he had developed what came to be known as 'muslin' glass. This crystal patterned glass, mere millimetres thick, was difficult to manufacture. It had to be hand-blown, cut, engraved and polished by hand, a process involving more than a dozen skilled craftsmen to ensure every last detail was exact. A whole range of muslin glass was produced, including objects from decanters and goblets to the 'Lobmeyr' Crystal Drinking Set. Wine aficionados loved it because it created the thinnest possible surface between the liquid and one's mouth. Unadorned and fragile, the glass has a timeless appeal that would not look out of place had it been designed a century later. Ludwig Lobmeyr was a founding father of the Arts and Crafts movement in Vienna, becoming something of a cultural patron in the city and counting many artists and sculptors among his friends. He retired from the business in 1900, having trained his nephew Stefan Rath to continue the pioneering glasswork. Rath later flourished in this role, positioning the company at the heart of the turn-of-the-century artistic collective, the Vienna Secession, and promoting good industrial design. The hand-produced range continues to be bought by collectors and fine restaurants today.

J. & L. Lobmeyr

KAISERL. KÖNIGL.

HOF-GLASWAARENHÄNDLER

KRONLEUCHTER u. KRISTALLWAAREN-FABRIKANTEN

13 KÄRNTHNERSTRASSE **13**

Wien.

KRISTALL u. FARBIGES GLAS, SPIEGEL, KRON-
ARM u. WANDLEUCHTER von GLAS u. BRONZE.
AMPELN u.d.m.

Michael Thonet and Sons, founder of Thonet

No name just a number. An unassuming entry in the extensive
catalogue of Michael Thonet and Sons cabinetmakers. This modest anonymity
however belies the fact that little No.14 is, in reality, a giant presence in the
history of furniture. The representative symbol of Thonet 'Bentwood', it is a
hugely influential and enduring icon. Designed by Thonet in 1859, what set this
chair apart was not its general form (it was similar in style to other chairs of the
period) but the new philosophy of manufacture that it represented. This simple
chair embodied innovative and radical methods of both processing and
construction. In the 1850s the cabinetmaker Michael Thonet pioneered and
developed a process of steam bending laminated and solid wooden rods and
strips. This 'bentwood' method allowed tight continuous curves to be produced
without the use of carving or of glued joints, and was hugely liberating in terms
of time and skilled labour. It was a process that enabled discrete, relatively
complex shapes to be fully formed. Simplified versions of the styles of the
period could be produced in component form and fixed together with screws.
In turn this allowed the furniture to be mass-produced, shipped as parts and
assembled at destination at very low cost. These issues, namely material-
processing innovation, kit of parts construction and mechanical assembly set a
precedent in the philosophy and production of furniture. No.14 and its retinue
anticipated by more than fifty years the essential themes and axioms that would
come to define Modernism in the early twentieth century. Michael Thonet died
in 1871 but by this time Gebrüder Thonet was the largest furniture factory in
the world. No.14 has another number attached to it – 50 million! This
astonishing figure represents the volume of No.14s manufactured and sold
between 1859 and 1930. Probably the single most commercially successful
chair ever produced, its success has done nothing to diminish its enduring
formal and conceptual charm. Today this manifestation of nineteenth-century
high technology still retains a fresh and elegant utility. Lyrical *and* restrained, it
is truly a classic 'classic'.

Claus, Peter, and Phillip Thonet, the fifth generation of Thonet

Since the fall of the Roman Empire no age has had a more classical cast of mind than ours. Take Puvis de Chavannes and Max Klinger for example. Have there ever been such Greek minds since the days of Aeschines? Take the Thonet chair. Is it not the same spirit as the Greek chairs with its curved legs and its back rest, without ornamentation, the embodiment of a whole age's attitude towards sitting?

Adolph Loos, *A Review of Applied Arts*, 1898

Sister Mathilde 'Tillie' Schnell at the Hancock Shaker Village, Massachusetts, 1935

The Shakers' commitment to absorbing oneself in labour as an act of religious devotion is manifest in the flawless precision of their creations. The Shaker Slat Back Chair is a prime example of an elegant object derived from a clearly articulated, principled system. The subtle and graceful upward ascension of the curved back splats, and the softened attenuation of finials, intentionally guided a path for the eye to pay homage to the heavens. It has been said that they sought to make their chairs so beautiful, that at any time an angel might feel welcome to come and sit in one of them. The finials were sometimes so delicate that they were reinforced with internal steel pins, revealed later in X-rays. The lightweight proportions of the turned legs and cross supports illustrate an expert understanding of materials, using the minimal material required to retain strength. The webbed seats of the Slat Back Chair were woven with tape, leather, wool or cane, over a soft inner matting to add function and durability. The rhythmic horizontal lines of splats, stretchers and rails allow for an extremely lightweight, yet durable structure. The Shakers, who came to America in 1774, established communities around New England. This chaste community organized its agriculture and woodworking, and handmade its furniture, clothes and home accessories based on the principle that cleanliness equalled godliness. The multi-purpose furniture had no adornments or ornamentation, thus preventing dust settling, and were hung up on wooden pegs, which ran the perimeter of the rooms, each time the houses were swept. Shaker furniture and agricultural and domestic tools were sold to outsiders, thus creating an economy and sustenance for the community. The Slat Back Chair was made by Brother Robert Wagan, and evolved from the Ladder Back Chair in the 1860s. A woodworking machine was adapted under his supervision, allowing for an increase in production, making 600 chairs annually. In 1872, a new factory was built with a steam engine and upgraded lathes, machines and jigsaws, which enabled ten workers to produce 144 chairs per week. As the production level rose, the need for standard designs emerged, which resulted in several styles of ladder back chairs, of which the Slat Back Chair was known as No.5 Dining Chair, and began to be sold through a mail-order catalogue. The evolution from handmade chair to factory-produced product by RM Wagan & Company did not detract from the quality of the chair, nor its beauty and elegance. The Shakers' firm belief in asceticism and austerity remains in the chairs produced in the Shaker-style, even today.

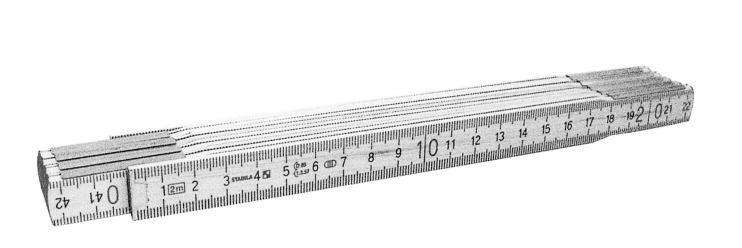

It is not clear when the Folding Ruler was invented, but examples are known from the mid-nineteenth century onwards. The purpose of folding rulers was to make them convenient to carry. They were made in various lengths, ranging from a 43 cm (1 ft 4 in), convenient for the shirt pocket, to a 268 cm (8 ft 8 in) folding ruler for the toolbox. Precision rulers have always been made from metal, usually brass or steel. Metal was expensive, difficult to work with and heavy, so common rulers were made from ivory or wood before plastics were introduced. Ivory is an inferior material for an accurate and durable ruler, as it was susceptible to humidity. It was purely used on account of its whiteness, which was attractive and provided a good contrast to the black graduation markings. Wooden rulers were traditionally made from boxwood, a hard, yellowish wood with an obscure, fine grain. Boxwood was originally obtained from Turkey, although North American rulers were later made from Maracaibo boxwood from Venezuela. This wood is not only durable, but has the essential property of not expanding or contracting with changes in humidity. Boxwood rulers were fabricated with brass hinges and fittings, while ivory ones generally used German silver (nickel silver), because brass stains ivory. It was vital that the hinges were well engineered so that when the ruler was unfolded it locked in position without any flexibility. Early rulers were graduated by hand, following a master pattern using a graduating square and graduation knife. The numbers and other legends were stamped into the surface, and all markings were filled with lamp black, with linseed oil rubbed into them. The introduction of Stanley's retractable metal tape Push-Pull Rule in 1932 marked a steady decline in the use of the folding ruler. The convenience of being able to carry a 3 m (10 ft) measuring tape in the palm of your hand was overwhelming, yet the impact and influence of the Folding Ruler lead the way forward to future developments. It is believed that Anton Ullrich created the Folding Ruler in 1865 for Stabila, which became the standard, produced even by other companies.

CASTLES'

HEAVY, STOUTLY CONSTRUCTED SEATS

COMFORT   DURABILITY

THE "APOLLO"

Height of seat, 1 ft. 4 in. ; depth of seat, 1 ft. 8 in.   Total height, 3 ft.

THE "WIDGEON"

Height of seat, 1 ft. 4 in. ; depth of seat, 1 ft. 6½ in. Total height, 2 ft. 9 in.

**SEATS SUPPLIED BY CASTLES'
FOR H.M. OFFICE OF WORKS, THE MALL, LONDON.**

THE HANNIBAL "B"

Height of seat, 1 ft. 4 in. ; depth of seat, 1 ft. 7½ in. Total height, 2 ft. 11½ in.

THE "SALAMANDER"

Height of seat, 1 ft. 4 in. ; depth of seat, 1 ft. 8 in.   Total height, 3 ft.

We have all enjoyed a rest on a park bench. Varieties abound, but the all-wooden version with vertical slatted back and horizontal slatted seat is the most ubiquitous and least affected by the various fashions of the times it has lived through. Its status as the archetypal bench was confirmed by its use in the famous statue on London's Old Bond Street, *The Allies*, where sculptor Lawrence Holofcener depicted Franklin Roosevelt and Winston Churchill as its occupants. Similar constructions can be seen on vernacular domestic benches or 'settles' dating back to the sixteenth century, but it was the Victorians that gave us the park bench as we know it today. When the Industrial Revolution brought expansion of the cities, industrial benefactors put money into the creation of public parks. Royal parks were also opened and expanded to satisfy the Victorian fashion for perambulation, which in turn provided the need for inexpensive but sturdy seating. The bench was made of oak, or occasionally teak, some of which came from boards reclaimed from wooden battleships. Its actual design is harder to trace. The eighteenth century saw the widespread publishing of pattern books, which enabled local craftsmen to serve the tastes of the gentry. During the exchange of designs, the humble bench became a staple of many firms. Pre-dating the Arts and Crafts movement, the bench embodies the honesty of Ruskin and Morris's approach to materials. Assembled with strong mortise and tenon joints cut into fat timbers with a minimum of decoration, the bench has an understated, reassuring presence. Commemorative plaques or engravings have become a common addition to the park bench. In the eighteenth century, seats in ornamental and landscape gardens were occasionally inscribed with lines of poetry in an attempt to aid contemplation of the vistas before them. The bequeathing of municipal park benches by private individuals in memory of loved ones extended this tradition. In recent years, designers have even electronically augmented benches, enabling users to listen to audio tributes, hear poetry or access the Internet.

Can you tell a YALE lock at three yards?

If shape settled it you could.

But that narrow slit which takes a small flat key does not finally identify either the lock or its key.

Go nearer—is the name YALE there?

The locks and keys that look like YALE at three yards are up against something else at three feet.

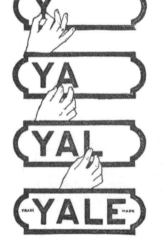

Up against the reason that made it worth while for them to look like YALE at all.

Up against the reason which makes it worth while to find YALE there. The name YALE on a lock is our signal to you that the lock is right.

That name is worth finding on any type of lock, on Builders' Hardware, Padlocks, Night Latches, Door Closers, Bank Locks, Chain Blocks, because it means that the goods will stand up when the going is the hardest.

Specify it   Check it up.   Don't let *shape* double-cross satisfaction.

Some Yale Products

Yale Cylinder Night Latches

Yale Door Closers

Yale Padlocks

The Yale & Towne Mfg. Co., *Makers of the Yale Locks*--General Offices & Works: Stamford. Conn. New York Office: 9 E. 40th St. Canadian Yale & Towne Ltd., St. Catharines. Ont. Chicago Office: 77 E. Lake St.

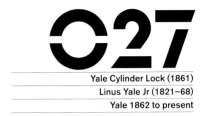
Linus Yale Jr was the son of a locksmith, and went on to invent locks whose basic principles are still in use for domestic small key locks, banks and vaults today. Yale was also a Victorian entrepreneur, and became a supreme self-publicist working for most of his career as a security consultant to banks and mints, and publishing essays and pamphlets on security. Yale created his first lock in 1851, and named it, with all the flair of a circus ringmaster, the Yale Magic Infallible Bank Lock. It was constructed around the principle of a key made of component parts, meaning that the combination could be endlessly changed and the key nearly impossible to copy. Internally, the lock avoided the use of springs and other components that had a tendency to fail in other locks. Yale also devised a mechanism that made the lock inaccessible to picking tools, and, he claimed, impervious to attack by gunpowder, concealing the pin-tumbler mechanism from the opening of the key hole. His second lock, the Yale Infallible Safe Lock was an improvement on this first model. His unpickable locks became famous in the 1850s through their reliability and they were used in the US Mint from 1856, through Linus Yale Jr's marketing expertise. He was, for instance, so confident in his mechanism that he offered a $3,000 reward to anyone who could pick the lock in his presence. This brash confidence of the entrepreneur coupled with a mechanical genius made Yale's the most famous name in lock design. In the 1860s, Yale developed the Monitor Bank Lock, the first combination bank lock, and the Yale Double Dial Bank Lock. He then began to rework the pin-tumbler mechanisms of the ancient Egyptians as a basis for his Cylinder Lock, patents for which were issued to Yale in 1861 and 1865. In 1868, Yale set up the Yale Lock Manufacturing Company in Philadelphia, with Henry Towne, which was intended to be Yale's big foray into small lock manufacturing, originally employing thirty-five people. However, he died just three months after construction began on the plant. But in 1879, padlocks, chain hoists and trucks were added to the production of locks, and the Yale name was carried forth into the twentieth century as the most established manufacturer of locks.

May 13 , 1924.

G. A. LEIGHTON

1,493,995

KEY OPENING CAN AND METHOD OF OPENING SAME

Filed Nov. 6, 1917

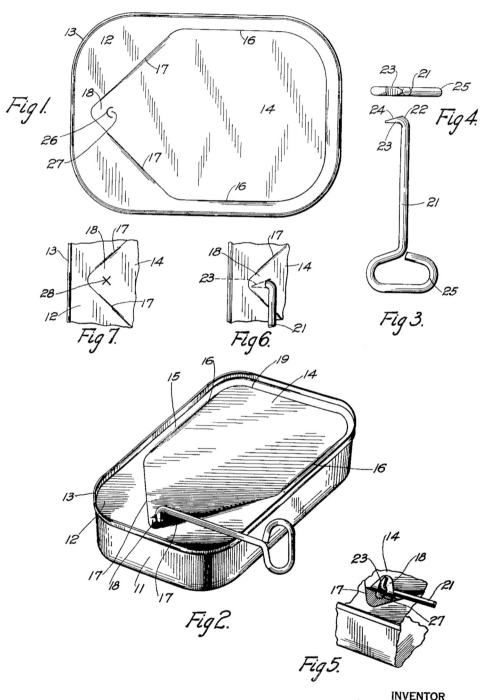

Fig 1.

Fig 4.

Fig 3.

Fig 7.

Fig 6.

Fig 2.

Fig 5.

INVENTOR

George A. Leighton

BY

Munday Clarke & Carpenter

ATTORNEYS

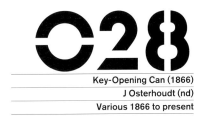

Key-Opening Can (1866)
J Osterhoudt (nd)
Various 1866 to present

In 1866 J Osterhoudt patented the first key-opening can. The key can's greatest asset was that, unlike its more generic cylindrical counterpart patented by Peter Durand in 1810, it could be opened with peculiar accuracy and easy manipulation without using a blade. Opening was achieved using a small metal 'key', which enabled the can's thin metal top to be peeled back. This simple, satisfying procedure led to many patents improving on the initial design. A patent by G A Leighton from 1924, featuring a slightly weakened 'x' point where the key was initially to be inserted and an arrow-shaped weakening line where the tin would be drawn back, shows particularly well how the 'key' worked. The key, replete with a delicate hook at its tip, is sunk into this weakened spot. By turning it and rolling it along the length of the can, the thin metal lid forms a curly roll at the end, revealing the can's contents. Although never as prevalent as the cylindrical tin can, these flimsier and shallower tins are best known as, and were perfectly designed to be, the receptacle for the humble sardine. In the Key-Opening Can, the little fish could be tightly packed together and yet not lose their shape or break up in transport. The slightly raised sides and relatively shallow depth of the key can meant also that the sardines could be accessed easily while at the same time preventing spillage of the oil they were preserved in. For this reason we can perhaps also thank the key can for the colloquialism, 'packed like sardines'.

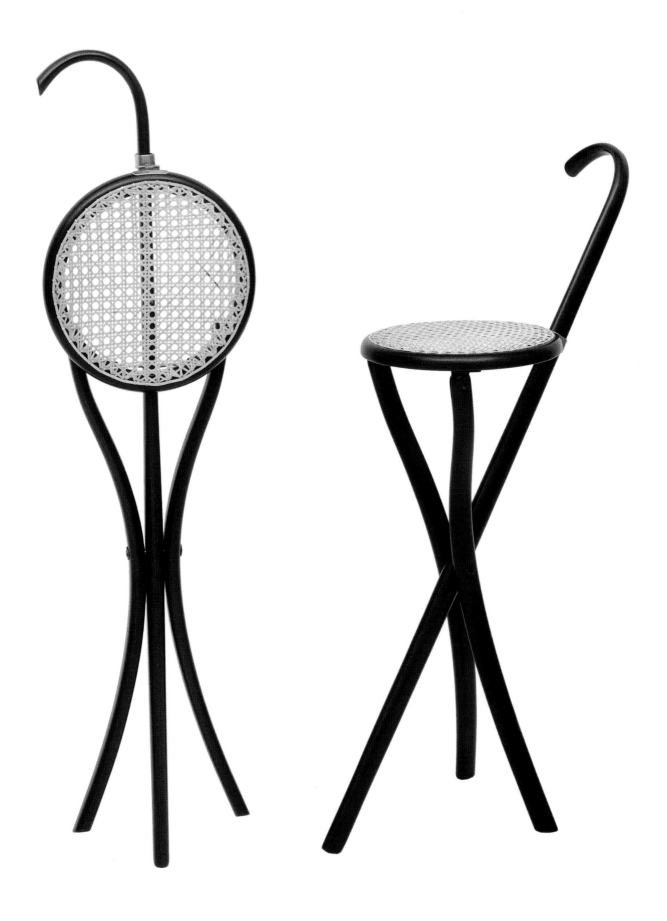

Damenstock (1866)
Michael Thonet (1796–1871)
Gebrüder Thonet 1879 to 1911
Gebrüder Thonet Vienna 2003 to present

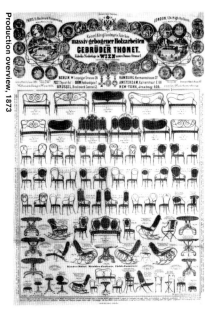

Production overview, 1873

Michael Thonet may be best known for the sinuous bentwood furniture that he created with his sons in Vienna in the late nineteenth century, but there are a number of objects that also came out of his workshop that are more playful than the standard coffee-house chair. Thonet's Damenstock, a two-in-one walking stick with a folding seat, for example, expresses its inherent split personality in the way its form resembles a combination umbrella and sporting rifle. For use in the city during long tram waits, or on a stroll in the near-lying Vienna Woods, Thonet's foldable contraption is an enduring example of a successful hybrid design that went elegantly from city to country. With two legs and a straight stick that turn around a central pivot and a seat that provides locking action, the piece is soundly and minimally engineered with a precise and relatively stripped-down aesthetic given that it pre-dated Modernism. Constructed out of hotbent beechwood and topped by a round seat of woven Viennese straw, the Thonet Damenstock first appeared commercially in the company's 1866 broadsheet. A leaner, more refined version of the traditional hunter's stool, Thonet's hybrid really came into its own in 1911, when it was displayed prominently in the company's catalogue and was offered in as many as twenty-four different variations, including a woman's version that replaced the object's thicker masculine lines with gracefully bowed legs and a handle turned the opposite way for certain differentiation. Although the fashion for walking sticks is, it would seem, at an end, the need for a portable seat that could be used anywhere from museums to sporting events still exists, which is what has made Gebrüder Thonet Vienna reissue the Damenstock, along with a number of other Thonet classics.

Typewriters were still a pretty unusual sight at the time of the introduction of this model, originally called the 'Sholes & Glidden Type Writer'. The designers, Sholes and Glidden, had licensed their invention to the gun, agricultural-implement and sewing machine-maker, E Remington and Sons, in 1870 and, although they had continued to make improvements where speed and accuracy were concerned, these early machines were by no means user-friendly. The majority of so-called typewriters at this time, including the Remington No.1, were 'blind-writer', or 'up-strike' designs, that is, the operators could not see what was being written until they either lifted up the carriage or the paper emerged from the feed mechanism. This must have compounded the frustration with what was already a fairly laborious process. Typing had only just started to catch on, this typewriter being the first machine that offered a potentially faster alternative to writing by hand. One design element that contributed to this increased speed was the now standard 'Qwerty' keyboard layout. A well-known, but almost certainly apocryphal story has Sholes devising this arrangement to hinder the typist's performance. It is more likely that he was organizing the mechanics to prevent the type bars (which held the letter at the end) of popular letter-combinations from approaching the platen (where the paper was struck) from angles likely to jam if used in quick succession. This should have had the effect of speeding up the typing. There were clearly many more innovations to be made before the archetypal form emerged, but the Remington No.1 was the first commercially successful machine, selling around 5,000 units in its various incarnations, at a price of $125. It helped to establish not only a market for typewriters, but also the reputation of the Remington company, which was to remain the biggest player for the next twenty years. Its legacy is strongly resonant even today, where all but a handful of keyboards in use have a 'Qwerty' layout. Research has shown alternatives (such as the Dvorak) to be quicker, but nothing approaches the popularity of Sholes's original layout.

Remington No.1 (1868)
Christopher Latham Sholes (1819–90)
Carlos Glidden (1834–77)
E Remington & Sons 1873 to c.1878

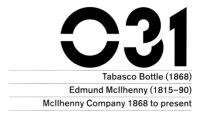

Edmund McIlhenny

The Tabasco Bottle is one of those ubiquitous and iconic products intrinsically linked with American life. The seemingly universal availability of Tabasco, a fiery chilli sauce, has been aided by a design that has changed very little since its inception in 1868, which is now sold in over 160 countries and territories. With 700,000 bottles being produced daily, and labels printed in twenty-two languages, the widespread popularity of this sauce is hardly surprising. When Edmund McIlhenny invented the hot pepper sauce, three years following the end of the Civil War, it was an entrepreneurial way to produce income from his war-ravaged land on Avery Island, in Louisiana. He bottled his first sample batch in used cologne bottles, which had a sprinkler filament attached to the neck – to slow the sauce as even the earliest recipe needed to applied with caution – and distributed the sauce to friends and family. The used cologne bottles were quickly replaced by new ones prior to making the first commercial batch, but they were to remain the blueprint for all future Tabasco Bottle designs. The 57 ml (2 fl oz) size was chosen as the optimum size, as it responded to the practical demands of the product. Sharp shoulders were replaced by rounded ones to lower the occurrence of breakages during shipment. Corks sealed in green wax were replaced by metal tops, and the embossed Tabasco trade name and two stars were added to the base of the bottle. The diamond-shaped label bearing the McIlhenny company name was devised and has changed only subtly since. McIlhenny's first choice of name for his sauce was Petit Anse Sauce, borrowed from the name of the family island (now called Avery Island), which lies 225 km (140 m) west of New Orleans. Ironically, the family was unwilling to have its island's name put to commercial use. The name 'tabasco', McIlhenny's second choice, was taken from the Native American word meaning 'land where the soil is hot and humid', and Avery Island, where Tabasco is still made today, is extremely well suited to the cultivation of chilli peppers. As pickers harvest the peppers, they compare the colour to a *petit bâton rouge*, a wooden dowel painted the exact shade of red that the company prefers for their chillies.

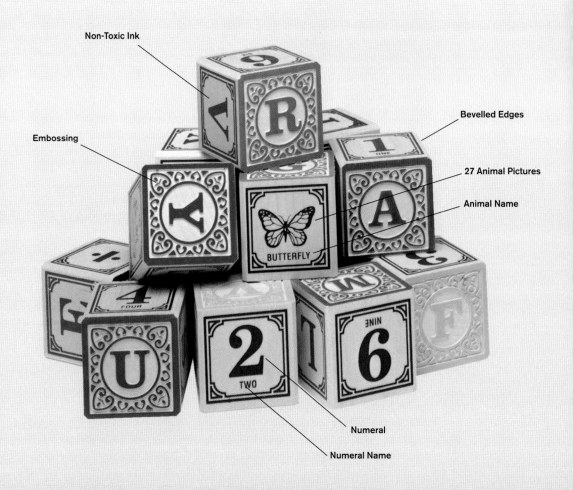

Non-Toxic Ink

Embossing

Bevelled Edges

27 Animal Pictures

Animal Name

BUTTERFLY

Numeral

Numeral Name

Learning to read is part of a rite of passage into a bigger world. How that is done seems almost magical and the best objects used in the process are imbued with a quality of wonder. For over a century Uncle Goose's ABC Blocks have been considered among the most fantastic of such tools. First manufactured in 1879, the set of twenty-seven 2.54 cm (1 in) wooden blocks were embossed with four alphabets, three sets of Arabic numerals, arithmetic signs and twenty-seven images of animals, with each brightly coloured image or symbol surrounded by a filigree pattern. Based on traditional toys originally carved by fathers and grandfathers as a winter pastime, the blocks were put into production by The Embossing Company of Albany, New York. For more than half a century these blocks were among the favourite toys of young children and even of adults like the notoriously selective Frank Lloyd Wright. When The Embossing Company of Albany closed it doors in 1955, production ceased. In 1983 William Bultman established his company, Uncle Goose Toys, to bring to market toys that developed motor skills and mathematical and language skills among children of preschool and kindergarten age. Bultman recalled the ABC blocks of his youth and reissued the toy sets, capitalizing on the sense of nostalgia they evoked, while at the same time making a commitment to improving the local economy by basing their production in Grand Rapids, Michigan. The blocks use the original surface design and colour scheme, but are made only with regional basswood and painted with child-safe, non-toxic inks. The blocks are available with Hebrew, Spanish and German alphabets, as well as in Braille and sign language, and Bultman has expanded the range of packaging to include boxes, bags, crates and wagons.

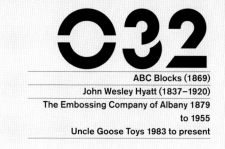

032

ABC Blocks (1869)
John Wesley Hyatt (1837–1920)
The Embossing Company of Albany 1879
to 1955
Uncle Goose Toys 1983 to present

Japan's rich cultural life may lay claim to a roll-call of iconic architectural, fashion and industrial design achievements that are specifically Japanese in style, but none have proved quite so pervasive as the humble disposable Waribashi Chopstick. Waribashi are an unavoidable fixture of daily Japanese life, and have proved to be the most widely used chopsticks not only in Japan, but also throughout much of the Westernized world. The name Waribashi translates as 'breakable', in reference to the snapping action needed to separate the two sticks before use. The pale wooden sticks measure approximately 15 cm (6 in) in length and can take on any number of variations, of which the Koban is most common. Usually Waribashi Chopsticks come enclosed in a hygienic paper sachet called *hashi bukuro*, set enticingly by each individual place setting. Waribashi were first introduced during the Meiji Restoration period between 1868 and 1912. During this time, Japan's cultural and social life was put through a fast-paced phase of modernization, which included establishing Shinto as the dominant religion. According to Shinto, chopsticks are given by the gods and provide a sacred bridge between human beings and the divine beings. In addition, the Shinto religion is heavily laden with the ideals of purity and renewal. Being both disposable and designed to be used only once, Waribashi fulfil both these Shinto stipulations. But interestingly, their latter day ubiquity contradicts another Shinto tenet – that of prudence. Originally Waribashi were made from scrap wood but in the twenty-first-century world they are made mostly from imported wood grown expressly for the purpose. Hence, in recent years these seemingly innocent utensils and their main producer, the monolithic Waribashi Company, have come under scrutiny from the environmental lobby. Annually, 24 billion pairs of Waribashi Chopsticks are produced, which amounts to roughly 168 pairs per person per year. Disposing of such an amount of waste wood poses severe ecological problems for Japan, but if anything the problem looks set to increase. In terms of design, however, the Waribashi Chopstick is possibly one of the world's most archetypal eating utensils. Although disregarded by most people as a simple accompaniment to a takeaway with little regard to the long and profound history that went to create them, their utility, elegance and function are indisputable.

Tuck under thumb
and hold firmly

Learn how to use your chopsticks

Add second chopstick
hold it as you hold
a pencil

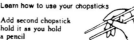

Hold first chopstick
in original position
move the second one
up and down Now you
can pick up anything

Considered the first professional industrial designer in Europe, Christopher Dresser designed a wealth of objects and decorative patterns throughout his fifty-year career. The most broad-minded designer of his time, Dresser studied botany and wrote books on decorative design while at the same time advocating the omission of decoration in certain objects for reasons of purity and formal elegance. One of his first metalware designs, this characterful three-legged Sugar Bowl appeared in his sketchbook in the mid-1860s and was manufactured by the Birmingham-based firm, Elkington & Company. The conical form points to Dresser's penchant for simplicity, gained in part from his study of Japanese metalware. His book Principles of Decorative Design, published in 1873, offers further insight. A self-help manual for the budding artisan, the author used the book to expound his theories upon the importance of 'fitness for purpose' and 'economy of materials'. The latter is given as the reason for the two ridges running around the top of the Sugar Bowl. The 'beads' strengthen the upper portion of the cone, meaning it could be constructed from thinner silver plate, saving money for both manufacturer and customer. In the book Dresser also explains the form of the bowl's legs in purely functional terms. Frustrated by the small handles applied to many bowls, which required the user to place their thumb inside the rim, and convinced a cone was the right form for the vessel as it helped to separate sugar dust from lumps, Dresser proposed three legs that would hold up the cone and also act as handles. The cartoon-like rendering of these legs and their feet lent a charm to the piece that has ensured its survival. In 1991 Italian company Alessi, who produce a silver reproduction of the piece, now with two legs, brought out versions in coloured resin. The green, yellow and blue versions of the bowl sat happily alongside the company's more frivolous anthropomorphic creations, their looks defying the original's 130 years of age.

Sugar Bowl (c.1873)
Christopher Dresser (1834–1904)
Elkington & Company c.1873 to 1890
Alessi 1991 to present

The 17.5 cm (7 in) Provence model may be only one of the eighty different options in wood, stainless steel and acrylic currently available in Peugeot Pepper Mills, but it is unquestionably the most recognized. This model, produced since 1874, is the most popular of the approximately two million pepper mills sold annually by Peugeot. For over 160 years Peugeot Pepper Mills, established in 1810 in eastern France, has set the standard for all competitors. The stature of this mill is based on converging factors of style, technology and association. It appears traditional, but the simple logic of its design, the technical innovation and the construction of the grinding mechanism all transcend style. The patented adjus-table mechanism uses double rows of spiral teeth, or two rows of helicoidal grooves, which channel and feed the peppercorns first through a cracking stage and then to fine grinding. Mechanisms are fabricated out of steel that is case-hardened to assure the reliability and durability for which the mills are famous. For

generations, these pepper mills have been associated with gourmet dining, preparing fine food and the attendant aura of the family gathering The lion, the emblem of Peugeot, first used in 1850 and formally registered in 1858, was adopted because of the association of the strong jaws of the beast with the cast steel blades originally used. Today, the internal mechanism is made of heavy-gauge processed steel, which is practically indestructible. This is the same Peugeot that has been renowned for racing bicycles and automobiles since the 1890s. In 1810 the Peugeot brothers converted a family grain mill into a steel mill and, by 1818, had been awarded a patent for tool production. In 1840 the company introduced its innovative coffee mills, followed later in the century by the pepper mills and by many other successful products like irons and sewing machines. In the twentieth century, the company's spice mills and salt mills, which use stainless steel for the mechanisms to resist corrosion, were popular, but since 1874, Peugeot has remained the leading manufacturer of pepper mills.

Christopher Dresser

Although looking precisely like the kind of object to come out of Germany's Bauhaus, this toast rack was designed by the British designer, Christopher Dresser, over forty years prior to the school's opening. Dresser's work was championed by Modernists of the early twentieth century, but although he designed many lines of silverware with sparse aesthetics, often using simple geometric forms, Dresser was not an advocate of one style of design or rigid doctrine. Working across a range of materials, he argued that ornament and construction ought not to be considered in isolation, but he was not averse to applying decoration where he saw fit. In his silverware, however, he concentrated upon economical use of the material and the majority of his surfaces remained unadorned, with structural details providing the focus. In the toast rack this economy is plain to see. Ten cylindrical pegs pierce through an oblong plate, with four

extending to make the feet. The remaining six are hammered over like rivets on the underside of the rack, a detail likely to have been inspired by the exposed rivets on Japanese metalwork. The T-shaped handle is another Japanese motif Dresser borrowed for a number of his designs and the collection to which the rack belonged is said to have been influenced not just by Japanese metal and lacquer stands but also by public metalwork, such as the country's railings and temple gates. Dresser was the first European designer to visit Japan, which he did in 1876 on the invitation of the Japanese government in recognition of his work promoting the country's goods in Europe. Originally manufactured in silver by the British company Hukin & Heath, for whom Dresser worked for many years, the piece was reissued in polished stainless steel by Alessi in 1991.

There are many things that the British view with fierce pride. Among them is the red pillar box, which English Heritage chairman Sir Neil Cossons has described as, 'a classic icon of British design inextricably linked to our national image'. Britain's first red free-standing cast-iron pillar box appeared in Jersey's capital, St Helier, in 1852, ushered in not by an engineer, designer or planner, but by the Victorian novelist Anthony Trollope. A surveyor's clerk for the Post Office at the time, Trollope had been sent to the Channel Islands to study ways of improving postal services and quickly arrived at the solution of the roadside post-boxes that are now regarded as Britain's first nationwide communication system. These first hexagonal boxes were designed by local designer John Vaudin and made their debut on mainland Britain in September 1853. But the shape of the boxes presented problems, including difficulty in emptying them. The mainland boxes were also painted in different colours, among them dark green, bronze and red, making identification on the street difficult, and they came in any shape or size that the relevant postal district desired. Some were 2.5 m (8 ft) tall in the form of fluted Doric columns with domes and ornate crowns, others were rectangular with an aperture in their roof, an obvious failing given the nation's inclement climate. The cylindrical National Standard, originally green but painted red in 1874 to aid visibility, was derived from an 1858 design by Richard Redgrave at the Department for Science and Arts, at what is now the Victoria and Albert Museum, London. In 1859 the design was improved in a number of ways. Among these was the introduction of a protective hood on the roof covering the repositioned aperture (from the top to below the rim) and a wire cage that held the post when the door was opened. Manufactured by Messers Cochrane & Company, the arrival of the first National Standard Pillar Box in 1859, as the name suggests, standardized the box across the country. In November 1875, a model for a cylindrical box was produced, which was to become the box we see today. The design was superseded by the iconic 'Anonymous' box without any royal cipher in 1879, which apart from a few recent experiments has changed very little since. The only addition has been the placement of the words 'POST OFFICE' on either side of the aperture. This is the now the National Standard and its key innovative design elements have remained almost untouched.

1/6

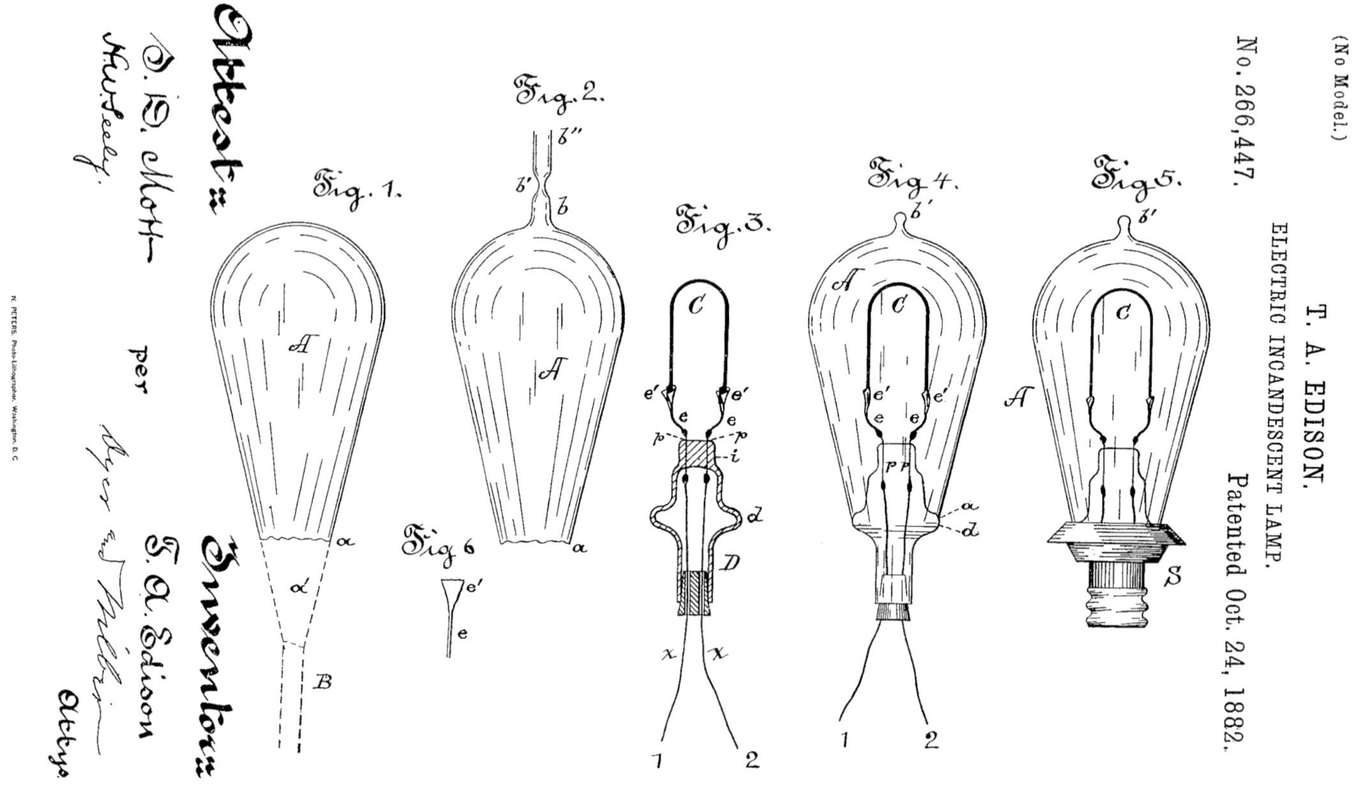

(No Model.)

No. 266,447.

T. A. EDISON.

ELECTRIC INCANDESCENT LAMP.

Patented Oct. 24, 1882.

Fig. 1.

Fig. 2.

Fig. 3.

Fig. 4.

Fig. 5.

Fig. 6.

The incandescent electric light bulb was the simultaneous invention of two scientists: Thomas Alva Edison in the USA and Sir Joseph Wilson Swan in the UK. In the subsequent histories of electric light, Edison's name has featured more prominently due to his ability to turn a scientific breakthrough into a commercial success. Developed at his laboratories in Menlo Park, New Jersey, Edison's light bulb used a carbon filament, made from cotton thread, inside a glass vacuum bulb. The glass bulbs were made in a glass-blowing workshop at Menlo Park. When electricity was passed through the filament, it burnt for a few hours, giving out a soft orange glow. The vacuum in the glass bulb delayed the filament from burning out, so that after further experiments Edison was able to produce a light bulb with a life of over 1,500 hours by the end of 1880. Sir Joseph Wilson Swan's version was produced and patented in England slightly earlier in 1879. Swan experimented with using electrical current applied to a conductive material, carbon wire, to produce a white-hot glow. He used a vacuum to slow the burning of the

filament, but his early experiments were too unstable to maintain the vacuum. Edison was able to perfect the technique and swiftly patented his invention (his light bulb was awarded US patent number 223,898 in 1880). On hearing of Swan's success, Edison also filed a patent infringement complaint against him. This litigious action backfired on Edison, who failed in his action and was forced to acknowledge Swan's earlier invention. As a result of the case, Edison was also obliged to enter into a joint commercial venture with Swan. Thus the Edison and Swan United Electric Light Company was established, with the conjoined brand name, Ediswan. The potential of Swan and Edison's invention could only be realized once an adequate power network was in place to bring electricity to the light bulb. First commercial and public, and later domestic uptake of electrical lighting created a huge global market for the incandescent light bulb. Although it has been in a process of continual technical improvement since its invention, the incandescent bulb today is still recognizable as the vision of its inventors.

Type Edison Lamp (1879)
Thomas Alva Edison (1847–1931)
Edison General Electric (General Electric)
1880 to 1890s

Almost as much a part of childhood play as the teddy bear, the brightly coloured Musical Spinning Top enjoys an enduring appeal in more or less its original design form. In 1888 Lorenz Bolz began production of the first hand-pressed zinc spinning tops at his firm in Zirndorf, Bavaria, to his own design. Traditional spinning tops had been wooden cones that rotated at their point and were propelled with a whip. The Bolz Spinning Top combined the body shape of the top with a wooden hand grip that allowed more control over the spinning action. Small incisions made in the metal body and the reaction of the airflow inside the top to the centrifugal force created a humming effect. Gradually Bolz changed the manufacturing material from zinc to tin plate, and in 1913, his son Peter Bolz further modified the design by introducing the plunger or pump mechanism drill bar feature. This metal drill bar, with spiral grooves and a wooden grip, effectively drilled into the top like a screw, and its repeated pump action was able to create a greater spinning momentum, which in turn heightened the singing effect of the top. Additional note chords were also incorporated to produce a more sophisticated and livelier sound. Later developments included a humming top patented in 1937 with twenty-note chords and in 1952, a top that could play a whole song. The tops are decorated in different designs. The dimensions of the basic model include a diameter of 19 cm (7 in), a height of 19 cm (7 in) and a weight of 230 g (8 oz). Despite the current dominance of conglomerates and homogenized global markets, this small family-run enterprise with its long history manages to maintain its position among the world's leading humming top manufacturers.

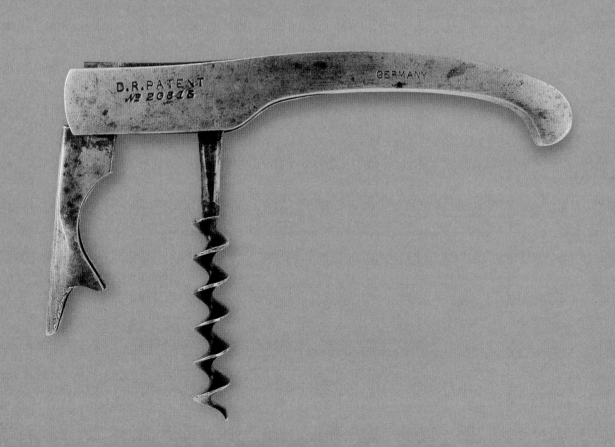

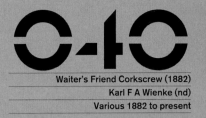

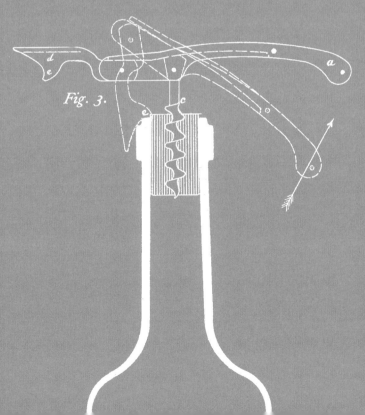

Fig. 3.

The original design of Karl F A Wienke's Waiter's Friend has remained more or less the same since it was first patented in Rostock in Germany in 1882. Unassailable in its combination of simplicity, practicality and affordability, this single-lever corkscrew is still mass-produced around the world. The Waiter's or Butler's Friend was so-called because it could be easily collapsed and, at 11.5 cm (4 in) in length, kept in a pocket, winning many fans among waiters. Wienke's patent drawings describe a steel handle-lever with three retractable appendages: a knife for cutting the foil seal, a wire helix corkscrew and a fulcrum that grips the rim of the bottle, allowing the lever action to remove the cork. Several German companies initially manufactured the Waiter's Friend, notably Eduard Becker of Solingen. The simple single-lever mechanism has inevitably been challenged by other corkscrew designs over the years, particularly the double lever rack and pinion corkscrew mechanism, which came to prominence with a model first patented by Dominick Rosati in Chicago in 1930. Despite the success of this rival design, Wienke's corkscrew continues to enjoy favour with wine connoisseurs and societies as well as waiters. A plethora of facsimile Waiter's Friends is available on the market, ranging from cheap steel versions to state-of-the-art models with solid ABS plastic handles, stainless steel micro-serrated knives, five-turn teflon-coated worms and in a wide assortment of colours. Yet all bear the same basic Wienke patent design and function in exactly the same way.

The distinctive nickel-plated brass barrel of the Metropolitan Whistle, with its ring at one end and bottle-like lip at the other, is familiar to the workforce of over 120 national police forces in the world. But it is the sound of the whistle that really distinguishes it as an intelligent design. The two-tone, discordant sound of the Metropolitan could be heard over two miles away from its user, and was adopted by the London Metropolitan Police in 1883 as a replacement for the awkward and quiet rattles they had used previously. The main advantage of the Metropolitan over its competitors was that it was the first whistle of its type to have a mouthpiece that could be held between the teeth, leaving the hands free. After tests on Hampstead Heath in north London in 1883, the Metropolitan Police ordered 21,000, which were to be delivered by the end of the year. Its inventor, Joseph Hudson, had to borrow £20 from the Metropolitan Police to buy the amount of brass required. The model is still in use today, virtually unchanged, and the majority have been produced at Hudson's historic Barr Street factory in the suburbs of Birmingham. Hudson was a tool-maker and amateur musician from Birmingham, who hit on the idea that a whistle could form a portable device to get the attention of people in a variety of different situations. The myth is that he came across the sound as he dropped his violin by accident, creating a sharp sound as the strings snapped. This noise, he felt, was exactly what the London bobby was looking for, and he finally patented the device in 1908. A staggering 45 million Metropolitan Whistles have been produced since it was first created.

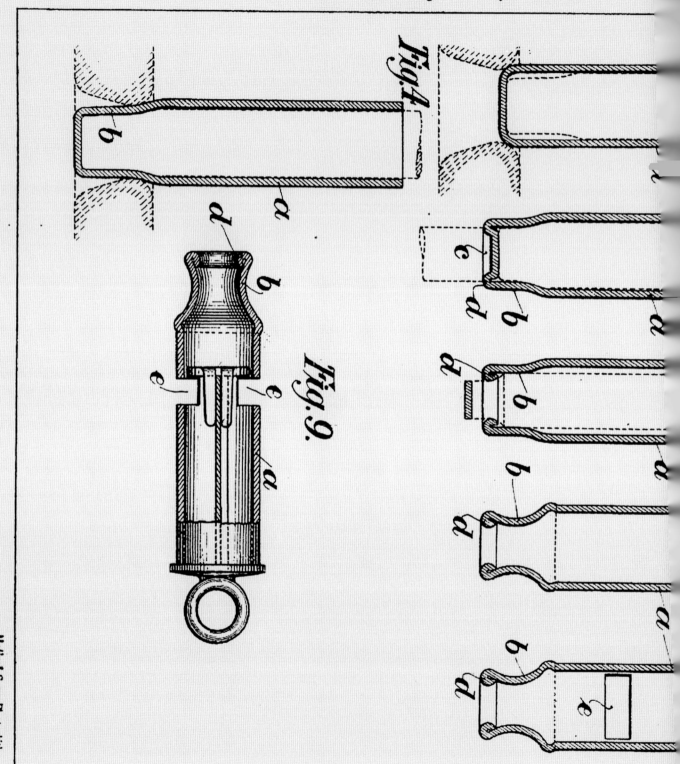

Fig.4

Fig.9.

A.D. 1911. DEC. 23. N°. 28,999.

HUDSON'S COMPLETE SPECIFICATION.

(1 SHEET)

al on a reduced scale.]

Fig. 1.

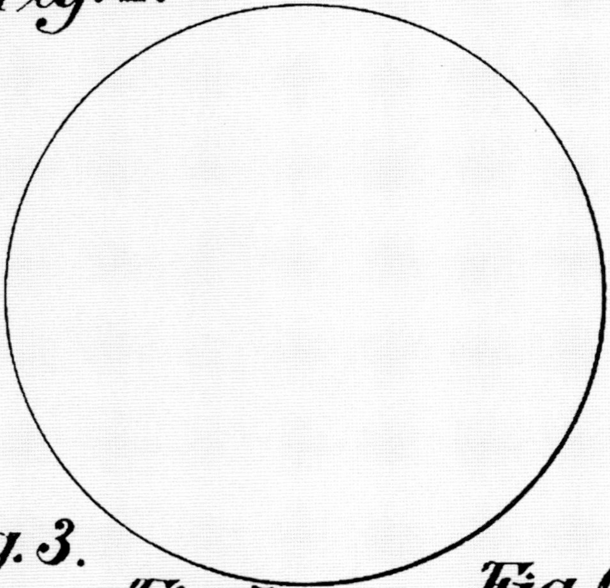

Fig. 2.

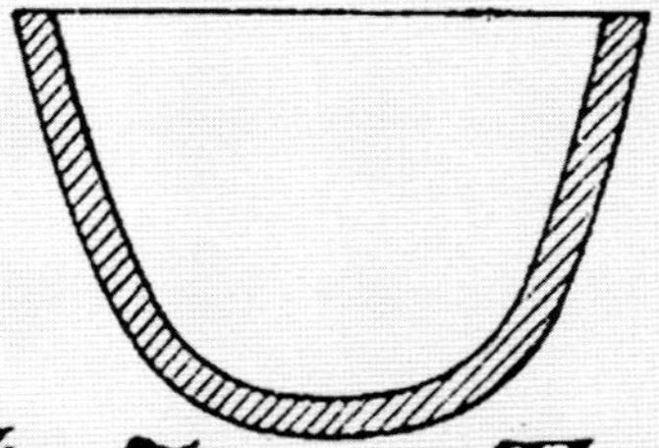

Fig. 3.

Fig. 5.

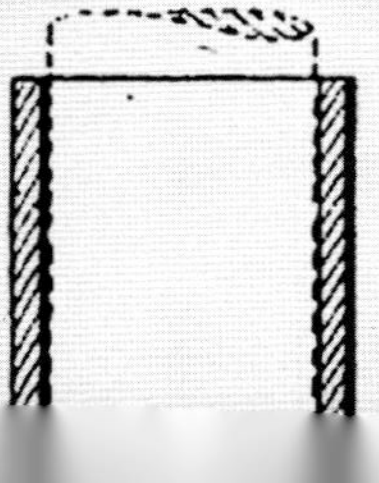

Fig. 6.

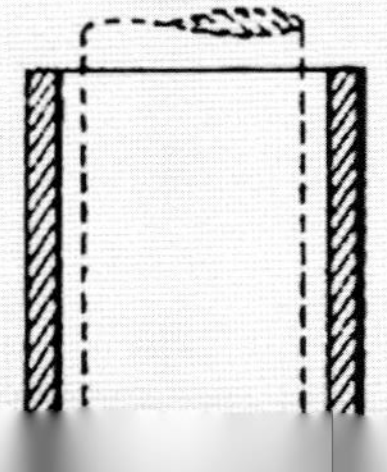

Fig. 7.

Fig. 8.

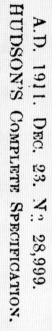

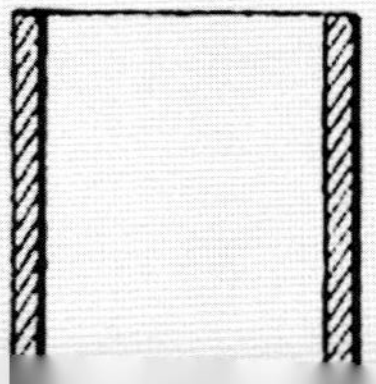

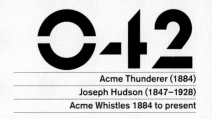

Acme Thunderer (1884)
Joseph Hudson (1847–1928)
Acme Whistles 1884 to present

A mark of a perfectly designed object is not only its ability to withstand the test of time, but also its ability to remain essentially unchanged in that time. Such an accolade goes to the Acme Thunderer. This little piece of metal has fulfilled its function as a referee's whistle so consistently well since its invention in 1884 that it is now the world's biggest-selling whistle, heard in more than 137 countries. The story of its invention and design is almost as beguiling as the object itself. Its maker, Joseph Hudson, chanced upon the sound of its predecessor, the Metropolitan Whistle. Having so firmly established the policeman's whistle, Hudson had to come up with a distinctly different sound when, a year later, he began to develop a whistle that football umpires could use in place of their decidedly ineffectual handkerchiefs or sticks. Where the Metropolitan Police needed to create a sound that would carry over a long distance, the Thunderer needed to penetrate through dense background noise. The solution, of course, was the insertion of a pea, which was actually a cork pellet, into the two manually joined, moulded brass pieces that made up the whistle. This produced a warbling sound as the air in the whistle chamber forced the pea-shaped cork around. Minor changes were made to the design in the 1920s, when the whistle was made smaller and the mouthpiece tapered to produce a higher pitch and more comfortable whistle, but it is still produced by Acme Whistles, and each one still tested before it leaves the factory. Its piercing sound is still heard today; both the Acme and the more recent Thunderer 2000, can be heard in sports stadiums around the world.

Fig. 1.

Fig. 2.

Fig. 3.

Fig. 4.

Fig. 5.

Fig. 6.

Fig. 7.

Fig. 8.

Fig. 9.

Fig. 10.

The Rover Safety Bicycle is considered to be the mother of the modern bicycle. It was designed and built in 1885 by John Kemp Starley in Coventry, England. His concern was, as the name suggests, to make his machine as safe as a tricycle, yet at least as light and fast as the penny-farthing. His bicycle, using two similar sized wheels, was the first step in the development of what soon became, and still remains, the most economic and efficient form of transport ever devised. This is arguably the world's first example of this standardized format, combining the key elements of what the word 'bicycle' conjures up in most people's minds. Beyond the decision to use two similar sized wheels, the next most pertinent feature is what has become known as the 'diamond frame'. The diamond (or trapezoid) shape which it refers to is formed by two triangles; the three larger diameter tubes which join the three nodes that hold the saddle, the handlebars/front forks and the bottom bracket, the point at which the cranks and pedals rotate around, together with the second, or 'rear' triangle, which is made up of smaller diameter tubes and which provides support for the rear wheel fixing. The increasing availablity of good quality steel tube, which was fantastically light and strong, meant it soon became the obvious material for frame building. Following a further twenty years of development in many countries, the basic form of the modern bicycle became standardized. The other key components that were developed during this period were; pneumatic tyres by John Boyd Dunlop, the free wheel by Ernst Sachs, crossed tangentially spoked wheels, and later cogs and gears. Together, these developments allowed the bicycle to go from experimental plaything of the wealthy, viewed with some suspicion, to a cheap, everyday, robust and convenient workhorse for all people. It was even argued at the time, that the safety bicycle was invaluable in assisting the emancipation of women.

O-43

Rover Safety Bicycle (1885)
John Kemp Starley (1854–1901)
JK Starley & Co (Rover Cycle Company)
1885 to 1897

Illustrated London News, 1899

STARLEY & SUTTON,

𝔐eteor 𝔚orks, 𝔚est 𝔒rchard,

COVENTRY.

" The 'Rover' has set the fashion to the world."—*Cyclist.*

18½ MILES IN THE HOUR; 30½ MILES IN 1 hr. 41 min. ON THE HIGH ROAD.

The "Rover," as ridden by Lord BURY, President N.C.U.

MANUFACTURERS OF THE CELEBRATED

"ROVER" BICYCLE,

THE "ROAMER" & OTHER TRICYCLES,

"COVENTRY CHAIR," &c., &c.

Price Lists and Testimonials Free.   *Full Illustrated Catalogue, 2 Stamps.*

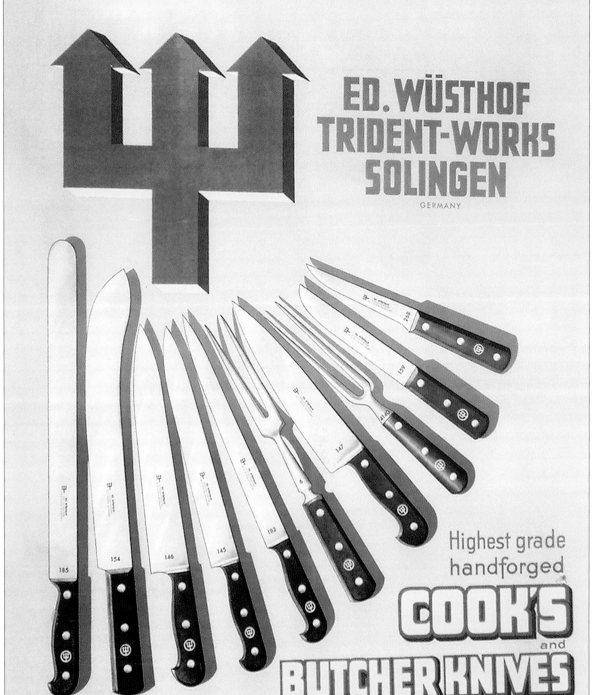

ED. WÜSTHOF
TRIDENT-WORKS
SOLINGEN

GERMANY

Highest grade
handforged

COOK'S
and
BUTCHER KNIVES

Advertisement, c.1950s

Wüsthof Classic Knives (1886)
Ed Wüsthof Dreizackwerk Design Team
Ed Wüsthof Dreizackwerk 1886 to present

2001

1886

The Wüsthof Classic Knife design has remained virtually unchanged since it first appeared in 1886. Designed and manufactured by Ed Wüsthof Dreizackwerk of Solingen, Germany, the Classic series was designed for and used by both professional and domestic cooks worldwide. Solingen is a city renowned for cutlery design, and the Wüsthof Classic plays a vital role in the origin of this reputation. The beauty and success of the design is in its simplicity of form and ease of use, combined with high standards in craftsmanship and materials. The ground-breaking construction and design meant that the common failing of the blade coming away or breaking off from the handle, became a thing of the past. Launched during the early days of the Industrial Revolution, the Wüsthof Classic Knife range references traditional styling combined with innovative design and production. Forged from a single piece of stainless steel, the tang is fully visible, forming blade and handle core. The precision forging and use of a single piece of steel means the manufacturing processes are reduced. There is no need for stamping, welding, or short cuts, thus eliminating any weak points in the form and construction of the knife and resulting in an end product that is a perfectly balanced cutting tool. Stainless steel is traditionally considered one of the most hygienic materials for use in the kitchen, and its bright surface create a modern, attractive appearance. Visually, the Wüsthof Classic Knives series stood apart from its competitors from the outset, with a core tang that is visible and sandwiched between the wooden handles. The characteristic three rivets along the handle provide a simple method for secure and safe attachment. The three-piece construction succeeds in presenting a knife that is cleverly designed for maximum strength, safety, balance and heft. The Wüsthof Classic is still in production today and used in both professional and domestic environments. New styles have been added to the range, but the basic construction remains the same. This cult object owes its enduring popularity to the minimal and unpretentious nature of its form and materials. The Wüsthof Classic has therefore enjoyed long-standing success through the loyalty of its users.

The only difference between a regular, or gentleman's, bicycle and a lady's bicycle is the design of the frame. The Raleigh Lady's Bicycle frame was developed without a crossbar, to enable ease of mounting while wearing a skirt. In other respects, it is the same as the regular or 'diamond-frame' bicycle, which was introduced in the 1880s. This landmark moment in the evolution of the world's most enduring form of transport was followed by many years of development. Most of this research was centred on the other components that would be attached to the now standardized diamond frame. Much of this early work was completed in Britain, but as the machine gathered popularity, further development and improvements took place in other countries, with France, Germany and Holland all particularly active. However, during the same period one of Britain's most interesting and dynamic industrial success stories, Raleigh, had grown into the world's largest bicycle manufacturer. Originally established in 1886 in Raleigh Street, Nottingham, England, Raleigh went through a number of different guises under different leadership and conditions. Its early growth and success was in part dependent on hub gears, which were developed by associated company, Sturmey Archer. This early specialist expertise allowed the company to go on to produce motorcycles, gearboxes and even three-wheel cars. In 1938 Raleigh Cycle Holdings Ltd had stopped the production of cars and motorcycles, and were building approximately 500,000 bicycles every year. The sheer scale of its manufacturing meant the company played a key part in the growing success of the bicycle and subsequently, the interwar years have become known as the golden age of bicycle touring. The classlessness of this means of transport, which gave the possibility of a new independence, especially for women, was the main reason for its unprecedented popularity. The industry realised the potential of this market and featured movie stars like Katherine Hepburn in their advertisements.

RALEIGH № 12.

LADY'S BICYCLE

O-45

Lady's Bicycle (c.1886)
Designer Unknown
Raleigh c.1886 to present

PRICES.

No. 12 N, Nottingham make,
          Specification same as No. 1 Lady's Bicycle,
                            £30   0 0

No. 12 L, Lenton make,
          Specification same as No. 2 Lady's Bicycle,
                            £26   0 0

No. 12 R, Radford make,
          Specification same as No. 13 Lady's Bicycle,
                            £22   0 0

Julius Maggi

Maggi Sauce, found in kitchens and dining rooms across the globe, is a fine example of what functional packaging can achieve alongside imaginative branding and marketing. The sauce, a mix of hydrogenated vegetable protein, salt and water, with a flavour similar to soy sauce, was actually created by Swiss-born Julius Maggi to add a savoury zip to his dried soups. Made from powdered peas, beans, lentils and other vegetables, these soups aimed to combat the plummeting standards of nutrition, particularly protein deficiency, among poor families uprooted from the countryside to work in factories in rapidly industrializing Switzerland. The first pea and bean soup of 1886 lacked flavour, but Maggi compensated later that year with the sauce. The distinctive quadrangular bottle design and eye-catching yellow and red branding were both Maggi's work. While its proportions have been tweaked slightly over time, the bottle design has remained essentially unchanged as an enduring expression of the Maggi brand. The most significant alteration came in the mid-1930s, when the company stopped tying the corked drop dispenser to the bottle's neck for the consumer to apply and made it integral to the design itself. The labelling, meanwhile, is a study in changing trends, with the text-heavy labels and extravagant fonts of the turn of the century slowly giving way to uncluttered simplicity and sans-serif lettering. But Maggi went beyond product innovation, supporting the sauce and soups from the start with the most creative poster artists and even recruiting playwright Frank Wedekind as his copywriter. The result was a stream of ingenious work that had catapulted the products to prominence by the time of Maggi's death in 1912. Maggi had also published recipe guides, which quickly led to the sauce being used not only with soups but also with stews, sauces, meat dishes, pasta and salads. Importantly, it was to find favour not just with budget-conscious shoppers but also with eminent chefs such as Auguste Escoffier, who praised the merits of Maggi Sauce in his cookery bible. Maggi Sauce is ingrained in all Germanic cultures. The bottle found its way into modern art in Joseph Beuys' 1972 work *Ich kenne kein Wochenende*, which featured a bottle of sauce attached to a black briefcase next to a copy of Kant's *Critique of Pure Reason*. Frankfurt artist Thomas Bayrle later wrote: 'It is an archetype in form and substance, elixir in modern industrial times … the Americans created Coke, the Germans created Maggi.'

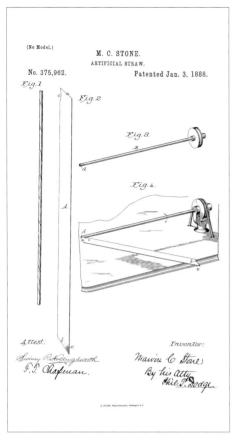

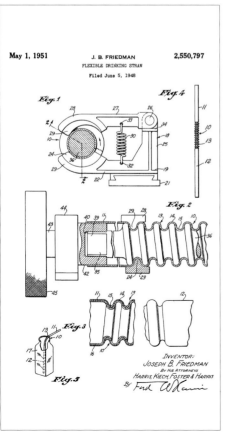

There are certain products that have worked their way into the fabric of our culture and become so commonplace that they are taken for granted. The Drinking Straw is one of them. More often than not, it is only fully appreciated when it is absent; only when it is missing do you realize how indispensable it is. The first paper Drinking Straw was created by Marvin Stone, a maker of paper cigarette holders. While drinking a mint julep after work, Stone became frustrated at having to use the traditional natural rye grass straws that would regularly break and often left a nasty sediment at the bottom of the drink. Instead, he thought he might be able to harness the paper technology used in his factory. He wound strips of paper around a pencil, then glued them together to create the first paper straw. The prototype was improved by using paraffin-coated paper to stop the straw becoming soggy, and the design was officially patented in 1888. Two years later the new product was Stone's main source of income. Since then there have been a number of material and technological innovations made to Stone's original. Arguably the most important has been the addition of the flex, introduced by Joseph B Friedman in 1937, and which meant that the paper straw could now be bent over a glass. This proved extremely useful for young children still getting to grips with drinking, and was useful for the bed-ridden as well. Indeed, the first sale of Friedman's company, the Flexible Straw Corporation, was to a hospital in 1947. Good design should make life just a little bit better, and this is why the Straw is simply ubiquitous.

This pocket knife, made of pearwood and carbon stainless steel, is a wolf in sheep's clothing. It is compact, has a graceful form with a pleasing tactile quality, and is completely functional, with a high-quality blade that really cuts – a surprise when it is extracted/removed from its innocent hiding place. This is an iconic knife that has not been superseded in over a century. This may be because, in addition to being sturdy and cheap, it does one thing extremely well, rather than many things badly, and gives pleasure while so doing, whether cutting branches or cutting an apple. Joseph Opinel was nineteen when he designed the knife. He wanted to make a pocket knife that was simple, robust and affordable, an integrity that was ahead of its time. Opinel was the son of a tool-maker from the Savoie region in France, an area locally renowned for its axes, billhooks and pruning knives. Initially Opinel produced the knives for a few friends. They quickly became successful, so Opinel decided to put the knife into production. Opinel combined very good design with the skills of generations of metalworkers. He solved problems such as how to create a split in the handle to house the blade without weakening it by inventing a machine to cut out the precise amount of wood required. The resulting tool with its organic form fits perfectly into, and acts as an extension of, the hand and comes in eleven sizes, from the no.2 with a blade of 3.5 cm (1.4 in) to the no.12 with a blade of 12 cm (4 in). As with any good tool, this knife needs maintenance and care; an interesting requirement in this day of disposable obsolescence. It demands a relationship, creating a connection almost like a pet.

Joseph Opinel

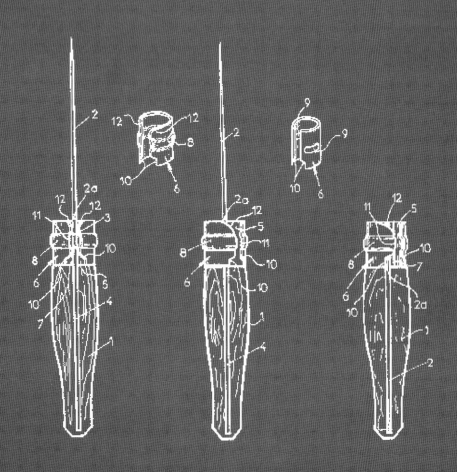

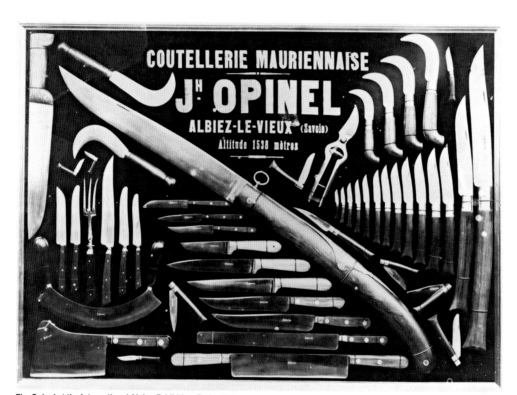

The Opinel at the International Alpine Exhibition, Turin, 1911

Dhabawallah, Mumbai, Maharashtra, 1992, photograph by Raghubir Singh

'Tiffin' is an Anglo-Indian

word describing a light luncheon. In the days before microwaves and fast-food restaurants, the Tiffin box was the only means by which Indian workers could enjoy hot, fresh, home-cooked meals at their place of work. The traditional Tiffin box consists of three or four round, stainless-steel containers that slot one on top of the other to form a compact stack. In order to make the stack portable, each container is fitted with metal lugs that allow it to slip onto a frame with a handle on top. The metal containers are extremely good conductors of heat, and consequently help keep each other warm, but the system is particularly successful in that it allows for a variety of different foods to be transported without their mixing. The delivery system of the Tiffin began under the British Raj over a century ago, and the *dhabawallah* (delivery man) evolved as a result of lunches being delivered to the British workers. *Dhabawallahs* continue a trade that is passed down through generations; wearing their Ghandi caps, long shirts and loose trousers, their distinctive identity and trade is unique to Mumbai, mostly to the upper-middle classes. That the Tiffin box has survived and prospered in India despite the invention of microwave ovens and the slow invasion of fast-food restaurants is due both to the efficiency of its design and the work of dhabawallahs, who pick up lunchboxes in the mornings and deliver them to the recipient's place of work for a charge of around $7 per month. Each box is marked with a coloured numeric code that ensures it reaches its intended recipient. The whole task of picking up and delivering the boxes takes roughly two hours, after which the process begins again, but this time to return each tiffin to the correct homes. Indeed, the system is so accurate that the American business magazine Forbes once awarded the dhabawallahs the highest performance rating possible. In Mumbai alone almost 200,000 meals are delivered by this system every day.

Tiffin (c.1890)
Designer Unknown
Various c.1890 to present

The Heinz Ketchup Bottle embodies many of the qualities that made the brand such a success. When Henry James Heinz introduced the world to his new product in 1876, most other ketchup manufacturers packaged their sauce in barrels in order to conceal the presence of additions such as leaves, fillers and wood fibre. Heinz insisted that his sauce be packaged in clear glass bottles so that he could visibly demonstrate its purity and tomato-rich redness. On a more practical level the glass is also very effective in protecting the product from excessive moisture and oxidation. Although the ketchup bottle effectively allows the sauce to promote itself, its design is also calculated to promote the idea that its contents are a fundamental part of a well-run household. The container's octagonal shape and long, fluted neck invite parallels with classical columns; and the implication that bottled ketchup (which was traditionally made via a rather arduous process of stewing) would provide support to the modern housewife was echoed in one of Heinz's many marketing slogans: 'Blessed relief for the mother and the other women in the household!' At the same time, that long neck served to regulate the flow of the sauce from the bottle, slowing it down, not only so that it did not flood out all over the plate, but also in order to further articulate the product's quality by making it seem even thicker and heavier. Early ketchup bottles were sealed with wax-dipped corks and hand-trimmed foil; the more familiar screw cap was introduced in 1890, along with the keystone label and neckband. More than anything else his patented tomato ketchup bottle provided a means by which Heinz could establish his brand identity, something that was particularly important as H J Heinz faced competition from rather brazen imitators such as the (unrelated) Heinz Brothers. After intensive advertising campaigns (most of which featured the bottle), its distinctive shape became one of the most recognizable food packages in America, featuring in Pop artist Claes Oldenburg's 1966–7 *Giant Soft Ketchup Bottle with Ketchup* and even being turned into a range of novelty telephones (with the earpiece on the neck and the numbers on the bottom). In 1983 Heinz introduced squeezable plastic containers in response to consumer complaints about the difficulty of getting the last drops of ketchup out of the traditional glass bottles. Glass bottles continue to be available to the 10 per cent of consumers who still prefer them.

Heinz Ketchup Bottle (1890)
H J Heinz Company Design Team
H J Heinz Company 1890 to present

Soldier's Knife, 1891

The renowned outline

of the Swiss Army Knife began life, as its name suggests, as a utilitarian tool for soldiers. The contemporary range using the recognizable motif of the Swiss cross is synonymous with a superior, functional, multi-purpose tool. Karl Elsener trained as a cutler and provided the Swiss Army with its first delivery of soldier's knives in 1891. He founded the Swiss Cutlers' Association, with twenty-five fellow cutlers, to facilitate production by sharing resources. However, the soldier's knife was not successful and the association disbanded, leaving Elsener heavily in debt. Undeterred, Elsener went on to redress the problems of weight and limited function. The developed design was registered again in 1897 and provided the template for the range as it is known today. The functionality and aesthetic of the small, pocket-sized knife was well received by the Swiss Army and soon found favour in the public market place. The redesigned knife had a more elegant outline than the original and employed only two springs for six tools, which was an advantage over other knives available at the time. This original format remains available today, though a host of variables born out of the original design are supplied to meet every user need. Elsener named his growing company after his mother, Victoria and later in 1921 added the international designation for stainless steel, 'inox' to create the brand name Victorinox. The name and motif of cross and shield are an identity proudly paralleled with the reliability and quality of Swiss design. Victorinox is associated with stories of knives used by soldiers, astronauts and explorers, providing the consumer with the confidence that they are buying into a reliable tool for camping and picnicking and at the same time creating the need for a pocket-sized tool for all even-tualities. Today, with a range of nearly 100 models bearing homage to Elsener's original design, the Victorinox brand enjoys the success of the original ideals of quality of design and function.

THE DEVELOPMENT OF THE SWISS SOLDIER'S KNIFE

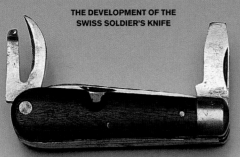

1891 – wooden scales, blade, punch, tin opener, screwdriver, 5 oz

1908 – fibre scales with embossed Swiss emblem, 4.4 oz

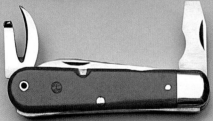

1951 – fibre scales with embossed Swiss emblem, 3.2 oz

1954 – fibre with bushings, with Swiss emblem, 3.2 oz

1961 – Alox red with Swiss emblem, 2.5 oz

1965 – Alox silver colour Swiss emblem, 2.5 oz

1980 – Alox silver colour with Swiss emblem in white on red, 2.5 oz

THE DEVELOPMENT THE SWISS ARMY OFFICER'S KNIFE, 8.9 CM

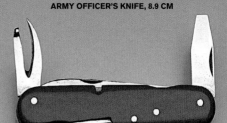

1897 – fibre scales, old can opener

1909 – fibre scales with cross and shield in white on red

1923 – stainless steel

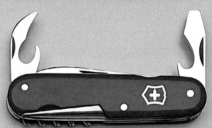

1942 – bottle opener

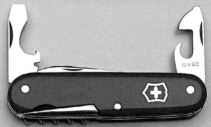

1951 – new can opener and Alox linings

1961 – new reamer, invisible rivets, shackle

1968 – attachment ring replaces shackle

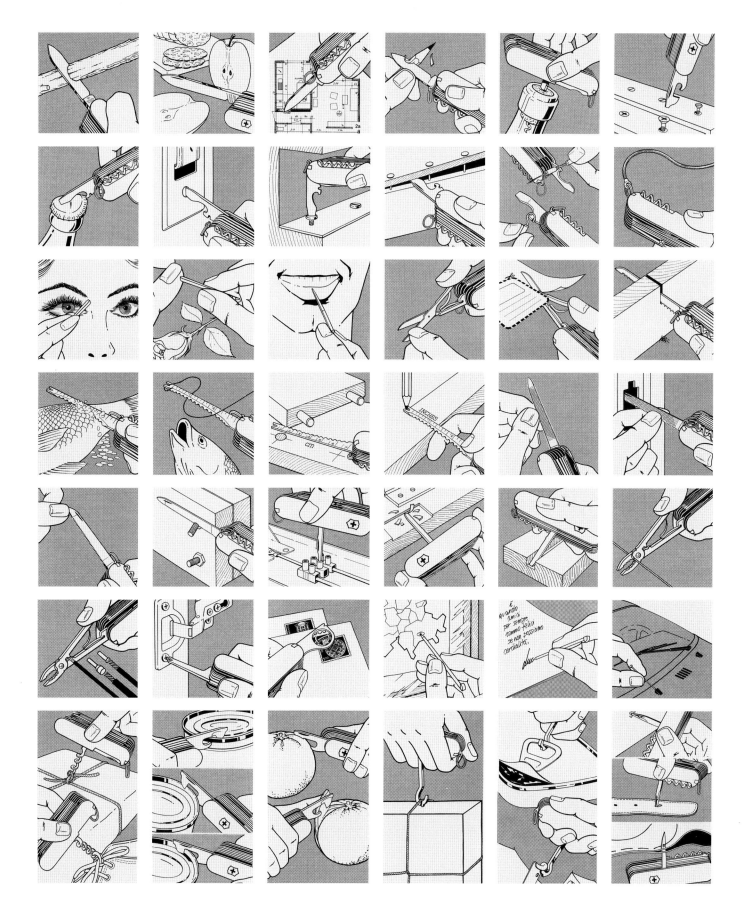

William Painter

The world of the soft drink or bottled beer would be unimaginable without the Crown Cap. It seems to evoke a bygone age, and yet it is still the most widely used method for sealing glass bottles. Bottles of fizzy drink had been available for some years prior to the invention of the Crown Cap, but the bottles often leaked, either the beverage or the carbon dioxide gas needed to keep it fizzy. Many attempts at preventing leakage ended in disaster if the metal stopper came into contact with the drink itself. William Painter saw the need for a better way of sealing bottles while allowing for contact between the metal cap and the drink inside. The Crown Cap, which he originally named the 'Crown Cork', has remained the solution for over a century. A very simple design, the Crown Cork was a metal cap with a corrugated-flange edge looking something like an upside down crown. Entirely leakproof, it was lined with a thin cork disc backed with special paper to seal the bottle and prevent any contact with the metal. After securing the patent for the Crown Cap on 2 February 1892, Painter formed the Crown Cork and Seal Company in Baltimore, Maryland (now Crown Holdings). By the 1920s the company had factories around the globe and began to shift its market focus from beer to soft drinks in order to survive Prohibition. For the remainder of the century the Crown Cap would occupy an essential role in the identity of some of the most famous soft drink brands. The 1960s saw the development of an industry standard for the 'Intermediate Crown Cap', which, until the appearance of the twist-off cap, had been the only bottle cap used for decades. Since then the Crown Cork and Seal Company of Baltimore has developed into one of the world's leading packaging companies. Although a number of other bottle caps have been invented, the Crown Cap still holds its position as the market leader. Changing only the lining in the cap, from cork to a more sustainable material, Painter's design has remained much the same for over 100 years. For reliability and simplicity the Crown Cap has remained a clever design, along with the satisfaction derived from removing the cap, with a quick flik of the wrist.

THERMOS

WHY YOU NEED IT

❡ Because it is the only flask in the world that keeps hot drinks hot and cold drinks cold.

❡ Because in the Sick Room it saves time and trouble.

❡ Hot remedies cannot lose strength and cold liquids are always icy.

❡ Because Baby's food can be kept ready at all hours of the day or night, and the food is sweet all the time.

❡ Because it is always ready for use.

❡ Because there are times when you absolutely cannot wait.

❡ It keeps hot drinks hot —24 hours.

PRICES
PINTS - - **21/-**

WHEN YOU NEED IT

❡ In any emergency that calls for **a hot** or a cold drink without delay.

❡ When you are travelling by Rail, Road, or Sea. When you are at play or at work.

❡ In the Sick Room and in the Nursery.

❡ When you come home fatigued from the Office, Theatre, Concert, Dance, or Reception.

❡ When you are cold and want a hot drink, or hot and want a cool drink.

❡ It keeps cold drinks cold—many days.

PRICES
QUARTS - **31/6**

The PATENT FLASK

(The adaption of the Vacuum principle)

ALL FLASKS GUARANTEED.

Of all Stores, Silversmiths, Chemists, Ironmongers, etc.

A. E. GUTMANN & CO.
8 LONG LANE, LONDON, E.C.

List of Retailers sent on application

Sir James Dewar

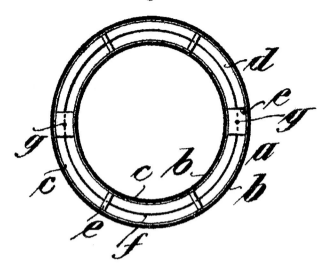

Fig. 2.

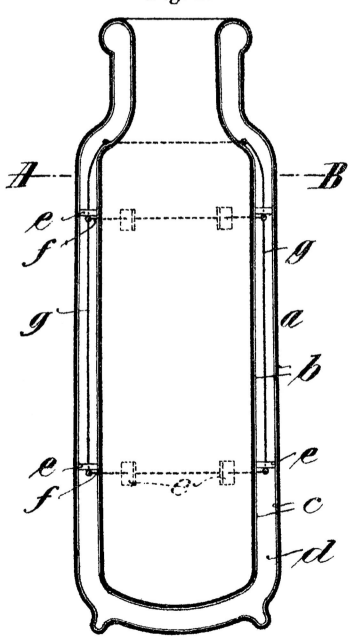

Fig. 1.

The Vacuum Flask was invented in 1892 by Sir James Dewar, a British scientist at Oxford University, to store chemicals at constant temperatures. The principle was to create an outer container separated from an inner container by a vacuum; the vacuum ensures the reduction of heat transfer. The first commercial use of the technique came in 1904, when German glass blower Reinhold Burger formed Thermos GmbH. The Berlin-based company held a competition to name its newly patented vacuum flask, and the result was Thermos, derived from the Greek word therme meaning 'heat'. In 1907, Thermos GmbH sold the Thermos trademark rights to three independent companies: The American Thermos Bottle Company of Brooklyn, New York, Thermos Limited of Tottenham, England and the Canadian Thermos Bottle Company of Montreal, who developed the Thermos Vacuum Flask into a widely sought-after product, which held many forms, most still using the Dewar flask's original glass structure, but coated in steel or later plastic. Thermos flasks developed a hardy reputation, and accompanied explorers such as Ernest Shackleton on his expedition to the South Pole and Robert E Peary on his trip to the Arctic. The Wright Brothers took a flask up in their aeroplane and Count Zeppelin carried one in his air balloon. The popularity of Thermos products grew tremendously after the advent of industrial machine-made glass fillers in 1911, and by 1923 Thermos had introduced the 24-pint (13.6 L) Blue Bottle and a new gallon-sized (4.5 L) insulated food jar known as the Thermos Jumbo Jug. The use of Pyrex rather than glass from 1928 allowed the creation of flasks as large as 28 gallons (127.25 L). These became extremely popular in 1928 and 1929, just prior to the advent of commercial refrigeration. The original Dewar flask had been made out of glass: two bottles, one inside the other, with air almost completely removed from the cavity between them. The same technique is still used today and is so effective that almost all heat loss occurs through the stopper. Because of this an insulating material is often used; often cork and latterly plastic. Plastic and steel were also used for the fillers in later models.

W. H. HICKS.
BOTTLE-CLOSING DEVICE.

No. 191,283.   Patented May 29, 1877.

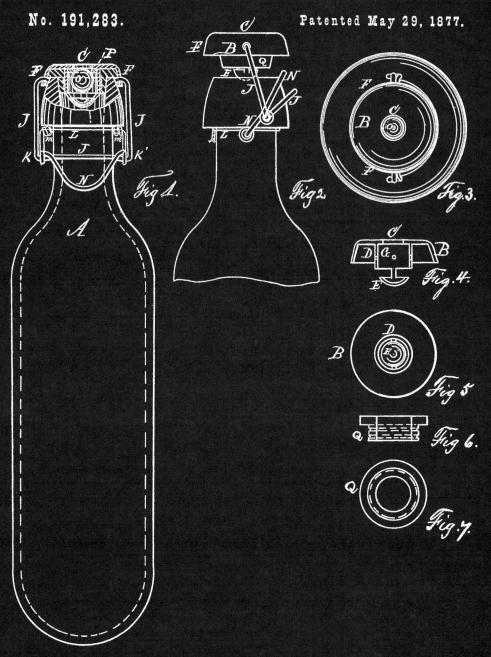

Fig.1. Fig.2. Fig.3. Fig.4. Fig.5. Fig.6. Fig.7.

Witnesses
James M. Hicks,
William G. Jenkins

Inventor.
W. H. Hicks.

Initially invented by Charles de Quillfeldt in 1875, the Lightning Stopper revolutionized the beer and soft drinks bottling industry. Until then beer and fizzy soft drinks manufacturers had tended to employ corks to stop their bottles. However, the pressure of the contents made this tricky. To seal the bottle effectively, the cork had to remain moist to prevent it from shrinking and the liquid inside going flat. Inevitably this effected the design of the bottles themselves. To make sure the cork remained damp the bottles were often made with rounded bottoms, meaning they had to be stored on their sides. However, too often they would simply leak. The earliest attempt at creating closures for soda or beer bottles was by Henry William Putnam, who invented a heavy wire bail in 1859 that would swing over the cork to secure it. Charles de Quillfeldt's design, which was much imitated and occasionally improved upon as he had sold the patent rights to several individuals, simply leveraged a rubber disc around a cork into the lip of the bottle, creating a seal. The mechanism was secured with a tie wire that had two complete loops on either side of the neck acting as pivots. The key improvement to de Quillfeldt's original patent came in 1893, when Karl Hutter added a tapered porcelain plug, fitted with a rubber washer at the bottom. As well as being extremely easy to refit, Hutter's improved Hutter Stopper, or 'swing-top' as it is commonly known, meant that the shape of beer and soda bottles could change. They no longer needed to have long, swan-like, necks to protect the cork and this gave makers a chance to experiment and differentiate their brands. By the 1920s the Hutter Stopper had been usurped when beer and soft drink manufacturing became completely industrialized by the Crown Cap – a simple metal cap with a corrugated edge that can be locked into position by a machine patented by William Painter in 1892. However, by then, the stopper had already made an indelible mark on the mass consciousness. A form of the Hutter Stopper – which has the fulcrums as an integrated part of the bottle – is still used by the Dutch brewer, Grolsch. The company has been employing the swing top since 1897 and has effectively made it a part of the brand experience. For an extremely brief period of time, the swing top bottle – as worn on the shoes of Matt and Luke Goss of UK Pop sensations Bros – became a vital fashion accessory for every teenage wardrobe across the country. A product that was iconic for very different reasons in the previous century moved centre-stage once again.

The Odol Bottle has remained unchanged for over a century and is unparalleled in the packaging industry. The white glass bottle for Odol mouthwash is one of the few designs that has survived the trend of frequent updates. From 1893 until 1954 the bottle has remained virtually unaltered: a flat oblong bottle with bevelled sides and a curved neck. From 1954 the shape was slightly softened, but the peculiar neck remained its trademark. This bent neck is not only a striking formal and useful solution for dispensing drops but also a marvel of technique, requiring a lot of ingenuity to produce on a glass-blowing machine. Most likely the bottle is the work of an inventive engineer but there are persistent rumours that the inventor of the mouthwash, Karl August Lingner, was also the creator of the bottle. Odol was not just a successful antiseptic mouthwash, it was a sophisticated marketing concept at a time when hygiene was not standard in daily life. At the end of the nineteenth century great strides were made in the study of bacteriology. Lingner started his Dresdener Chemisches Laboratorium in 1892 and with the assistance of Dr Richard Seifert, a friendly chemist, he developed an antiseptic substance that has remained the secret ingredient of Odol. It was a promotion campaign in the United States, which included advertisements in magazines, on zeppelins and on buildings, that turned Odol into one of the first world-established brands. Because of its unique packaging and its, for the time, revolutionary emphasis on its proven effectiveness, the product was an immediate success. Very soon after its launch Odol was available in sixty countries and produced in twenty, which led to instant imitations. In 1907 over thirty similar products were known, of which six used a bottle with a curved neck. Over the years, various patents have been granted for the manufacture of Odol's curved neck. One of the most striking dates from 1919, when Adolf Schiller, from Berlin Schöneberg, devised a means of pressing air directly from the sides of the mould. This was a revolutionary glass technique, because bottles until then were always produced from the top. Today the bottle is produced by GlaxoSmithKline, which owns the Odol brand. How it is manufactured remains a secret.

Odol Bottle (1893)
Karl August Lingner (1861–1916)
Odol (GlaxoSmithKline) 1893 to present

Nach dem heutigen Stande der Wissenschaft ist

Odol

nachweislich des beste Mittel zur Pflege der Zähne und des Mundes

½ Flasche: 1,50 Mark.

Dresdener Chemisches Laboratorium Lingner.

Probably 80% of the gum consumed in the world is made of these three brands.

WRIGLEY'S SPEARMINT has real mint leaf flavor.

WRIGLEY'S DOUBLEMINT has strong peppermint flavor.

There are two samples of **WRIGLEY'S JUICY FRUIT CHEWING GUM** as, while this brand has been sold for 24 years, it is not so well known in your section as the other two. It has an odd flavor and is a great favorite with the ladies.

All three brands are of the well known

"WRIGLEY QUALITY"

the difference being only in the flavor.

WRIGLEY'S is sold all over the world and the constantly increasing demand must prove that the goods are made right, wrapped right, and are the right thing for 80% of the world's chewing gum users.

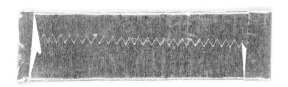

According to legend, twenty-nine-year-old William Wrigley Jr arrived in Chicago in 1891 with only his natural gift as a salesman and $32 to recommend him to the big city. He soon realized that he could make his mark in the pre-existing but dormant chewing gum business. He set about doing this with a very modern understanding of the importance of advertising, using newspaper space, posters and promotions to sell his product. Wrigley's Spearmint Gum was introduced in 1893 with its distinctive red lettering and leaf green arrow on a bright white background. The brand, along with other classics like Juicy Fruit (1893) and Doublemint (1914), is still immensely popular today and propelled Wrigley to worldwide commercial success. Chewing gum occupies a strange hold on popular culture considering it is a synthetic gum-based product with minimal taste and lack of any nutritional content. However, it has become an habitual activity for many, with uses ranging from a stress-buster for football managers to a handy postprandial breath freshener.

It also became associated with a rebellious 'cool', via a suitably nonchalant chew, making it popular with and symbolic of youth culture. Subsequently, once the satisfyingly flat piece of gum was unwrapped from its perfect shiny foil jacket it became a common game for kids to see who could fold it into their mouths and chew it most like their favourite film or TV star. Not surprisingly then, clever advertising has continued to play a large part in the company's success, most famously in the early 1990s when a Wrigley's advertisement appeared featuring another mainstay of US iconography, the Greyhound bus. Two beautiful strangers, exchanging slightly salacious glances on a bus travelling through the United States, ponder how best to divide the final stick of Wrigley's Spearmint Gum to the sound of Free's 'All Right Now' (which subsequently rocketed to No. 1 in the charts). Its tag-line, 'Great to chew, even better to share', became an irresistible catchphrase whenever chewing gum was offered round.

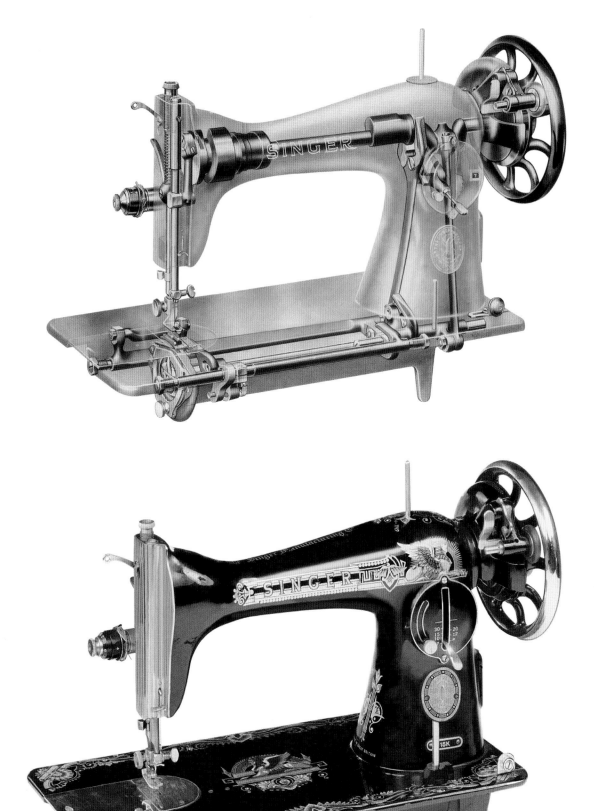

Singer is to sewing machines what Hoover is to vacuum cleaners, but contrary to popular belief the sewing machine was not invented by Isaac Merritt Singer. In fact, Singer's machine was introduced into what was already a crowded field of competitors and although the Singer had its merits, it was not designed along radical new lines. Indeed, the designs on sale in the 1850s were often so similar in certain elements of their assembly that the nascent industry was fraught with lawsuits, claims and counterclaims of patent infringement. The sewing machine manufacturers of the 1850s often seemed to be more familiar with the courtroom than the inventor's shed. In this early litigation with his rivals, Singer was unable to demonstrate primacy for any one element of the design. But the real strength of Singer's machine was, in some ways, a product of the absence of primacy. The machine was a synthesis, cleverly combining elements from previous models.

Its superiority stems from that, and also from what drove Singer to develop a machine in the first place: he saw another machine being repaired in a Boston shop and considered its design inelegant, not inoperative. Elegance is a quality that the Singers undisputedly possess and this refinement reached its apotheosis in the Singer Model 15K. The Singer 15K transcends mere effective design by simply being beautiful. Its action is similarly pleasing and the name Singer is appropriate as the treadle-powered machine purrs like a cat when in use. The Singer 15K is outstanding not for doing something new, or even for doing something differently, but for doing something very well and doing so with grace and dignity. Furthermore, Singer machines were not placed out of reach of the average consumer and the story ends with an interesting footnote in the history of innovation.
In order to make his earliest models available to as wide an audience as possible, Singer created the world's first hire-purchase scheme.

Bloemenwerf (1895)
Henry van de Velde (1863–1957)
Société Henry van de Velde 1895 to 1900
Van de Velde 1900 to 1903
Adelta 2002 to present

Henry van de Velde

Derision greeted Henry van de Velde at the unveiling

of his Bloemenwerf House in the Brussels suburb of Uccle in 1895. But what curious onlookers cannot have known was that this was an important articulation of a new ideal of the house as a single work of art, prefiguring the Gesamtkunstwerk exploits of the Vienna Workshop as well as providing an early marker for Art Nouveau. Backed by his wealthy mother-in-law, who bankrolled Bloemenwerf, the former painter turned to decorative and applied arts in the early 1890s. His concept kicked against both the low quality of mass production and the prevalent historicist tendency to embellish basic forms with gratuitous decoration that was unrelated to function and frequently masked poor workmanship. The furniture was guided by this rational perspective: the sideboard and centre element of the dining table, for instance, featured brass plates to prevent hot dishes marking the surfaces. The beechwood dining chairs, meanwhile, evoked harmony and comfort, echoing English 'rustic' designs of the eighteenth century but also suggesting a distinctive contemporary departure

with their curves. The dining chairs were available in versions with and without arms, as well as a smaller variant for children. Van de Velde received frequent orders for the furniture, including from art dealer Siegfried Bing, who featured them in his Paris shop L'Art Nouveau. From 1895 the furniture was produced by the artist's own business, Société Henry van de Velde. Bloemenwerf formed the basis of Van de Velde's reputation. He later directed the Arts and Crafts School in Weimar and in 1907 co-founded the Deutscher Werkbund, where he championed the creativity of the individual artist as the route to quality in manufacture. This was not a popular view at the time; his opponents claimed aesthetic and economic success was only possible through forms compatible with mass production. Eventually, he was forced out of Germany in 1914 by anti-foreign sentiment at the start of World War I. The Bloemenwerf chair was resurrected in 2002 when the German company Adelta launched a series of eleven Van de Velde reproductions.

By the second half of the twentieth century the dartboard had become a prerequisite for any self-respecting pub, yet its origins remain a mystery. The game is believed to have been invented by medieval archers throwing cropped arrows at an upturned cask of wine, and although the construction of the board has changed since the Middle Ages, for many it still remains connected to the drinks industry. Whether the original board was a barrel of wine or the cross-section of a tree, the modern image of a dartboard is instantly recognizable. The classic 'clockface' dartboard, with a diameter of 45.72 cm (18 in), was invented in 1896, by Brian Gamlin, a Lancashire carpenter. His numbering sequence, now the international standard, though seemingly random, was a deliberate design intended to minimize the proportion of lucky shots through the juxtaposition of high and low numbers. The board itself is made from compressed sisal or rope fibre, the centre spot is called the 'bullseye', and dividing the twenty red and green numbered segments is a wire frame called the 'spider'. Representing a seemingly dangerous sport that can be played with relative safety in small confines, the board takes up little space and can even be used in a bedroom. Darts themselves are still often referred to as 'arrows', and it was as an indoor form of archery that the game had grown in popularity through-out the Middle Ages, particularly among the nobility; in 1530, Henry VIII was given a set by Anne Boleyn. Since its medieval beginnings, the dartboard has been linked historically with off-duty soldiers. A game of accuracy in shot was no-doubt useful in sharpening skills when waiting for battle and would have been an opportunity for soldiers and officers to interact. In fact, during World War II most training and POW camps were issued with boards. It was after World War I that the modern game began to take form, with breweries organizing local leagues, leading to the establishment of a national darts association in 1924. The game was particularly popular in Britain in the early 1980s, largely due to televised matches that made stars of champions such as Eric Bristow and Jockey Wilson and brought darts to the attention of aspiring players. The game also inspired a television gameshow, *Bullseye*, which made great use of the symbolic dartboard image.

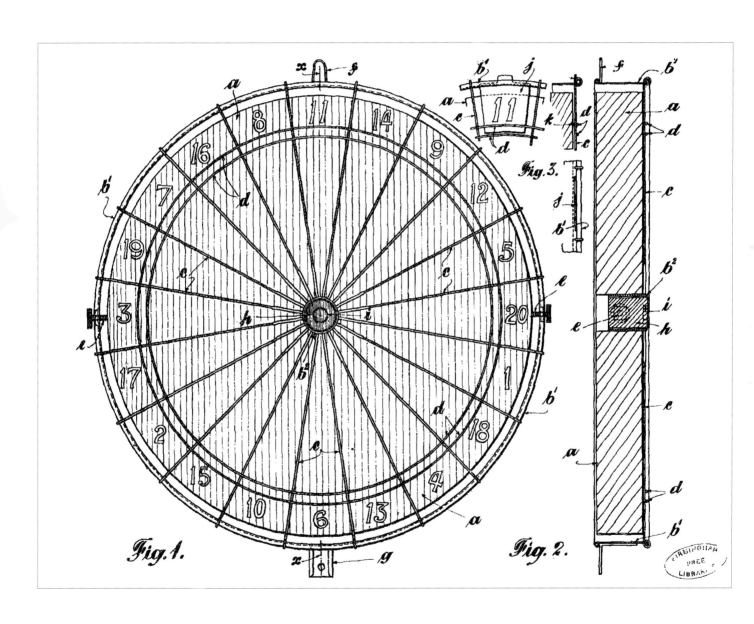

Fig. 1.

Fig. 2.

Fig. 3.

Emil Berliner

Thomas Edison may have been the first person to successfully reproduce sound in 1877, followed by Alexander Graham Bell with his wax-cylinder-playing gramophone, but it was the US-based German immigrant Emil Berliner who designed, and eventually popularized, the gramophone between 1885 and 1899. He created a method of recording that could be used many times and, in so doing, he created an entire industry that would go on to be worth millions of dollars and would help to change the face of popular culture. During his extraordinary career, the gramophone was actually the second of Berliner's great innovations (the first was a transmitter he made for Graham Bell's telephone). By 1887 he had perfected the now familiar system of a needle vibrating from side to side in a groove on a flat disc made from shellac (instead of the earlier wax cylinder) and in the same year he produced the first recording. It was a system that remained in place until the emergence of the compact disc in the 1980s. In 1895 he set up the Gramophone Company to market and sell his new product. However, sales were initially sluggish and it was not until the classic Berliner Model B gramophone arrived, complete with a wind-up spring motor designed by Eldridge R Johnson, which allowed the turntable to revolve at one speed, that the gramophone really began to take off. The gramophone no longer required hand-cranking to wind the motor. The product's iconic status was assured when Berliner used the now-familiar painting, *His Master's Voice*, by artist Francis Barraud as his company's trademark. The image of the dog listening to a gramophone was used for more than seventy years, easily outlasting the popularity of the Model B, and is still used today by the music retailers HMV. Ever restless, Berliner did not rest on his laurels: in 1926 he obtained the patent for a new acoustic tile, while he also found time to establish the Society for the Prevention of Sickness, which played a key role in the campaign to pasteurize milk across America.

060

Berliner Model B (1897)

Emil Berliner (1851–1929)

Gramophone Company 1897 to c.1901

Peter Behrens

The career of Peter Behrens

followed an interesting trajectory in which he trained as a painter, but became a highly successful industrial designer, working most notably for the German industrial giant AEG. His Glass Service designed for the Bavarian manufacturer Freiherr von Poschinger, glass makers since 1568, marks a notable turning point in his career. At the time, Behrens was a member of an influential group of reforming designers based in Munich, and the service was designed shortly after he decided to give up painting to concentrate on designing objects for use in the domestic interior. For its plain but elegant simplicity, the service also marks a turning point in the design of large services of glass. The service was conceived as part of a dining room, also designed by Behrens, shown at one of the group's exhibitions held at the Munich Glaspalast in 1899. The service was notable

for its integrity to materials and for simplifying the kind of glass service then popular, both factors that made it relatively inexpensive to produce. First, Behrens simplified the design by reducing the number of objects that comprise a traditional service. He omitted objects such as decanters, jugs and finger bowls, and instead designed only twelve glasses of different sizes. He also simplified the design by removing all surface decoration such as etching, engraving, carving or enamelling, which were traditional on artist-designed pieces. But Behrens did allow himself some decoration his careful design of the taut but gently serpentine line that marks the understated outline of each piece was a masterstroke for the simple vitality it conferred on the service. The service was only produced for four years, and finally reissued by the original company in 1998, proving its enduring simplicity and timelessness.

061

Glass Service (1898)
Peter Behrens (1868–1940)
Freiherr von Poschinger Glasmanufaktur
1898 to c.1902, 1998 to present

Richard Riemerschmid

Many believe that Richard Riemerschmid's Musiksalon Chair is confirmed as one the first examples of flat-pack furniture, due to its simple components, and it is certainly part of its history. Riemerschmid is associated, more than anything else, with the Deutscher Werkbund, of which he was a founding member, with Hermann Muthesius, in 1907. As an early champion of quality serial production and the machine made creating a standard for industrial design, the Deutscher Werkbund had a huge influence on Modernism and the Bauhaus movement, which were to take up many of its ideals. But prior to this, Riemerschmid was also one of the most important representatives of German Art Nouveau, co-founding in 1897 the Münchner Vereinigte Werkstätten für Kunst im Handwerk (Munich Unified Workshops for Art in Handicraft), which was modelled on English Arts and Crafts precedents. As part of this movement, in 1898, Riemerschmid was commissioned to design a music room for the Munich piano manufacturer J Mayer and Company. The room was subsequently exhibited at the 1899 Dresden Art Exhibition and then a year later at the 1900 Paris Exhibition. The chair Riemerschmid created as an integral part of this room is regarded as one of his most original designs. The Musiksalon Chair is typical of Riemerschmid's pre-Werkbund style, which successfully married expressive curvilinear decoration with the constructive elements of an object. The chair's diagonal side arms, sweeping down from the top of the chair's back to the bottom of its front legs, provided support with a graceful, understated decoration, but skilfully left the seated musician's arms and body unimpeded. A matching chair for the audience replaced the diagonal support with armrests. With a frame in golden natural or ebonized beech and the seat a studded cushion in leather or fabric, the chair was a superior example of German design of the period. While it did not have a direct impact on the German Modernism that was to come, it must have played a part in the march towards the range of *Maschinenmöbel* – simply styled, machine-made, hand-assembled furniture – designed by Riemerschmid for his brother-in-law Karl Schmidt's Dresden workshop, and created in the same year as the Musiksalon Chair. No longer manufactured in its original form, it was redesigned for Lucas Schnaidt by Ernst Martin Dettinger in 1983, and that version is still available.

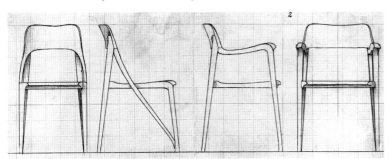

The Paperclip is one of those low-tech inventions that support the cliché that the

simplest ideas are often the best. Today's Paperclip has been honed to the optimum

dimensions – a length of steel wire 9.85 cm (3.9 in) long and 0.08 cm (0.31 in) in diameter

provides just the right tension of firmness and give. This thin twisted rod of steel slips so

unobtrusively yet so essentially into our everyday lives that it's hard to believe it was ever

actually invented. We never stop to marvel at the perfection of its simple loops and bends,

the fitting straightness of its parallels, or the perfected flexibility. And yet somehow we have

this mysterious urge to destroy the perfection, to experience the delicious joy of unpicking

a Paperclip. We know it's an empty and wasteful act, and yet few can resist the desire to

straighten what more industrious minds have bent. We are actually destroying the work of

Johan Vaaler, a Norwegian inventor, who developed the clip in 1899, but patented it in

Germany because Norway had no patent laws. Although by 1900 American inventor Cornelius

J Brosnan had filed for his own Paperclip, the 'Konaclip', it was Gem Manufacturing of England who first designed the double oval-shaped clip that we recognize today. This is different from Vaaler's original in that it has one extra corner, giving the paper added protection from scratches by the metal. At the time, steel wire was only just becoming available following technological advances that enabled a machine to bend the wire into place quickly, reliably and cost-efficiently. Other designs proliferated, among them the non-tangling 'owl', the 'ideal' (for thick wads of paper) and the self-explanatory 'non-skid'. Norway, though, is still the spiritual home of the clip: and one story of defiance proves it. When, during World War II, the occupying Nazi forces banned Norwegians from wearing any buttons bearing the likeness of their king, the Norwegians started wearing Paperclips, even though the flaunting of such peaceful mechanical superiority brought the risk of arrest.

Adolf Loos was one of the first twentieth-century architects to modernize the spatial concepts of architecture. He introduced split levels, and stripped architecture of any historical decorative references. He was also a very influential critic and wrote theoretical essays and manifestos on architecture, design and modern life. In 1899 Adolf Loos designed a café at the corner of the Operngasse and the Friedrichstrasse in Vienna, which has been open ever since, and was recently restored, in 2003, to its original style. He also took care of the complete interior turning the V-shaped café into an avant-garde hot spot. He was inspired by 1830s coffee-houses, which were popular meeting places, and wanted to create a space with no style reference. Instead of using a red plush interior, the standard for coffee-houses at that time, he stripped the building and used simple self-designed furniture. The café was nicknamed 'Café Nihilismus', referring to the rejection of all values. When Adolf Loos designed his Café Museum Chair, bentwood furniture was very fashionable. Firms like Thonet and Jacob & Joseph Kohn were world producers in the field. Besides creating a range of products that were designed by company technicians, the firms collaborated with artists and architects. This broadened their horizon and laid a solid base for future collaborations of art and industry. At first glance the chair can even compete with the best-known bentwood chair, Thonet No.14. Loos took the standardized production of the existing chair for granted and worked with carpenters to strip parts of the round beech stick into an oval. He also thinned some parts, like the back and the legs, in order to create a more elegant appearance. He drew inspiration from the shapes of two chairs produced earlier by Jacob & Joseph Kohn, using the three-part back, and corner parts under the seats to ensure greater firmness. The natural beech was stained red, giving the impression of mahogany or rosewood. It came with either a woven cane or a saddle-shaped wooden seat. Loos is probably best known for his essay 'Ornament und Verbrechen' ('Ornament and Crime') of 1908. In this paper he condemns the use of ornament since it hides the qualities of true craftsmanship and the natural beauty of the materials used in contemporary design. His Café Museum Chair is, in this respect, an early, three-dimensional manifesto.

Café Museum Chair (1899)
Adolf Loos (1861–1933)
Jacob & Joseph Kohn 1899 to 1922
Gebrüder Thonet 1922 to 1930
Gebrüder Thonet Vienna 2002 to present

Smith & Ellis

Folding

Garden

Chairs.

No. 780.   No. 710.

No. 780. This Chair is most useful where storage space is valuable as it folds perfectly flat. Oil polished. Size, 14-in. by 15-in. Height, 33-in. **4/11** each.

No. 710. Perforated Seat. Extra Stout. Strongly made. **7/6** Polished.

Park Pattern Folding Iron and Wood Chairs.

No. 70.   No. 70A.

No. 70. Strong Chair, folding flat for storage. Ironwork and Pitch Pine splines. Painted Green all over. Price **7/6.**

No. 70A. Light Folding Chair with iron framework and wood splines, painted Green all over. **Price 5/11.**

Carriage on single chairs, 1/6 extra ; on two chairs, 2/6 extra ; one dozen lots, Carriage Paid England and Wales.

This now ubiquitous Garden Chair first appeared in the public spaces of Paris around the turn of the twentieth century. The chair is used in gardens, parks and bistros and its popularity is related to the success of the design, in terms of its functionality and style. Historically, the folding chair was considered an important and valued item of furniture, representing a status symbol for the owner. The folding chair, as opposed to the stool, first appeared shortly before the Renaissance, and evolved through variations on the folding mechanism, with the principal methods being the pincer arrangement and the scissor construction. As the folding chair itself became more common, the folding variety and its technical achievement followed naturally. While this reduced the status of the object, it led to the development of new uses and new design solutions. By the nineteenth century folding chairs were a widespread utilitarian feature of public spaces where there was a need to rearrange or regularly remove seating. Folding chairs also allowed for large numbers to be stored in a small space when not in use. The folding design of this Garden Chair has a simple side X-pivot mechanism, positioned below the seat level. This chair's slender metal frame made it noticeably lighter than its predecessor, which was made entirely of wood. Furthermore, its narrow metal structure allowed for reduced dimensions, imbuing the chair with a previously unseen elegance and space-saving benefits. It has no attributed designer, but the classic French folding garden chair has proven to be an enduring source of design inspiration, with its influence clearly visible in many subsequent chairs. The design is flawless, as is proved by its adoption as the archetypal form of outdoor chair with its understated style and highly practical design.

065
Garden Chair (1900s)
Designer Unknown
Various 1900s
Habitat 1998 to present

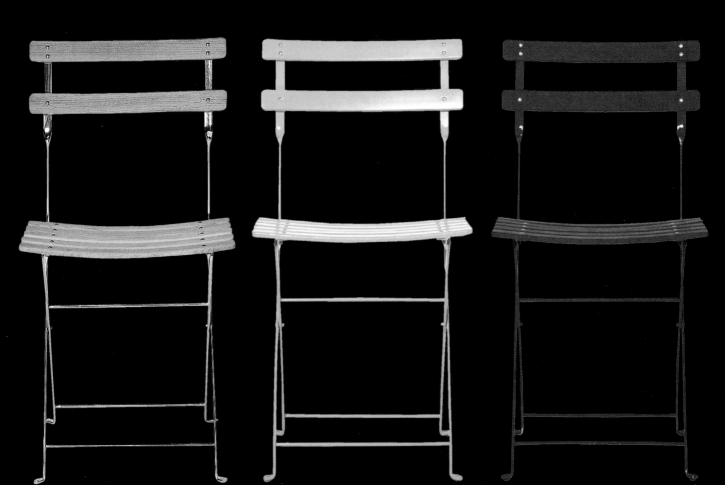

Since the nineteenth century the Honey Swivel Stick has tested the skills of woodturners. Its elegant and efficient design comprises a deeply incised wooden globe that gathers honey, attached to a thin shaft. While the origins of its design are difficult to establish, its effectiveness has made the honey dipper a staple among kitchen utensils. Sometimes round, sometimes elliptical, sometimes egg-shaped, the Honey Stick is generally made of a fine-grained wood. It can also be found as more expensive versions in silver, porcelain or other materials, which are more easily cleaned and more durable. Why the Honey Stick has endured with only minimal stylistic changes is a mystery. Its efficacy in relationship to the simple spoon is debatable. Unlike the spoon, the Honey Swivel Stick is only useful with runny honey, not the buttery or crystallized variations. The swivel stick creates more surface area for the honey, but unless it is mixed in hot liquids, the sweetener becomes lodged in its crevices and is difficult to clean. Nevertheless, with the growing interest in, and enjoyment of, traditional culinary and dining practices, tools like chopsticks and honey swivel sticks escape qualitative judgements and are incorporated into daily life adding value to home economics. As honey rode the wave of the organic, back-to-nature lifestyles of the late twentieth century, so did the Honey Swivel Stick. Sometimes adorned with bees or blossoms, it has been subject to sentimental excesses. However, like the yogurt spoon, fish knife or fondue fork, the longevity of the Honey Swivel Stick is as linked to social context as it is to function.

Oddly for a piece of furniture that is widely regarded as being utilitarian, the Folding Director's Chair has a rather illustrious history and has traditionally been something of a status symbol. The chair is first believed to have been developed by the Egyptians between 2000 and 1500 BC for the commanding officers of its army. The basic design had barely changed by the early twentieth century, when it gained its iconic status as the chair for directors in America's rapidly expanding film industry. There are more than a few parallels between the two professions: both the military commander and the movie director are in charge of vast numbers of people and both tend to find themselves on the move for much of the time, the commander from battlefield to battle-field and the director from set to set. Between its ancient antecedents and its present-day incarnation, the typology of the folding chair was also adopted by the Church. The decorative Savonarola, named after the former ruler of the Florentine Republic who was responsible for instigating the 'Bonfire of the Vanities' in the late fifteenth century, was used by travelling bishops before the Renaissance, for example. Made from wood, with a canvas seat and back, the classic Director's Chair frame is shaped like the letter 'X' with pivots below the seat at the front and back that allow it to be folded away like a concertina. Over the years it has become an item that has fascinated designers. In 1928 Marcel Breuer produced his take on the folding chair, while the likes of Erik Magnussen, Enzo Mari and, inevitably, Philippe Starck have also created their own interpretations of the classic design. However, ultimately it is a product that will always be associated with a particular era and an industry rather than any specific designer.

O67

Folding Director's Chair (c.1900)
Designer Unknown
Various c.1900

MRS. BATES

Alfred Hitchcock

068

Kodak Brownie (1900–1)
Frank A Brownell (1859–1939)
Brownell Manufacturing 1900 to 1902
Eastman Kodak Company 1903 to 1916

The Brownie Camera was innovative in simplifying the camera to a bare minimum. It was made of jute board reinforced with wood and covered in black imitation leather. The few controls were nickel-plated. At one end was a simple meniscus lens of 100 mm focal length and aperture of f/14 and a simple single-speed rotary shutter. The camera back was held on by two metal springs and was removed to allow a newly introduced roll film to be inserted. The shutter release and winding key to advance the film were located on top of the camera. With no controls, it was the first point-and-shoot camera producing competent results in sunshine. Frank Brownell had been working with George Eastman making the Eastman-Walker roll film holder from 1885 and undertaking woodworking for cameras. In 1892 Eastman built a factory next to his own that he called the Camera Works and rented to Brownell, who began designing and making cameras for Eastman's rapidly expanding company. By the time Brownell retired in 1902 and Eastman bought the factory, more than sixty new camera models and designs had come out of the Camera Works. Eastman described Brownell as 'the greatest camera designer the world has known'. By 1899 Eastman had asked Brownell to design a camera that was cheaper and easier to use than any Kodak had yet produced. The original Brownie was shipped to dealers on 1 February 1900 and, following feedback, was redesigned, with a new version sold in June. By the time the original Brownie was superseded by the No. 1 Brownie in October 1901, around 245,000 had been sold. If the original Kodak camera of 1888 had taken the photographer away from the darkroom, then the Brownie brought photography within the reach of everyone. The camera was sold for $1 and was deliberately marketed at children through the use of Palmer Cox's well-known Brownie characters. Kodak organized competitions for photographs taken with the camera and established Brownie clubs to encourage picture-taking and, of course, sales of film, where the real profits were to be had. Between 1900 and 1980 a vast range of camera models that were well designed, simple to operate and cheap was sold under the Brownie name, making it the most successful camera range of all time.

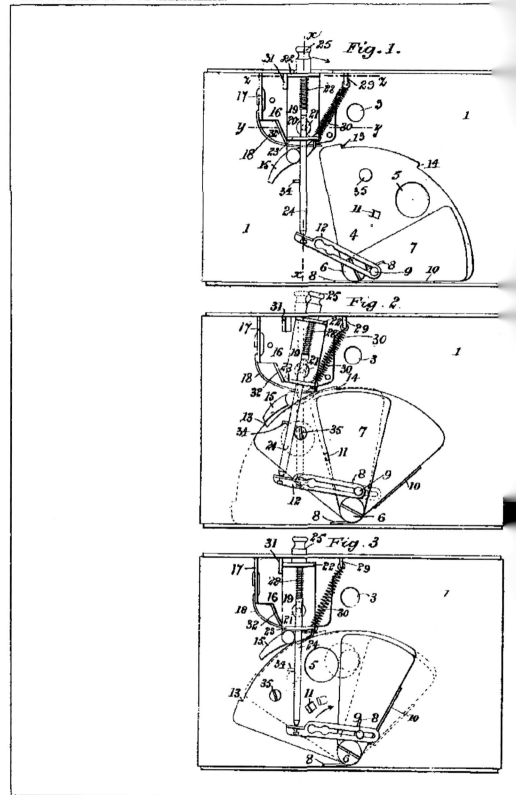

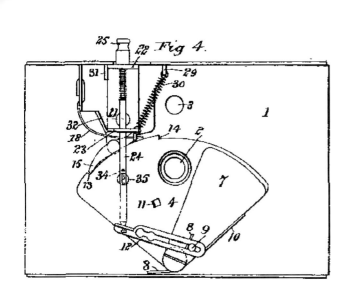

Fig 4.

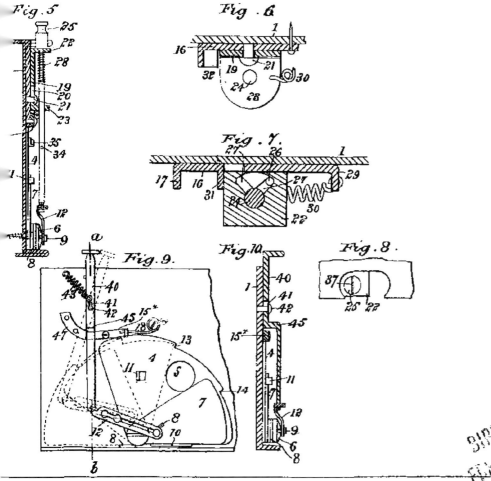

Fig. 5   Fig. 6

Fig. 7.

Fig. 9.   Fig.10.   Fig. 8.

With its rationalist design and engineered precision, inventor Frank Hornby's Meccano is a proto-modernist toy that was originally based on fifteen prefab elements that included perforated strips and plates of tin simply pieced together with nuts and bolts. Rendered at various times over the century in tin and nickel plate featuring bold primary colours, and in kits with different themes, Meccano was the twentieth century's archetypal construction toy, and a source of youthful pleasure for many a nascent designer. Comparable in influence to Friedrich Froebel's nineteenth-century wooden blocks, Meccano unleashed the imagination through its very prefab simplicity. Alvar Aalto, the great Finnish designer, was once described by a Swedish critic as treating 'architecture as a big Meccano box'. And Joe Colombo, a generation later, spent his childhood creating fantastical worlds using Hornby's kit of parts. Hornby was an English inventor whose day job as a meat importer was balanced out by a fervid after-hours interest in providing healthy, constructive pastimes that would raise young boys into clean-living men. Hornby's most famous creation was brainstormed during a train trip in which he gazed out the window at the industrial scenery surrounding his native Liverpool. The childhood dream of creating a crane that could lift heavy things took shape on paper, and soon the idea of a modular construction toy comprised of metal strips and bolts became reality in his back-garden workshop. Hornby's sons responded enthusiastically to the model of this first crane, complete with base, jib, cord, pulley and gear wheel, and even more so after dismantling it into a base with four wheels that was transformed into a truck. After refining his idea to include the possibilities of building all manner of structures and vehicles using correct mechanical principles, Hornby patented what he at first called 'Mechanics Made Easy' but later became Meccano. With seed money from an acquaintance, Hornby designed the construction set with the help of a single assistant and farmed it out to manufacturers around Liverpool until, two years later, he could afford larger quarters to begin manufacturing Meccano himself.

The remarkable Catalan architect Antoni Gaudí's
first foray into furniture design was a desk for his own use, designed
when he graduated in 1878. Subsequent furniture designs were
always specifically for the interiors of his own buildings. The Casa
Calvet was built for Don Pedro Mártir Calvet, a textile manufacturer
at 48 Calle de Caspe, Barcelona, between 1898 and 1904, and Gaudí
was given the Barcelona City Counsel Award in 1900 for the artistic
merits of this building. Oak furniture, including desks and this armchair,
was designed in 1902 for offices in the building and made by the firm
of Casa y Bardés, and the magazine *Arquitectura y Construcción*
published images of the furniture in the same year. Gaudí also designed
a gilded salon for the same building, which housed luxury flats. Gaudí's
previous furniture had overtones of the Gothic Revival derived from
designers such as Viollet-le-Duc, and even incorporated naturalistic
decoration such as foliage. This chair, however, marks a departure from
reproductions of historic precedents and decorative traditions, which
Gaudí achieved by synthesizing the decoration with the structure of the
chair, rather than applying it to the surface. Most notable is the organic,

plastic character of the design whereby the elements appear to grow out of one another. On closer inspection there are references to architectural motifs, 'C' scrolls and a suggestion of a cabriole leg, for example. But these baroque elements are subsumed into the overall coherent vegetative form of Gaudí's exuberant chair, in the same way that the building for which it was designed expressed organic principles of design. It is this organic quality, which makes it stand out as a classic. Gaudí is sometimes regarded as an Art Nouveau designer because of his sinuous, organic forms. Indeed, some of his furniture bears comparison with the work of Art Nouveau masters like Hector Guimard. However, perhaps more than many of his contemporaries, he abstracted principles of organic design so that his furniture and buildings appear to have lives of their own. Because of this, Gaudí is often regarded as a forebear of the Surrealism movement later in the twentieth century.

Antoni Gaudí, Casa Calvet, Barcelona, 1898–1904

Of all the objects to emerge from Germany's industrial age, the Steiff Teddy Bear 55 PB may be the only one to be universally regarded with affection. Invented by Richard Steiff, the much-loved nephew of company founder Margarete Steiff, the teddy bear was inspired by sketches the former art student created of the bears at the Stuttgart zoo. Fashioned from mohair plush and a stuffing of wood shavings, the somewhat awkward-looking bear was an addition to the company's ever-increasing menagerie of children's toys. The glass-eyed bear differed in that its joints were articulated and attached by strong thread so they could be moved independently of the torso. Dubbed the 55 PB for its material (*Plüsch*), its movability (*Beweglichkeit*) and its height (55 cm), the bear was at first rejected by the Steiff family matriarch as uncomely,

Richard Steiff

and the initial public reaction was similar. It was the last-minute purchase of 3,000 bears by an American buyer visiting the 1903 Leipzig Trade Fair, however, that cemented its place in toy history. A subsequent American debut at the St Louis World's Fair in 1904 increased the popularity of Steiff's creation, which became aligned in the popular imagination with the then president, Theodore Roosevelt, who, despite his reputation as a hunter, was said to have spared the life of a bear cub during a shooting party. However, the convergence of presidential myth and design ingenuity served to launch a thousand teddy bear imitators, leading Steiff to brand its creation with a hallmark brass button in its left ear, a tradition that continues to identify Bear 55 PB's progeny to this day.

Freunde fürs Leben

Surely it would be misusing language to say that the function of the Teddy bear is to represent a bear. It does not. It is a new kind of bear, a creation of this century and maybe one of its few lovable ones. I do not think that Christopher Robin ever wondered who had made his dear Winnie whom he called Pooh, but with the distance of time, scholarly curiosity and the greed of the market have also invaded the nursery. The Teddy can now confidently be attributed to two independent artists: the German toy maker Margarete Steiff with her product, but the inventor of the name Teddy bear and thus of the toy was an American called Morris Milton, who in all sincerity wrote to President Theodore Roosevelt in about 1902 asking for permission to call one of his stuffed toys after him, which was graciously granted. But Milton was not swollen-headed; he obviously felt that his bear lacked a certain *je na sais quoi* and when, on a visit to Leipzig, he saw a bear called Petz made by Mrs Steiff, he at once ordered 3,000 copies, much to her amazement, and so began Teddy's career in earnest. I say began, but it is only in the last few years that this creation has received the accolade of being auctioned at Christie's, where on 5 December 1994, £110,000 was paid for a specimen from around 1904.

But what may be called the aestheticization or sterilization of the Teddy bear happened a few centuries after the aestheticization of paintings of saints. Surely the original demand for the bear was not the demand for a work of art but for a creature to play with, a companion to share the child's pillow or plate, in other words to become vested with something like a soul. It is difficult to find a word to describe this capacity of three-dimensional images to be drawn into the world of the living, to become not representations of something else but almost individuals in their own right. 'Personalized' might have fitted, if it had not been so horribly abused. Perhaps animation is the best I can do. For the child, the image is charged with a life of its own, not a dangerous life, but a fictitious life of make-believe.

E.H. Gombrich, *The Uses of Images: Studies in the Social Function of Art and Visual Communication*, Phaidon, 1999

Charles Rennie Mackintosh enjoyed an influential career as one of Britain's most important contributors to twentieth-century design. After qualifying from Glasgow School of Art, Mackintosh started working for the newly founded architectural firm of Honeyman and Keppie in 1890. A few years later, his early furniture and decorative designs helped him win the prestigious competition for a new Glasgow School of Art, which in turn attracted the attention of the editors of influential design journals *The Studio* and *Dekorative Kunst*. Given instant credibility through the magazines, Mackintosh earned an invitation to exhibit his work in Vienna at the 1900 Secession exhibition, gaining international respect and an equal footing with the likes of Koloman Moser and Josef Hoffmann. Meanwhile, as the art school unfolded in Glasgow at the turn of the century, publisher Walter Blackie approached Mackintosh to design his home, The Hill House, in Helensburgh outside Glasgow. Blackie was drawn towards Mackintosh's approach to designing, whereby the one person created everything from the building down to the cutlery and door handles. It was for Blackie's bedroom that Mackintosh designed the Ladder Back Chair. Turning away from the organic naturalism of Art Nouveau, for this chair Mackintosh adopted abstract geometry inspired by the rectilinear patterns of Japanese design. He was interested in the balancing of opposites, choosing a dark ebonized ashwood frame in contrast to the designated white wall behind. The seemingly unnecessary height of the chair was a feature to enhance the spatial qualities of the room. For Mackintosh, the visual effects of a wholly integrated scheme was more important than the quality of craftsmanship and truth to materials that his Arts and Crafts contemporaries were advocating in Britain at that time. He applied similar principles in the design of several tea rooms for Catherine Cranston in Glasgow. Mackintosh left Honeyman and Keppie in 1913. He struggled as an independent architect and found it difficult to attract many more commissions for furniture. He took up painting, then retired to the south of France in 1923, and died in 1928 in London. The Ladder Back Chair was originally handmade, and was then reissued by Italian manufacturer Cassina, who have also produced a number of chair and table designs by Mackintosh.

Crayola Crayons are the most recognizable brand of crayon in the world. Made with paraffin wax and colour pigments, and originally sold in boxes of eight, there are now 120 colours in the Crayola collection, and after a hundred years of production they are as popular as ever. In 1903, having recently expanded their company to create crayons and drawing materials for educational use, co-inventors and cousins Edwin Binney and Harold Smith deliberately set out to create a set of colourful crayons that would be safe for children to use in schools. When they were satisfied with the safety and reliability of the crayons, they added two more essential ingredients to ensure success: good packaging and a catchy name. Alice Binney, Edwin's wife, named the crayons 'Crayola' from the French words for 'chalk' and 'oily', and throughout its 100-year history Crayola has retained the familiar yellow and green packaging and still uses the same design on the paper wrapper of each crayon. Crayola moves with the times and is constantly updating its collection, introducing new, contemporary colours and retiring unpopular shades. The first set, priced at a nickel, was introduced in 1903 and contained eight colours: red, blue, yellow, green, purple, orange, brown and

O73

Crayola Crayons (1903)
Edwin Binney (nd)
Harold Smith (nd)
Crayola 1903 to present

black. Between 1949 and 1957 forty new colours were introduced, such as apricot and silver, along with lemon-yellow and maize that would later be removed in 1990 to make space for new colours. The discontinued crayons are exonerated in the Crayola Hall of Fame and no doubt sought after by collectors. Fluorescent crayons like ultra pink and hot magenta were popular in the 1970s and 1980s and, in 1993, 'macaroni and cheese' was added to an already impressive menu of colours. Part of Crayola's success may be due to its ability to engage with those buying or using its crayons: listening to teachers' and parents' suggestions and adapting to their needs. In 1962 the 'flesh'-coloured crayon was renamed 'peach' in recognition that it did not represent everybody's skin colour. Later, washable crayons were introduced, as well as crayons that are visible only on special paper. These innovations and a policy of allowing the public to name new colours keep the crayons popular with consumers. A recent study by Yale University found the smell of Crayola Crayons amongst the twenty most recognizable scents for American adults. For children, however, they remain the first recognizable steps towards artistic expression.

While experimenting with the newly invented electric light bulb, Mariano Fortuny y Madrazo created the Fortuny Moda Lamp. Sometimes technology, science, materials and the designer's interests and concepts come together to create an ingenious design. This is the case with the Fortuny Moda Lamp. Fortuny y Madrazo's life was dedicated to all forms of art, from interior and set design to photography, architecture, painting, textiles, clothing and lighting. He is perhaps best known for his spectacular luxury fabrics; his Delphos robe, in pleated silk and inspired by Greek gowns, is considered a legend in fashion design. His insights into the way light could transform stage sets led to his experiments with indirect lighting in interiors. Reflected light was softer and produced a glow rather than a glare; by reflecting light off fabric he was able to create whatever mood he wished. Fortuny y Madrazo patented his system of indirect lighting

for the stage in 1901. The refinements of the system lead him to design the Fortuny Moda Lamp, which was patented in 1903. It was the fortunate converging of seemingly unrelated ideas that created this unusual shape. The lamp's form also speaks to Fortuny y Madrazo's varied interests. Camera tripods probably influenced the lamp's base, with its adjustable central column and swivelling head and the lamp's shade is a simple inversion of traditional shades of the time, with the added function of tilting. Fortuny y Madrazo's genius is in his combination of these elements into the form, which continues to remain contemporary. His concepts of reflected light have greatly influenced how designers, to this day, use light as a tool, rather than using the light merely as an object in itself. Conceptually, Fortuny y Madrazo's Lamp was clearly ahead of its time, and when seen, either in a studio or the home, it is still distinctive.

Purkersdorf Sanatorium, Josef Hoffmann and the Wiener Werkstatte, 1903–04

O75

Purkersdorf (1903)
Josef Hoffmann (1870–1956)
Koloman Moser (1896–1918)
Franz Wittmann Möbelwerkstätten
1973 to present

This chair, designed by Josef Hoffmann and Koloman Moser, was designed for the lobby of the Purkersdorf Sanatorium on the outskirts of Vienna, an elegant, spa-like resort for wealthy patrons. The sanatorium was designed by Josef Hoffman and the Wiener Werkstätte and was a place where elegant black tie dinners were served in the large dining room, with famous figures of the day, including Arnold Schönberg, Gustav Mahler and international royalty. Both Hoffmann and Moser often painted their furniture white, which was unheard of until the late nineteenth century. Many designers of the period, including Charles Rennie Mackintosh, were preoccupied with the notion of creating a total, cohesive environment in which interior, furniture and architecture all complemented each other and added to the experience of the building. This chair, an almost perfect cube, is the ideal complement to the strong rectilinear quality of both the architecture and the interior decoration of the sanatorium. The use of white and black and the geometric motif also enhances the sense of order and calm that one might expect from a visit to a sanatorium. The chair's strong, underlying geometry suggests rationalism and an encouragement of contemplation, while the use of white also reflects the contemporary fascination with new ideas about hygiene. The Josef Hoffmann Foundation has granted the sole rights to Franz Wittmann Möbelwerkstätten to reproduce his furniture, and the Purkersdorf has been reproduced since 1973. Both Moser and Hoffman were members of the Vienna Secession, a group who aimed to replace the excessive ornamentation of Art Nouveau with a more precise, orderly and less bourgeois style. The austere architecture of the sanatorium, with very slight decoration on the exterior, contrasts with an interior of adornment and detail, such as the checkerboard pattern used for the seat, representing a departure from the overly decorative styles of Art Nouveau and the Victorian era. The sanatorium has gone through several owners, from the original builder, Victor Zuckerkandl, to the National Socialists after Zuckerkandl's death, and at a time when Jewish property was overtaken, to the Russian military as a hospital for their forces, then slowly returned back to the original families. The building was in a ruinous state, as it had been looted; attempts were made to use it until 1975, when it entirely abandoned. In 2003, the building was gently restored, and is now used as a home for the elderly, with the original furniture.

This cutlery was an early product of the Wiener Werkstätte, founded by Josef Hoffmann and Koloman Moser with the financial backing of Fritz Wärndorfer in 1903. The business shared Art Nouveau's preoccupation with craftsmanship in the face of industrialization and its urge to banish superfluous decoration from the design of everyday objects. But its preference for stricter forms was all its own. The design for the Flat Model cutlery is a fine example of that aesthetic in action. There is no ornament at all, except for a row of round beads at the end of the handles, though personalized versions for Hoffmann, Moser and Wärndorfer would each feature monograms on the handles. Evidently, the smooth, broad surfaces and regular geometric shapes were a little too far ahead of their time for some tastes. Reviewing the Wiener Werkstätte's 1906 exhibition 'Der Gedeckter Tisch' ('The Laid Table'), the newspaper *Deutsche Zeitung* accused Hoffmann of creating geometry instead of art, while the *Hamburger Fremdenblatt* called his cutlery 'uncomfortable', likening it to anatomical instruments. Moser took rigour at the dining table to such lengths that he even designed new pastry shapes, though few bakers could realize them to his specification. The critic Armin Friedmann commented scathingly in 1906 that, 'the new grace will have to be "Bless these lines that we are about to receive"…to carve beef

with stylistic correctness you
need a ruler and dividers…here
madness marries geometry.'
The thirty-three-piece service,
Hoffmann's first attempt at this
particular form, came in silver,
plated silver and gilded silver and
was produced at a time when the
output of the metalwork, gold and
silver workshops was the most
important branch of the Wiener

Werkstätte enterprise. It had
a relatively limited life, being
produced only until 1908, but its
stylistic approach survived in
other forms, remained influential
for many years and still appears
modern today.

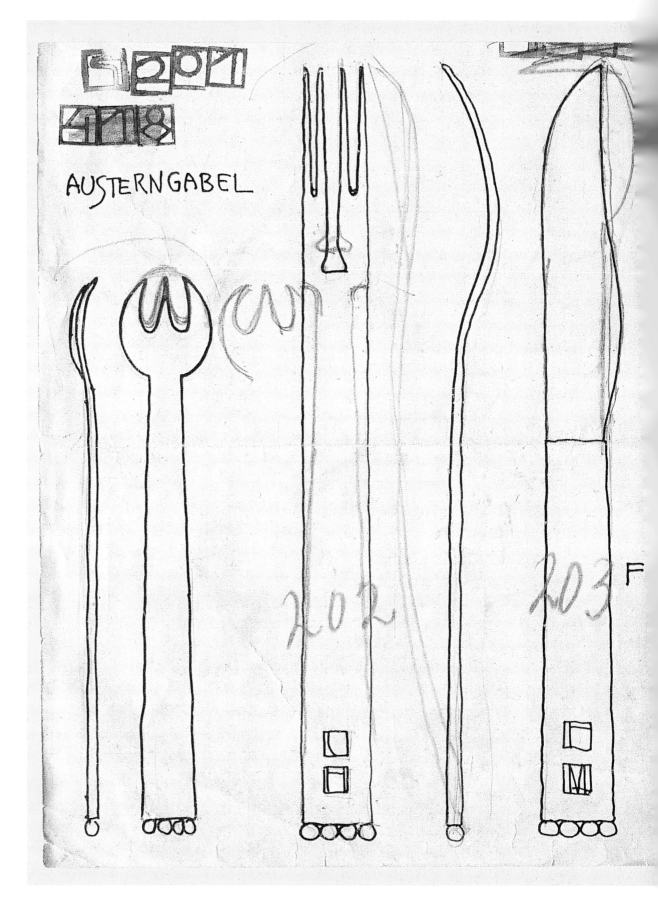

AUSTERNGABEL

202

203 F

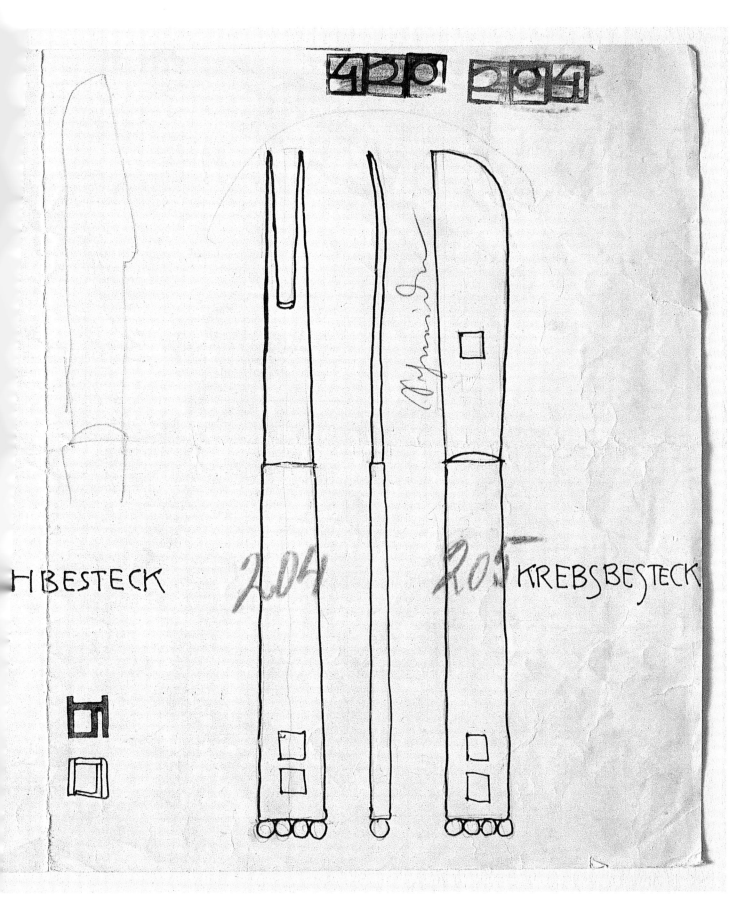

H BESTECK

2,04

RO5 KREBSBESTECK

Its simple design and seductive lapis lazuli colour has made La Boule Bleue an icon of the modern game of *boules*. While its success is partly due to its idiosyncratic appearance – a blue enigma in possession of a 'closely guarded production secret' – it appeared with perfect timing, just as *pétanque*, today the most popular form of *boules*, was taking off. The origins of La Boule Bleue can be traced back to 1904 when one Captain Félix Rofritsch established a bowl-making venture in Marseille. Rofritsch's first bowls were made of wood and studded with nails hammered in one by one and he could only make two pairs per day. But *boules* was not a particularly popular sport until *pétanque*, a version from the south of France, captured the nation's imagination. The word derives from the provençal 'pèd tanco', which means 'feet together'; marking an area out on rough terrain, players stand in a circle scratched in the dirt and throw their bowls with no run-up. The first official *pétanque* competition was held in the town of La Ciotat, a port east of Marseille, in 1908. The traditional Rofritsch hand-made wooden bowls were eventually superseded by bronze and brass models in the mid-1920s; the defining moment for the company came in 1947, however, when Félix's two sons Fortuné and Marcel created a bowl out of tempered Swedish carbon steel. This highly resistant alloy develops blue highlights during thermal oxidization of hardening, thus establishing the distinctive and defining characteristic of La Boule Bleue as a chance by-product. The production secret of La Boule Bleue involves a particular firing and hardening technique that affords each meticulously crafted steel and carbon bowl an exceptional hardness and makes it durable on all terrains. Diameters range from 70.5–80 mm (2–3 in). Many *boules* champions, including Lovino, Locatelli and Charly de Gémenos, have been particular fans of La Boule Bleue. The Boule Bleue plant in Marseille continues to be run by the Rofritsch family, with Maurice Rofritsch in charge since 1967. And with an estimated 600,000 licensed *pétanque* players worldwide there is clearly a market for this unique product.

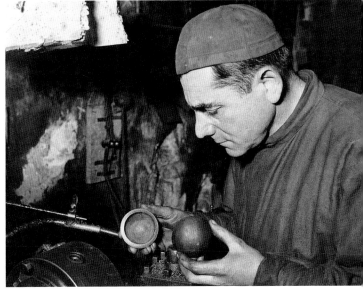

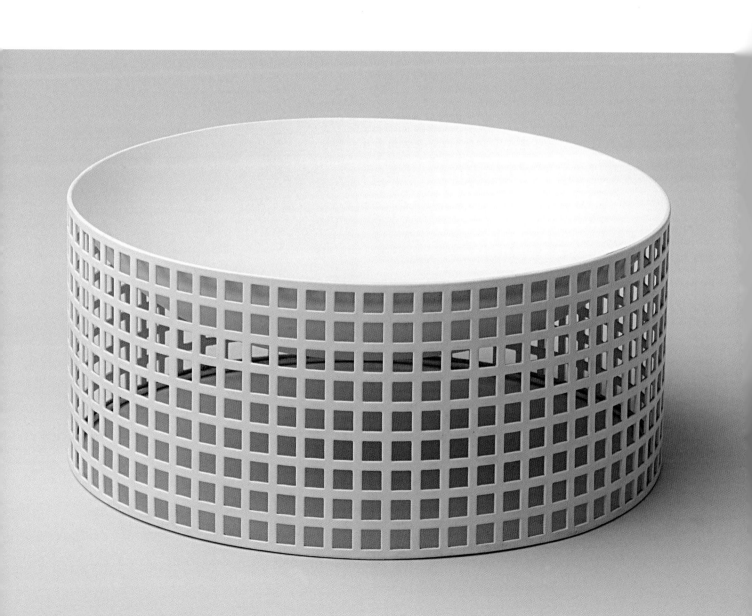

O78

Fruit Bowl (1904)
Josef Hoffmann (1870–1956)
Wiener Werkstätte 1904
Franz Wittmann Möbelwerkstätten
1970 to 1985

This Fruit Bowl is a relatively early product of the Wiener Werkstätte, founded in 1903 by Hoffmann, Koloman Moser and their patron-turned-financial backer Fritz Wärndorfer to realize a new approach to uniting handicraft and art. The enterprise grew out of the earlier Vienna Secession, which had been founded as a reaction to the conservatism of the Viennese art establishment. The movement, whose founders included Gustav Klimt as well as Moser and Hoffmann, was allied to Art Nouveau in rejecting what it saw as the lazy use of historical decorative devices, but it stopped short of its French counterpart's wholehearted use of natural forms. Much of the Wiener Werkstätte's output exemplified the strikingly modern, restrained aesthetic that flowed from this thinking. Hoffmann applied it to architecture, interiors, furniture, glassware, jewellery and other decorative objects, frequently designing whole buildings and their contents as a single integrated work, or *Gesamtkunstwerk*. Hoffmann resorted readily to geometric, rectilinear forms to the extent that he acquired the nickname 'Quadratl'. Hoffmann's Fruit Bowl of 1904, made from sheet iron with a decoration of punched squares and painted white, is typical of the Wiener Werkstätte's striving for simplicity and functionality. At the time it was a bold departure but it was later to become a key principle of the Bauhaus and the Modern movement. The piece also illustrates how the organization made a virtue of exclusivity: its metalwork shop yielded just two of these bowls in 1904, one white and one black. It is possible that one of them featured in the Wiener Werkstätte's first exhibition, held at Berlin's Hohenzollern Kunstgewerbehaus in 1905, as one of the buyers was the Hohenzollern Kaufhaus. The bowl would reach a considerably wider clientele more than sixty years later thanks to Franz Wittmann Möbelwerkstätten, based in Vienna, which produced it for fifteen years from 1970 until 1985, and now produces many of Hoffmann's chair designs.

Benjamin Holt, a peat farmer with a vast knowledge about agricultural steam engines, living in the deep south of the United States, realized the enormous economic potential for a vehicle capable of working in the soft, spongy native soil. This soil would not support horses or the heavy, steam-driven, wheeled tractors on the market at the time. Holt began testing his first humble conversion of a steam-powered, wheeled vehicle fitted with two continuous wooden tracks on his personal farmland in 1904. The machine's ability successfully to manoeuvre over the soft soil due to its increased surface area in contact with the ground led him to invest in developing the machine. It was soon dubbed 'Caterpillar' by the company's photographer, in response to the machine's unusual propulsion method of simultaneously laying its own track and rotating back up as the wheels turn. Holt replaced the steam engine with a petrol combustion engine two years later, and went on to develop a clutch and braking mechanism, which enabled the design to become a viable commercial product. It soon became apparent that this machine could serve many purposes, most notably in road building, earth moving and military service. The challenge of moving artillery and supplies across the demanding trench-laden terrain of the French battlefields of World

Benjamin Holt pictured meeting British officer Ernest Swinton, whose military tank design was inspired by Holt's track-type tractor, April 1918.

War 1 led the Allies to use a series of Holt-designed, petrol-powered, tracked tractors on the Western Front. As the war progressed, the British army decided to explore the possibility of armour-plating a tracked vehicle to create a machine capable of destroying the German barbed-wire entanglements. To ensure that the enemy did not get wind of the project, the new machine was code-named 'water tanks', or the 'tank', as it is now universally known. The device, launched in 1915, helped to break the military deadlock and created a template for tracked vehicles that continues to this day. The British company Hornsby modified Holt's design to create tracks that could be driven separately on either side, which also allowed the whole vehicle to turn on one spot. It sold this patent to Holt in 1913, but he died in 1920, only five years before the Holt Manufacturing Company merged with rival tractor manufacturer, the CL Best Tractor Company. This formed the Caterpillar Tractor Company (formerly known as the Holt Manufacturing Company), based in Preoria, Illinois, USA. Today, Caterpillar is a highly successful multinational company producing the trademark yellow-liveried machines that continue to play a vital role in the creation of almost every structure in modern society.

Caterpillar Tractor (1904)
Benjamin Holt (1849–1920)
Caterpillar 1904 to present

Holt's Steam Traction Engine No.77 with the new track system installed, 1905

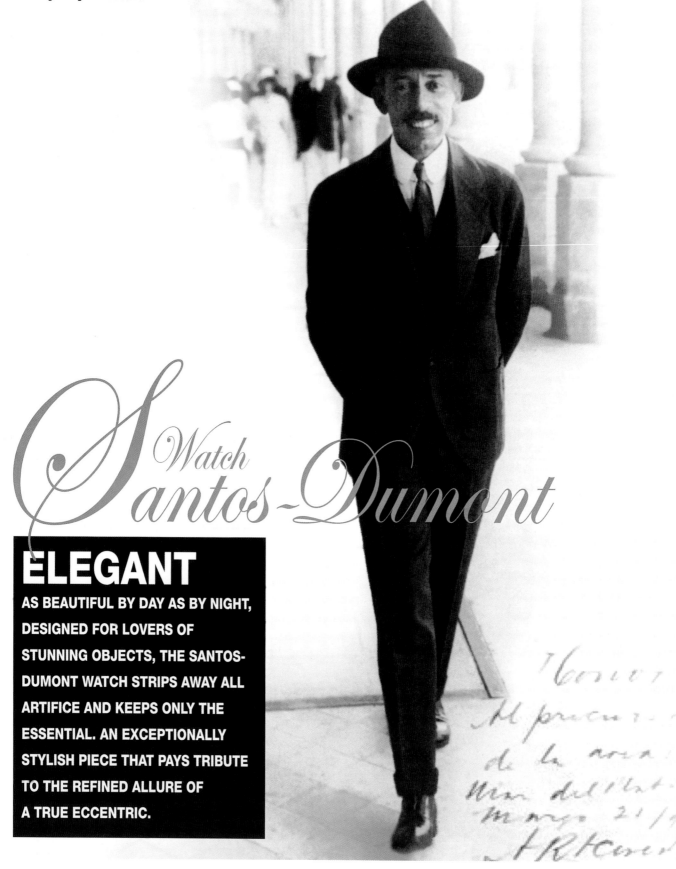

Cartier catalogue image of Louis Cartier

Watch
Santos-Dumont

ELEGANT

AS BEAUTIFUL BY DAY AS BY NIGHT,
DESIGNED FOR LOVERS OF
STUNNING OBJECTS, THE SANTOS-
DUMONT WATCH STRIPS AWAY ALL
ARTIFICE AND KEEPS ONLY THE
ESSENTIAL. AN EXCEPTIONALLY
STYLISH PIECE THAT PAYS TRIBUTE
TO THE REFINED ALLURE OF
A TRUE ECCENTRIC.

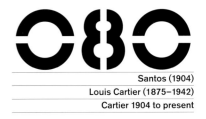

The history of the watch goes back to the sixteenth century, but wristwatches date from only just over a century ago, and the Cartier Santos watch has a good claim to being the first commercial model. It was among the first 'true' wristwatches and its design, which has endured unchanged to this day has been extremely influential and much imitated. Timepieces began finding their way onto wearers' wrists halfway through the nineteenth century, but these were essentially round pocket watches with straps. By the 1880s English ladies out hunting wore pendant watches strapped to their wrists in leather cases, but as yet no gentleman would be seen with anything other than a pocket watch. Industrialization and a faster pace of life would gradually change this, but it was World War I that finally signalled the ascendancy of the wristwatch. Soldiers in the trenches needed something less cumbersome than a pocket watch tucked under several layers of uniform and so it was that wristwatches finally became acceptable gentleman's apparel. By then the Santos had been available commercially for some years, while the design itself had been around for a decade. It was devised by Louis Cartier, grandson of the Cartier company's founder and the driving force behind the company becoming an international name and its cultivation of blue-blooded clients. It was with good reason that Edward VII dubbed Cartier the 'jeweller of kings, king among jewellers'. The client behind the Santos (and the watch's name) was the Brazilian pilot Alberto Santos-Dumont, who wanted a timepiece he could see easily while engaged in airborne daredevilry. He first donned the watch for a 220 m (720 ft) flight in 1907. The Santos's origins explain its robust, masculine appearance and the pronounced screw-like rivets that punctuate the steel strap and quadratic face, and this has surprisingly added to its unisex appeal and the company continues to make numerous versions for women.

O81

Armchair for the Postsparkasse (1904–6)
Otto Wagner (1841–1918)
Gebrüder Thonet 1906 to 1915
Gebrüder Thonet Germany 1987 to present
Gebrüder Thonet Vienna 2003 to present

Austrian architect Otto Wagner won a competition to design a number of public facilities in 1893, among which the Postsparkasse, the Austrian postal savings bank, was included as the last building to complete Vienna's Ringstrasse. This grand project gave the city the allure of a modern metropolis. The Postsparkasse was designed as a unified work, with a glass ceiling in the entrance, detachable office walls and an exterior wall made of aluminium, the material which was also used for the interior fittings and furniture. This project allowed Wagner to apply his philosophy of moving away from historical formalism towards a modern, rational style. Around 1902 Wagner designed his first chair in bentwood for the telegraph office of the newspaper *Die Zeit*, in collaboration with the Viennese firm Jacob & Joseph Kohn, a company who at that time was very keen on collaborating with architects. In 1904 Wagner slightly modified his Zeit Chair for the Postsparkasse, and Thonet produced the design. The chair was the first to use a single length of bentwood to form the back, arms and front legs. U-shaped braces were added to support the D-shaped seat and back legs. This chair, which came with or without arms according to where it was used in the building, is still recognized for its efficient use of material and the great comfort it provides. Metal decorative details, like studs, sabots and plates to prevent the chair from wear, were used to customize the chair for specific uses. The most luxurious version, embellished with aluminium, at that time a rare material, was used for the directors' offices. The chair's popularity was such that by 1911 many versions, produced by various companies, were on the market, and is still being produced today.

The Diabolo is a circus game made from two cast-rubber domes joined in the middle with a metal axle. By spooling a length of string around the axle, the Diabolo can be spun and propelled into the air, whereupon, with skill, it can be caught on its return and used to perform a series of gravity-defying tricks. Gustave Phillippart's design draws inspiration from a traditional Chinese toy, which can trace its history back over 3,000 years. It was originally called a 'Kouen-gen', which loosely translates as 'make the hollow bamboo stick whistle'. During the Han dynasty the use of the toy became a formal circus skill. These

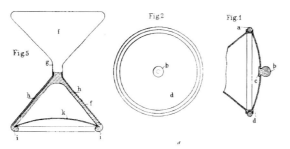

traditional Chinese toys were made with two round pieces of bamboo held together by a horizontal stick. Two sticks held together with string made up the rest of the toy. These forerunners of the modern Diabolo often had small holes or grooves in the wooden elements, which made a howling sound when spun at speed by skilled jugglers. The toy was imported to Europe during the eighteenth century by French and English traders, and given the name 'Diaballo', from the ancient Greek *dia* (through) and *ballo* (to throw). It gained widespread acceptance in France during the nineteenth century, as clubs and competitions sprung up promoting the toy's use. Phillippart was the first manufacturer to realize the toy's potential, and his design crystallized the toy's form and established it as a universal childhood activity. After World War I the Diabolo's popularity faded, only for it to enjoy a remarkable comeback during the 1980s,

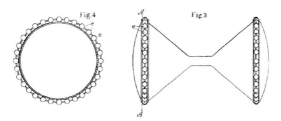

as circus acts and juggling enjoyed a creative renaissance through the re-emergence of street performance. Since its introduction, there have been many different design interpretations and sizes of Diabolo manufactured in a variety of materials, although most commonly in plastic, rubber, wood and metal. While newer materials and greater precision in production have allowed jugglers to explore a far greater repertoire of tricks, such as wrapping the Diabolo around their arms, legs and body, the modern Diabolo continues to refer back to Phillippart's archetypal design.

Every part of this chair was designed to tell us that it was machine made and that, in fact, we are to regard it as a machine itself. The mechanical impression is achieved through the absence of any historical or traditional decorations. Geometry and the play of lines, curves and planes, solids and voids, appear to govern the form of the chair. The back and seat are two oblongs (echoed in the side panels) suspended between simple D-shaped runners. The machine-like character is reinforced by the mechanism to raise and lower the back that is clearly evident. A rod, fitted against domes mounted on the frame, dictates the slope of the back. In all parts this chair appears to be the epitome of logic and functionalism. Chairs with adjustable reclining backs had been known since the mid-seventeenth century, and in the late nineteenth century they were popularized by the design reformer William Morris. He gave his name to a chair reliant on the same simple rod mechanism that controls the rake of this chair. The English Arts and Crafts movement enthralled Viennese designers and from the 1880s Thonet had produced bentwood versions of Morris chairs. Along with Thonet, Kohn was one of the leading pioneers of mass-produced bentwood furniture and the design of this chair clearly exploits the potential for repetitive production of simple units for assembly that bentwood technology embodied. The Sitzmaschine, or Sitting Machine, was designed by the leading Viennese designer of the early twentieth century, Josef Hoffmann. Perhaps influenced by the geometric patterns of Charles Rennie Mackintosh, Hoffmann championed a similar style in Vienna that could be easily translated to mass-production processes, as shown here.

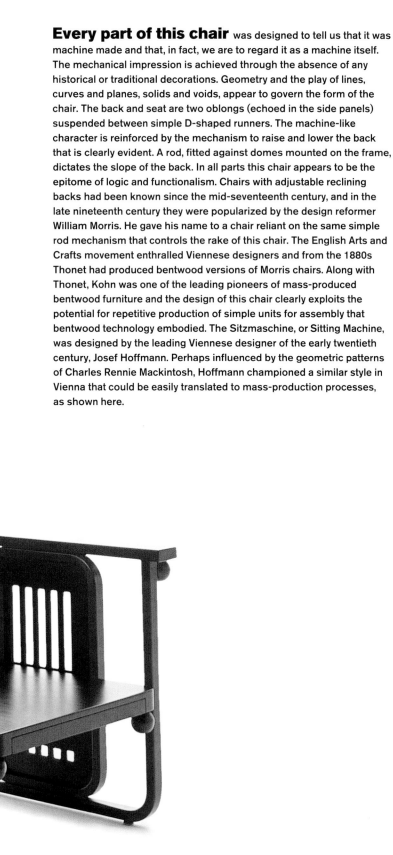

Sitzmaschine (1905)
Josef Hoffmann (1870–1956)
Jacob & Joseph Kohn 1905 to 1916
Franz Wittmann Möbelwerkstätten
1997 to present

Josef Hoffmann

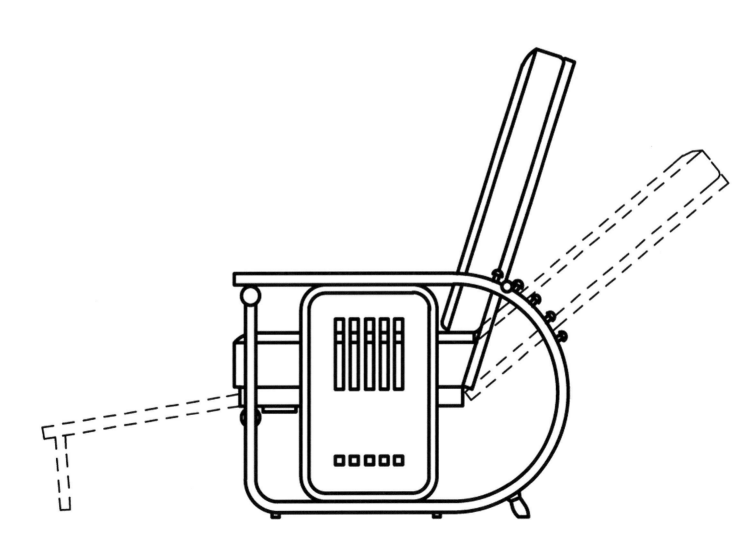

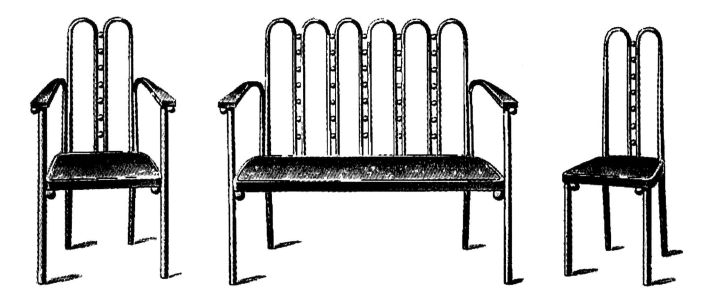

Josef Hoffmann's No. 371 Chair illustrates the subtle decorative style synonymous with progressive Viennese design movements at the turn of the last century. It was to be influential in seating design for many years after. The 371 is a spare and reductionist form, with token decorative elements provided by the turned wooden balls that link the two crested uprights of the back support. The strong geometry of this arrangement typifies Hoffmann's ability to create a significant aesthetic in architecture and design. Similar decoration with geometric forms would later be copied by lesser designers, in many cases without reference to an integrated theme or structure as in the 371. For example, the wooden balls on the back and under the seat also provide structural strength and linkage between the seat components,while they are important decorative additions to the design. Furthermore, the plywood saddle-shaped seat predates the mass-produced designs by the Eameses and Alvar Aalto. Hoffmann studied architecture under Otto Wagner and co-founded the radical group the Vienna Secession in 1897. His strikingly modern designs made no reference to historical precedents and he created truly original work in architecture, interiors and furniture whose influence is still felt today. The 371 was designed for the porch of a Secessionist villa Hoffman displayed at the 1908 Kunstschau in Vienna and remains a testament to his ability to marry functional simplicity with geometry that rejected historical models. The 371 Chair utilizes mass-production materials and processes forged by Jacob & Josef Kohn, and was put into production for a short period. It is unfortunate that in an increasingly competitive marketplace, the 371 remained a purely site-specific design, as it shows sensitivity towards decoration, the potential for mass production and the individualistic talent of Josef Hoffmann.

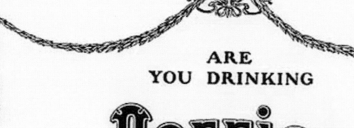

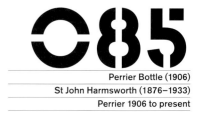

Today, the Bouillens Estate, the site of a spring of naturally carbonated mineral water in Vergèze in south-east France, is home to a production plant capable of bottling 750 million bottles of Perrier water per year. In 1863 Napoleon III approved spring water as a mineral water, which led to a variety of scientific studies that verified the merits of the water. Dr Louis Perrier, a physician from Nîmes, took ownership of the estate in 1898 with a mission to bottle and sell this natural resource. His ambition came at a time when his countrymen were more likely to drink beer, wine and absinthe over the healthier option of water. Proper investment was needed to build the facilities he was planning and it was while searching for backers that he ran the site as a spa and dedicated much of his time to the development of a bottle with a hermetically sealed cap that would enable correct packaging and shipping of his product. In 1902 Dr Perrier met St John Harmsworth, who had travelled to the area to learn French. Harmsworth, who came from a wealthy Irish family, was immediately drawn to the potential of the spring and leased the property a year later, eventually buying it. His mission was to convert the entire British Empire to the benefits of mineral water, but first he needed to attract customers by positioning the Perrier brand as a high-end product. In 1906 the Perrier glass bottle was conceived, an elegant, curvaceous drop-like form that bestowed on the product an instantly recognizable visual identity. Harmsworth took the shape from the Indian exercise clubs he used, and decided that the best way to sell the product was through the British army in India and other colonies. The demand for the bottled water grew and was then accepted onto the dining tables of the discerning, including at Buckingham Palace. Nineteen million bottles a year were produced by 1933, and between 1948 and 1952 production rapidly increased from 30 to 150 million bottles. From 1973 onwards the bottles were made only by the Verrerie du Languedoc glassworks factory, following the purchase of a sand quarry in Mont Ventoux that supplied the silica sand used to create the green glass. The sparkling water came with the slogan 'Champagne des eaux de table' ('The champagne of table waters'), resulting in rapid uptake by consumers. The bottle and green colour have become synonymous with the brand; even with all labelling removed, people around the world can successfully link the bottle to Perrier. Only minor changes have been made to the bottle since its creation in 1906, mainly in the form of new caps and label designs.

Georg Jensen

The Continental silver cutlery range was the first major cutlery pattern to emerge from the workshop of Danish silversmith Georg Jensen, who was hailed in a *New York Herald Tribune* obituary of 1935 as 'the greatest silversmith of the last 300 years'. Jensen's meticulously handcrafted silverware has become synonymous with the global luxury goods market, yet when he first set up his silversmith studio in Copenhagen in 1904, his business was both niche and radical. With an apprenticeship as goldsmith and sculptor behind him, Jensen rejected the popular taste of the time for romantic and historicist ornamentation and ostentation, instead embracing the avant-garde Art Nouveau style with its simple organic forms and craft-based approach to production. The Continental range has been one of the company's most popular and enduring silver cutlery patterns, and is still in production today after almost a hundred years. Characteristically understated in its refinement, the range uses simple decoration and delicately beaten surfaces to create knives and forks that are sensual and sculptural. Jensen's design also pays homage to the traditional wooden utensils of the centuries-old cottage industries of Denmark. Jensen was instrumental in defining the character of twentieth-century Scandinavian design by drawing on indigenous Danish traditions and infusing them with a progressive design rationale. He was also pivotal in the transition from Art Nouveau to Art Deco in design, adding crisp geometric forms to his existing repertoire of undulating organic forms as early as 1915. Jensen's craftsmanship caught the eye of newspaper tycoon and art collector William Randolph Hearst at the Panama-Pacific International Exposition in San Francisco in 1915. Hearst was so impressed he bought the entire exhibit.

Venturing into boot polish production in 1904 from a small factory in Melbourne, Australia, Scottish innovator William Ramsay and his co-worker Hamilton McKellan refined and improved their polish formula until they were able to launch and market Kiwi in the surrounding city two years later, selling predominantly to ranchers who wanted to protect their boots against the elements. Naming their product after the bird from Ramsay's wife's homeland of New Zealand, they hit on a simple, memorable and recognizable brand identity, which remains an important factor in the marketability and success of Kiwi shoe polish today. Before 1906, shoe polish was not widely available to buy, and domestic polish was hand-prepared using a base of lanolin or beeswax. Kiwi polish was a significant improvement on these inconsistent and ineffective home-produced forms; it could restore the colour and shine of leather, protecting shoes and enhancing their durability. When Kiwi introduced a dark tan variant in 1908, it incorporated specific chemical agents that added suppleness and water resistance. As a combination of non-soluble liquids and solids, shoe polish ingredients often comprise naphtha, lanolin, wax, gum arabic and sometimes an added colour. The almost insoluble naphtha evaporates on contact with air, drying out and hardening the polish after application, while retaining its shine. Lanolin acts as a waterproofing wax, giving the polish a greasy texture and improving application, as well as working to delay the evaporation of the naphtha until the polish has been applied and buffed evenly over the leather surface. Kiwi became a globally significant brand during World War I when millions of leather army boots required simple, quick and efficient polishing, and Kiwi polish was traded as a commodity throughout the British Commonwealth and the United States to meet this huge demand. Soldiers returning from service in both world wars continued to use the polish, and as shoe fashions changed from the 1950s onward, Kiwi polish became a staple household brand. Today Kiwi remains the global leader in polish production, selling to over 180 countries worldwide.

"Kiwi" KEE-WEE

AUSTRALIA 1919

"Hail Shining Morn"

The Quality Boot Polish.
In Black & all shades of Tan

The spreading of communicable diseases has spawned the invention of many a vaccine, but it also motivated the creation of the individual paper cup used at water coolers the world over. In the late nineteenth century, drinking water in public places was accessed with a tin dipper from which people would quaff, an unhygienic practice that only started being abolished in the United States in 1909. A few years earlier, a Boston-based entrepreneur named Lawrence Luellen conceived of a paraffin-treated paper cup and dispensing apparatus that would address this pernicious health problem. Teaming up with his brother-in-law Hugh Everett Moore, a Harvard student with a keen business sense and a penchant for socialist thought, Luellen started a business crusading against the common drinking cup, and unwittingly created the standard against which all throwaway cups would be measured in the future. The disposable cup went through a number of iterations, starting out life as a 0.15 L (5 fl oz) form constructed from two pieces of paper with a flat bottom and straight drinking edge treated in wax. Further improvements included the recessed bottom for better stackability and a rolled lip for greater structural integrity. After the team secured a $200,000 capital investment by a group of New York bankers, the main obstacle to success was distribution. Luellen's initial idea was to sell territorial rights to various companies across the country, which worked well at first. The partners also leased water dispensers with an attachment for stacking cups in bulk to railway stations, schools, offices and other public places where drinking water was needed. Finally, in 1910, Luellen and Moore founded the Individual Drinking Cup Company of New York, which became Dixie in 1919. Such events as the flu epidemic that swept the country after World War I and the need for portable water dispensers during World War II served to establish further the Dixie in the public imagination. Peacetime pleasures like individual ice cream servings also contributed to the unassuming container's wild success, as did the product's blank sides, which became the perfect medium for conveying branding and advertising messages. Aided by the convergence of historical events and a sharp use of marketing techniques, the two men built an empire based on nothing more complicated than wax and paper.

088

Dixie Cups (1908)
Hugh Everett Moore (1887–1972)
Lawrence Luellen (nd)
Dixie 1908 to present

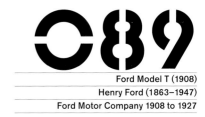

Henry Ford

Between 1908, when the Model T was released, and 1927, when production was discontinued, Ford factories around the world manufactured an amazing 15 million cars: only the Volkswagen Beetle would break this production record. With the introduction of the assembly line, production rates soared from one car every twelve hours and seven minutes to one car every twenty-four seconds. Designed to be lightweight and flexible to cope with rough roads, the Model T had a standard 254 cm (100 in) wheelbase chassis that could be fitted with different body styles ranging from a five-seat touring car to a two-seat runabout or a seven-seat town car. The engine had its four cylinders cast in a block with the cylinder head detachable for easy access and, producing 20 hp, it could achieve a top speed of 72 kph (45 mph). A hand crank was used to start the Model T until 1920 when some models were finally equipped with a battery-powered starter. As the petrol was fed to the engine purely by gravity, the only way to drive a Model T up a steep hill was in reverse; incidentally the reverse gear was much more powerful than the two forward gears. It came in just one colour: black. When Henry Ford said, 'An idealist is a person who helps other people to be prosperous,' he must have been referring to himself. He revolutionized society by cheaply and efficiently creating the Model T, the world's most successful car, while paying his employees a very good wage. In 1914 he was able to pay his employees $5 a day, nearly twice the wages offered by rival manufacturers. The rise in rapid production led to a drop in the market price from $850 in 1908 to under $300 in the 1920s, transforming the car from a means of transport only for the well-to-do into a mass phenomenon. Assembly-line production also allowed Ford to cut the working day from nine hours to eight and convert to a three-shift working day in his factories. Today it is estimated that 100,000 Model Ts survive around the world.

VEREINIGTE
WERKSTÄTTEN
FÜR·KUNST·IM
HANDWERK·A.G.

Kleiderständer MODELL: 4522
ENTWURF: V. W / O. Blümel

AUSFÜHRUNG:

MOD. 4522. KLEIDERSTÄNDER· M·1:10

Designed by Munich-based
Otto Blümel, the Nymphenburg Coat Stand is
a classic example of Jugendstil, the German
Art Nouveau style. Avoiding the fussy excess
of some Art Nouveau decoration, the coat
stand favours a more restrained approach,
anticipating the crisper rectilinear ornament
of Art Deco and the pared-down simplicity of
the Modern movement. The refinement,
simplicity and clean lines of Blümel's brass
and nickel plated coat stand, which stands
at 180 cm (71 in) high and 48.5 cm (19 in)
wide, lend themselves to the philosophy of
mass production. Its 'contemporary' design
credentials have ensured its continued
popularity and it remains a key ClassiCon
production piece today. Something of a *fin-
de-siècle* renaissance man, Blümel studied
both architecture and painting before in 1907
becoming head of the design department
at the Vereinigte Werkstätte für Kunst im
Handwerk (Unified Workshops for Art in
Handicraft), founded in 1898 in Munich.
Prominent in the Jugendstil movement,
the Workshops promoted the exploration
of simple organic forms and a craft-based
approach to design as well as pioneering the
exploitation of the commercial potential of
their designs, even building their own factory
to make some of the products in their design
portfolio. Students were encouraged to
present and offer their products to the public
via permanent or temporary exhibitions,
often earning a percentage of the proceeds.
Blümel's relationship with craft, which is
explored at its most stylized, rationalized
form in the Nymphenburg Coat Stand, took
on a more literal aspect for the designer,
when after World War I he helped establish
the Heimatmuseum branch of the
Museumsverein Werdenfels, a museum
dedicated to the celebration and promotion
of indigenous German arts and handicrafts
designs.

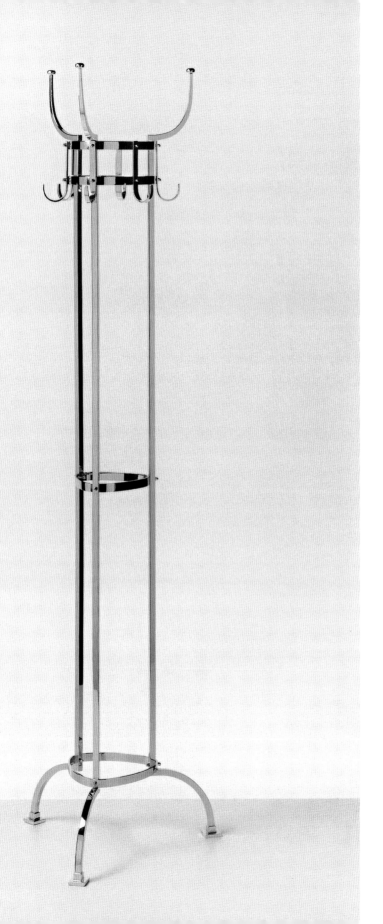

Toblerone is one of the earliest brands that exists almost unchanged from its origins in the mid-nineteenth century. Its name and distinctive pyramid shape are recognizable the world over as icons of Swiss chocolate-making. Jean Tobler opened his first chocolate shop, the Confiserie Spéciale, in Bern, Switzerland, in 1867. By 1899 Tobler's chocolate was in such demand that he was able to open a chocolate factory. But it was not until Tobler's son Theodor and his cousin Emil Baumann came up with the recipe for milk chocolate with honey almond nougat in 1908 that Toblerone was born. The name was coined as a play on the name Tobler, and the Italian word for the nougat, *torrone*. Theodor patented the manufacturing process in 1906, and registered the brand in 1909 along with its distinctive pyramid shape and packaging. Toblerone was then the first chocolate to be patented. The form of the chocolate has changed little since then. The pyramid shape of the segments of chocolate are said to resemble the distinctive triangular profile of the Matterhorn mountain in the Swiss Alps. The pyramids of chocolate are each stamped at their base with a letter spelling out the name Toblerone. Many different versions of Toblerone are now available. In 1969 a dark chocolate version was released, followed by white chocolate Toblerone in 1973 and the first filled Toblerone in 1996. The packaging has gone through several changes, with the inclusion of an eagle and heraldic symbol being replaced by the contemporary version that depicts the Matterhorn and the distinctive Toblerone font. The original Toblerone factory in Bern has now been turned into part of Bern's university, but its new factory is still in the city, and still produces every Toblerone bar for distribution throughout the world.

Toblerone ® (1908)
Theodor Tobler (1876–1941)
Emil Baumann (1883–1966)
Berner Chocoladefabrik Tobler & Co
1908 to present

Advertising poster, 1925

Advertising poster, 1926

The history of aviation might have been very different but for the unstoppable determination of Louis Blériot to fly. In the face of a host of biplane designs, Blériot's X1 was a monoplane, meaning it had one wing, and one that became the very symbol of aviation for a generation. After a gaining a degree from the École Centrale in Paris, Louis Blériot began his quest to fly. But his first effort was not promising. In 1900 he built what he called an 'ornithopter', which was supposed to

fly by flapping its wings. It never got off the ground. Nor did Blériot's next ten planes, built over the course of eight years. A lesser man might have given up, but Blériot persisted – spurred on by the emerging fame of the Wright brothers' flight across the Atlantic. In October 1908 the *Daily Mail* in London offered a prize of £1,000, a very hand-some sum for those times, to the first aviator to cross the English Channel. It was just the encouragement Blériot needed. Blériot enlisted

his friend and fellow aviation enthusiast, Raymond Saulnier, who himself would go on to make a major impact on early aviation. Recognizing that his time aloft would be limited by the poor reliability of the engines available to him, Blériot, with Saulnier's help, built a monoplane, hoping that its light weight and low drag, and its relative simplicity, would be the keys to crossing *La Manche* in the shortest possible time. Remarkably, and countering every disappointment he had felt in the previous years,

BLÉRIOT MONOPLANE

Blériot's X1 Monoplane actually flew, on a wintry day in 1909, at Issy-les-Moulineaux, France. Over the next six months, Blériot and Saulnier improved the plane's handling and reliability, the latter achieved by using a lighter 25 hp Anzani engine. On 25 July 1909, and in rainy, blustery conditions that kept his Anzani engine cool, Blériot crossed the Channel from La Baraques in France, to Dover in England, making the journey in just over 37 minutes. It was a monumental achievement, and one that ignited the public imagination. The crossing brought Blériot wide renown to go along with the £1,000 prize. At a time when the whole world seemed to be taking to the air, it was Blériot's achievement as a pilot and an aeronautical pioneer that enshrined his X1 in popular culture as the most famous design of its day.

092

Blériot X1 Monoplane (1909)
Louis Blériot (1872–1936)
Blériot Aéronautique 1909 to 1914

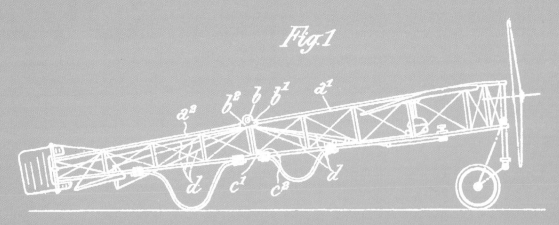

Fig.1

Fig.2

Fig.3

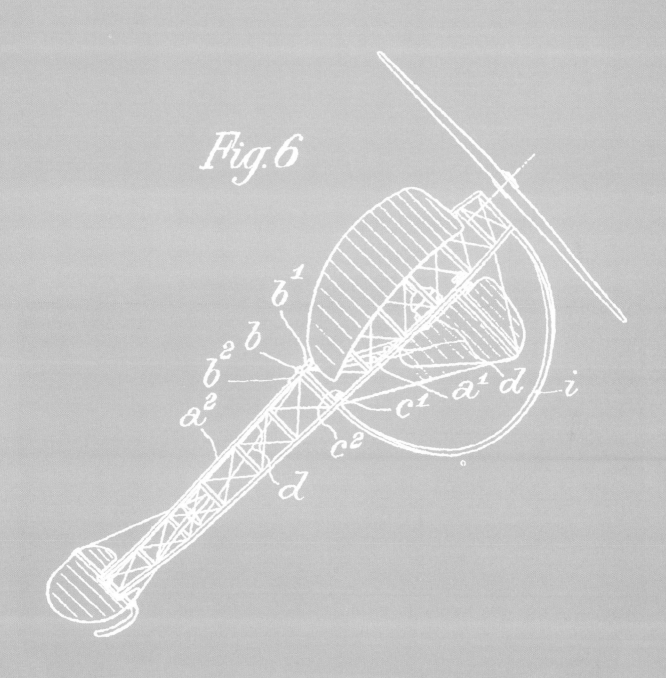

Fig.6

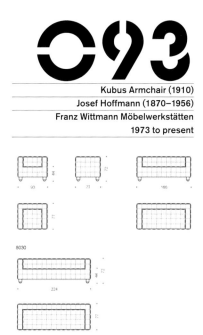

Looking at the Kubus Armchair, one could be forgiven for assuming it was produced later than 1910, the year it was exhibited in Buenos Aires. Its similarities to Le Corbusier's LC2 Grand Confort Armchair of 1928 are striking. Its abstract purity, functional clarity and geometric use of ornamentation would suggest a place within the Modernist movement. In actuality, it was designed within the alternative reform ideals of the Arts and Crafts movement of the late nineteenth century. Its designer Josef Hoffmann played an important part in shaping Viennese Modernism. He co-founded the Wiener Werkstätte in 1903 out of a desire to save the decorative arts from their aesthetic devaluation through mass production. Hoffmann had trained as an architect under the influential figure Otto Wagner at the University of Vienna. Here he came into contact with the idea of the 'complete work of art', whereby the architect/designer would be involved in all aspects of design. 'I believe that a house has to be made from one piece and that its exterior should reveal its interior.' Both his architecture and furniture were inspired by time spent in Italy after graduating, particularly the cubic, white-washed country houses with windows carved irregularly out of the walls. The chair is composed of polyurethane foam over a wooden frame and is upholstered in black leather. Its square pads and its austere, straight form are a true representation of the Hoffmann style, for whom the plain cube was the preferred form. The work of the Wiener Werkstätte, however, embodied a fundamental conflict. Its primary aim of bringing good design into every part of people's lives was at odds with its commitment to the high-quality production of unique, handcrafted designs and emphasis on artistic experimentation. The projects were necessarily costly and exclusive, but they were the precursors of Modernism. In 1969 the Josef Hoffmann Foundation granted the manufacturer Franz Wittmann Möbelwerkstätten sole rights to recreate the Kubus Chair.

J. C. HAWKINS.
PAPER FASTENER.
APPLICATION FILED NOV. 3, 1911.

1,130,594.

Patented Mar. 2, 1915.
2 SHEETS—SHEET 2.

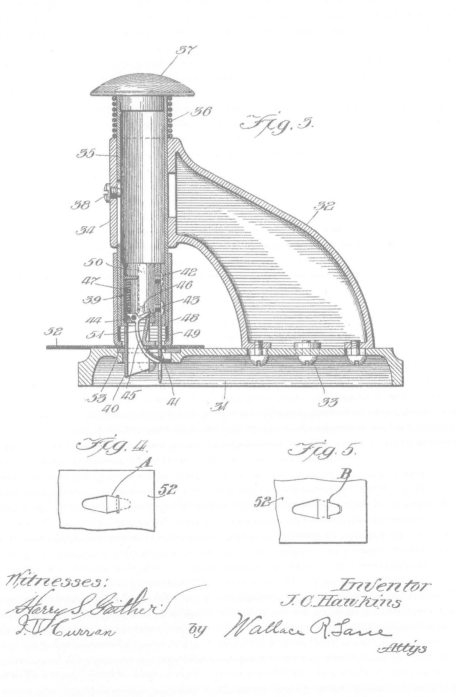

Fig. 3.

Fig. 4.

Fig. 5.

Witnesses:
Harry S. Gaither
J. V. Curran

Inventor
J. C. Hawkins
by Wallace R. Lane
Attys

The Clipless Stand Paper

Fastener looks like a highly polished piston, a relic from the steam age or a spare part belonging to a brass band. In fact, it was the first staple-less paper fastener, which was available both as plier-shaped 'hand' model from 1909 and as 'stand' (desk-based) version from 1910. Advertised as products that would 'make money by saving money', these devices use the paper itself as a fastening element (thus sparing their owners the expense of having to go out and buy metal staples). The Clipless works by punching and then folding a triangular section of the paper (as the tool is pressed down), before drawing this section back through a slit, 0.6 cm (0.25 in) wide, in the paper (as the fastener is released) and in effect almost 'stitching' it shut. Clipless owner, J C Hawkins, believed in an aggressive marketing strategy and highly trained sales team. He wrote 'Salesmanship, or How to make Money' to motivate his staff and sent his fasteners out for trial (upon request) with a no-obligation to purchase policy. The products were expensive for the time as they were retailed for $5, the equivalent of $95 today. Clipless's chief competitor was the La Crosse Wisconsin-based Bump Paper Fastening Company founded in 1910. Although Clipless produced the first device to enter that market, Bump filed a patent for its fastener seven months before its competitor. Curiously, Bump's patent was granted after Clipless's and named Clipless's founder as the assignee for half of the patent. The precise reasons for this are unknown. Clipless's aggressive marketing tactic and a drastic reduction in prices (by 1911 the price had dropped to $3.50) were not enough to compete with the bargain offered by Bump ($2.50). Eventually in the early 1930s the Clipless Paper Fastener Company was acquired by its rival. Bump's fasteners remained in production until 1950, always (somewhat bizarrely) with the words 'patent pending' on its base.

Workers seated at desks in the
office of Charles W Mackie Jr,
New Orleans, 1917

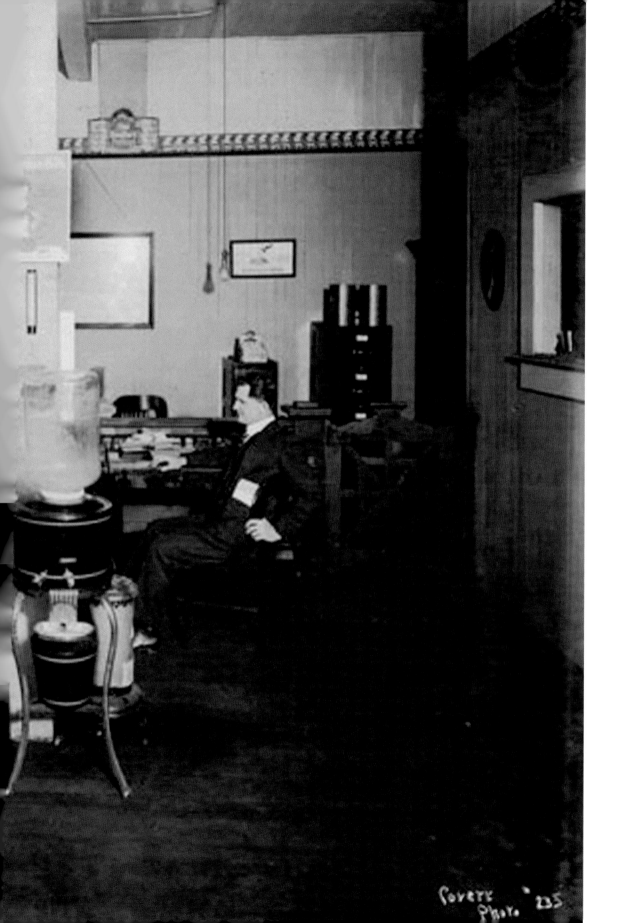

In 1912, two years after French engineer and chemist Georges Claude presented his improved neon lamp at the 1910 Paris Exposition, the first neon sign was sold to a barber in Paris. The idea soon crossed the Atlantic and the stage was set for neon to become a glittering, gaudy symbol of Western consumerist culture. The idea itself is simple: when a high voltage is passed through a bent glass tube containing neon, or another suitable inert gas, at low pressure, light is then produced. Neon naturally emits a red glow but the use of other gases, coloured tubes and phosphor coatings ensure that a spectrum of different coloured lights can be created. In the 1950s and 1960s, neon's popularity grew rapidly in a commercially expansive United States. The enthusiastic employment of neon for shop and motel signs and billboards nationwide saw neon simultaneously becoming an important part of America's youthful aesthetic heritage and a symbol of transitory postmodern experience. This dual association is epitomized in the giddy neon wonderland of the Las Vegas strip, a location much used in American literature and film as a symbol of both American wealth and optimism and vacuous greed and individual disappointment. Neon's more practical cousin, the fluorescent lamp, works on very similar principles. Straight, thicker tubes filled with low-pressure mercury vapour and argon gas produce ultraviolet light when electrically charged. A coating of phosphor inside the tube, filters out harmful UV rays leaving a practical light source. This uniform strip lighting is used all over the world in large public spaces such as hospitals, schools, and offices, making up for its stark unflattering quality with a long life expectancy, low maintenance and subsequent cost-effectiveness. Fluorescent light has also found its way into visual culture, most famously in the work of Minimalist artist Dan Flavin. The incandescent allure and sense of the sublime imparted by his light sculptures seem in direct conflict with their construction from mundane industrial light units. Flavin exploited this tension to question both the traditional concept and physical limits of the flat picture plane and to consider the individual's relationship to these 'icons' of technology.

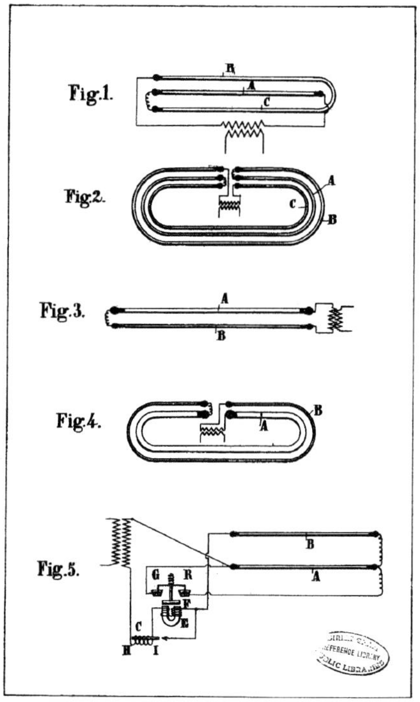

Neon Gas Light (1910)
Georges Claude (1870–1960)
Various 1912 to present

Fig.1.

Fig.2.

Fig.3.

Fig.4.

Fig.5.

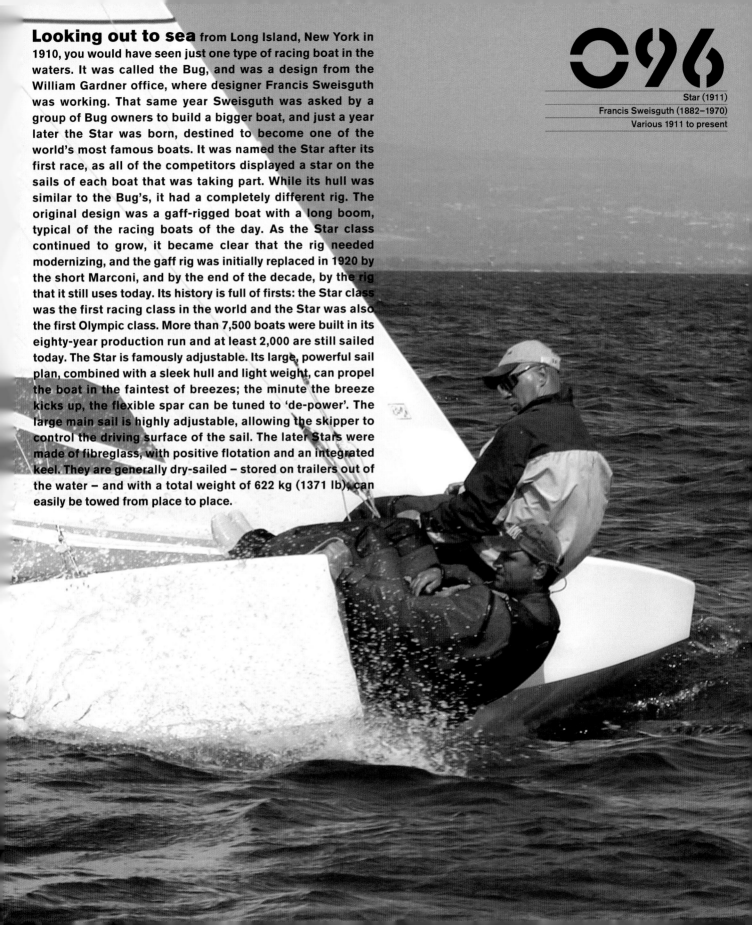

Looking out to sea from Long Island, New York in 1910, you would have seen just one type of racing boat in the waters. It was called the Bug, and was a design from the William Gardner office, where designer Francis Sweisguth was working. That same year Sweisguth was asked by a group of Bug owners to build a bigger boat, and just a year later the Star was born, destined to become one of the world's most famous boats. It was named the Star after its first race, as all of the competitors displayed a star on the sails of each boat that was taking part. While its hull was similar to the Bug's, it had a completely different rig. The original design was a gaff-rigged boat with a long boom, typical of the racing boats of the day. As the Star class continued to grow, it became clear that the rig needed modernizing, and the gaff rig was initially replaced in 1920 by the short Marconi, and by the end of the decade, by the rig that it still uses today. Its history is full of firsts: the Star class was the first racing class in the world and the Star was also the first Olympic class. More than 7,500 boats were built in its eighty-year production run and at least 2,000 are still sailed today. The Star is famously adjustable. Its large, powerful sail plan, combined with a sleek hull and light weight, can propel the boat in the faintest of breezes; the minute the breeze kicks up, the flexible spar can be tuned to 'de-power'. The large main sail is highly adjustable, allowing the skipper to control the driving surface of the sail. The later Stars were made of fibreglass, with positive flotation and an integrated keel. They are generally dry-sailed – stored on trailers out of the water – and with a total weight of 622 kg (1371 lb), can easily be towed from place to place.

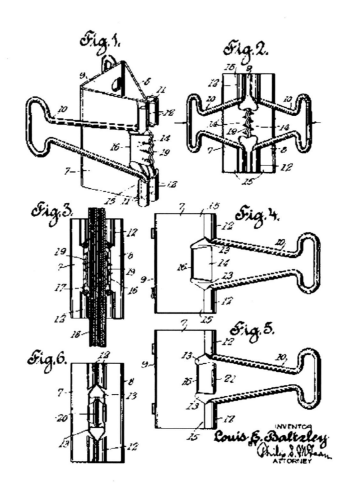

Fig. 1.
Fig. 2.
Fig. 3.
Fig. 4.
Fig. 5.
Fig. 6.

INVENTOR

Louis E. Baltzley

BY

Philip S. McLean
ATTORNEY

Louis E Baltzley

The Binder Clip, invented by Louis E Baltzley in 1911, is a simple but inspired design for holding loose paper together. It takes over from its more diminutive counterparts, the paperclip and staple, which can hold only moderate amounts of paper by comparison. Baltzley was born in Washington DC in 1884 into an already remarkable family: his father Edwin Baltzley held eight US patents for different devices; his uncle Henry Hawson Baltzley two; and his grandfather Elias Howe invented the first practical sewing machine. The inspiration for this elegent fastener came from Baltzley's father Edwin, who was also a prolific writer. He needed a way of keeping the pages of his manuscripts in order without resorting to the traditional method of the time, which involved punching holes along the pages and sewing them together with needle and thread. This could keep the pages securely bound, but meant that inserting or removing pages involved a laborious rebind each time: hardly practical for a writer at work. Louis came up with the perfect solution in the Binder Clip. The clip can stand upright on the flat of its hollow, triangular-shaped black base, which is made of a sturdy but flexible metal. Attached to it are two moveable metal handles that slot like hinges into the top. These can flex back flat, becoming strong levers to prize open the base and firmly clamp the paper. The handles can then be folded back to lie flush along the sides of the manuscript for easy stacking and storage or can be pushed back again for reading purposes. It is this combination of the base's hollow volume and the adjustable levering handles that give access to it that are the key to the Binder Clip's capacity and therefore its versatility. Baltzley began manufacturing the clip at his own company LEB Manufacturing, and later licensed the design out to other companies. He also revised and modified his 1911 design a further five times between 1915 and 1932. By 1934 Baltzey held over twenty patents including a Machine for Snelling Fishhooks (1931) and a Ping-Pong Racket (1934). Baltzley could not have predicted the lasting ubiquity of his Binder Clip in today's workplace. However, the clip's status is confirmed by its practical and ingenious simplicity, which makes it a stationery standard in modern offices, studios and classrooms around the world.

The Chester Armchair and Sofa looks back to the classical armchairs of Edwardian England's clubs and country houses for its inspiration. However, its design strips away all unnecessary materials and decoration to focus exclusively on the fabric, structure and construction of the chair, allowing simplicity of form and complexity of craftsmanship to shape the design of the object. So the leather covering is folded into a series of pleats, or plissés, on the bulbous arms to create the range's trademark look, the backrest and arms are hand-quilted to create the distinctive Chesterfield diamond-pattern motif and leather-covered tacks are the only 'decoration'. And the upholstery and construction are equally important. A suspension system of steel springs, which are tied by hand on jute belts, helps create the structure and shaping for the hand-moulded horsehair padding, ensuring the correct amount of weight absorption and very small movement of the seat – resulting in a sofa whose shape and contours are perfectly attuned to the human body. It is such attention to detail that makes the Chester such an enduring design; every element of it – from its solid, seasoned beechwood frame to its goose-feather-filled seat cushions and hand-selected hides cut with a shoe maker's knife – is lovingly crafted, which may go some way to explaining why the model has consistently remained Poltrona Frau's best-known model, although it is also made by a number of manufacturers.

Chester Armchair and Sofa (1912)
Designer Unknown
Poltrona Frau 1912 to 1960, 1962 to present
Various 1912 to present

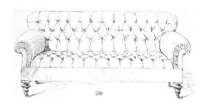

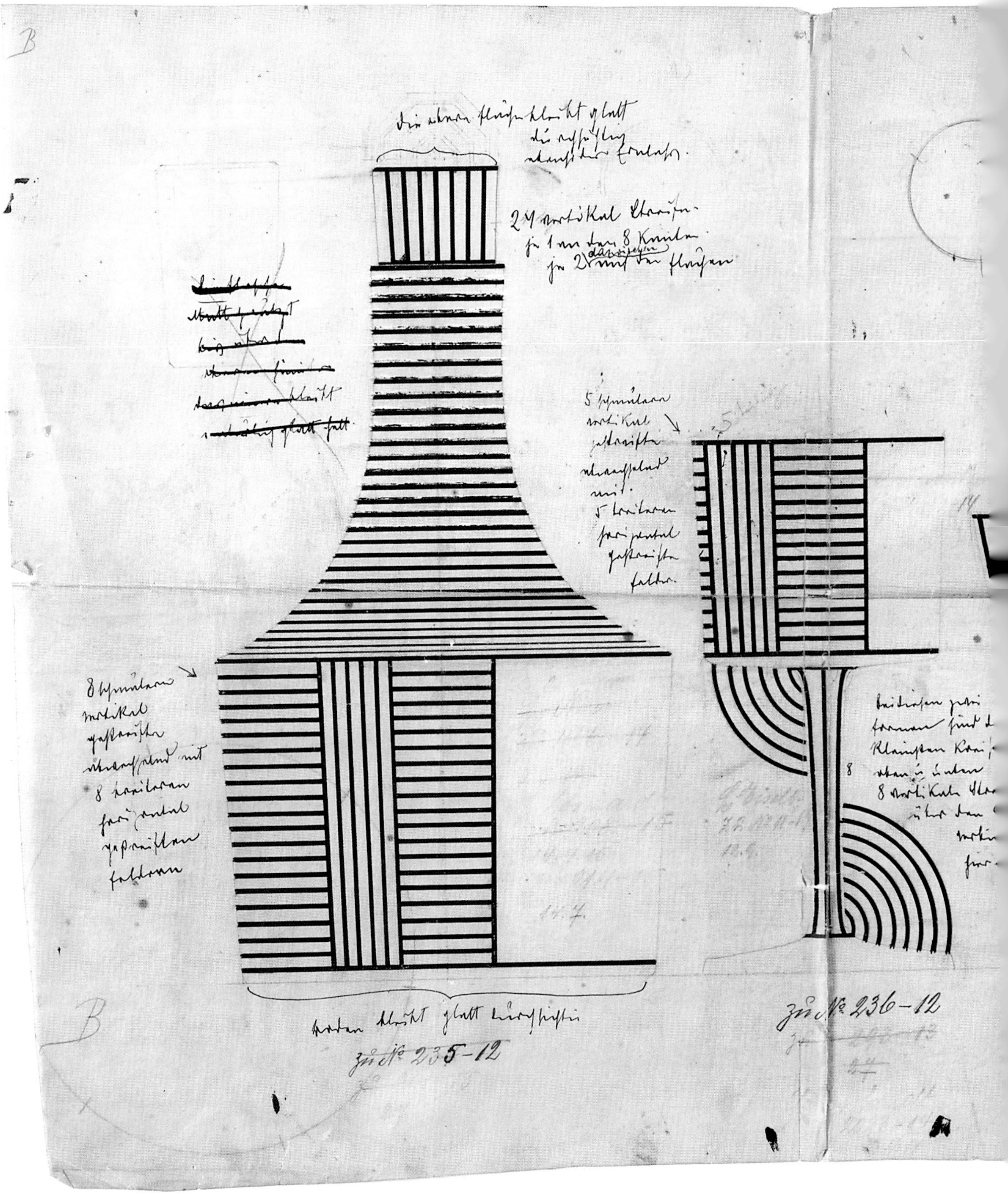
zu № 235-12
zu № 236-12

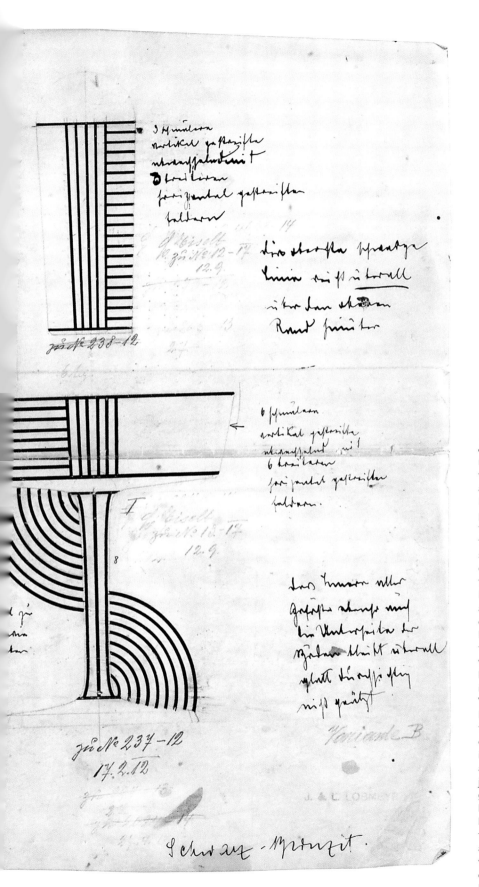

Josef Hoffmann enjoyed a lengthy relationship with the Viennese glassmaker J & L Lobmeyr, which was deepened by a friendship between the architect and designer and the then head of the business, Stefan Rath. The Series 'B' glassware was an early product of this partnership, which began in 1910. Lobmeyr was one of the most enthusiastic supporters of Hoffmann's strict forms, and still makes Series 'B' today. In its modernity, simplicity of form and deployment of black and white, the design carries the hallmarks both of Hoffmann's work and the output of the Wiener Werkstätte, which Hoffmann and Koloman Moser had founded in 1903 as a co-operative of applied arts. In particular, they strove both to promote craftsmanship in everyday objects and reject gratuitous, historically based decoration, which they felt obscured function. By the time of the Series 'B' glassware, Hoffmann's vision of the house and its contents as a single work of art had reached its zenith in the Palais Stoclet of 1911, built in Brussels for the banker and art lover Adolphe Stoclet. Wiener Werkstätte never had its own glass workshop. Instead, its designs were taken up by external manufacturers. The Series 'B', in common with several other designs from the Hoffmann-Lobmeyr partnership, is made from blown crystal, decorated with black bronzite and frosted. The bronzite technique had been developed just two years earlier in Bohemia, the traditional home of glassmaking. In this process the glass was coated with a layer of bronzite, on to which the decorative design would be painted with varnish. Any unvarnished bronzite was then removed with acid, leaving a decorative pattern with a metallic sheen. Lobmeyr sustained a lofty reputation, with its products included as early as the 1920s in collections such as The Museum of Modern Art, in New York and London's Victoria and Albert Museum.

A peculiarly British phenomenon, Marmite Yeast Extract is a by-product of the brewing industry transformed into a savoury spread commonly enjoyed on buttered toast. The yeast used to ferment sugars into alcohol provides the basis for the paste that was invented by a German chemist named Liebig. However, it was in Burton-on-Trent in England, an area popular for beer production due to the properties of the water, that the product first became commercially available, a patent being acquired for it in 1902. Broadly similar in taste to Bovril, a beef extract intended to be made into a hot drink, the vegetarian Marmite is thought to have been named after either a French soup or the pot in which it is cooked, an image of which appears on the product's label. The bright red banner of the label, with its white lettering and yellow surround, has become so iconic that the company has rolled out versions with different wording ('My Mate') to coincide with its advertising. Both the label and the jar have undergone only subtle changes since the product was introduced. The jar superseded the original earthenware pots around 1912, and appears to have borrowed heavily from the Bovril jar of the time, having the same brown glass, dumpy form and flattened oval areas for labels. The Marmite Jar, however, had a shorter neck, perhaps alluding to the 'marmite' pot of its origin. Relief lettering disappeared and inevitably the once-metal lid was replaced by plastic, although not without dissent from the product's fanatical consumers. Despite this, like the product itself, the essential ingredients remain the same: a satisfyingly heavy, well-proportioned and rounded jar that is pleasant to hold, a bright yellow lid and a colourful label that demands attention on the supermarket shelf.

Plaubel Makina

PLAUBEL Feinmechanik und Optik · Frankfurt am Main

Plaubel & Company of Frankfurt, Germany, was founded in 1902 by Hugo Schrader, the son-in-law of the renowned camera designer Dr Rudolf Krügener. The Makina range of cameras was introduced in 1912 and was a long-lived design that continued in an updated form until 1958, when production of the Makina IIIR (produced during 1953–58) ceased. The firm was taken over by the Japanese Doi group headed by Kimio Doi in 1975, who produced a series of specialized wide-angle cameras under the Makina name until 1986. These were produced in Japan, but had little continuity with the original range. The original Makina camera model was made from 1912 until around 1928 and took 4.5 × 6 cm (1.8 × 2.4 in) plates. A stereoscopic model was made taking 4.5 × 10.7 cm (1.8 × 4.2 in) plates. The camera was a precision-made lazy-tongs collapsing camera, with the struts placed above and below the bellows. The pivoting struts connected the front lens board to the back section in a rigid way, and was a design that had been tried with varying degrees of success since the 1880s. Importantly, Schrader's design was rigid and kept the front section exactly parallel to the back, which was essential for sharp photographs. The design was popular and a larger model for 6.5 × 9 cm (2.6 × 3.5 in) negatives was introduced in 1922 to the range of cameras which had interchangeable lenses, taking photographs on either glass plates, cut film or rollfilm. The Makina II of 1933 added a coupled rangefinder for precise focusing. With interest in small collapsible cameras of the Makina type limited after 1946 and unable to compete with large-volume camera manufacturers in Germany and, increasingly, from the Far East, Plaubel concentrated on producing good-quality professional studio cameras of different designs before being taken over in 1975.

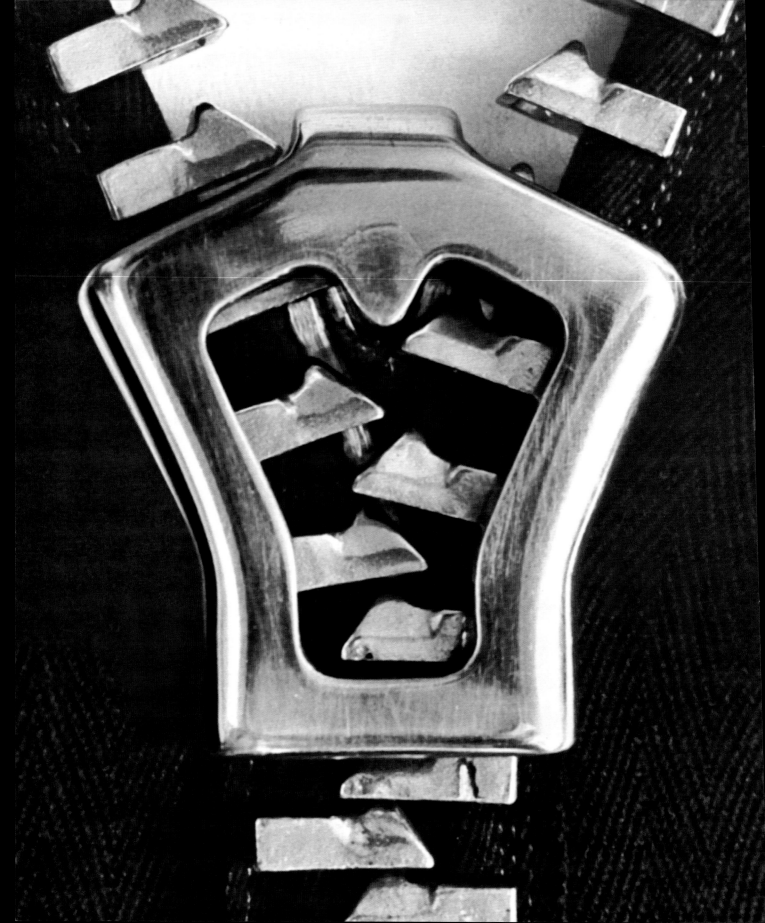

1O2

Zip Fastener (1913)
Gideon Sundback (1880–1954)
Hookless Fastener (Talon) 1913 to present
Various 1930s to present

The zipper began life as Whitcomb Judson's 'clasp locker', a fastener intended for shoes and patented in 1893. Its parallel rows of vicious-looking metal hooks closed by a metal slider more closely resembled a torture device than the smooth, fine zips of today, and did not meet with wide success. It was, however, recognizably the 'zip' concept. The credit for perfecting the zip must be given to Swedish immigrant Gideon Sundback, who was employed by the Universal Fastener Company of Chicago. Over the course of five years Sundback miniaturized and refined Judson's design, increasing the number of 'teeth' per inch to ten, and developed a method for mass-manufacturing the result. He called the result the 'hookless fastener', a slightly misleading name as the teeth on the design were, and are today, effectively tiny hooks, a little like train carriage hitchings. The hookless fastener's move from novelty to widespread acceptance and use came in 1923, when the BF Goodrich Company decided to use it for its range of galoshes. As the new range was being developed, one of Goodrich's marketing people suggested the name 'zipper' based on how quickly it closed and the sound it made. From there, the zipper spread into clothing in the 1930s via childrenswear and men's trousers, and then on to its current global omnipresence. But the zip has gone beyond being a simple fastener; it has made a deep impression on fashion and social consciousness itself. Certain iconic fashions such as biker chic and the 1970s punk designs of Malcolm McLaren and Vivienne Westwood are almost impossible to imagine without numerous, often purposeless, zips. With some help from these trends, the very feeling and look of a zip opening or closing has been invested with an image of sensuality: think of the moment in many romantic films where the zip at the back of a dress slides down.

In 1860 most people still wrote using quills; by 1872 the Joseph Dixon Crucible Company was producing 86,000 pencils a day, and by 1892 Dixon Crucible had manufactured more than 30 million pencils. Dixon did not invent the first pencil or design its classic characteristics, the yellow-painted wooden casing with the cast-graphite lead. Pencil history points to Nicolas-Jacques Conté (1755–1805) as the inventor of the modern lead pencil. Prior to Conté, pencils had almost all been made from lumps of pure graphite, mined from the Borrowdale mine in England and sawn into strips that were then encased in wood. In 1794 there was a call to invent a substitute for the now expensive and difficult-to-come-by pure English graphite. The Conté process was invented as a way to make pencil leads from powdered graphite and is still, essentially, used today. The origin of the yellow-painted coating is attributed to the fact that the best graphite in the world comes from the East, or, to be precise, from the Alibert mine near the Chinese border in Siberia. This association was used by companies such as Koh-I-Noor and, although their pencils contained no Siberian graphite, they nevertheless started a trend in the US that has persisted to this day. The reason Dixon is associated with the dry, clean, portable writing instrument is for the superior mass-production and quality he developed in reaction to market demand during and after the American Civil War. Joseph Dixon (1799–1869) started off as a printer and photographer, interested in new technologies and innovation. It was while developing his own typeset-casting letters that he came upon graphite, and also discovered its merits as a stove polish. His biggest contribution was to the US steel industry, primarily through the graphite industry and the development of crucibles. Dixon produced his first pencils in 1829; by the 1890s he was a leading producer. The ingenious design of his tooling, such as a wood-planing machine for shaping pencils that produced 132 pencils a minute, the advanced technology of his crucible plants and the integration of sought-after all contributed to the reduction by 50 per cent in the cost of pencils during the 1890s. The sheer mass-production and sustained high quality of Dixon's pencils have ensured their status as timeless objects. The name 'Ticonderoga' was not given until 1913, and was originally made with a brass ferrule, or a metal ring used as a reinforcement to prevent splitting, and with two yellow bands. During World War II, the metal ferrule was replaced by a green plastic one, due to the shortage of metal. However the yellow bands remained, establishing the trademark for the pencil and giving us the archetypal yellow pencil we recognize today.

Advertisements, 1910

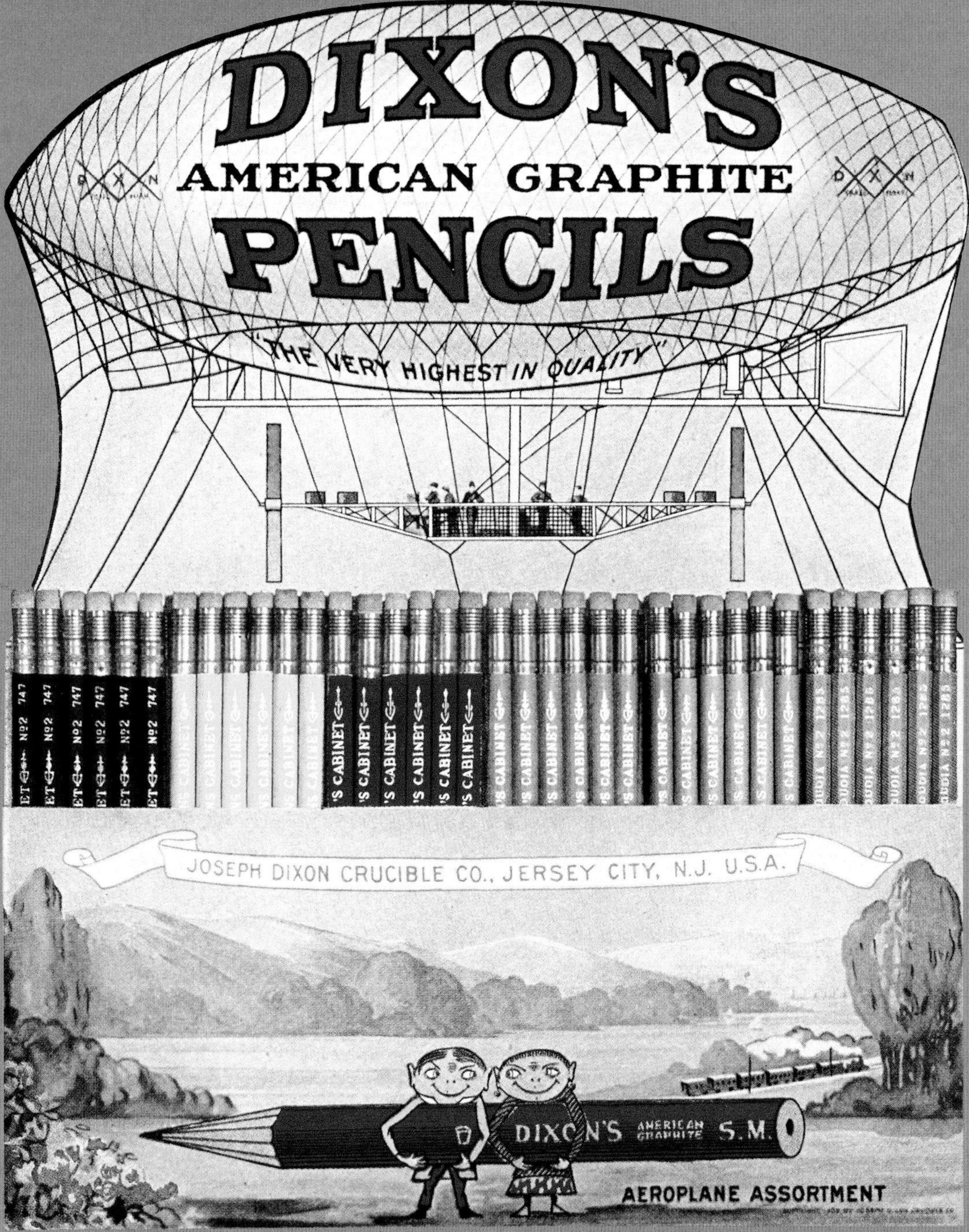
DIXON'S
AMERICAN GRAPHITE
PENCILS
"THE VERY HIGHEST IN QUALITY"
JOSEPH DIXON CRUCIBLE CO., JERSEY CITY, N.J. U.S.A.
DIXON'S AMERICAN GRAPHITE S.M.
AEROPLANE ASSORTMENT

Fig. 3.

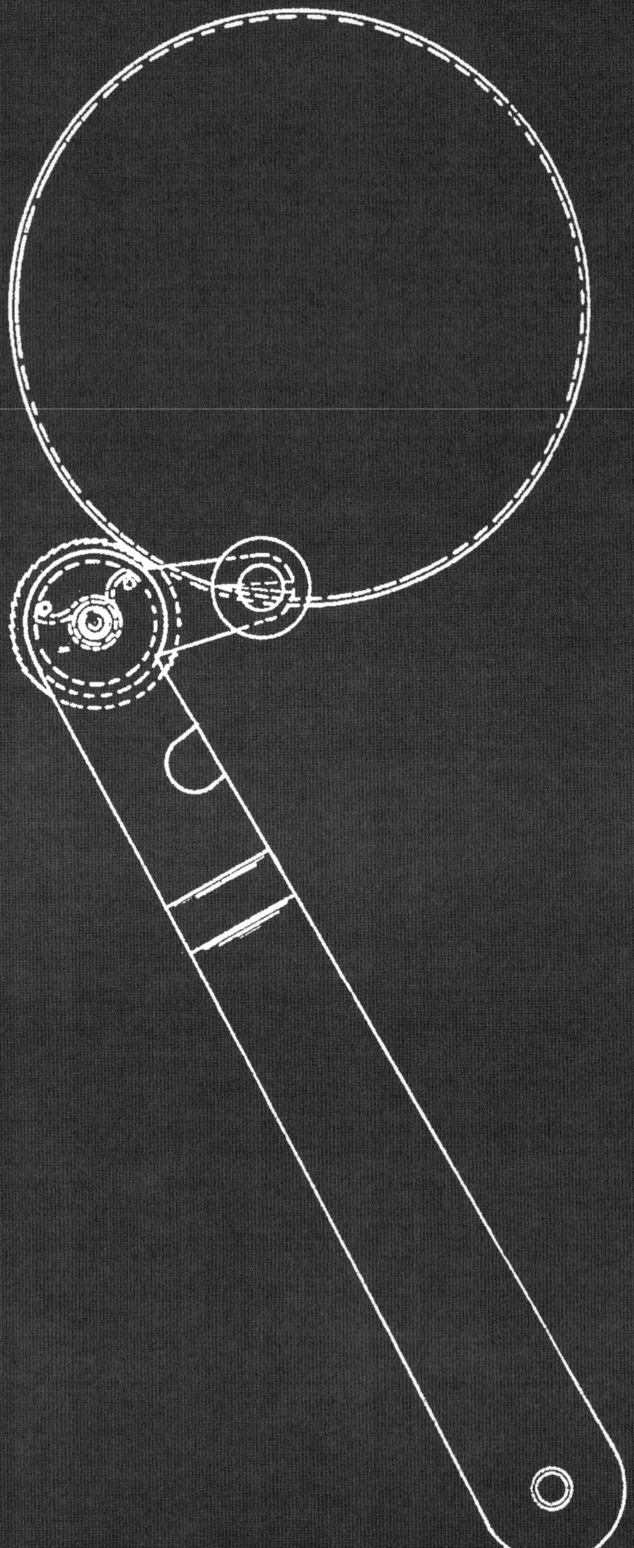

Fig. 1.

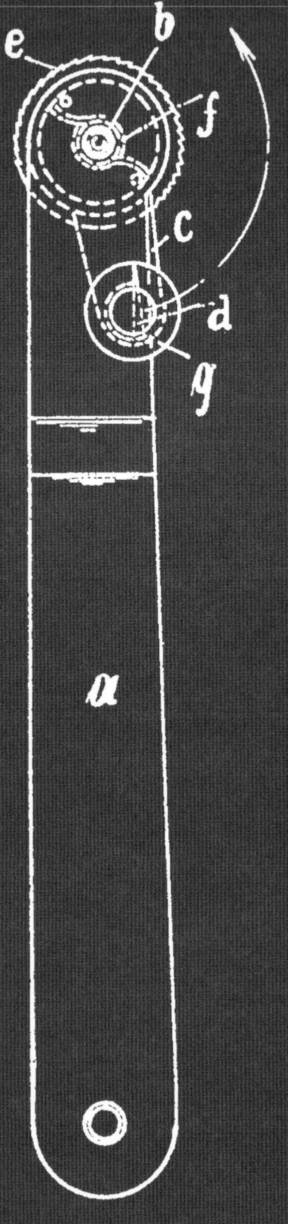

Fig. 2.

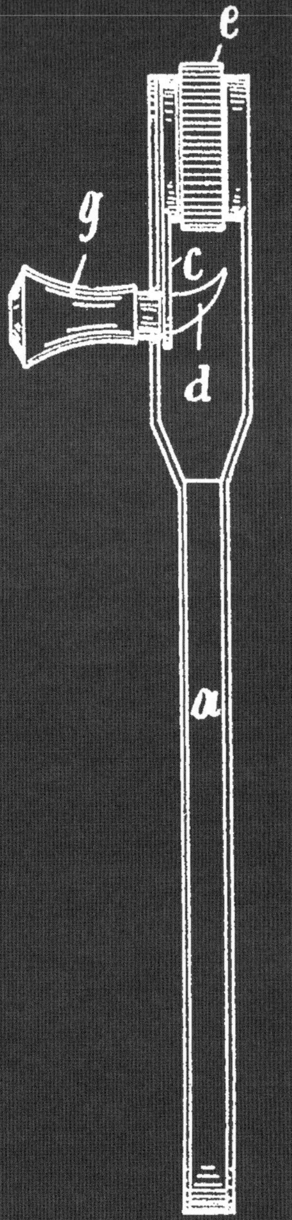

e b
f
c
d
g

a

e

g

c

d

a

e

SIEGER®

The Sieger Can Opener is a lesson in mechanical economy and an object with a functionalist appeal that has endured throughout its history. The Sieger, which translates as 'victor' in German, was first invented in 1913 (after which a number of patents were given), and has changed little since its first incarnation. It became highly popular after World War I, before which tins were opened with a hook-like stick. The Sieger transformed this task and became instantly popular. Its ratchet, a shiny nickel-plate surface, now has a riveted plastic layer in the middle, which operates the opener. Tempered steel is used for the cutter blade, the transport wheels or cogs, and the cap lifter, making an impenetrable surface. The device is a compact 15 cm (6 in) long, 5 cm (2 in) wide, with the handle a slim 2.2 cm (0.8 in), and weighs just 86 g (3 oz). The August Reutershan Company, founded in 1864 in Solingen, has had the same location for its production, with building additions throughout the years, since 1906. The company originally produced pocket knives, with corkscrews as accessories, but stopped producing corkscrews until 1975. The Can Opener instead became the driving force behind the company, and various styles were added to the original design – the Eminent in 1949, the Gigant in 1952, the Zangen-Sieger in 1961, and the wall-mounted version, the Der große Sieger in 1964. Despite these variations, the original remains an international best-seller to this day. The company even changed its name from August Reutershan to Sieger, in order to emphasize the connection between the famous brand and its manufacturer.

The story of the Dinghy begins

in 1913, when George Cockshott won a boat-designing competition. The idea behind the competition was to produce a tender for big yachts that yacht-owners could race in fashionable bays across the world. The only rule for the competing boat builders was to follow the brief with extreme precision. The great surprise was that Cockshott, the winning designer, was neither boat designer nor architect; he was just a passionate sailor. Because Cockshott's boat was fast, easy to sail and cheap, it was immediately successful, especially in Britain and Southern Europe. In 1919 the Dinghy was chosen by the International Yacht Race Union as the first International Class, and in 1920 and 1928, it achieved Olympic recognition in the *en solitaire* class. From the 1930s the Dinghy appeared on seas around the world, always with its wood thoroughly polished and a well-dressed owner at the helm. The Dinghy was 'clinker-built', a technique whereby the hull is constructed so that each wooden plank overlaps the one below. A transom stern, low freeboard and a fractionated mast were also employed to ensure maximum stability and strength in this comparatively small vessel. The Dinghy is one of the first racing boats and now is probably the only one with a fractionated mast. Two little benches are used to stiffen the hull, and when it is racing, two special stools are needed to make the boat more rigid. Most of today's dinghies are made in fibreglass, with only a few boat builders following traditional methods. There are separate racing classes for the classic and the modern, and surprisingly little difference in performance. They are widely used in Southern Europe, and particularly Italy and Turkey, with the most important dinghy race taking place annually in Portofino, organized by the Italian Yacht Club.

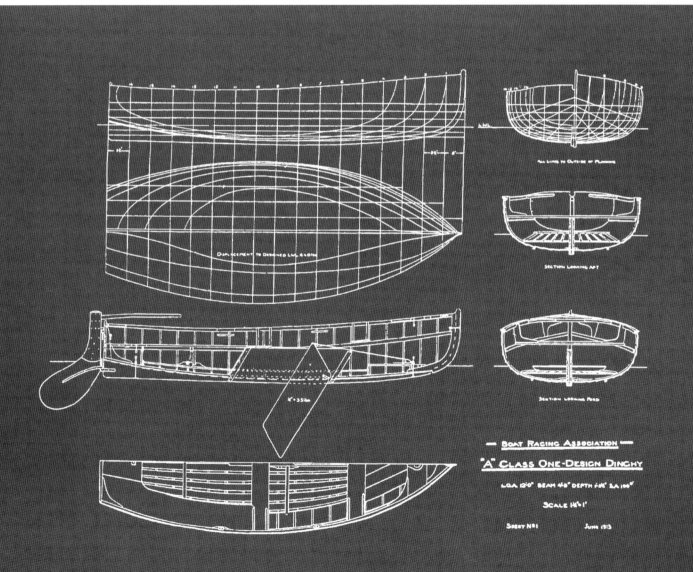

The humble pint glass, with its familiar bulge, has become a potent symbol of British pub culture, a friendly reminder of good times and a weapon for hooligans. Comfortably chubby yet elegant, the Nonic's lack of affectation in its design ensures its timelessness. Available in a number of capacities, the UK standard being 20 fl oz (to hold a 16 fl oz pint of beer with room for the head), Nonic glasses are ideally adorned with the government stamp and a fill level line. Seen as too ordinary for many modern bars, the Nonic glass is beginning to lose out to more flamboyant designs specific to particular brands of beer. However, in its time the Nonic also blazed a trail. Nonic Safe Edge Glassware, named because it did not nick or chip, was a range of non-stacking glasses first produced by Albert Pick & Company of Chicago in 1914. The distinctive bulge made the glasses less prone to chipping when two or more were nested together, allowing the bulges to clash rather than the fragile rims. The next innovation was heralded by the introduction of factory-blown glass using metal moulds, which superseded pressing and enabled the mass production of glass vessels with thinner wall sections. Belgian Jean Viatour patented a number of designs for stacking glasses in 1938 that incorporated the Nonic bulge. The designs solved the common problem of tapered stacking glasses wedging inside one another, often cracking them. The bulge spaced the glasses so only the rim was in contact with the glass stacked into it. In 1948 British manufacturer Ravenhead Glass began production of the Nonic we know today, offering a modern alternative to the heavy, dimpled pint mugs with handles. The company has since ceased trading but the Nonic continues to be produced by manufacturers in the UK and abroad.

106

Nonic Pint Glass (1914)
Albert Pick & Company Design Team
Albert Pick & Company 1914 to 1920s
Ravenhead Glass 1948 to 2001
Various 1989 to present

The Western Electric 20 series had been in production for over a decade by the time the improved No.20 AL Desk Stand was introduced in 1914. It was developed by the joint engineering department of Bell Telephone and the Western Electric Company, later to become Bell Telephone Laboratories. The 20 AL was very similar in form to its predecessors, with the main differences being its fabricated, rather than cast receiver cradle, and the wires for the transmitter, which were now routed through the base and shaft of the device. The overall effect was more elegant and less machine-like than previous models, although it would still have been installed with a separate oak 'ringer-box', or 'subset', which housed the generator, induction coils, batteries and bells. This iconic 'candlestick' configuration was a far cry from the first generation of telephones, which were wall-mounted and required the user to wind a handle during conversation. The separate earpiece and transmitter lent an informality to the telephone's use, although in order to work effectively it still needed to be placed on a level, stable surface. This was because of the still rather limited electronics technology: the transmitter component, made from a sandwich of carbon granules, was prone to crackling if moved too much, so the only solution was to mount this on a base where it would be subject to less vibration. The handset, stem and 'daffodil' transmitter were all made of brass, and the majority of these were painted with a black 'japan' finish. After World War I, when brass was scarce, the 40 AL came out with all the same features, but with a steel shaft and grey finish. The dial system was not introduced until 1919, and was only available to the inhabitants of New York in 1922. The candlestick format remained the standard for Bell's subscribers until the first combined handsets were introduced in 1928, following improvements to transmitter technology. It became very popular when featured in many Hollywood films such as *Sob Sister*.

James Dunn and Linda Watkins in *Sob Sister* (1931), directed by Alfred Santell

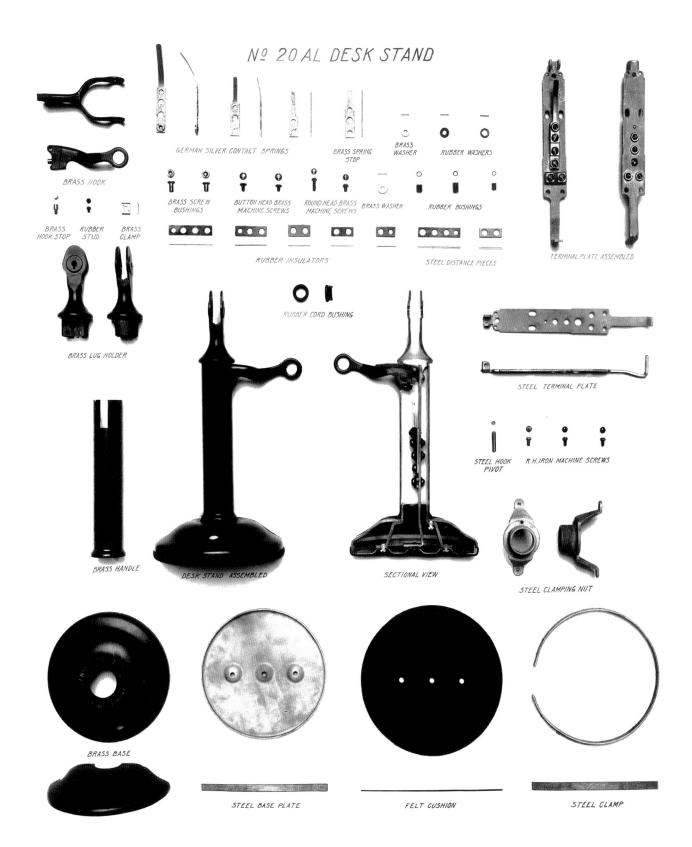

Nº 20 AL DESK STAND

BRASS HOOK

BRASS HOOK STOP   RUBBER STUD   BRASS CLAMP

BRASS LUG HOLDER

GERMAN SILVER CONTACT SPRINGS

BRASS SPRING STOP

BRASS WASHER   RUBBER WASHERS

BRASS SCREW BUSHINGS   BUTTON HEAD BRASS MACHINE SCREWS   ROUND HEAD BRASS MACHINE SCREWS   BRASS WASHER   RUBBER BUSHINGS

RUBBER INSULATORS   STEEL DISTANCE PIECES

TERMINAL PLATE ASSEMBLED

RUBBER CORD BUSHING

STEEL TERMINAL PLATE

BRASS HANDLE   DESK STAND ASSEMBLED   SECTIONAL VIEW

STEEL HOOK PIVOT   R.H. IRON MACHINE SCREWS

STEEL CLAMPING NUT

BRASS BASE   STEEL BASE PLATE   FELT CUSHION   STEEL CLAMP

Disassembled components of the No.20 AL, 1916

In a way, Roy Joroleman's Tunnel Mailbox originated as a model to standardize US mail delivery on rural routes. When free, rural delivery of US mail began in 1896, mail boxes were homemade, usually from some sort of discarded container, oil cans, for example, often with remains of its original contents, slapped onto a pole and set along the road. To resolve this situation, in 1901 the US Postal Service created a commission for a standardized mailbox and reviewed sixty-three designs submitted by prospective manufacturers. The guidelines established that the mailboxes should be made of sheet steel, preferably galvanized, and should have a durable sign that would signal the presence of mail. The committee initially approved fourteen of the submitted designs. In 1915 another committee was set to review new and existing designs in order to update and improve the service. The committee agreed that mailboxes needed further standardization and turned to postal engineer Roy Joroleman, whose proposal for a tunnel-shaped mailbox was to become the standard. The design was approved by the postmaster general in 1915 and was not allowed to be patented in order to encourage competition between manufacturers. In 1928 a larger version was approved, the No.2 Size Box, which could also accommodate parcels. Both designs have remained in production ever since. What makes the design so appealing is its sense of effortless simplicity. In a way it is not very different from its predecessors, a mutated can that has now become the perfect mailbox. It grew in depth to accommodate both letters and newspapers, yet still remained a 'can', although one with a flattened side that allowed it to be securely fixed to a pole, and a hinged end to open and close. It retained its fabrication ethos, both because it is a structurally efficient shape and because there was already a large manufacturing industry that could easily manufacture it at competitive prices. And finally it grew its trademark flag, which signalled incoming or outgoing mail. Today, in the digital world, the Tunnel Mailbox has been appropriated as the symbol for email. Its iconic status is assured.

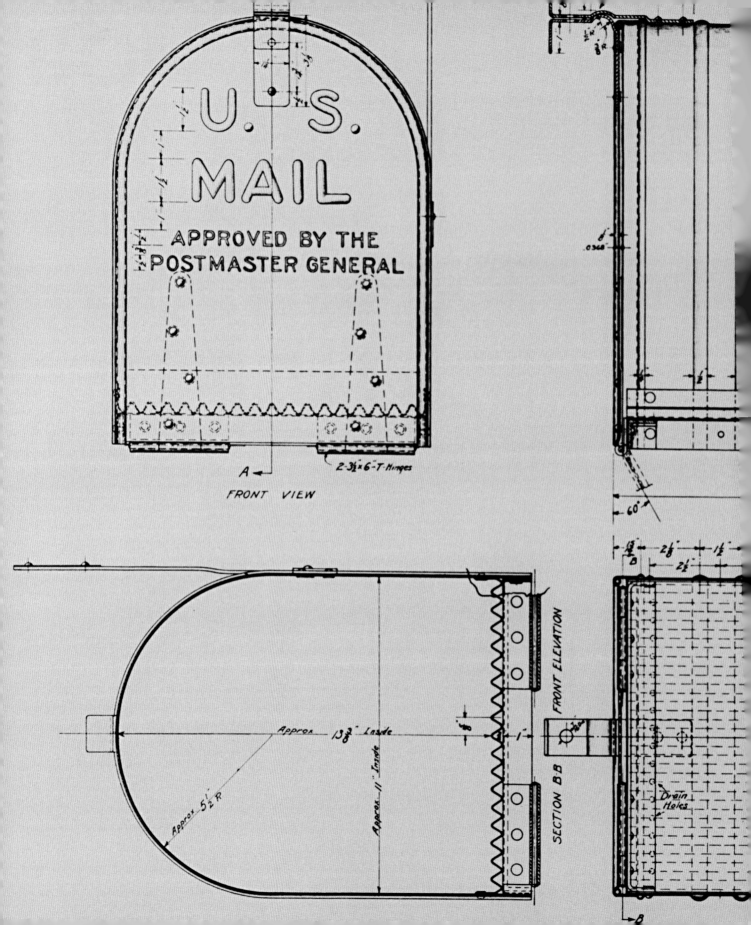

U. S.
MAIL

APPROVED BY THE
POSTMASTER GENERAL

A

FRONT VIEW

2-3½x6-T-Hinges

Approx 13⅜ Inside

Approx 5½ R

Approx 11" Inside

FRONT ELEVATION

SECTION B-B

Drain Holes

60°

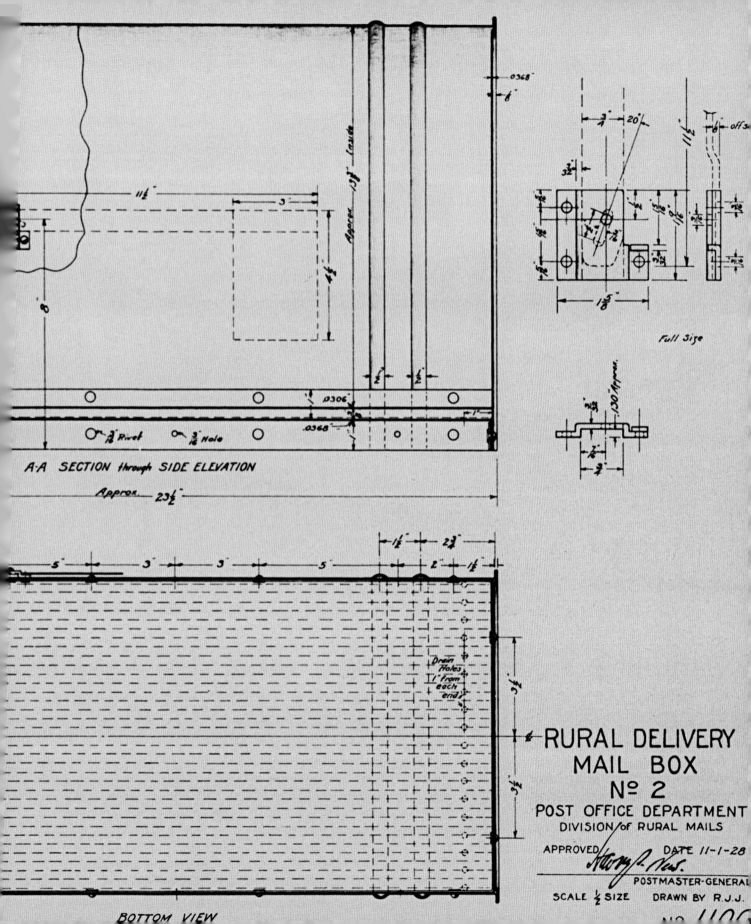

RURAL DELIVERY
MAIL BOX
Nº 2
POST OFFICE DEPARTMENT
DIVISION of RURAL MAILS
APPROVED   DATE 11-1-28
POSTMASTER-GENERAL
SCALE ½ SIZE   DRAWN BY R.J.J.

John Pemberton

The internationally beloved Coca-Cola Bottle was designed by Alexander Samuelson, a Swedish glass blower employed by the Root Glass Company based in Terre Haute, Indiana. His contoured shape was patented in 1915 and introduced to the market in 1916. Samuelson drew inspiration from an illustration of a cocoa bean pod in the *Encyclopædia Britannica*. Further, the fluted form was intended to distinguish the bottle from its competitors, to be recognizable in the dark or even when broken. The parallel vertical grooves, bulging middle and tapered ends allowed for the glass container to be patented and trademarked on the basis of its distinctive shape. Originally containing sand that produced a greenish glass, the colour of the glass has changed over time, though the design remains faithful to the original form. Coca-Cola was first sold in 1886 in an Atlanta drug store. The drink was created by pharmacist Dr John Pemberton, and named by his bookkeeper, Frank Robinson, who also drew the first sign in its recognizable script, creating one of the most lasting logos. In 1899, Coca-Cola was bottled for the first time, after being sold only as a soda fountain drink for more than a decade. Because of its common bottle, Coca-Cola was often imitated. The contour bottle changed that. By this time, the drink had become one of the most popular drinks to have at soda fountains across America. The Coca-Cola Bottle illustrates the power of brand identity. As the drink spread across the globe, demonstrating the boundless reach of American culture, the bottle appeared with its Spencerian script in countless languages, offering relevance to the brand around the world. There are few comparable packaging designs that have endured economic, political and cultural cycles. The bottle has become a collector's item, a cult object, a subject for fine art and essential subject matter in the study of brand awareness. The waisted design has endured several reincarnations, including various updates in its shape. The most well-known example of this is when the king-size larger bottle was introduced in 1955 by Raymond Loewy's firm, who had a consulting role in the design. Samuelson's design is frequently used as the template for marketing exercises and many designers have been approached to apply their creative personalities to the iconic form. Coca-Cola sells over 47 billion bottles a year, the original bottle being retained for image-building purposes. In 1993 Samuelson's classic contour design was translated into plastic, thus proving this cultural icon's ability to outlast material and technological change.

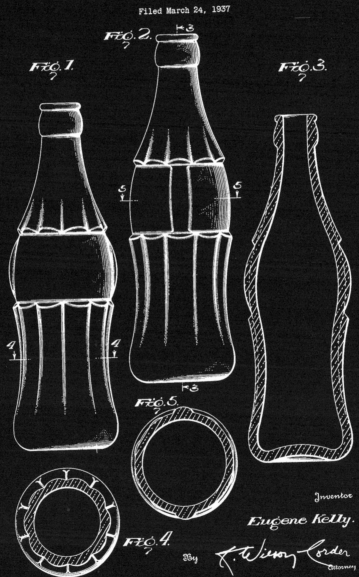

Aug. 3, 1937.   E. KELLY   Des. 105,529

BOTTLE

Filed March 24, 1937

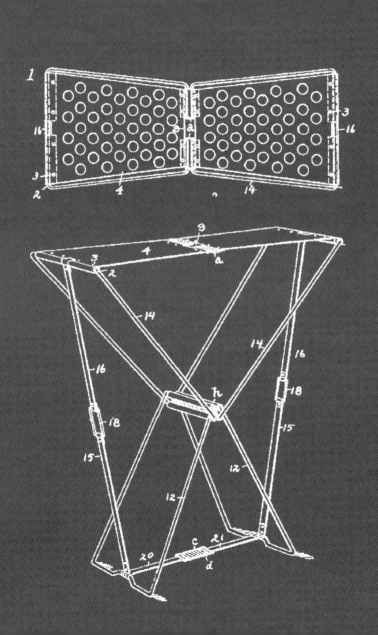

While choosing a folding stool as a seating option may be considered a last resort today, this has not always been the case. In ancient Rome such a seat, known as a *sella curulis* (chair of state), was considered to be a symbol of authority and dignity. With seating reserved for the wealthy and powerful, the folding stool implied social importance. Perceptions of the stool, particularly the folding stool, have changed since ancient times and such stools as this 1915 design are now associated with a range of outdoor activities. The interwar period saw an increase in popularity for outdoor pastimes, which was reflected in new products and designs. Popular activities ranged from picnicking to fishing, and with the increased accessibility to the motorcar for many, portable furniture found a new and relatively wealthy market. As an advance on the classic X-frame construction, which simply consisted of two crossed supports, and where the tension and support was all held in the seat, this design saw a more refined design and engineered approach to the folding mechanism and support structure of the seat. The more complex configuration of the folding legs allows the weight to be distributed evenly, and the metal seat, which still is the key to the stool's stability, is easy to clean, can be wiped dry in an instant, and leaves no opportunity for fraying or tearing and subsequent collapse of the stool. The stool folds flat, and with its bent metal legs and coloured metal seat is a utilitarian example of functional modernist European design.

The most significant features of Corning's Pyrex range are its design and its material, both of which have remain unchanged. The material used in its manufacture, heat-resistant glass, made its function possible. Most glass, for instance, that is used to make windows or bottles, cannot tolerate significant or rapid changes in temperature. The internal composition of such glass means that it would expand on heating, inevitably leading to fracture. From the end of the nineteenth century, originating in the pioneering research of Otto Schott in Germany, serious attempts were made to find recipes for glass mixtures that could be used in various technically demanding settings, such as in kilns, for optical use, for thermometers and for light-bulb casings. Although Corning originally specialized in ornamental glass and tableware, by the late nineteenth century the company had started to manufacture glass for technical use. In 1908 a research laboratory was set up for the company by Eugene Sullivan and William Taylor. Building on Schott's original discovery of the heat-resistant properties of borosilicate glass made during the period 1887–93, in 1912 Sullivan and Taylor were able to create a new glass they called 'Nonex', which was also heat-resistant and suitable for use in certain types of lighting. By 1915, with the help of Jesse Littleton, they had improved the recipe to the point that the glass, registered under the trade name 'Pyrex', could be used for laboratory glass and items such as glass battery containers (an important market because they were used with electricity generators). Littleton took one of these battery containers, cut the top off it and asked his wife to bake a cake in the wide dish that he had made. Unlike Schott, who was largely interested in the technological and industrial applications of his borosilicate glass, Littleton had recognized the potential domestic use of the material. Corning did not look back.

Publicity Shot, 1916

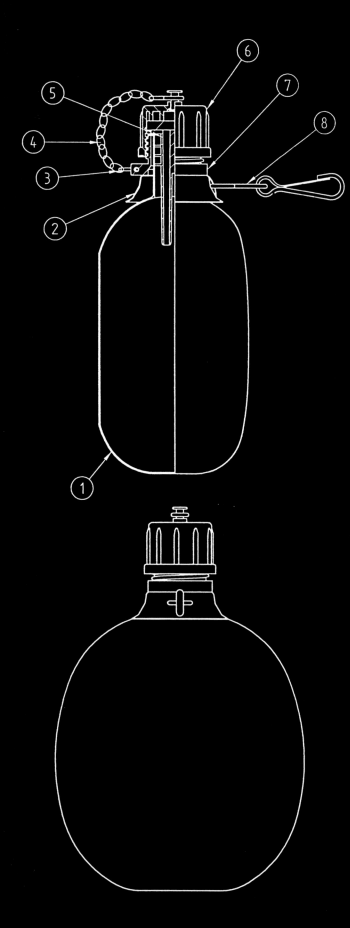

Top of any expedition equipment list is a Laken water bottle. The Laken company pioneered the design of aluminium drinking-water bottles with the Clásica model in the early twentieth century. It was immediately popular and remains so today. Spanish designer Gregorio Montesinos became aware of the manufacturing potential of aluminium, then a new metal, when he was working in France in the emerging aluminium industry. The modern aluminium industry was effectively born in 1886 when two unknown young scientists, Paul Louis Toussaint Héroult, from France, and the American, Charles Martin Hall, simultaneously invented a new electrolytic process, the Hall-Héroult process, when they discovered that if they dissolved aluminium oxide in a bath of molten cryolite and passed a powerful electric current through it, then molten aluminium would be deposited at the bottom of the bath. This is the basis for all aluminium production today. Returning to Spain, Montesinos established his own company in Murcia, and began to design water bottles as a cheap and lighter alternative to the ceramic and glass drinking bottles available at the time. Aluminium is strong and lightweight, and remarkable for its resistance to oxidation, properties that Montesinos was keen to harness. Designing for the armed forces and with mass production in mind, he came up with the Clásica. Made from 99.7 per cent pure isotope aluminium, it is anti-corrosive and hygienic, as well as extremely light and durable. An external textile cover (either felt or cotton) not only keeps the water fresh and protects the bottle from breakage, but can also be soaked in order to cool the water inside by evaporation. The Clásica stands at 18.5 cm (7 in) high and comes in two diameters of 13.8 cm (5.4 in) and the smaller 8.2 cm (3 in). Resilient to extremes of temperature, the Laken water bottle has been taken on expeditions to the North Pole, to Antarctica, to the Sahara and to the Amazon, and is still favoured by armed forces around the world. The Laken company, founded by Montesinos back in 1912, was one of the first manufacturers to process aluminium for the production of drinking containers, kitchenware and utensils, and a remains market leader in Spain today.

FOKKER TRIPLANE 110 HP.

LE RHONE.

There were certainly better aeroplanes in World War 1 than the Fokker DR1 Triplane. Its successor, the Fokker DV11, also designed by Reinhold Platz, would be the most obvious candidate, with more than 1,000 built before the war's end. Not to mention the Albatrosses, Nieuports, Spads and Sopwith Camels that preceded these. But there is no plane more famous than the DR1 Triplane, and for one reason only. Painted a menacing scarlet, the Fokker Triplane was the plane in which the great ace-of-aces, Manfred Albrecht Freiherr von Richthofen, the famous Red Baron, was shot down and killed. He was twenty-five at the age of his death in 1918, but he would become one of the century's enduring pop cultural heroes. The Baron's Triplane would go on to become an icon of heroic adventure for young boys all over twentieth-century Europe. Without doubt the greatest fighter pilot of the time, von Richthofen is remembered as the scarlet nemesis by Allied pilots. By the time of his death von Richthofen had accounted for eighty Allied fighters, an astonishing number, even for those days when battlefield casualties were numbered in the tens of thousands. That he recorded the majority of those 'kills' in fighter planes other than the Triplane is lost in the mists of legend. Anton Fokker was an entrepreneur, a showman and a very good pilot, quite capable of impressing steely-eyed military procurement officers with his flying prowess. Although Dutch by birth, Fokker took advantage of the war to build aeroplanes, and great wealth, at a factory in Berlin. Immediately after the war he moved his base to Holland, where production continues to this day. Fokker's abilities as a development engineer allowed him to refine his planes so that they were reliable by the standards of the day, and were easy to fly. None of Fokker's business acumen and flair would have mattered, but for the work of Reinhold Platz, one of the great designers of aeronautical history. The triplane's design, with three short wings, made it very manoeuvrable and strong. But, while the Triplane is remembered in legend, it had a relatively small production run of little over 300 aircraft before being replaced by Platz's vastly improved biplane, the Fokker DV11.

Having originally avoided the manufacture of watches (as opposed to selling bought-in ones) Cartier claims to be the first in France and the third in the world to produce wristwatches. Its first collection, launched in 1888, was aimed only at the women's market. This was typical of the era, as wristwatches were initially thought of as pieces of jewellery – as ornamental bracelets set with a watch. But the public was initially reluctant to embrace the new style: the fashion for long gloves kept the wristwatch hidden from view, and so it was consequently less showy than the pin or brooch watch, for which there was an established market. The wristwatch was only to prove its worth as an acceptable form of timepiece for men when it was realized how invaluable it was for reading the time during warfare, motoring or aviation, when one's hands were already engaged and so not able to access and open a pocket watch. Meanwhile, following the lead provided by the aviator Alberto Santos-Dumont's demand in 1904 for a robust wristwatch, Cartier started offering men's pocket and wristwatches as part of its regular range of stock. The pocket watches were typically geometric in shape and included models that were square with rounded corners, or pure circles, rectangles, hexagons or octagons. In this context, the design of the Tank watch was revolutionary. Its form is based on the horizontal plan (looking from above) of the armoured tanks of World War I. Its case is rectangular, with the sides, representing the tank's straight-line caterpillar tracks, extending beyond the main body and so providing the lugs for attaching the wrist band. Developed in 1917, the Tank's launch was delayed until 1919, when it became an immediate success. It remains in production, although now with a quartz movement. The Tank is in some ways a victim of its own esteem: it has earned the unfortunate accolade of most imitated wristwatch of all time.

115

Red and Blue Armchair (c.1918)
Gerrit Rietveld (1888–1964)
Gerard van de Groenekan 1924 to 1973
Cassina 1973 to present

The Red and Blue Armchair is one of a handful of seating designs that is universally recognizable. With no direct precedents, the chair is symbolic of Gerrit Rietveld's career and epitomizes his theories. Conceptually, the design was enormously influential at the time and through to present day. The construction of the chair is simply and clearly defined through the standardized wood components meeting and overlapping. In the first model the oak remained unpainted and was suggestive of a stripped-down sculptural version of a traditional armchair. Within a year Rietveld had slightly modified the design and painted the components. The geometry and structure were defined by colour; black was used for the frame, yellow for the cut ends of these elements and red and blue for the back and seat. The desire to inform its structure as well as examine how this structure reacted with the space around it was a key theory expounded by the journal De Stijl and the group of artists and designers of the same name. The Red and Blue Armchair formed part of De Stijl's evolution of Cubism into a purer form of fine and applied art. Rietveld was only twenty-nine when he created this seminal design and began his search for furniture designs that translated the two-dimensional painting system, Neoplasticism. His experimentations were to continue until they reached their fullest expression with his architectural work at Schröder House in 1924, where the exterior, interior and furnishings were wholly integrated through colour and the use of structure and planes. The Red and Blue Armchair greatly influenced the building's structural composition and the definition of spatial and colour-informed volumes within. The Rietveld Chair has always been a key reference point in the design of furniture and applied art, as well as their teaching. Although produced only intermittently until 1973, when Cassina made a licensed reproduction, the chair remains in production today – a mark of its importance and influence in the history of Modernism. It should be noted that the Red and Blue Armchair is demonstrative of theory and has often been misunderstood as being symbolic of the uncompromising comfort levels offered by modernist furniture.

The Brown Betty has the archetypal teapot form. It originated in the seventeenth century, when British potters copied the spherical designs of teapots imported from China, during the Ming period. It took some time before the formula for bone china, the fine white china that would not crack under repeated exposure to boiling water, was discovered. Prior to this, red clay was a reliable alternative used for such purposes. The Brown Betty evolved from unglazed teapots made from red clay discovered by the Dutch Elers brothers at Bradwell Wood in Staffordshire. Since then it has become a much-loved icon of the British tea table despite 'finer' china becoming available, and the chubby form and sturdy feel make it charming and dependable as an everyday tool. Alcock, Lindley and Bloore, a small factory in Stoke-on-Trent which employed only 100 people, put the Brown Betty into production from 1919 to 1979, when it closed down. Royal Doulton took over this company in 1974, manufactured a similar version, and well in excess of a million a year were sold. Since then a number of other manufacturers have brought out their own interpretations. Although many claim to make 'the original Brown Betty', not all have the features that have endeared the real thing to generations of consumers. A high-quality Brown Betty has the handle and spout added after the body has been cast rather than being cast in one piece. This allows a grid of holes to be pierced in the body, behind the spout, to catch the tea leaves. The lid does not fall when the pot is poured and the tip of the spout is sharpened to reduce drips. If the deep brown Rockingham glaze is chipped, the red clay body is revealed, which is much easier on the eye than if a white clay had been used. Available in a family of sizes from two to eight cups, the Brown Betty has conquered the mass market by striking a perfect balance between elegance and utility.

The history of wooden spoons dates back to around 1000 BC in Egypt and they were still being used in the early seventeenth century when they were listed on the inventories of early settlers of America. However, as mining and manufacturing techniques improved, wooden cutlery was inevitably replaced on dining tables by pieces crafted from materials such as iron, brass, pewter and, of course, steel. Yet despite this, the wooden spoon remains an essential part of the kitchen today. And there is at least one very good reason why. As our pots and pans have become high-tech, non-stick objects, ironically one of the best ways to keep them scratch-free is to use this defiantly low-tech product. Add to this the fact that they just feel more organic, are warmer to touch and do not conduct heat, it becomes apparent why they refuse to go out of fashion. Traditionally the spoon was hand-carved from indigenous woods. This changed after the Industrial Revolution, however, when companies realized they could be mass-manufactured and exported. Bearing in mind its abundance of beech, as well as a stripped down, economic aesthetic which lent itself well to industrial processes and crossed international borders, it's perhaps not surprising that Scandinavia established itself as the manufacturing centre of the product. Arguably, the company best known for the wooden kitchen spoon is ScanWood. Based in Denmark, it was founded in 1919 with the aim of producing 'functional wooden tools, with a nice modern design'. Proving how lucrative the export market is, since 1996 all its production has been performed on its own machines in other countries, creating an array of wooden kitchen equipment from beech, maple, cherry and olive trees.

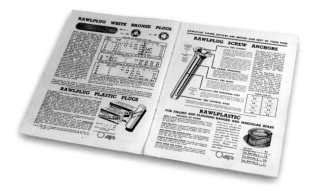

Original Rawlplug Product Guide, 1939

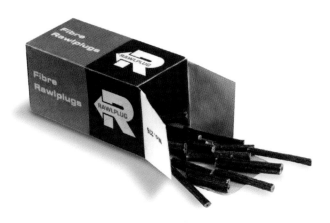

.ed patents throughout the world nearly distributors for Nobel Chemical Finishes, Ltd.

Every week over 3,000,000 RAWLPLUGS are fixed in England alone

THE RAWLPLUG COMPANY

Rawlplugs (1919)
John J Rawlings (nd)
Artex-Rawlplug (BPB Group)
1919 to present

For as long as threaded screws have existed, time and effort has been devoted to the problem of how to fix them securely into certain substances, notably plasterboard and masonry, but also reinforced concrete. A building contractor John J Rawlings applied himself to finding a solution before just before World War I, when he was doing some work for the British Museum. Museum officials asked that he fix screws to the walls with as little damage to the masonry as possible, meaning that Rawlings had almost immediately to reject the common method of fixing at the time: blocks of wood tightly fitted into relatively large holes, into which screws were driven. His answer was a fabric plug the length of the threaded section of screw, which had a hollow core. The material was a coarse fibre, such as jute or hemp, and was bonded with glue or sometimes even animal blood. A hole approximately the diameter of the screw was drilled in the masonry and the plug inserted. The screw was then screwed into the plug, pushing it outwards and securing a very firm grip against the sides of the hole. Rawlings named his invention after himself: the Rawlplug. Although far smaller than the wooden plugs, the Rawlplug was far more effective at fixing. Rawlings was satisfied enough with it to patent it. In 1919, after the end of World War I, Rawlings established the Rawlplug Company to manufacture and market his product. In 1914 Black and Decker patented the world's first 'pistol grip' power drill, which made drilling quick and easy. After World War II the power drill began to establish itself in the home market and, as consumer incomes and leisure time increased in the 1960s, the home improvement craze took off. Now made from extruded plastic, Rawlplugs embedded themselves in the habits and vocabulary of the domestic consumer. Simplicity and effectiveness have made the Rawlplug ubiquitous.

Johan Rohde was an architect, painter and writer who created a range of high quality silverware for Georg Jensen, whose workshops were established in Copenhagen in 1904. In 1906 Rohde first asked Jensen to execute various designs in silver for his own use and later was given permanent employment at the workshop as a designer. The Pitcher Model No. 432, designed in 1920, is one of Rohde's finest works. Rohde's designs were often characterized by curving lines and flower, fruit and animal forms in tight clusters appear on his tea services, bowls and candlesticks. By contrast the Pitcher shows a remarkable simplicity of form and functionalism of design that anticipates the development of a more streamlined and undecorated style in the 1930s. The pitcher was designed in 1920 but did not enter production until 1925 as it was felt to be too avant-garde and would not appeal to the consumer. However, tea and coffee sets were much in demand during this period and the Pitcher proved to be a huge success. It was originally produced with a silver handle but later versions incorporated an ivory handle. Silver was often combined with ivory adding a much sought after touch of luxury that characterized work produced during the Art Deco period. Many designers during this period felt that industrialization had brought about a marked deterioration in the quality of Danish silver and had encouraged large imports of cheap, inferior foreign silver. Only a few Danish silver workshops, such as the outstanding metal workshop of Georg Jensen, were attempting to maintain the traditions of their craft and to raise aesthetic standards. Rohde designed the interior of Georg Jensen's first shop, and created a range of hollow ware for Jensen during the 1930s which were decorated with a quasi-naturalistic style popular at the time. Many of Rohde's designs are still in production by Georg Jensen's studio, which has been part of Royal Copenhagen since 1985.

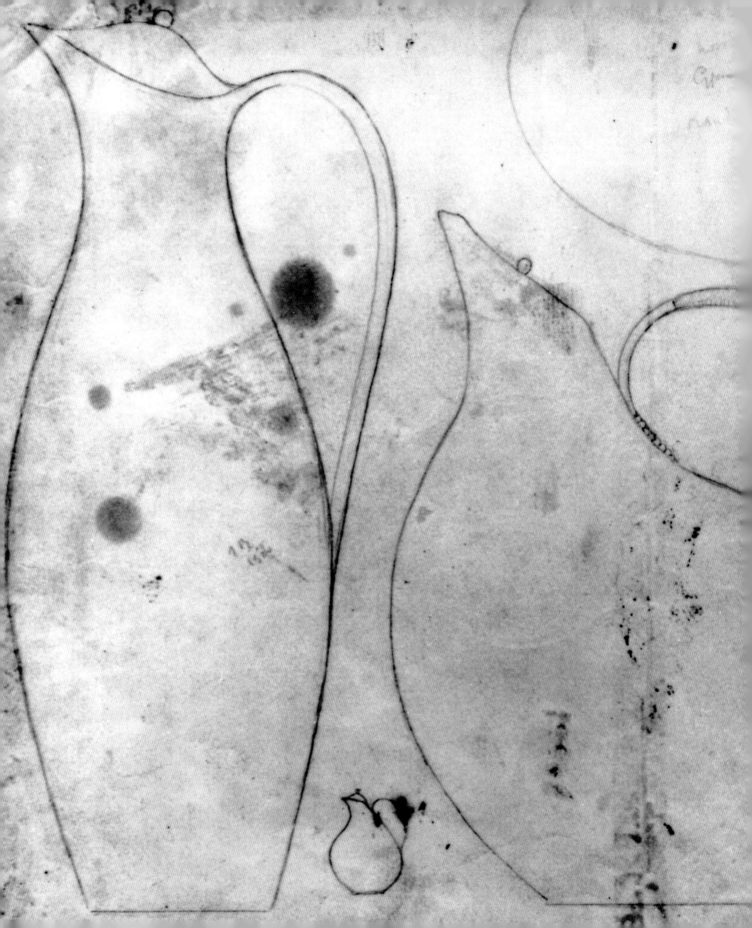

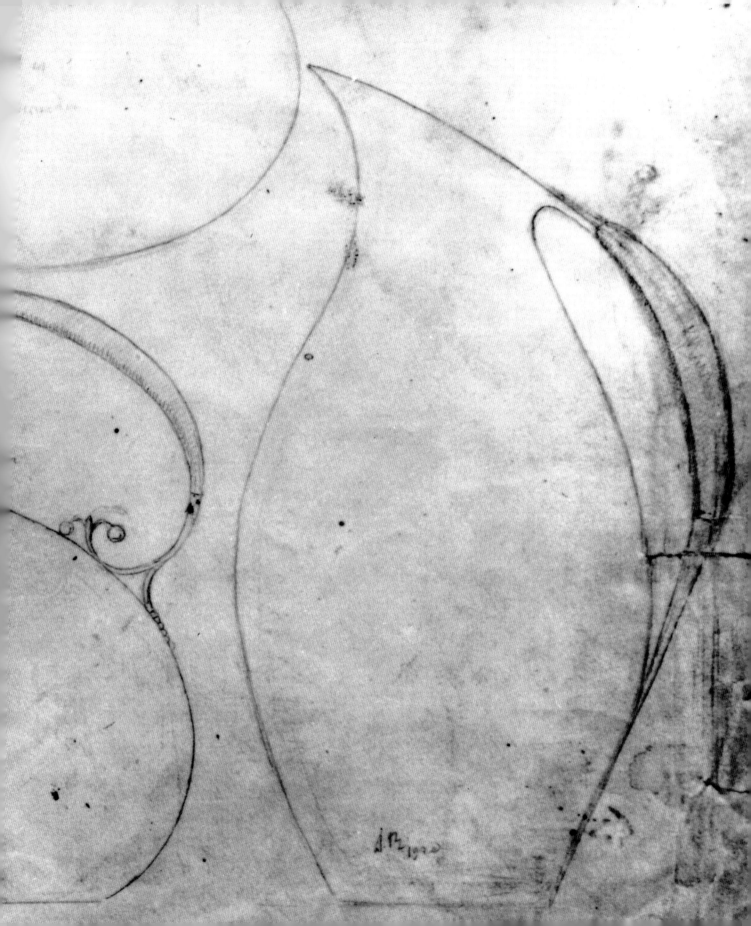

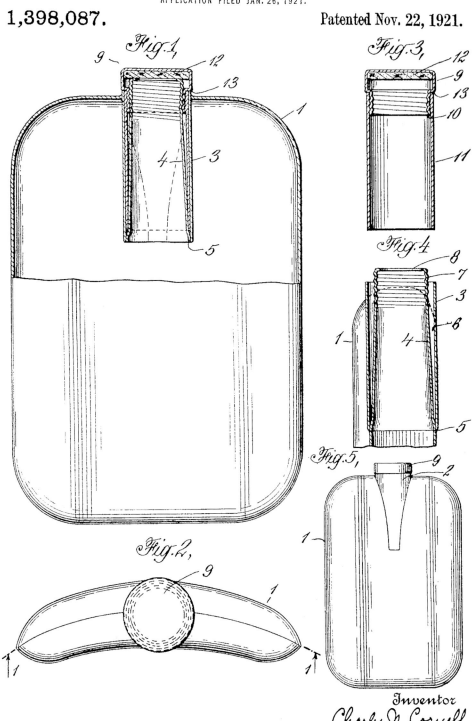

Fig.1

Fig.2

Fig.3

Fig.4

Fig.5

Inventor
Charles N. Coryell
By his Attorneys
Pennie, Davis, Marvin & Edmonds

Until well into the twentieth century, before the advent of modern palliatives, chronic pain was a factor in the lives of many people. Alcoholic spirits were used not only for the pleasure they provided as intoxicants, but for their medicinal and pain-relieving properties. In the first decades of the twentieth century, the medicinal role of alcohol took on a whole new dimension with the outbreak of World War I, as severe trauma became a part of the lives of countless young men. The medicinal role soon changed to one of recreation with the introduction of Prohibition in the United States in 1920 and the subsequent advent of the Jazz Age. This last factor, aided by the American film industry's glamorous portrayal of alcohol consumption, significantly contributed to the new phenomenon of women as public alcohol consumers. Given the illegal nature of the industry, the reusable vessel became a common personal accessory. Flasks to carry whiskey or other spirits had been popular accessories since the eighteenth century. Changing social circumstances, however, made their use and ownership common practice in the 1920s. Before that time, flasks were usually made of silver, designed to be carried in a pocket and held with one hand. Most had a hinged, bayonet-fit lid but others had a pull-off cup or screw-off lid attached with a security chain. They came in sizes ranging from 0.03L to 1.14L (1 fl oz to 2 pt) and were shaped to the contours of the human body. Most were relatively unadorned but, depending upon the styles of the era, some were engraved or shaped to resemble animals or objects. For today's collectors, such novelty flasks are the most valuable. In the 1920s, a slim version of the flask that could be hidden in a hip pocket or handbag or held by a garter became the preferred standard. Because of its ease of production, the two-part, twist-off lidded hip flask became a common and elegant example of the period's metalwork.

The Pendant Lamp depicted is often referenced as an unattributed design by one of the students or tutors attending the Bauhaus between 1919 and 1933. The design was indeed widely used and favoured by eminent architects including Josef Hoffmann and Adolf Loos, but these applications predate the Bauhaus era. The basic outline of the Opaque Globe was used by many Bauhaus designers; in particular, both Marianne Brandt and Hans Przyrembel created lighting designs that could easily be seen to be part of the same family as the Pendant Lamp. The form was also widely used within interiors built during and after the Bauhaus era by Peter Behrens and his contemporaries. It is a design that traversed Europe in the period before World War II, being used in modernist interior landscapes. Although the creator is still unknown, the appearance of a simple suspended opaque glass globe can be traced to as early as the first decade of the twentieth century. With the advent of electricity, the need to devise new fittings to hide or decorate the light source was quickly addressed. The Globe Pendant Lamp appears as an almost Minimalist design, without decoration and in the purest geometric form, the sphere. On a functional level, the light diffuses evenly and the size of the sphere can easily be adapted to suit the volume of space in which it is hung. The design works equally well singularly, or en masse in rows or a grid. Typically, this low-cost, mass-produced design has been specified in large numbers in school or factory locations and it found favour with many prewar architects designing such buildings and interiors. As with many classic designs, particularly those without attributed designers and licences, it has been widely produced to various levels of quality. Its production has been intermittent since the early twentieth century. The simplicity of the Globe Pendant Light has been highly influential as a template for similar lighting designs from early Marianne Brandt table and pendant lights to the more contemporary elegant Glo-Ball series by Jasper Morrison.

Kugelleuchten

Leuchte Nr.	Watt	Länge etwa cm	Ø etwa cm	Preis* RM Messing kupferbraun galvanisiert	Preis* RM Messing matt vernickelt
810	40—100	72	25	14,—	15,—
811	60—200	76	29	17,—	18,—
812	300	84	37	23,—	24,—
813	300—500	87	40	26,—	27,—

* Preise und Längenmaße gelten für Leuchten mit etwa 40 cm Pendelrohr (Zusatzbezeichnung: P 40). **Mehrpreis** für Leuchten mit etwa 80 cm Pendelrohr (Zusatzbezeichnung: P 80) 2,— RM.

Doppelzylinderleuchten

Leuchte Nr.	Watt	Länge cm	Ø etwa cm	Preis* RM Messing matt vernickelt
806	40—100	81—84	27	37,—
666	75—200	88	37	45,—
666	300—500	98	37	52,—

* Preise und Längenmaße gelten für Leuchten mit etwa 40 cm Pendelrohr (Zusatzbezeichnung: P 40). **Mehrpreis** für Leuchten mit etwa 80 cm Pendelrohr (Zusatzbezeichnung: P 80) 2,— RM.

Körting & Mathiesen catalogue, 'Kandem Innenraumleuchten', Leipzig, 1930

Now a standard feature

in any home decor that acknowledges retro influences and kitsch styling, the design of the Insulated Teapot is as much about practicality as it is style. When first launched in the late 1920s the insulated stoneware tea service was adopted as the standard for a high tea service at hotels and restaurants across Europe. The reason was aesthetic and functional; the styling was in keeping with the desire for a modern look and the integrated tea cosy would keep tea warm without stewing for up to an hour. Like many of the most successful classic designs, the idea and construction is simple. Consisting of a plain stoneware teapot, the insulating element is the brushed stainless steel jacket that either sits over the pot, or surrounds the body of the pot, depending on the design. This 'cosy' element is lined with an insulating fabric that insures piping hot tea for more than the first pouring. This teapot design

embraced the burgeoning popularity for Art Deco style and the adoption of a machine aesthetic. Teapots are classically either stoneware or porcelain, and, until this design, heat-preserving covers were unconnected with the design of the pot, and were usually quilted fabric or knitted, making them more part of a craft sensibility than a design process. The Insulated Teapot with its chrome-looking cover challenged this tradition and allowed the beauty of the modern design to be uncompromised by its functional quality in everyday use. The further innovation of this design is that, while keeping the contents of the pot warm, the handle, being outside the insulated cover, remains cool.

122

Insulated Teapot (1920s)
Designer Unknown
Various 1920s to present

As its name indicates, this utilitarian, light and curvaceous glass tumbler was originally designed to be used at the soda fountain in the 1920s. Its wide top allows for ease of pouring, and the thinner lower part, combined with a curved side to prevent the hand from slipping, ensures a good grip. The shape is perfect for ice cream soda, as the broad rim allows the ice cream to be easily added. It is made by the glassware pioneers Libbey of Ohio, renowned for their 'Brilliant Cut' glass. Usually located in American drugstores, the soda fountain was a popular place to socialize from the late nineteenth century. The advent of new bottle making technology in the early twentieth century saw bottled soda become more common. The hobble skirt Coca Cola bottle was introduced in 1916, and the sale of bottled Coca Cola had overtaken fountain sales by the end of the 1920s. As a companion to their bottle, the soda fountain tumbler, usually printed with their logo, was adopted as a part of Coca Cola's corporate image in 1929. Prohibition was introduced in 1919 and the soda fountain filled the void caused by the closing of bars. When Prohibition was abolished in 1933, the soda fountain and ice cream parlor were taken over by teenagers. During the 1950s the soda fountain became an important icon of American culture. The soda glasses printed with various logos and commemorative designs from that period have become collector's items. The soda fountain age had passed by the 1960s, but the glass has survived. They are still commonly found in bars and restaurants. When we look at this design with fresh eyes, we notice the beauty of its form and how practical it is. This is a familiar type of American icon; it is essentially raw, anonymous, and ultimately ephemeral and timeless.

The strong, clear-cut shape of the Pushcan, and its shiny flap that simply reads 'PUSH', all add up to an archetypal product by the German company, Wesco. The Pushcan design was closely based on the American 'PushCan', created in the 1920s by Sam Hemmer, although it took the Germans to transform the design in 1989 into the global favourite that it is today as the bin is exported to over fifty countries world-wide. Made from powder-coated sheet steel and a base of reinforced plastic, it is hard to imagine how this design could be further improved. The flap of the Pushcan is spring-loaded, ensuring the bin is closed at all times, keeping smells inside and pests out. The bin comes in a range of vibrant colours, although the matt silver finish of the stainless-steel version, in keeping with the product's industrial look, is always likely to prove the most popular. Wesco, which stands for Westermann & Co, was founded in 1867 as a metal manufacturer dedicated to making

12-4

Pushcan (1920s)
Sam Hammer (nd)
Various 1920s to present
Wesco 1989 to present

stable lamps and coffee flasks for miners. For over 100 years the company continued to make functional, sheet-steel products that sold modestly across Germany. It was only at the end of the 1980s, with a conscious effort to ape the success of big-thinking US firms, that the name Wesco became rather better known. Not only did an American attitude become incorporated into the company's business practice, but it influenced its product range too, as the Pushcan proves. Today, still part-owned by the Westermann family, the range has expanded considerably, although waste disposal products are now the company's primary concern. Since the world's waste production has grown ever larger, so Wesco's focus on bins has grown ever stronger. Indeed, it was Wesco that first introduced bins that encouraged recycling and waste separation. The Wesco Pushcan is the perfect marriage of American style and German craftsmanship. So universal is the Pushcan's design that it seems right at home in many different settings; in the kitchen or in the office, in its hometown of Schwarzenberg, Germany or on the other side of the globe in its spiritual home of the USA.

Peacock Chair for the Imperial Hotel (c.1921)
Frank Lloyd Wright (1867–1959)
Manufacturer Unknown

Frank Lloyd Wright, the legendary American architect, believed that furniture design could enhance and amplify the quality of his architecture, and that through it the whole aesthetic of a building could be unified. He famously designed a swivel armchair for the offices of the Larkin Company Administration Building in Buffalo in1904, and the desks for one of his masterpieces, the Johnson Wax Administration Building in Racine, Wisconsin in 1939. In between those projects he also designed this chair, called the Peacock, for the Imperial Hotel in Tokyo, in around 1921. This is a complicated, perhaps even slightly cluttered chair, made from an oak frame with its seat and back upholstered in oilcloth. Its striking upright back, reminiscent in shape of the proud open feathers of its avian namesake, is bluntly angular and was intended for multiple rooms in the hotel. The hexagons on the back and sides reflected the interior of the building, indeed they were even repeated in a coffee set Wright created specifically for the hotel. The construction of the Peacock Chair means it is quite fragile and, according to the Vitra Design Museum, it seems likely that the chairs had to be replaced at least three times before the hotel was finally demolished in 1968. The earliest models would almost certainly have come with wicker seats, sides and backs as well as loose upholstered cushions. The chair is highly stylized in form and unmistakably from the 1920s era. As such the Peacock remains an evocative piece of design from one of the architectural greats. Wright had been interested in Japanese culture for a number of years, and therefore, lobbied for the opportunity to build the hotel as a merging of Japanese and Western architecture.

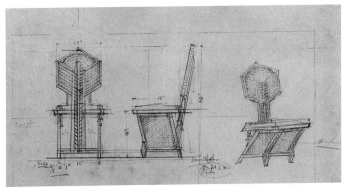

CHANEL

Marylin Monroe made Chanel No. 5 legendary when she coquettishly announced that all she wore in bed were a few drops of the fragrance. This anecdote played a large part in creating the perfume's legendary status and sex appeal. Launched in 1921, Chanel No. 5 was a revolutionary product for its time, a combination of a unique scent composition, a strikingly modern bottle design and a recognizable brand. It was the first perfume to bear its designer's name. The innovative package sets the tone. A luxurious product is enclosed in a simple, square Art Deco bottle, a reflection of Coco Chanel's maxim 'always remove, always strip away, never add'. Since its conception, the only really significant change in design came in 1924 when the original rounded edges of the bottle and stopper were replaced by bevelled edges. The look of Chanel No. 5 is safeguarded by Jacques Helleu, artistic director at Chanel. Imperceptible changes

are made perhaps once every ten or twenty years to reflect contemporary requirements. For example, one change in the design has been the addition of an atomizer, and over the years the lines have become more defined, the sides more rectilinear, and the glass heavier, adding to No. 5's luxurious appeal. This attention to detail has made Chanel No. 5 the top-selling perfume in the world, with estimated annual retail sales of $100m (£60m). In 1959, the packaging secured a place for No. 5 in the permanent collection of The Museum of Modern Art in New York. In the 1960s the bottle was immortalized as an icon of the twentieth-century in a series of nine silkscreen prints by Andy Warhol. Advertising campaigns by director Jean Paul Goude using Catherine Deneuve and most recently, the employment of actress Nicole Kidman as its new face, have insured that Chanel No. 5 is always in the spotlight.

Catherine Deneuve for Chanel

CHANEL

erfume in the classic bottle from 8.50 to 400., Eau de Chanel from 7.00 to 20.00, Eau de Cologne from 4.00 to 20.00, Spray Perfume and Spray Cologne each 6.00.

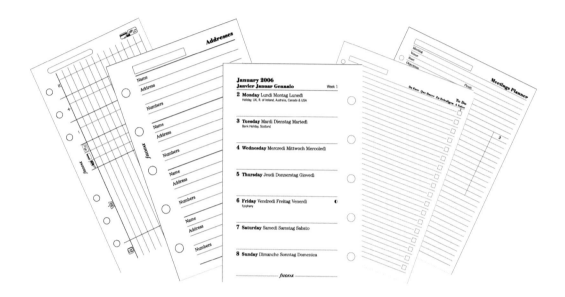

This stylish personal organizer was an obligatory accessory for any upwardly mobile executive in the 1980s, and thus seems the perfect embodiment of the decade. The Filofax had good looks, class and a price tag that perfectly suited its luxuriant leather jacket. If you were not fortunate enough to own one of the new mobile phones, then you could at least display your prowess by jotting down the number of a client in your Filofax. The story of the Filofax actually began in 1921. An Englishman working in the US had come across a file containing technical notes for engineers; literally a 'file of facts'. He recognized its potential and the idea was marketed in London, initially by mail order, through Norman & Hill and designed by William Rounce and Posseen Hill. In 1930 the name Filofax became a registered trademark. At first, it proved popular with the military and was a compulsory purchase at the British Army Staff College. Undoubtedly a useful item during World War II, the Filofax almost did not survive the Blitz. When Norman & Hill's offices in Aldersgate Street, London, were destroyed in 1940, the company was only able to be rebuilt because a secretary named Grace Scurr had listed all the company's supplier and customer details in her own Filofax. She went on to chair the company until it was bought by Pocketfax in 1976, which is when the Filofax really came into its own. It was sometimes referred to as a personal organizer, and the often personalized case was large and eye-catching, forcing others to imagine the importance of the busy life hidden within its pages. The success of Filofax was remarkable. From 1979 to 1985, revenue increased dramatically from £75,000 to £12 million. The global popularity of the Filofax is unquestionable. Essentially a diary and notebook, it is crammed with useful information, from addresses and telephone numbers to maps, CD or business card holders and even a calculator. Today you can also update your Filofax by adding inserts downloaded from a computer. According to a recent survey a large percentage of managers still prefer to write important information in a Filofax than to enter it into one of the many electronic organizers available today. It is good to know in an age where a phone smaller than your hand can store your record collection, videos, photos and an entire Bible, while recognizing your handwriting and storing notes, that, for sheer style and reliability nothing compares to the classic Filofax.

127

Filofax Personal Organizer (1921)
William Rounce (nd)
Posseen Hill (nd)
Norman & Hill 1921 to 1976
Pocketfax 1976 to c.1979
Filofax 1979 to present

Marcel Breuer

One of the most prolific

members of the Bauhaus school, Hungarian designer and architect Marcel Breuer established a concern with unit construction and mass-produced design early on in his career. As an apprentice at the school he designed the Lattenstuhl in 1922. The chair was very obviously inspired by the abstract aesthetic of the Dutch De Stijl movement, and in particular by the work of designer Gerrit Rietveld. The final version was constructed from a single wooden joint and envisaged by the young Breuer as a suitable model for mass, factory production. The ergonomics of the slatted oak and leather chair was based on anatomical research to support the heaviest bones of the human body in maximum comfort. These very modern concerns engaged Breuer throughout his career. He famously went on to investigate mass production with his long-running tubular steel range and later experimented with the same disciplines through plywood with his work for Isokon Plus. While an apprentice at the Bauhaus, Breuer was favoured by director Walter Gropius, who encouraged Breuer's investigations in design by making him the head of carpentry at the school. Both men considered the application of mass-produced furniture an essential element of modern life and a cornerstone of the Bauhaus mission. Breuer went on to become one of the best-known designers in Europe, with a string of international commissions, including UNESCO in Paris and the Whitney Museum in New York. But throughout his highly acclaimed career Breuer remained true to the ambition of creating a democratic design that had coloured his very earliest work and inspired the form of one of his primary pieces, the Lattenstuhl.

New York and yellow taxis are synonymous; when we think of the city, we can immediately picture millions of taxis streaming down its avenues. The pair have formed an inexorable link, reinforced by movies such as Martin Scorsese's *Taxi Driver* (1976), or the 1970s sitcom *Taxi*, starring Danny DeVito and Andy Kaufman. The cab management company Yellow Cab was founded in 1915 by John D Hertz, who created the booming business by recycling used cars as taxis. Hertz chose the colour yellow after reading a study published by the University of Chicago that asserted that yellow was the easiest colour to see at great distances. In 1929 Hertz sold the company to move on to the rental business and Morris Markin, a Russian-born immigrant bought sixty percent of the Yellow Cab Company and all of Hertz's shares. Morris had arrived at New York's Ellis Island at the age of nineteen with little money and barely speaking English. He initially worked as a tailor and only entered the automobile industry by lending money to a friend who owed debts to a car manufacturer. In 1922 Markin founded the Checker Cab Manufacturing Company (later became Checkers Motors Corporation) in alliance with Checker Taxi, a taxi drivers' association. With his latest purchase from Hertz, Markin ran both Checker Cab and Yellow Cab in Chicago and by 1935, Checker Taxi was established as a corporation. Although Chicago was the city in which the cab's story began, Checker Taxi's distributor Henry Weiss brought the cars to New York City soon after. Most significantly, Markin produced the mainstay of the taxi industry, the Checker Marathon Cab, with its wide grille and sleek line of checkers down each side, which went on to be used throughout the United States by most cab companies until 1954, when smaller vehicles were permitted to be used as cabs. Up until the 1950s, taxis had to accommodate five people – seated behind the driver – as well as a luggage rack. The Checker Marathon was produced until 1982, but was sadly retired from the streets of New York in 1999 and the very last cab was auctioned through Sotheby's by its driver, Earl Johnson, for a hefty sum. Although the Checker Cab is no longer on the streets of New York, the distinctive yellow hue has remained the iconic colour of all New York taxis and is still used today on the city's 12,053 modern cabs. Many taxi firms across the United States still operate under the name Checker Cabs, despite the fact that they have no affiliation with the legendary company.

Robert De Niro in *Taxi Driver* (1976), directed by Martin Scorsese

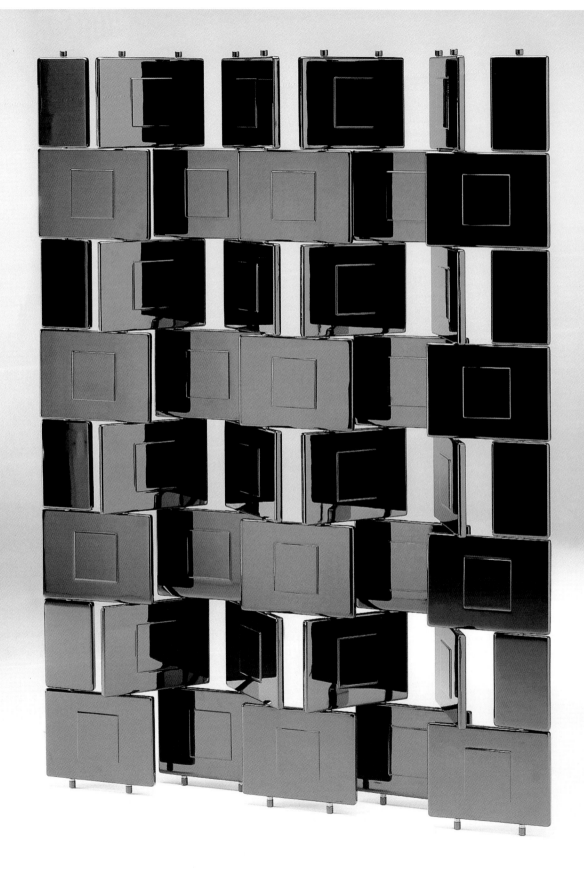

130

A commission from the hat designer, Madame Mathieu Lévy, in 1919 for an apartment interior on rue de Lota in Paris was a milestone for the Irish-born designer and classically trained painter, Eileen Gray. This project allowed her to explore her very personal and distinct aesthetic on an architectural scale rather than through individual objects. The heart of her design was a screen stretching through the apartment made of 450 small panels. Each panel was painstakingly created in matt-grey lacquer with gold and silver highlights. This initial design was not entirely freestanding, unlike the many brick screens that were to follow; rather it existed as both architectural feature and functional object. Only a small length of the screen was freely moveable. Having worked closely for many years with Seizo Sugawara, one of the very few remaining masters of the ancient Japanese art of screen-making, Gray approached her earliest screens more as canvases than as items of interior design. The later brick screens were altogether different; self-sufficient and functional, they were largely devoid of decoration save for the occasional use of a simple geometric raised form. As the rue de Lota was nearing completion, Gray also created an exhibit for the 1923 Paris Salon des Artistes Décorateurs. Representing a wholly uncompromised vision of her designs, her strikingly stark 'Boudoir for Monte Carlo' included two white freestanding brick screens. Displayed alongside more conventional exhibits by Brandt, Lalique and Chareau, her room was controversial and a clear departure from the then popular, more decorative French design. It was also a philosophical departure from the past and an implicit adoption of many of the tenets of the Dutch De Stijl movement, where 'all beautiful forms are mechanical or functional, showing the thing without décor'. For several years following 1923 and before immersing herself in architecture, Gray continued to create further versions of the brick screen although only eleven known examples were produced between 1922 and 1971, and there are even imitations being produced today. While several of these screens were finished with paint, others were made of Japanese lacquered wooden bricks. Gray employed a team of artisans to make these bricks, using a time-consuming process of applying and polishing layer upon layer of a specially formulated resin. The resulting screens of either white or black were striking and functional, devoid of decoration yet sumptuous, complex in construction and useful across varied formats.

Gustaf Dalén

An object of affection, and sometimes obsession, since its introduction in 1922, the enamelled cast-iron Aga Stove has become a symbolic lifestyle appurtenance for generations of people in northern climes for its dual-purpose use as an oven and secondary heating source. With its standard design remaining more or less the same over the years – with two ovens and two covered heating plates, or a larger version with four ovens – the Aga is one of the century's most enduring icons of hearth and home. Like many inventions, the Aga was created amidst less than ideal conditions. Gustaf Dalén, a Swedish physicist and managing director of Svenska Aktiebolaget Gasaccumulator (AGA), lost his eyesight from an explosion during an experiment, which left him housebound and restless. With nothing to do all day, the physicist – who was even unable to attend the awards ceremony for the Nobel Prize, which he had won earlier in the year –

honed all of his attention on figuring out a way to aid his wife, who he noticed spent a good portion of the day in the kitchen stoking their wood-burning stove and tending to food preparation. Dalén wondered whether there would be a way to construct an oven that would burn more steadily with less intervention necessary. Dalén's design was based on the principles of heat storage. Constructed of cast iron coated with three layers of enamelling, the burner unit was placed next to two stacked cooking chambers, with the lower one for slow cooking, and the upper one for roasting and baking. He designed the cooker's surface with two hotplates insulated by lids that give off warmth when not in use, providing a source of heat for northern winters. With an even transfer of heat from the inner core to the ovens and covered surface areas – despite the fuel source – the Aga does away with knobs or dials with an internal thermostat that regulates the temperature, making the cooker both sleekly uncluttered and unconditionally yielding in its readiness to serve; a warm, maternal figure for even the chilliest and busiest of households.

The

"New Standard"
AGA COOKER

(Regd Trade Mark)

gives you
better cooking, more leisure . .
a Guaranteed maximum fuel cost
of less than £4 a year

**Some points of the
"New Standard"
AGA Cooker:**

The most economical in the world.

Independent of gas or electricity.

Burns day and night.

No morning fires to light.

Easy to clean, simple to manage.

Always ready for immediate use.

No fumes, or cooking smells.

Extremely rapid boiling, safe
simmering.

All cooking temperatures
automatically controlled.

Two big ovens, two large hot-plates.

Unusually even heat in the ovens.

Fuelling and riddling only
twice a day.

Absolutely safe and fool-proof.

Guaranteed fixed fuel cost.

Easy to install.

Width 3 ft. 3 ins.

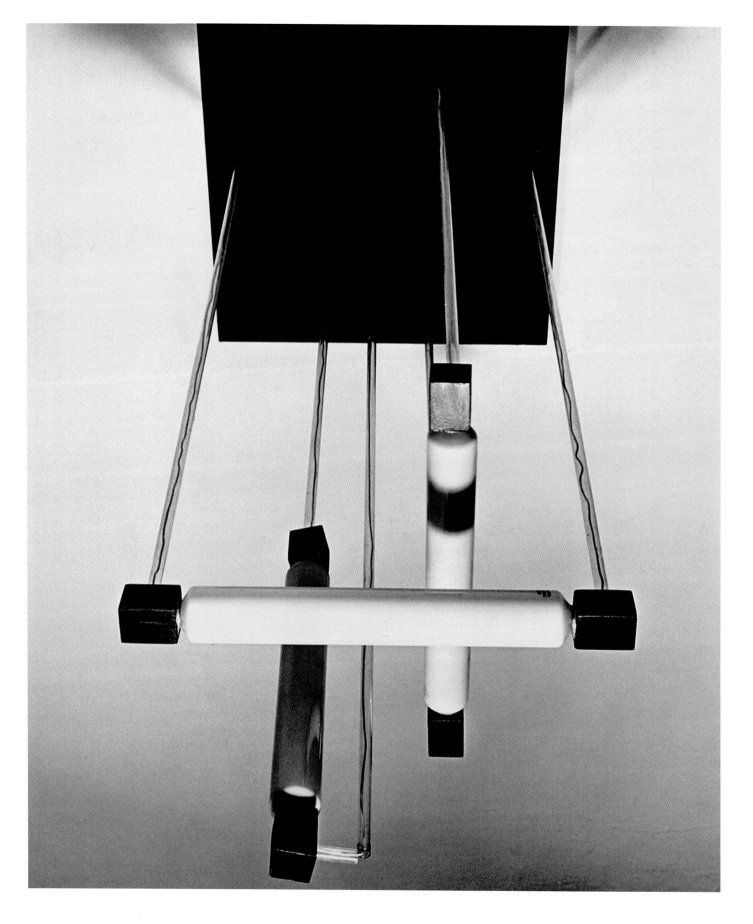

The Hanging Lamp was designed by Gerrit Rietveld for one of his most important early commissions: an interior for Dr A M Hartog, a general practitioner in Maarssen, near Utrecht. The lamp comprised four standard incandescent lighting tubes, which were manufactured by Philips, arranged in a spatial composition. Two of the tubes were hung vertically, and two horizontally, with each intersecting at different points to form an arrangement rather like Rietveld's slat furniture. The tubes were fixed at either end into small blocks of wood, suspended from rods attached to a ceiling plate. The light hung over the desk in Hartog's office until the interior was destroyed after his death in 1939. The Hanging Lamp is designed according to an arrangement Rietveld had experimented with in previous commissions. In a shop interior of the early 1920s he had hung a cluster of bare round bulbs from a square ceiling plate, and he repeated this idea in a 1921 apartment interior for Truüs Schröder-Schrader. In the interiors for the Utrecht House Rietveld designed with and for Mrs Schröder in 1924, known as the Rietveld-Schröder House, the Hanging Lamp was redesigned with three, rather than four, tubular lamps. Another version, even more minimal, with only two tubes, appeared in the Elling interior of around 1925. Rietveld's explanation for the different configurations was pragmatic: the number of tubes was due to the fact that different regions of Holland used different voltages. In notes added to a sketch, he commented that 'if voltage used is 220 v, either three or four tubes can be used. If voltage is 110 v, three lamps have to be used.' However, the revolutionary arrangement of the lamp shows how he was able to apply his ideas of spatial elemental composition to fittings as well as furniture and architecture. The interplay of lines and the clear articulation of individual elements is characteristic of the De Stijl movement to which Rietveld belonged. The lamp form was also highly influential: it was a likely source for the design of a similar tube lamp, which hung in the office of Walter Gropius at the Bauhaus school in Dessau. Two original versions of Rietveld's lamp are in the collections of the Stedelijk Museum, Amsterdam and Centraal Museum, Utrecht.

Hanging Lamp (1922)
Gerrit Rietveld (1888–1964)
Van Ommen Electricien 1922 to 1923
Tecta (licenced by Cassina) 1986 to present

Indian 1348"

1948 MODEL OF
...'S FINEST MOTORCYCLE
...OFFERING
...RTANT IMPROVEMENTS

It is no accident that European motorcycles are short, quick handling and sporty, while their American counterparts are long, somewhat lumbering, and possessing handling characteristics that can best be described as ponderous. A quick comparison of the terrain characteristics shows Europe to be a mass of narrow, winding roads, while a glance at any map of the United States shows long, straight roads, that go on and on, seemingly forever. So there is an irony in the fact that America's iconic cruiser, the Indian Chief, was designed by an Irish design engineer, Charles Franklin. Franklin had been brought from Dublin to the Indian factory in Springfield, Massachusetts, partly because of his record as an Indian racer, but largely because of his reputation as an engineer. He worked a miracle at Indian, designing a new side-valve engine that started out at 600cc for the Scout in 1920, and was bumped up to 989cc for the first Chief in 1922. Reliable and powerful, Franklin's engine was the core of the Indian for thirty years, and established his reputation as one of the great figures of American automotive design. Engine aside, what distinguishes the Chief among the throng of American cruisers is its ineffable style. Where its competitor, the Harley-Davidson 'Knucklehead', was all muscle and grunt, the Chief, with its flowing lines, its wide-brimmed saddle, and the glorious, skirted fenders of its final years, seemed like a dandy, a boulevardier for the open road. This fugitive spirit is the very heart and soul of American popular culture. The Indian Chief, a perfect evocation of the cowboy's horse in mechanical form, is the bike on which to ride to the horizon and beyond. The Chief remained in production for thirty-one years, until the demise of the great Indian name in 1953.

Alma Siedhoff-Buscher

These Bauhaus Bauspiel (Bauhaus Building Blocks) are part of a collection of Bauhaus toys developed during the 1920s. The set consists of 22 wooden pieces of different shapes, sizes and colours. They were carefully designed to stimulate children's imaginations through exploring the unlimited combinations of forms and colours available. Now made by Naef Spiele, a Swiss company renowned for educational toys, each piece is cut from wood and coated with non-toxic paint. Following the original specification, the pieces are painted in beautiful shades of red, blue, green and yellow as well as white. Alma Siedhoff-Buscher included white because 'white heightens the cheerful colours and the pleasure of the children'. The proportional relationships between the parts, from the biggest, ark-shaped block (25 cm/10 in long) to the smallest flat square (2 cm/1 in), allows them to be fitted together in infinite combinations to make a boat, a house, a bridge or anything at all. It is interesting to see that whatever is made, it appears to be original and meaningful. When no longer in use, the pieces can be packed away in the beautifully labelled cardboard box.

Siedhoff-Buscher was involved with the Bauhaus between 1922 and 1927. Along with Marianne Brandt of the metal workshop, she was one of only a few women to be successful at the Bauhaus outside the textile workshop. She believed strongly in the educational impact design could have on children, and all her early work was in this area. She rejected fairy tales as 'an unnecessary burden for small brains' and tried to create toys that were 'clear and specific' and 'as harmonious as possible' in their proportions. The blocks were created after she had designed a children's room and furniture for the

Bauhaus exhibition of 1923. Siedhoff-Buscher died prematurely, killed during a bombing raid during World War II, but her Bauspiel design continues to fascinate not only children but adults as well.

Bauhaus Bauspiel (1923)
Alma Siedhoff-Buscher (1899–1944)
Bauhaus Metallwerkstatt 1924
Naef Spiele 1977 to present

The second oldest toy in the world, after the doll, the yo-yo's classic design and versatility has preserved its popularity over the past 2,500 years. The yo-yo is almost as old as the wheel itself. In ancient Greece it was made of terracotta and painted with decorative images of gods. By the 1800s the yo-yo had travelled the world from the East to Europe where Prince Louis XVII and even Napoleon had reportedly toyed with one, possibly as a means of relieving stress. In the 1920s the word 'yo-yo' first gained recognition when Pedro Flores, from the Philippines, started the Flores Yo-Yo Company and began making and selling the yo-yo on the streets of California. The name 'yo-yo' was coined because it is a Filipino term meaning 'come-come'. Flores's yo-yo was made from two rounded halves of wood connected by an axle to which a string was tied, allowing it to roll up and down. In 1929 the technological revolution of the yo-yo began with the introduction of a looped slip-string. This allowed it to 'sleep' or spin continuously at the end of the string for the

Pedro Flores demonstrating the yo-yo, c.1930

first time. That same year the entrepreneur Donald F Duncan bought and trademarked the yo-yo and began a series of competitions and events, thus launching the yo-yo craze. In the 1950s Duncan introduced the first plastic model and the Butterfly yo-yo. The Butterfly allowed the player to catch the yo-yo on the string, essential for complex tricks. Tricks such as 'Walk the Dog' where the yo-yo rolls along the ground behind the user, the string acting as a 'leash' and 'Around the World', in which the player swings the yo-yo around in an orbital-like motion, began to catch on and sales continued spinning upwards. Flambeau Products, manufacturers of the plastic yo-yo, purchased the Duncan name in 1968 and continue to produce it today. The 1990s saw a resurgence of the yo-yo's popularity when, in addition to new light and sound effects, technological advancements such as high-performance axles, rim weighting and Brake Pad Technology put a new spin on yo-yo design. From the original design to the recent high-performance models, the yo-yo remains one of the most popular toys in history.

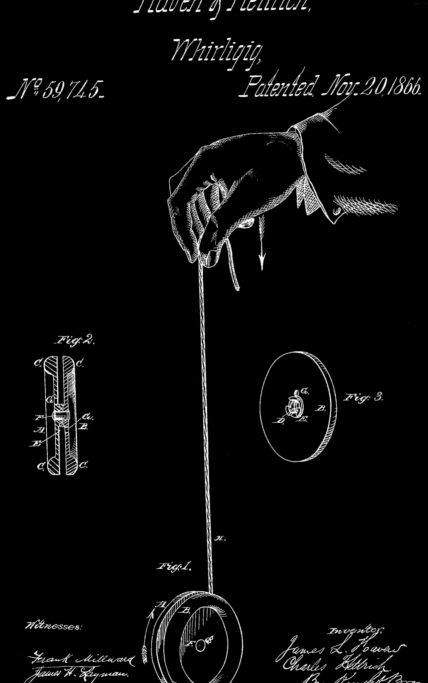

Haven & Hettrich,

Whirligig,

Nº 59,745.

Patented Nov. 20, 1866.

Fig. 2.

Fig. 3.

Fig. 1.

Witnesses:
Frank Millward
James H. Layman.

Inventor:
James L. Haven
Charles Hettrich
By Knight Bros
Attys.

AM. PHOTO-LITHO. CO. N.Y. (OSBORNE'S PROCESS)

Walter Gropius

This Door Handle is one of the first truly mass-produced door handles, with a clear, distinctive design, and is one of the defining fittings of Modernism, designed by Walter Gropius and Adolf Meyer. Its conception came as a direct expression of the modernist ideals of Gropius, who was one of the founders of the Bauhaus in Dessau, Germany, the most important institution during the early modern period of architecture. The Bauhaus itself advocated the use of mass-production techniques in architecture and design, and maintained a firm belief in the power of new technology to improve society and the lives of ordinary people. The Bauhaus celebrated the idea of the *Gesamtkunstwerk,* which meant that the architect should control the aesthetics of every element of the building, from structure to furniture to fittings. The Door Handle was created in 1923 to be part of the design for

136

Gro D23 E NI Door Handle (1923)
Walter Gropius (1883–1969)
Adolf Meyer (1881–1929)
Bauhaus Metallwerkstatt 1923 to 1933
S A Loevy 1923 to 1933
Tecnoline 1984 to present

the Faguswerk shoe factory in Alfeld an der Leine, Germany. Created by Gropius and Meyer in 1911, the building was considered a pioneering design, comprising a 'glass envelope' on a classical brick and concrete structure. The Door Handle went on to feature in the Dessau Bauhaus building itself. It was a geometric, abstract design consisting of a cylindrical handle, which joined an orthogonal section that met a small square door plate. German historian Siegfried Gronert called it 'the first mass-produced handle consciously designed with a primary stereometric form.' The material was polished nickel-plated steel, and the Berlin company S A Loevy began manufacturing it that same year. Versions were also available with long door plates, and with a lock. The handle swiftly became well-known, and is still manu-factured under license by Tecnoline. The Door Handle is now in important design collections all over the world, including the permanent architecture gallery of the Victoria and Albert Musuem, in London.

In the years following its defeat in World War I, Germany might have been a vacuum of design talent and industrial innovation, but such institutions as the Bauhaus, founded in 1919, proved that new ideas, creativity, and aesthetics could prevail. Shortly after the war, BMW, a company which was a manufacturer of planes, began instead to produce automobiles and motorcycles. The change was a lucky one, because the best aeronautical design minds of the day turned their considerable skills to more earth-bound work. The best of these was Max Friz and he was the perfect man for the new design direction at BMW. One of the great designers of his day, Friz designed both the six- and twelve-cylinder aircraft engines that, between them, set a total of ninety-eight world records. There is an adage in the aircraft world that if a plane 'looks good, it flies good'. It might have been coined for the work of aeronautical designer Friz, who in his new role at BMW was charged to design BMW's second motorcycle, the R32. Not only does it look good, it worked so well that it set design and mechanical standards for BMW motorcycles that continue to this day. The influence of the Bauhaus on Friz's design is clear. There is wonderful fluid harmony between the circular shape on the wheel fenders and the triangles of the frame and tank. The shaft drive from gearbox to the rear wheel has become a signature of BMW, and is elegantly engineered on the R32. The transverse horizontal twin cylinder motor, nicknamed the 'boxer', was light, powerful and efficient. The R32 was an enormous success when it was introduced at the Paris Motorcycle Salon in 1923. In all, over 3,000 R32s were produced between 1923 and 1926, when production ended, thus guaranteeing BMW's reputation as a leading producer of motorcycles, a reputation that it holds to this day.

137

BMW R32 Motorcycle (1923)
Max Friz (1883-1966)
BMW 1923 to 1926

In the 1920s, a series of toys were designed at the Bauhaus to reflect a growing interest in the educational impact of good design on children. This Spinning Top or 'Optischer Farbmischer' was one such design. It consists of a wooden top with seven different 10 cm (4 in) discs made from cardboard. Each disc is printed with different colours and patterns, and has a small hole in the centre to insert the rod onto the spinning top. When the top is spun, each disc creates an interesting effect of mixed colours. Since 1977 the toy has been made by Naef Spiele, a Swiss company renowned for educational toys. Ludwig Hirschfeld-Mack came to study at the Bauhaus in 1920, where such figures as Johannes Itten, Paul Klee and Wassily Kandinsky were teaching pictorial form and colour theory. Itten in particular was a seminal influence on colour theory, having developed a colour wheel that transformed how colour was related to by, for example, describing blue-green hues as 'cold'. He formed a colour circle with seven contrasts, based on the emotional, psychological, religious, psychic and philosophical relations associated with each colour. Kandinsky's investigation into colour began with the three primaries, red, yellow and blue, and the elemental forms of circle, triangle and square. He asked Hirschfeld-Mack to co-organize the 'colour seminars' and together they developed a series of exercises to investigate the nature of colour, light and dark, black and white and the relationship between colour and form. This Spinning Top is a distillation of this research. Hirschfeld-Mack also investigated the connections between colour, light and music, and along with Itten, he is recognized as a pioneer of light art. Forced to flee Germany in 1936 because of his Jewish background, Hirschfeld-Mack went first to Britain and then in 1940 to Australia. There he began a successful and respected career as an art educator, spreading the Bauhaus principles of art and design to this continent. This Spinning Top is perhaps a suitable summation of his work and as such can be seen as symbolic of his achievements.

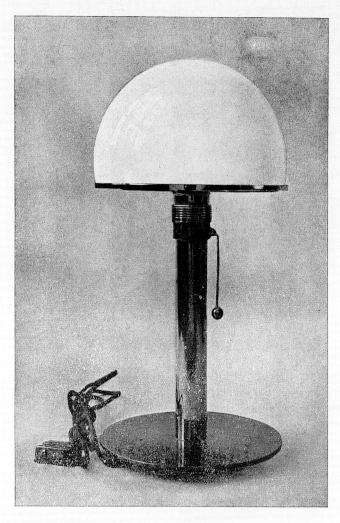

gesch.
Höhe ca. **35 cm**
AUSFÜHRUNG

Messing vernickelt, Glasschirm, Zugfassung

TISCHLAMPE AUS METALL

VORTEILE

1 beste Lichtzerstreuung (genau erprobt) mit Jenaer Schottglas
2 sehr stabil
3 einfachste, gefällige Form
4 praktisch für Schreibtisch, Nachttisch usw.
5 Glocke festgeschraubt, bleibt in jeder Lage unbeweglich

The MT 8 Table Lamp, often referred to as the Bauhaus Table Lamp, was first produced in the metals workshops of the Weimar Bauhaus under the guidance of László Moholy-Nagy. It was made of metal with an opaque glass shade, circular base and a glass shaft through which the electrical cable is visible. This distinctive design feature had been used by Carl Jacob Jucker (1907–97) in a number of lamp prototypes of 1923. Jucker's earlier lamps, which demonstrate the idea for the lamp's base and shaft but with different shades and bulb casings, were developed before Wilhelm Wagenfeld joined the Bauhaus in 1923. Wagenfeld, also given the task of designing lamp forms, developed the idea for the opaque glass shade edged with nickel-plated brass. The two design ideas were fused into one, and in some subsequent versions Wagenfeld replaced Jucker's glass shaft with a nickel-plated metal shaft, set into a metal base. The first versions of the lamps were handmade, using traditional craft techniques such as burnishing the metal plates by hand. At this stage the lamp was extremely expensive to produce. The workshop had difficulty in creating a glass shade that would not shatter from the heat of the bulb. The early versions also varied considerably in size. However, the basic arrangement of components never changed. 'A round plate, a cylindrical pipe and a spherical shade,' said Wagenfeld in 1924, 'are its most important components.' With modifications, the lamp continued to be produced by the Bauhaus, Dessau, until the late 1920s, when the licence to produce Bauhaus lamps was passed to Schwintzer and Gräff until 1930. The subsequent history of the copyrighted design is highly complex. Wagenfeld appears to have obtained the copyright from the Bauhaus, and a version of the metal lamp with a smaller base and a reduced dome was produced under his name. Similarly, Jucker licensed a version of his lamp to an Italian manufacturer in the 1970s. Added to this, many replicas and plagiarized versions have come on the market since its first production. Despite this claim to ubiquity, the original MT 8 was never produced in large quantities, and its enduring history is as a museum piece and collector's item. An exclusive licensed nickel-plated version, granted by Wagenfeld, is now produced by Tecnolumen.

MT 8 Table Lamp (1923–4)
Wilhelm Wagenfeld (1900–90)
Bauhaus Metallwerkstatt Weimar 1924
Bauhaus Metallwerkstatt Dessau 1925
to 1927
Schwintzer and Gräff 1928 to 1930
Wilhelm Wagenfeld & Architekturbedorf
1930 to 1933
Tecnolumen 1980 to present

In Germany a *Meisterstück* is a kind of final-year project for a young craftsman, marking (if good enough) his or her transition from apprentice to master. As such, it is an extravagant title for something as simple as a pen, yet the Mont Blanc Meisterstück 149 has cleverly managed to fulfil the prophecy of its name to become not only Mont Blanc's most successful product, but for more than eighty years now, a powerful global icon representing luxury, tradition, culture and power. Each pen is individually crafted rather than mass-produced, and can be specially tailored to the user's desires with various point sizes and ranges of flexibility in the nib. The pen itself is 148 mm (5.8 in) long by 16 mm (0.63 in) in diameter – a sleek torpedo of polished black resin circled with bands of gold. A white star on the tip of the cap represents the snow cap and six glacial valleys of Mont Blanc. The height of the mountain in metres, 4810, is inscribed amongst decorative swirls on the pen's 18 carat hand-ground gold nib, each one hand-tested by individual craftsmen. The name of the pen is also etched into the widest gold-plated band of the three iconic gold rings found on the cap. People say the Meisterstück 149 is the epitome of elegance, with its heavy shiny black resin barrel highlighted by the gold rings and clip. Its fans talk of the warmth and individuality of the pen, the way its flexible nib, with platinum inlay, adapts to the owner's writing style like a pair of leather shoes. The company was founded in Hamburg, Germany, in 1906 under the much less evocative name, Simplo Filler Pen Company. The name Montblanc was registered in 1911, although it was not until 1924 that the company began producing particular lines of pens and the Meisterstück 149 was issued. The pen has changed little over the years – a specially developed resin has replaced the original celluloid and ballpoint models and a highlighter pen has even been introduced, but functionally and aesthetically the design has endured, making it a true legend.

Mont Blanc Meisterstück 149 (1924)
Mont Blanc Design Team
Mont Blanc 1924 to present

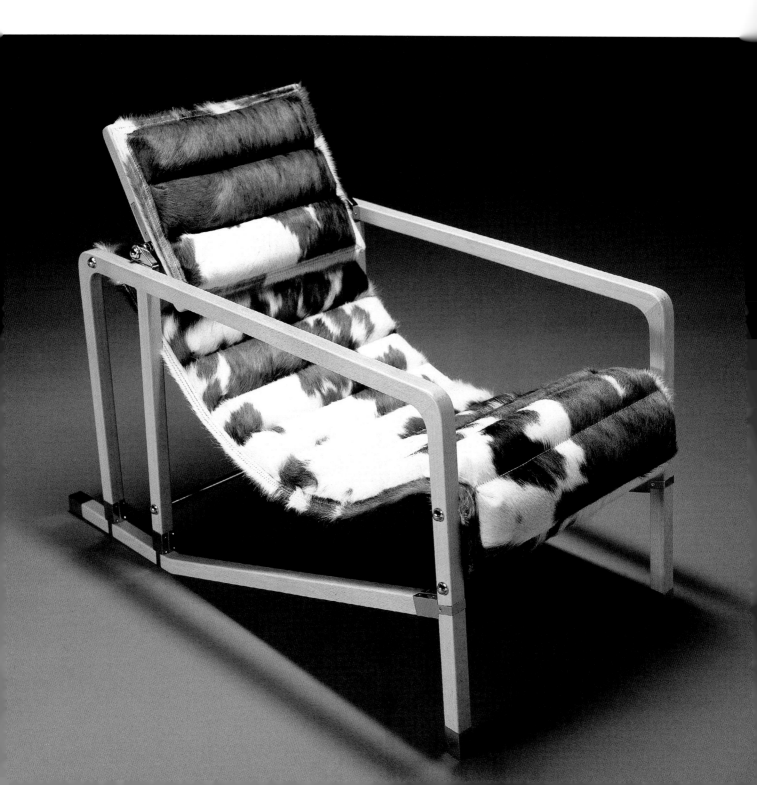

Though based in Paris, Irish-born designer Eileen Gray was already taking an interest in the Dutch De Stijl movement's pure geometric forms by the time she turned to architecture in the mid-1920s. Teaming up with architecture critic Jean Badovici, she designed her own modernist house, E1027, by the Mediterranean at Roquebrune in France. It was for this house that she conceived a number of individual items of furniture, including the Transat Armchair. Appropriately for a chair in a house located at the water's edge, the Transat plays with the form of the deckchair – known as a *transatlantique* in French, hence the name. The chair also demonstrates a typically idiosyncratic fusion of the then popular Art Deco style and the functionalism espoused by the Bauhaus and De Stijl, which Gray had come into contact with while exhibiting work in Amsterdam in 1922. Functionalism is suggested by the angular frame, whose lacquered wood is at the same time a nod to Art Deco. Gray learned lacquering from Seizo Sugawara, whose apprentice she became in Paris, and perfected the skill which changes the furniture's surface and provides the illusion of various layers. Certainly, comfort was Gray's priority and she remained suspicious of any approach that was preoccupied only with form. The frame could be disassembled, and its wooden rods were joined with chromed metal fittings. The headrest was adjustable and the seat was pliable, slung low and suspended from the lacquered wooden frame. Black leather and lacquer were used for the Transats appearing in E 1027, though versions in other colours were sold through Gray's Paris shop, Galerie Jean Désert. At this time, Gray's designs were relatively expensive to produce and not intended for mass production and only twelve editions were originally made. Two of these were specially commissioned by the Maharaja of Indore, for which a special glue had to be applied to the wooden pieces in order to withstand the heat. There was also an authorized copy of Transat for the painter Frank Stella, by Max Ott. The chair was originally patented in 1930, yet it was not until 1986 that the Transat Armchair received wider attention through a reproduction from Écart International. This triggered a renewed interest in Gray's work, which had initially been stimulated by both critics and collectors.

Marianne Brandt

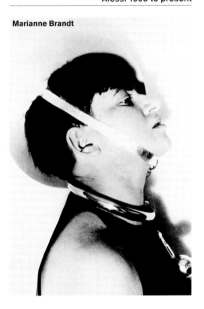

Marianne Brandt is best remembered today for the numerous designs that she produced during her time in the metal workshop at the Bauhaus. She worked under the tutelage of László Moholy-Nagy, who took over from Johannes Itten as director of the workshop in the summer of 1923. As one of six people, Brandt thrived in the creative environment of the workshop, producing nearly seventy products at the Bauhaus's Weimar and Dessau sites in Germany. Along with her peers in Weimar, Brandt began experimenting with geometric forms as the creative starting point for her tableware and lighting designs, inspired by Cubism, De Stijl and Constructivism. Elementary forms such as spheres, cylinders, circles, and hemispheres were considered easy to mass produce at a time when industrial processes were still insufficiently understood. Conceived as sections of circles and spheres, the base, body, lid, and cigarette balance of this Ashtray are each clearly defined and constructed with mathematical exactitude. Brandt was passionate about metal, especially steel, aluminium, and silver, and her energetic experi-mentation gave rise to the unusual combination of different metals in the same product, as this brass and part nickel-plated Ashtray and her equally influential Teapot of 1924 exemplify. While most creations were handmade in the workshop, Brandt and her contemporaries were unveiling products that coupled materials from industry with a mass-produced aesthetic. The teams were achieving refined simplicity of form that consumed minimum materials and labour time, and providing an economic role model for mass production. Indeed, between 1928 and 1932, Brandt led the metal workshop to financial success by securing suitable manufacturers for several of its designs, namely lighting. In 1933, Brandt returned to her parents and chose to live a private life painting. She died in 1983, and it was only in 1985 that her name and designs became well known when the Italian manufacturer, Alessi, reissued certain products on licence from the Bauhaus Archiv in Berlin, including this Ashtray.

Walter & Ise Gropius sitting in living room of their house, Dessau, 1927

ges. gesch.

AUSFÜHRUNG

Silber, Neusilber, Messing vernickelt.

TEEKUGEL

ME
3

VORTEILE:

1 Jeder macht sich seinen Tee so stark wie er will!
2 sauberes Öffnen, leichtes Einfüllen, sicheres Schließen
3 bequeme Reinigung
4 einfache, handliche Form.

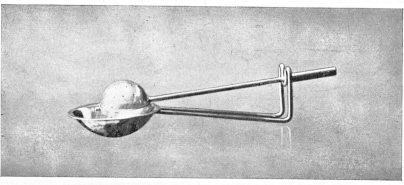

ges. gesch.

AUSFÜHRUNG

Silber, Neusilber, Messing vernickelt.

TEEKUGELHALTER

ME
4

VORTEILE

1 saubere und sichere Lagerung der Kugel
2 schützt den Teetisch vor Flecken
3 Geringe Raumbeanspruchung.

The early twentieth century witnessed a tension in German manufacturing between two fundamental positions: one, rooted in the English Arts and Crafts movement, aspired to goods imbued with the artist's personality and craftsmanship, while the other was dedicated to rational blueprints for mass manufacturing. This dichotomy would spill over into the workshops of the Bauhaus from 1919. Seeking a unity between art, handiwork and industry, the school's training initially favoured applied arts, with students moving from a preliminary course based on free experimentation with form, colour and materials to specialized work in one of the various workshops. The arrival of the Hungarian László Moholy-Nagy to run the metal workshop in 1923 signalled an abrupt change of direction there and Rittweger and Knau's design is a good example of the results. Out went predecessor Johannes Itten's preoccupation with spirituality and philosophy, along with handicraft materials like silver, wood and clay, and in came an emphasis on functionality and pragmatism, expressed in materials such as tubular and sheeted steel, plywood and industrial glass. Moholy-Nagy saw the machine as a democratizing force, rather than the threat to humanity perceived by the Bauhaus's artists. He even communicated his intent in his appearance, preferring simple industrial overalls to the more rarefied image Itten cultivated with his flowing robes. The clean-lined, simple shape of Rittweger and Knau's Tea Infusers and Stand, which was nickel-plated, expresses the sobriety that replaced what one student described as the 'spiritual samovars and intellectual doorknobs' of the old workshop. The new approach would help the school generate much-needed income through commissions and by selling designs and patents rather than by producing expensive one-offs. At the time the Tea Infusers and Stand were produced, work was being geared to trade fairs and exhibitions. The design has been reproduced, but today it is manufactured in stainless steel.

1·43

Tea Infusers and Stand (1924)
Otto Rittweger (1904-65)
Josef Knau (1897–1945)
Bauhaus Metallwerkstatt 1924
Alessi 1995 to present

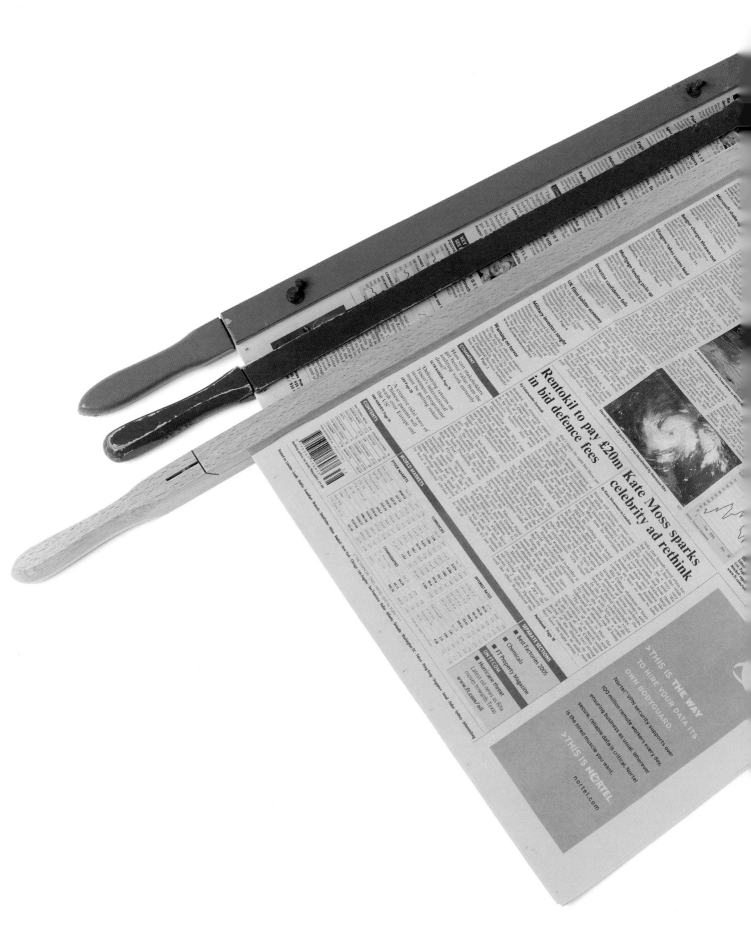

The Newspaper Holder initially appeared more than two centuries ago in coffee houses in Germany and Switzerland, but became forever associated with the Viennese coffee house culture in Austria at the end of the nineteenth and the beginning of the twentieth century. It was a ubiquitous object and therefore numerous designs were patented in the early part of the twentieth century. The design of the holder today is centred on two elongated wooden sticks that slide open to reveal four nails placed inside, which grip the newspaper once closed. This version, by Fritz Hahne, one of the earliest and only manufacturers still producing holders, is based on a variety of designs. Each design over the years has been slightly different: some have two wing-nut screws at either end, which open to allow a small gap, others have a hinge at one end so that one side opens. Yet despite these differences in design, all versions shared the key aim of easing the activity of reading a newspaper, a format known for its awkwardness. The company founded by Fritz Hahne, is a family-run business and still produces the holders in pine. They are sold almost exclusively to newspaper publishers in Germany, Switzerland, Austria, the Netherlands and Belgium, imprinted with the insignia of each various newspaper. Recently, Kuno Prey revisited the design because he felt that the sticks would sometimes hide part of the text in the paper. Prey came up with a design that holds either magazines or newspapers between three round bars, and Alessi has been producing this since 1996.

STAATL. BAUHAUS zu WEIMAR
MEISTER JOSEF HARTWIG
NEUE SCHACHSPIELE
GES. GESCHÜTZT

XIV

Chess Set (1924)
Josef Hartwig (1880–1955)
Bauhaus Metallwerkstatt 1924
Naef Spiele 1981 to present

Josef Hartwig

While the exact origin of chess is not known, it is first mentioned in the sixth-century Persian manuscript, *Shahnama* ('Book of Kings'), among gifts sent by an Indian rajah to Shah Khusrau Nushirwan, a Persian king. The manuscript details the character of the game's pieces and the way in which the game was played. With relatively minor differences, chess has since remained the same representation of great powers on a battlefield, played to test one's intellectual agility. In the 1,500 years since then the chess board and players have been developed around the world and have mutated through every period. So great was the variation that a stylistically reductive set designed by Howard Staunton was selected by the World Chess Federation in 1924 for use in all international tournaments. That year also brought the design of one of the most elegant versions of the chess set, encapsulating the aesthetic concerns of the first two decades of the century. From the Bauhaus sculpture workshop, Josef Hartwig designed the set itself, and out of the joinery workshop came the corresponding chess table by Heinz Nösselt. Hartwig embraced modernist principles, rejecting the figure in favour of a formalist adherence to function. Their pieces were simply constructed of geometric forms, and were conceived as a graphic representation of the ways in which various pieces might move across the chess board's sixty-four squares. Made of pear wood in its natural colour or stained black, cubes move horizontally or vertically, X's move diagonally and polygons indicate more complex movement possibilities. The king, represented by a cube topped by another diagonally placed cube, is able to move in all directions, with certain limitations, while the queen, a cube topped by a sphere, may move freely, without boundaries, as indicated by the sphere's lack of borders. Originally manufactured by the sculpture studio at the Weimar Bauhaus, Hartwig's set is still being produced by Naef Spiele, a manufacturer of toys.

Small and precisely made,

the Leica was unlike any of its contemporaries. The rounded corners of the body and top plate containing all the camera made for easy and discreet picture taking. The pull-out lens permitted easy carrying while retaining excellent optical quality. The Leica was not the first 35 mm camera, but it was the culmination of a long period of gestation by its designer and it became the first commercially successful 35 mm hand camera. Oskar Barnack was brought from the German optical city of Jena to work for the Leitz company in 1911 and began work on developing a cine camera. This led to the development of a camera taking single pictures using movie film, and by 1913 a prototype camera, the later-named Ur-Leica, had been designed and built. After World War I, as the Leitz company searched for new products to improve its financial base, the Ur-Leica

was improved and a run of thirty-one cameras produced. The decision to produce the Leica camera commercially was taken after much discussion in 1925 and the Leica I camera was launched at the Leipzig Spring Fair. The Leica design brought together a number of different developments into one camera. Advances in film emulsion meant that the small 24 × 36 mm negative was able to hold its own against larger roll film and plate negatives. The Leica was supplied with a new lens designed by Max Berek, using new optical glasses with better refracting power. Soon after, the camera was offered with a range of inter-changeable lenses and accessories, making it a 'system' camera suitable for many different applications. Although the camera was expensive, it quickly found favour among professional photographers and amateurs. The Leica I design was continually updated, and Barnack's basic

design continued with refinements until the Leica IIIg of 1957. In 1954 the Leica was redesigned, with the introduction of the Leica M3. The M3 was substantially re-engineered internally, with the most obvious benefit being the use of quick-changing bayonet-fitting lenses. A Leica single-lens reflex range was introduced with the Leicaflex in 1965, but this had much less success and was far removed from Barnack's original concept of the Leica as a compact and easy-to-handle camera. The early Leicas and M-series cameras established a reputation as a camera for photo-journalists, and they were championed by Erich Salomon, Bert Hardy, Henri Cartier-Bresson, Leni Riefenstahl and David Duncan Douglas among many others.

1·46

Leica I (1925)
Oskar Barnack (1879–1936)
Leica Camera 1925 to 1932

The Wassily Chair is Marcel Breuer's most important and iconic design. The sitter is offered all-encompassing support whilst being virtually suspended within this tubular frame, which acts as a modernist interpretation of the club chair. The relatively complex tubular steel frame was designed to provide comfort without the traditional timber, spring and horsehair seating construction of the period. The use of Eisengard upholstery 'straps' and tubular steel was part of a revolutionary movement to create mass-produced 'equipment' for modern living; designs that were to be affordable, hygienic, light and strong. Marcel Breuer designed the Wassily in 1925, having apparently been inspired by the fine frame of a newly purchased bicycle. The result followed studies in timber furniture at the Bauhaus and formed part of his project to furnish the apartment of painter Wassily Kandinsky. It was a bold and unprecedented design that inspired architects and designers throughout Europe. Breuer went on to produce a considerable number of furniture designs in tubular steel. Later, after he fled Germany, Breuer worked in several other materials including aluminium and plywood. Although subsequent seating designs were important and remain historically relevant, the Wassily encapsulates the key attributes of tubular steel furniture. The Wassily was reintroduced in 1962 by Gavina, which was then taken over by Knoll in 1968 and produced as part of Knoll International's collection of classics. This anticipation of the longevity of prewar designs as 'classics' of the future was a cornerstone in the cementing of the chair as an emblematic design for corporate and domestic interiors. The Wassily remains part of the Knoll collection today and has endured changing stylistic tastes through the postwar period. Produced with leather upholstery, its attachment to the slick, high-value office foyer has unfairly compromised the democracy of the original design. With its origins, often confused with the high-tech movement of the late 1970s, the Wassily continues to maintain a highly relevant position in modern seating.

Wassily Chair (1925)
Marcel Breuer (1902–81)
Standard-Möbel 1926 to 1928
Gebrüder Thonet 1928 to 1932
Gavina/Knoll 1962 to present

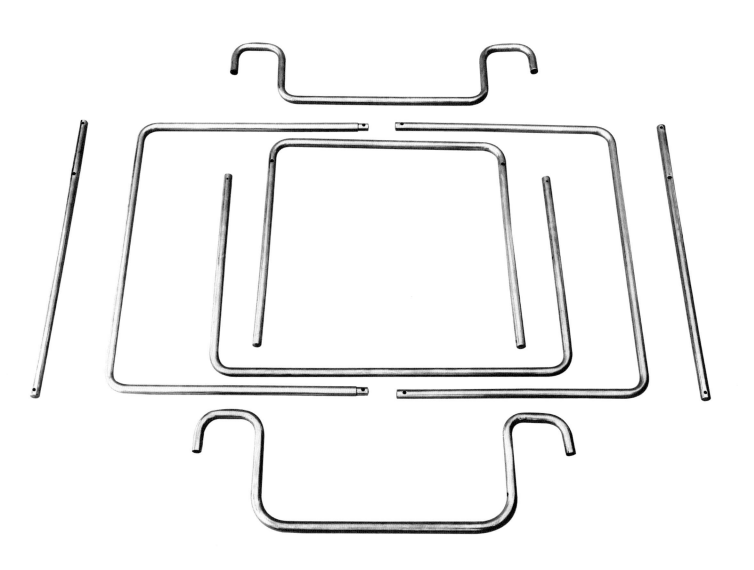

Ise Gropius with a theatre mask by Oskar Schlemmer,
photographed by Erich Consemüller, 1926

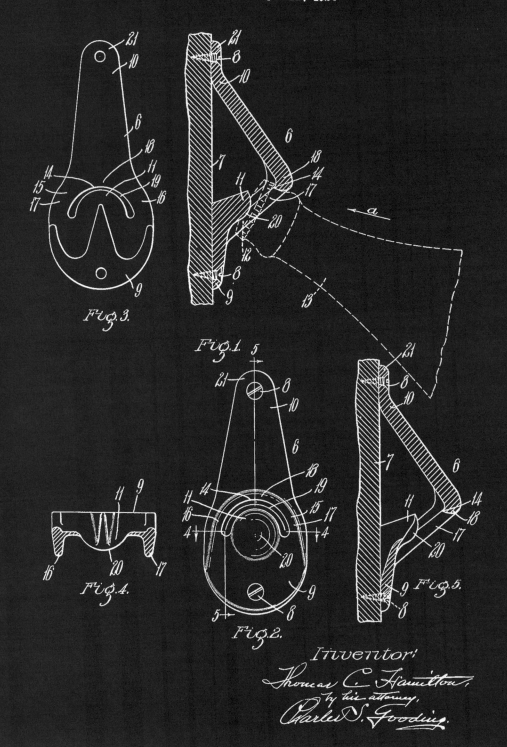

Fig.3.

Fig.1.

Fig.4.

Fig.2.

Fig.5.

Inventor:
Thomas C. Hamilton,
by his attorney,
Charles S. Gooding.

As a man who had made his fortune bottling and distributing Coca Cola, Raymond Brown would have been familiar with one of the key drawbacks of glass containers: they chip and break, especially while being opened. So when a failed attempt to manufacture recording equipment left him with some spare factory capacity, it is hardly surprising that he offered it to Thomas C Hamilton, who had developed a wall-mounted bottle opener that was guaranteed not to chip the bottle neck. Hamilton's opener consisted of a small plaque with a hole for it to be screwed to the wall. Over this was an eyelid-like hood that gripped the outer edge of the bottle cap, and beneath the hood was a small metal protuberance that pressed against the middle of the cap. The top of the bottle was inserted under the hood at a 45 degree angle, and then pushed towards the vertical; as the hood gripped the edge of the cap and levered it against the central protuberance, the cap was prised off. The design is simple enough, requiring only one cast and containing no moving parts. Its early success, however, was more to do with canny marketing. Firstly, the new opener was presented to luxury hotels not just as a way of opening bottles but as a way of preventing the damage caused to rooms by their occupants banging metal bottle caps against doors and furniture. Earlier models of the opener included a razor strap hook for the same reason, so that hotel patrons would not drive hooks into walls. But perhaps the real secret behind the desirability and lasting appeal of the opener as a collectable is its hood. The hood provided a perfect eye-level space for branding and, rather than putting any Starr logo there, it was left open for buyers to insert their own. The result is that hundreds, if not thousands, of separate designs of the same item exist, each unique. And over the years the logos and devices embossed onto the opener have not been limited to beer and soda companies; patriotic imagery, college sports teams, proverbs, witticisms and the simple instruction, 'open here', have all appeared.

Made from clear, colourless glass, the geometrically inspired shape of the Martini Glass is a drinking vessel as iconic as the cocktail it was designed to celebrate. It is so well executed that no one has yet succeeded in improving on the original, nor are they likely to in the future. The decisive outline of the glass, comprising a straight-flared V-shaped cup supported by a tall stem and an elegantly proportioned base, is now the kingpin of cocktail motifs. Yet, despite its fame, the precise origins of the Martini Glass remain difficult to establish. It is known to have originated during the mid-1920s, born from the changing currents influencing both high-class entertaining and the glassware designed to maintain it. Around this time, tastes in cocktails were moving away from the extravagances of the early 1920s towards a refined simplicity exemplified by the Martinis and Manhattans already being consumed by a dynamic following. As these cocktails reflected the shift in taste, decorative glassware gave way to a streamlined modernism. These new glasses were decidedly avant-garde, and specifically, the Martini Glass was a geometrically refined variation on the saucer-shaped champagne glass, which had replaced the flute at the turn of the century. What catapulted the design from its esoteric origins, enjoyed by a discerning few, to mainstream success was the evolution of the home cocktail set. The Martini and its associated cocktail paraphernalia were depicted on film, in café culture, and in print. Soon to capitalize were the marketing minds at the large-scale manufacturers, designing the Martini set as an accessible domestic alternative for a society feeling the effects of the Depression. The sleek cocktail shakers, stirrers, sieves and Martini glasses that went to make up these sets were bought in large volumes and provided a glimpse of the lifestyle enjoyed by the New York and Hollywood Hills social elite. Katherine Hepburn embodied this glamour not only in life, but on screen in *Philadelphia*. Both the Martini and the Martini Glass were then established in the mainstream as symbols of a new-found modernism. The Martini Glass remains cemented as an icon of 1920s glassware: accessible, instantly recognizable and endlessly revisited by illustrators, artists, filmmakers and the like.

Katherine Hepburn and James Stewart in *The Philadelphia Story* (1940), directed by George Cukor

Bauhaus Cocktail Shaker (1925)
Sylvia Stave (1908–94)
C G Hallbergs Company 1925 to 1930
Alessi 1989 to present

This Cocktail Shaker, a perfect sphere with a looped arc handle, was produced in the metal workshop of the Bauhaus when it was under the direction of László Moholy-Nagy, at the height of the school's revolutionary aesthetic and social agenda. Postwar German design was a reaction against prewar luxury, and the socialist ideals of the Bauhaus informed its desire to create a new language of design suitable for the machine age. Stripped of its cultural and social associations, this shaker became a statement of the new order. The design was commonly believed to by Marianne Brandt, but, after much research by Peter Hahn, director of the Bauhaus Archiv, it is now attributed to Sylvia Stave. It is as far from the traditional form of the cocktail shaker as it is possible to achieve. Firstly, it is horizontal rather than vertical: in searching for fresh forms, the Bauhaus looked to a new language of squares, circles and straight lines. Uncompromising and geometric in its form, this was a wildly innovative piece that pushed the limits of metal manufacturing at the time. In 1989 it was reintroduced by Alessi under licence from the Bauhaus Archive, proving its enduring style. Its seamless metal sphere, now produced in mirror-polished 18/10 stainless steel instead of the original nickel-plated version, is still a difficult object to produce, requiring two halves of the orb to be stamped separately then welded together and polished by hand. The resulting mirrored sphere is undeniably beautiful and enhances the idea of containing and pouring, treating its contents as a precious liquid. While there is a removable strainer hidden under the stopper for ease of pouring, it suffers from a common Bauhaus flaw in that it confuses geometry with functionality. It is more an object of admiration than one to use; an iconic piece that represents the gigantic leap that the Bauhaus made in the language of form. In its design language, with its languorous looped handle, the shaker represents more a static object than one that is shaken. And it is questionable how far a cocktail shaker could be considered the most appropriate contribution to a new order of mass production. It was objects such as this that opened the Bauhaus up to accusations of being 'just another style', although this shaker's style has gained momentum through the years.

Following a tradition that dates back to the Middle Ages, all Le Creuset Cast Iron Cookware is made from enamelled cast iron. Based at Fresnoy-Le-Grand, in northern France, the Le Creuset factory began producing cast iron in 1925. This was originally done by hand-casting molten iron in sand moulds. The process was extremely delicate and, even when using a similar technique today, each mould is destroyed prior to the cookware being polished and sanded by hand. Le Creuset cookware enjoys an enduring success and popularity. It is practical and utilitarian in style and material, and its reputation is a result of high standards in traditional manufacturing techniques and the quality and suitability of the materials used. The cast iron has a double enamel coating that, due to its extreme firing process of 800°C (1470° F), makes the pans hard and durable and virtually resistant to damage through everyday use. This process of production, which has been developed and refined over years, has meant that Le Creuset cookware has a name for both quality and hard-wearing endurance. Its simplicity of form and design combined with its construction and innovative use of materials have ensured Le Creuset cookware's reputation. The porcelain-enamelled cast iron spreads heat evenly, retains heat longer and does not react to acidic foods. This, combined with the precise, tight-fitting lid, forms a blanket of heat that cooks food gently. The material allows the pans to be used on all heat sources and reassures the consumer that the investment made in the pans will endure any change in stove or cooker. A favourite of cooks, the cast iron is energy-efficient, and as much of the finishing is done by hand, each Le Creuset Cast Iron Cookware piece is completely unique. Available in a range of colours, including blue, green, orange and red, Le Creuset Cookware has become a symbol for home cooking, quality and the culture of the kitchen as central to domestic life.

Although Eileen Gray designed buildings, she had no formal architectural training, and her work concentrated on a small number of highly influential interiors. She would design custom-made furniture, hand-woven carpets and lighting to create exclusive interiors for wealthy, forward-thinking clients. Progressive in her outlook, her iconic designs possessed an almost alchemical flair with materials and structure. Her Bibendum Chair was created in 1925–6 to furnish Madame Mathieu-Lévy's apartment in rue de Lota, Paris, and finally achieved the recognition it deserved when Zeev Aram, a London-based furniture company, put some of Gray's archive back into production in the 1970s. Aram Designs now holds a sub-license for all of Gray's works, and it is only with this license that her pieces were and still put into production. The chair was named after 'Bibendum, the living tyre', the mascot created in 1898 by the poster artist O'Galop for the tyre company Michelin. The rounded form of the cheerful giant was echoed in the armchair. The leather-clad chair, with its distinctive tubular upholstered form housed within a chrome-plated tubular steel frame, was an opulent, luxurious approach to modernist aesthetic concerns. Unlike her contemporaries and colleagues such as Le Corbusier, Gray did not share a rigid aesthetic preoccupation with machine-age Functionalism. Instead, she used the Bauhaus-inspired Functionalism emanating from Germany, and fused it with the more sumptuous materiality of Art Deco. Gray's furniture designs were never intended for even limited mass production, and were expensively hand-built in her Paris workshop. Because of this, her designs remained elitist and relatively unknown until they were reissued, when they finally gained the widespread influence and appreciation they undoubtedly deserved. Her voluptuous leather and tubular steel Bibendum Chair is now a familiar icon of the International Style. Unfairly neglected for most of her considerable career, Eileen Gray is now recognized as one of the most influential designers and architects of the early twentieth century. She was almost unique in the 1920s and 1930s as a successful, practising female designer in the male-dominated world of architecture and design.

152

Bibendum Chair (1925–6)
Eileen Gray (1879–1976)
Aram Designs 1975 to present
Vereinigte Werkstätten 1984 to 1990
ClassiCon 1990 to present

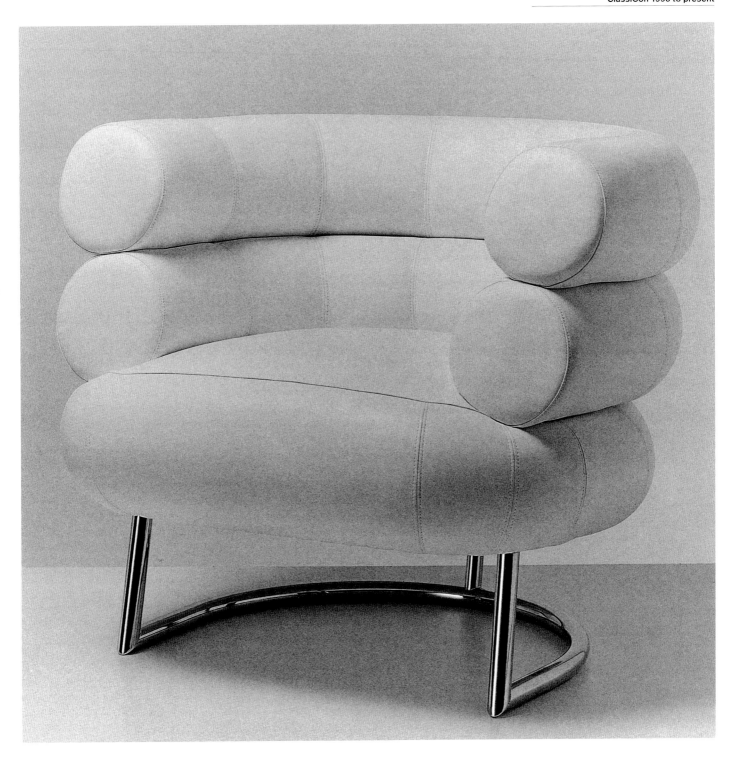

Marianne Brandt's Tea and Coffee Service is an iconic example of the progressive teachings of the Bauhaus. University lecturers and curators pay regular homage to it, and collectors are frustrated by the fact that there remains only one complete original set. Comprising Kettle, Teapot, Coffee Pot, Sugar Bowl, Cream Jug and Tray, the set is made from 925/1000 silver with ebony details. The basic geometric forms of the circle and the square from which the ensemble is constructed lend the design a feeling of strength, born of a well-defined profile. The Teapot gives an initial impression of stoicism mixed with serious intent, which in turn yields an almost accidental beauty. Supported by a low stand made of two straight cross members, the elegantly polished bowl rounds upwards to half its potential height, only to be stopped short and squared off, forming a clean, decisive surface. A tall silver handle incorporating an inlaid grip of dark ebony arcs up and over the lid continuing the curve of the bowl beneath. The handle can move left and right over the lid, joining the back of the teapot with a hinge that juts out from the lid. The circular lid sits in relief on the pot and has an ebony handle, a small elliptical lip that mirrors the rise and fall of the pot handle above. The only woman to work in the Bauhaus metal workshop, Marianne Brandt was a versatile designer in the spirit of the Bauhaus, becoming known for her adjustable metal lamps, paintings and witty photomontages. Her Tea and Coffee Service is a classic example of the Bauhaus philosophy that emphasizes manual working practices and where form is determined by the intended use of the piece.

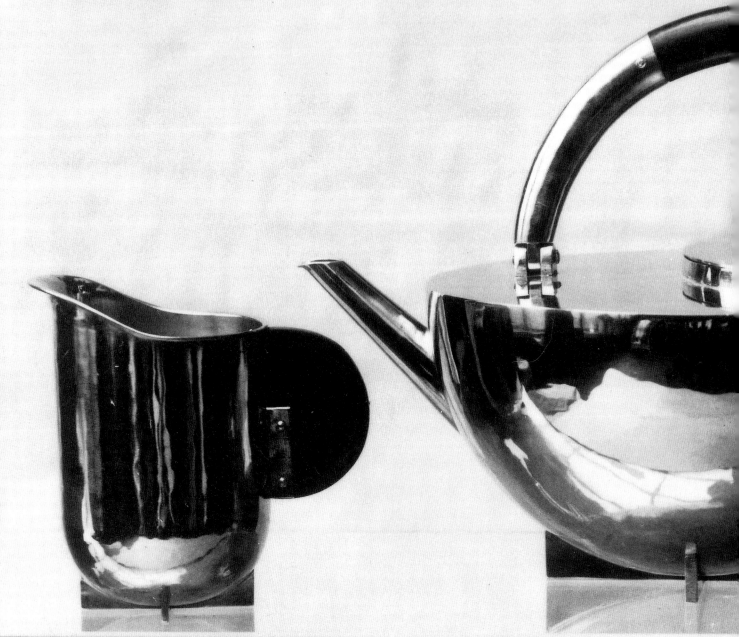

The glass Sintrax Coffee Maker is a piece of laboratory equipment, explicitly functional and more about the laboratory bench than the kitchen. It expresses the chemistry of coffee making as personal alchemy and elevates the black liquid to the status of an elixir. Its design was revolutionary in that it is transparent in every sense. The design is almost all glass, including the filter, the lid for the funnel and the stopper for the jug. It was one of the first domestic products to be designed for the German glass company Schott & Gen Jena, a company that specialized in laboratory instruments and baby bottles. One of the founders, Otto Schott, had discovered a type of heat-resistant glass, borosilicate glass, in 1887. In 1922 the company launched into household products. Its aim was to create practical, everyday objects in a simple, modern style, and this made the company a natural partner for the Bauhaus visionaries, whose mission was to bring together creativity with industry and science. Gerhard Marcks and Wilhelm Wagenfeld were the first outside designers to be employed by Schott. This vacuum Coffee Maker was one of the first of many to use heat-resistant glass in a radical new way. Marcks was a sculptor and artist who was the director of the pottery workshop at the Bauhaus School in Weimar from 1919 to 1925 and then taught at the Giebichenstein School at Halle from 1925 to 1930. The original Sintrax Coffee Maker was designed in 1925, available in three sizes: 0.5 litre, 1 litre and 1.5 litres (17, 34, and 51 fl oz). Wilhelm Wagenfeld added a straight wooden handle in 1930 because the original angled handle by Marcks burned when used on a gas stove. The Sintrax is considered the prototype for modern kitchen appliances. The notion of the modern kitchen as an efficient, hygienic workspace, a laboratory for preparing food, had just begun. Servants and grimy kitchen ranges were a thing of the past and this elegant glass coffee percolator set the tone for a new future.

154

Sintrax Coffee Maker (1925)
Gerhard Marcks (1889–1981)
Schott & Gen Jena 1925 to 1967

Early brochure, 1933

Marcel Breuer's side and coffee table combines a satin-finished, black or white plastic laminate top with polished chrome-plated tubular-steel frame and legs. The tables can be used separately or as a set. While heading the Bauhaus furniture workshop in the 1920s, Hungarian born Breuer had started to experiment with tubular steel to produce chairs, stools and table structures, creating some of the most influential furniture to come out of the Bauhaus. He conceived the low 'Laccio' as a companion to the Wassily Chair, the first tubular chair, based on a bicycle frame, combined with the form of a constructivist sculpture. Breuer's linear, multipurpose nesting tables reflect his rationalist aesthetic and accomplished technique. The construction is extremely stable, the materials are of exceptional quality and the forms are sculptural. The tubular-metal technology used in Laccio embodies the impact of the Bauhaus School on the development of modern design and architecture in the twentieth century. For Breuer metal became the material with which he could change the image of furniture. As he himself said, 'In my studies on mass production and standardization I very quickly discovered polished metal, luminous lines and spatial purity as new constructional elements for our furnishings. In these luminous, curved lines I saw not only symbols of modern technique, but technique in general.' Historically and socially, Breuer's furniture indicates a changed relationship between furnishings and the house. Furniture was no longer a static domestic ornament, but a useful object, one which could be light, manageable and flexible as well as economical to produce. The Laccio represents Breuer's belief in combining elegant lines with extreme functionalism.

155

Laccio (1925)
Marcel Breuer (1902–81)
Gebrüder Thonet 1929 to 1945, 1978 to present
Gavina 1962 to 1968
Knoll 1968 to present

Interior view of canteen, Bauhaus Dessau, 1925–6,

For many years designer Eileen Gray collaborated with the Romanian architect Jean Badovici, who encouraged her to go into architecture as well as furniture. design One of their first and most important projects was an informal house on the coast of Roquebrune near Cap Martin in the south of France, which was completed in 1929. For this architectural project, known as E1027, Badovici focused on the construction and Gray on the definition of space and the interior. The multi-purpose living room is the centre of the house and Gray designed many new pieces of furniture for this room. Some of it is multi-functional and can be adjusted to suit specific needs. Other pieces, like the Bibendum Chair and the Daybed, were designed for a more specific purpose, to repose and rest. The house and its interior are perfect examples of French modernist Art Deco and a very personal statement of Gray's intuitive and non-theoretical ideas on how modern people should live. The Daybed is as simple as one can imagine. It is made of a double, padded, rectangular leather mattress, supported by a chrome-plated frame. Its uniqueness is embodied in the fact that Gray does not use the tube for mere construction, like many of her modernist contemporaries, but that it is a decorative line framing the mattresses in right angles. This framing element in conjunction with a

massive padded structure can be seen in many of her designs, as can the desire for comfort. In the Daybed, for example, the frame pops up at the back to serve as a support for a cushion, a rug or a fur. Its asymmetric shape carries echoes of the past, and is reminiscent in some way of a classic Biedermeier chaise longue. In contrast to other modernist designers Gray liked the combination of opposites; of hard and soft materials and of machine-made and handcrafted parts. The bed remained a prototype, like many of her designs. In the early 1980s Aram Designs reintroduced the Daybed into their collection of classics and today they hold the worldwide licence for all Eileen Gray designs. They granted the Munich-based company Vereinigte Werkstätten the rights to reproduce the Daybed in 1984, but the company closed down and ClassiCon took over the production of many of Gray's designs under sub-licence from Aram.

156

Daybed (1925)
Eileen Gray (1879–1976)
Aram Designs 1984 to present
Vereinigte Werkstätten 1984 to 1990
ClassiCon 1990 to present

Prototype by Mart Stam

The B33 is certainly the most radical example of the tubular steel furniture developed and designed by Marcel Breuer. This cantilevered chair with only two 'legs' evolved from a series of experiments inspired by the metal frame of Breuer's bicycle. The B33 is also the natural consequence of the Laccio table/stool designed by Breuer in 1925. With its tubular steel legs, the Laccio was the precursor to the B33 and Breuer's first step towards the creation of a continuous cantilevered structure. When turned on its side, the table/stool takes on the same form as the base, legs and seat of a cantilevered chair. All that remained to make the transformation was to enlarge the radius of the tubing and add a backrest. Breuer then honed the initial design so that the structure became lighter but kept its resilience and strength as well as maintaining its comfort. The history of the B33 is also the history of a long-standing dispute. In 1926 the Dutch architect Mart Stam showed a cantilevered chair at the Weissenhof Exhibition in Stuttgart. Stam's chair was built with clumsy standard pipe fittings. A horizontal bar had been added to the front of the chair to increase its stability. Although Stam was the first to actually produce a metal cantilevered chair he had appropriated the idea from Breuer who, in the same year, discussed his on-going project with Stam. At the time Breuer was still struggling to find the solution whereby he could create a continuous, light structure, which was also strong enough to support the weight of a person. There are no formal records of this conversation, but it is more than likely that Breuer's research and ideas, once discussed with Stam, inspired the latter to take the matter forward. Breuer's final design is superior to Stam's in several ways: his chair did not require an additional supporting bar, is proportionally balanced and finally, is more comfortable than Stam's. The B33 was designed in 1926 and produced by Thonet from 1929 onwards. The legal dispute concerning the authorship of the cantilevered chair began almost immediately afterwards. Thonet lost the dispute to Anton Lorenz, who had previously registered an armchair version of Stam's version. As a consequence, Breuer did not receive any royalties on the B33 due to the fact that 'officially' his was not considered the original design.

The hairpin or hairgrip, or bobby pin as it is known in the United States, is a simple utility design, many different versions of which are still produced. However, like the best designs, it is a little gem of functional engineering. The brilliance of the grip is that it is made from one piece of bent metal and has no additional open/close mechanism to secure the hair. Made of resilient but thin and flexible metal (now usually plastic coated) it is bent round so that a longer straight base leg lies directly beneath a crimped upper leg. These two prongs only touch at one point, just before the grip's wider opening, which allows the user to pull the clip apart easily and push it into the hair. On release, the contact point is the key to keeping the grip secure, while the three gentle undulations offer varying degrees of give and take. The success of the design comes therefore in the balance it creates between space and compression, flexibility and grip,

allowing the pin both to be secure and yet to be inserted, adjusted or removed easily and with minimal damage to the hair shaft. Solomon H Goldberg invented the crimped hairgrip in 1926 with a specific hairstyle in mind. Very short hairstyles, particularly a sharp, near-sculptural bob, were all the rage in the 1920s as women used a short, sleek cut to show greater intellectual and sexual freedom. Ironically, like many 'empowering' fashions, the perfect bob was not easy to achieve and the grip was particularly useful for securing the thick waves that were commonly worn at the front. Help was sorely needed by most of the population and Goldberg had found a brilliant, cheap styling aid that was easy to mass produce. Today the hairgrip is still a universal item, as indispensable in front of the bathroom mirror in the early morning as it is in frantic backstage preparations at haute couture shows.

Oct. 22, 1929.   S. H. GOLDBERG   1,732,808

HAIRPIN

Filed July 17, 1926

Fig.1.

Fig.2.

Fig.3.

Inventor:
Solomon H Goldberg,

Frank L. Belknap

by   Atty.

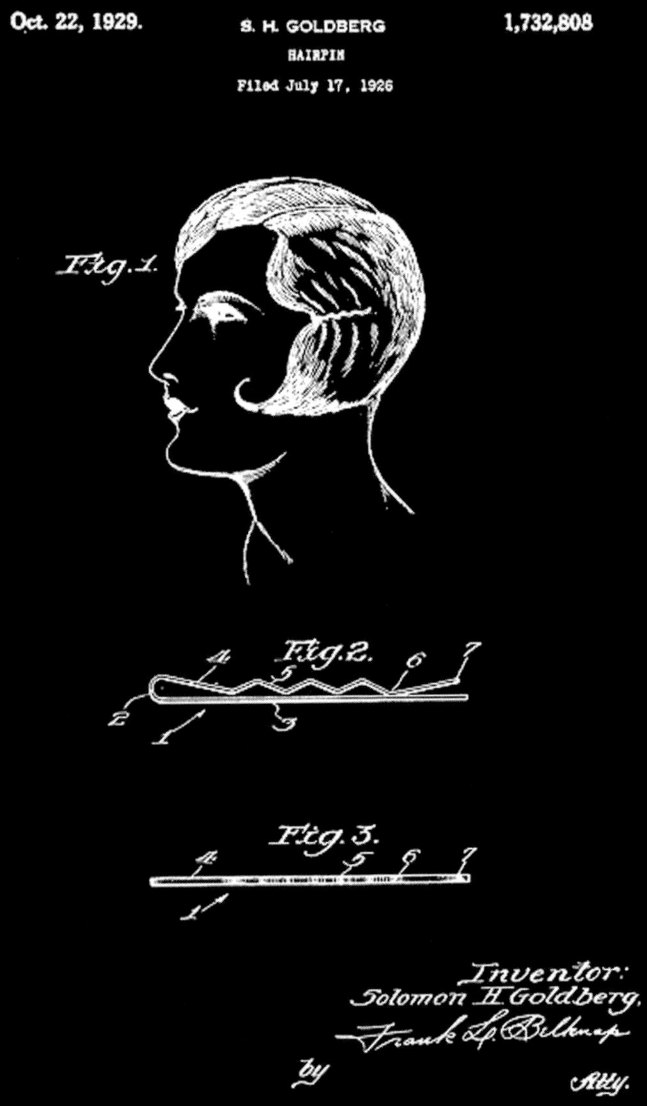

Max Ernst Haefeli was a founding member of the Federation of Swiss Architects together with luminary designers Karl Moser, Werner M Moser, Rudolf Steiger and Emil Roth. As designer and architect Haefeli developed a design language that brought together techno-logical innovation and artistic tradition in a way that is typically Swiss. It is no surprise, therefore, that he developed a partnership with Swiss furniture manufacturer horgenglarus. Established in 1882, horgenglarus adhered to the highest standards in craft tradition, using only hand methods in its furniture production. The Haefeli 1-790 Chair was a product of this union and illustrates both the designer's and the manufacturer's shared creative ideologies. First designed and produced in 1926, the Haefeli 1-790 is incredibly modern for its time. Its form and materials inspired later

Scandinavian designers such as Soren Hansen. Haefeli's chair is made in accordance with the high standards of the craft tradition. Made from solid wood with ply, the chair stands out from the bentwood ply and tubular steel designs that were becoming more common at the time, due to its rigid structure. The chair references Haefeli's architectural training in its simple form, perfect proportions and clean lines. The gently curved legs and the frame are constructed in solid wood, with the flat, wide back and seat machined in ply. The ergonomic seat and back result in a chair that combines traditional shapes with a craft sensibility and architectural sensitivity and results in a timeless, practical and comfortable seating solution.

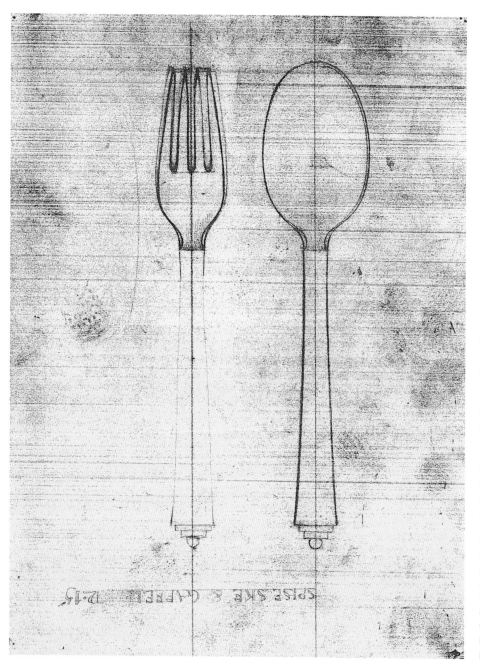

SPISESKE & GAFFEL D·15

Pyramid Cutlery, designed by Harald Nielsen for the silversmith Georg Jensen, epitomizes the look and essence of Art Deco, yet also represents an early example of Modernist cutlery. Pyramid was designed and first produced in the mid-1920s, and is still in production today, proving to be one of the Georg Jensen company's most popular silver designs. In 1935, the year of his death, the *Herald Tribune* described Georg Jensen as 'The greatest silversmith of the last 300 years.' This was a claim that few disputed. Georg Jensen had a skill for creating designs based on contemporary and historical sources, and for setting standards in form and design. Jensen recruited associates who worked for his firm as designers, among them his brother-in-law, Harald Nielsen, one of a number of people Georg employed from his own family. Harald's work played a major part in defining the Jensen style between the wars; his contribution is most clearly seen in the Pyramid design. Nielsen's silver Pyramid Cutlery illustrates the restrained Art Deco aesthetic that was to become prevalent in design of the 1930s. Of his designs, Nielsen remarked 'The cutlery's ornamentation is designed to accentuate the overall harmony of the piece but at the same time exists completely for its own sake and must never dominate.' The design's simplicity allied it with modernism and was a forerunner of the era of Functionalism. It was reproduced in *Les Echos des Industries D'art* as an example of modern silver, with its broad, flat surfaces characterizing the style. Pyramid was described in *Les Echos* as an example of 'a newer and simpler set of cutlery which is easy to clean' and was praised for its 'balance and proportion and inherent beauty of material rather than perfunctory ornamentation.' The combination of organic and geometric forms was used by Nielsen in an attempt to streamline Jensen's more naturalistic forms and became characteristic of his work for the firm.

160

Pyramid Cutlery (1926)
Harald Nielsen (1892–1977)
Georg Jensen 1926 to present

This cylindrical Tea Doser is simple in form yet invites the user to partake in the ritual of tea drinking. It appears to be nothing more than a narrow cylinder 20.5 cm (8 in) tall and 6 cm (2 in) in diameter, with a reflective surface without decoration. Yet the cap slides off to reveal a spout fashioned in an arc around the inner sleeve. This spout acts as a spoon to measure the tea leaves required. The design thus addresses the delicate balance between interior and exterior, between light and dark. When closed it is quite enigmatic; when open it is practical and useful. During the early period from its foundation in 1919, the Bauhaus metal workshop, under Johannes Itten's artistic guidance, took a traditional handicraft approach to making objects, but László Moholy-Nagy initiated change by developing a range of prototypes intended for industrial production. Wilhelm Wagenfeld was then an assistant instructor in the workshop, and his inspiration was a critical catalyst for this work, as he said 'every object has to find its formal solution in its functional use'. It was in this spirit that Przyrembel developed his Tea Doser. The Tea Doser, like so many other designs from the Bauhaus, never reached production until 1995, when it was reissued by Alessi, along with eight other Bauhaus designs. Przyrembel's original prototype was made of silver; the Alessi version is fabricated from stainless steel.

THE WRISTWATCH FOR SPORTSMEN AND SPORTSWOMEN

Patent Nos. 260554—274789—281315

THE WORLD-FAMOUS ROLEX MOVEMENT

'Sealed against the Elements'

The Rolex movement holds 25 World's Records for accuracy at Kew, Geneva and Neuchatel Observatories. No other wrist watch so small has ever secured the coveted Kew "A" certificate for accuracy, and the 'Oyster' is the same famous movement effectively 'sealed against the elements.'

THE ROLEX 'OYSTER' IS WATERPROOF SANDPROOF—PROOF AGAINST ALL EXTREME CONDITIONS.

SIZES FOR MEN AND WOMEN
Snowite £6-5-O
9ct. £11-5-O   18ct. £16-10-O
LUMINOUS DIAL 5/- extra

Obtainable from Authorised ROLEX Agents throughout New Zealand

25 WORLD'S RECORDS FOR ACCURACY

THE ROLEX WATCH CO., LTD.
(*H. Wilsdorf, Managing Director*)
GENEVA AND LONDON

MISS MERCEDES GLEITZE THE WORLD FAMOUS SWIMMER WEARS A ROLEX OYSTER

There's something about the Rolex 'Oyster' that appeals irresistibly to sportsmen and sportswomen. Perhaps it is the sturdy yet neat design of this wristlet or its unique waterproof and dustproof qualities. Certainly its undeviating accuracy is well appreciated by those who use time wisely.

"The reason I wear a Rolex Oyster Wrist Watch when swimming is because it is the only watch I know that is absolutely waterproof and also immune to damage from sand or salt air. Furthermore, I know that no other watch would stand up to the severe conditions experienced during long distance swims.

Yours faithfully,

Insist on seeing the name Rolex on dial and movement.

THE ROLEX 'OYSTER' WRIST WATCH

The Rolex brand name was registered in 1908 to feature on the dials of the watches distributed by a young Bavarian entrepreneur since 1905. Having received the first official chronometer certification ever awarded to a wristwatch in 1910 in Switzerland, the company continued to concentrate on ensuring the accurate timekeeping of its wristwatches, even in the most arduous conditions. This quest led to recognition by London's Kew Observatory test laboratory in 1914, sealing Rolex's international reputation for quality. The Oyster Watch was created by Rolex in 1926. It was the first truly water-resistant and dustproof wristwatch. Its rapid success was assured by the perfect time-keeping of the model worn by Mercedes Gleitze when she swam the English Channel in just over fifteen hours in October the following year. The Oyster was heralded as the 'Wonder Watch that Defies the Elements'. It is truly waterproof thanks to a screw-down waterproof case back and winding crown. The case is crafted from a solid piece of stainless steel, 18ct gold or platinum. The crystal is cut from synthetic sapphire, which is extremely hard, making it highly shatter- and scratch-resistant. The Cyclops lens over the date indicator magnifies the date, making it easily legible. The year 1931 witnessed the birth of the Perpetual rotor, a self-winding mechanism later found in every automatic watch. By eliminating the need to hand-wind the watch, thus reducing wear on the winding crown, Rolex made the Oyster case even more resistant in both normal and extreme conditions. In fact, the Oyster was used in the first successful ascent of Everest by Sir John Hunt's team in 1953. The Oyster Perpetual Watch has long maintained its status as one of the most revered wristwatches in the world. Epitomizing the values that have made the brand world famous, the Oyster is first and foremost an archetype, a symbol of a way of life, a benchmark for style.

The rectangular Club Chair is one of the most familiar products from the Art Deco period. Still in production today, the Club Chair has avoided becoming outdated thanks mainly to its angular form, which still manages to look modern today. Parisian designer Jean-Michel Frank was responsible for creating this timeless piece of furniture design, the simplicity of which is characteristic of his influential aesthetic. Frank designed the Club Chair as part of a series of upholstered cubic seating. The chair then appeared in several of Frank's high-profile interior designs. These ambitious projects ranged from a mansion for the Viscount Charles de Noilles on the Place des États-Unis in Paris to the Hotel Llao Lao in Bariloche, Patagonia. For each project the Club Chair would be adapted and reworked. Frank had a penchant for applying unexpected materials to his designs, with bleached leather and sharkskin being particular favourites. Frank's well-documented style was marked by spare, rectilinear details and elegant, pared-down forms. He himself claimed to be influenced by Neo-Classicism and Primitive Arts as well as by Modernism. The invention of much of what we now recognize as Art Deco style is widely credited to Frank and his original designs of the 1930s. So popular were these designs during the Art Deco period that Frank was propelled into the upper echelons of European creative society. Among his close friends and collaborators were Alberto Giacometti and Salvador Dalí, with whom he worked on numerous interior designs and products. Frank's glittering lifestyle took him to the United States and Argentina, where he continued to design extravagant interiors and sophisticated products for elite clients. His designs retain some of that sophistication, which might explain the continued popularity of one of his most basic but necessary pieces, the Club Chair.

16-4

Adjustable Table E1027 (1927)
Eileen Gray (1879–1976)
Aram Designs 1975 to present
Vereinigte Werkstätten 1984 to 1990
ClassiCon 1990 to present

Eileen Gray

The Adjustable Table E1027 is constructed from stainless steel and glass, with circular steel tubes forming the base and boundary for a spherical glass top; the table leg is also telescopic, controlled by a key in the back so that the table's height can be altered. This table must be one of the most plagiarized pieces of furniture of our time. While it is rigorously modernist in form and materials, it has a timeless appeal and just manages to avoid the cold rationalism of the movement, with its grace and flexibility. Legendary modernist architect Le Corbusier described it as 'enchanting and refined', which is more than was said about its designer, Eileen Gray, described by design historian Philippe Garner as 'a quiet but determined loner'. The table was part of a revolutionary series of furniture pieces, all designed for her house, E1027, in Roquebrune on the French Riviera. It is said that the 'E' stands for Eileen, while the numbers correspond to their sequence in the alphabet: the '7' therefore standing for G[ray], whilst '10' and '2' are said to allude to her friend and mentor, the Romanian architect Jean Badovici (1892–1956). Eileen Gray was born in Ireland, studied at the Slade School of Fine Art in London and then lived and worked in Paris for most of her life. She is considered to be one of the most important designers of the first half of the twentieth century and is among only a handful of women to get a mention in the male-dominated movement that is Modernism. Her output ranged widely from luxury decorative items in her early years, which she sold to private clients from the world of fashionable society, to simpler, modernist pieces of furniture as she grew older.

Coccoina ®

With its sweet almond aroma and stylish packaging, it might seem strange to find it in the stationery department, but Coccoina glue has been looking pretty on our shelves for over seventy years. This in itself might not seem remarkable, were it not for the fact that it has kept its original packaging since it was first launched in the 1920s. Made in Italy by Balma, Capoduri & C, Coccoina quickly became the adhesive of choice for Italian secretaries and librarians when production began in 1927. It was marketed as an office glue, but its packaging was more reminiscent of a beauty product, accompanied by advertising posters that suggested the height of style and modernity, and were as attractive as the packaging itself. With an eye-catching blue logo wrapped around a small silver package, the Coccoina Tin was and still is a beautiful and simple design. It comprises a metal canister with a screw-top lid, in the centre of which is a separate compartment with a tube for storing a small metal brush. Although it is now a common feature of glue containers, it was unusual for the time to include an applicator, especially one that fitted the design so perfectly. Coccoina *colla bianca*, or white glue, is made from potato starch (dextrine) in water, and is therefore non-toxic. The addition of almond oil ensures its position as the glue with the most appealing fragrance. It is ideal for many craft uses and, being solvent free, it is especially suitable for children. Coccoina is now available as a liquid glue and the paste is available in a plastic pot as well as the original aluminium container; the simple design remains unchanged since it was first launched almost a century ago. A range of new products bearing the Coccoina logo, including spiral bound notebooks and address books, as well as reproductions of Coccoina advertising posters from the past seventy years are available for purchase, and are all testaments to the enduring appeal of Coccoina's packaging. With attractive and simple packaging and a unique but functional design, it is not surprising that the Coccoina Tin and paste remain a favourite and are constantly being discovered by new fans.

QUESTA É LA VERA

Coccoina

BALMA, CAPODURI & C. s.a.s. - VOGHERA

Ludwig Mies van der Rohe

166

MR10 and MR20 Chairs (1927)
Ludwig Mies van der Rohe (1886–1969)
Berliner Metallgewerbe Josef Müller 1927
to 1931
Bamberg Metallwerkstätten 1931
Gebrüder Thonet 1932 to present
Knoll 1967 to present

Such is the apparent simplicity of Ludwig Mies van der Rohe's MR10 Chair that, seen from the front, it is easy to imagine that it is made from a single, continuous piece of tubular steel. The 'free-floating' seat, supported by the front legs alone, was a revelation when the chair was first shown in Stuttgart at the 1927 exhibition, 'Die Wohnung' (The Dwelling), of which Mies was the artistic director and for which the influential Weissenhof settlement of model public housing was created. Mies was not the first person to design and produce a cantilevered tubular steel chair. Also on show at Weissenhof was the Dutch architect Mart Stam's S33, for which a production contract had already been signed. When the two architects had met the previous year to discuss plans for the Weissenhof exhibition, Stam had drawn Mies a sketch of his idea for a cantilevered chair. Mies immediately saw its potential and, by the time of the exhibition, had come up with his own version. Where Stam's was cubic in form and rigid and heavy in construction due to the internal re-enforcement of the tubes, Mies's chair was lighter and had a springy resilience aided by the graceful curve of its legs. When Mies came to add arms to the chair to create the MR20, also first shown at Weissenhof, he made no attempt to disguise or aestheticize the junction of arm and leg, opting for a simple cuff joint. Perfectly complementing the austere modern interiors he created at Weissenhof, both versions of the chair met with critical success and were soon selling in large numbers. Variations in upholstery included separate leather or iron-yarn slings for back and seat or a one-piece seat/back in woven cane designed by Mies's partner Lilly Reich. Originally the chairs were available with a red or black lacquered finish as well as the nickel-plated versions that remain so popular today.

DIE FORM

ZEITSCHRIFT FÜR GESTALTENDE ARBEIT

4. JAHR

HEFT 5

1. MÄRZ 1929

VERLAG HERMANN RECKENDORF G. M. B. H. BERLIN W 35

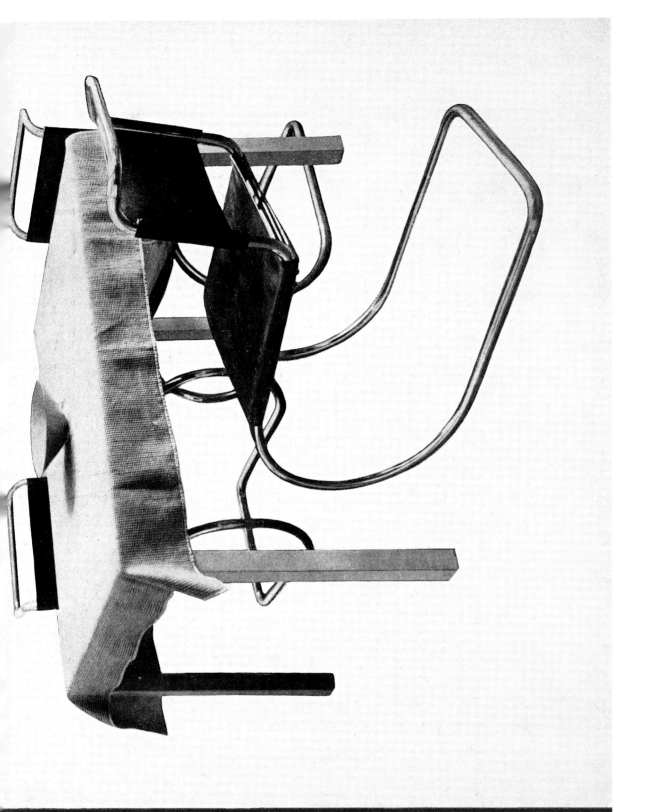

The 1927 Tube Light was the creation of the early modernist designer Eileen Gray. Gray studied fine art at The Slade School of Fine Art in London, but moved into interior design shortly after her studies. In 1925 she bought a plot of land at Rocquebrune-Cap Martin on the French Riviera, in order to build a house for her close friend, the architect Jean Badovici. She would name the modestly sized, but hugely influential house, E1027, the name derived from a numerical code based on Gray and Badovici's names. It followed Le Corbusier's five points of architecture established in 1926, but through its sense of interiority and Gray's bespoke furnishings, the result moved beyond the overly didactic results of most early modernist houses, creating not a 'machine for living', but a house with a 'spiritual glow'. A number of iconic objects were designed for E1027, with the Tube Light arguably the most radical. Rejecting the notion of a shade for the recently invented fluorescent filament, it took the then unheard of step of proudly displaying a naked light, revelling in its manufactured inherent beauty. The Tube Light's perpendicular form, enhanced by the elegant chrome-plated steel upright, created a wholly new minimalist form of floor lamp. A simple tube light, two sockets, a chromed metal foot, a switch and a chromed metal pipe to both attach the lamp and hide the wire are the most essential thing one needs for this particular lamp. Today's designers owe much to the design of their pioneering predecessor, Eileen Gray, whose breaking of convention by using naked lights inspired the likes of Ingo Maurer and the Castiglionis. Leading furniture manufacturer, Aram, reissued the design in the 1984, and Aram Designs sub-licensed her work to future manufacturers.

Tube Light (1927)
Eileen Gray (1879–1976)
Aram Designs 1984 to present
Vereinigte Werkstätten 1984 to 1990
ClassiCon 1990 to present

The Frankfurt Kitchen

represents one of the earliest attempts at creating a truly efficient domestic space. Driven by the ideal of providing good design within mass housing, it also pioneered the use of standardized, low-cost prefabricated elements in what was arguably the first fitted kitchen. Germany's inflation-wracked economy had to overcome a severe urban housing shortage in the 1920s by providing affordable accommodation for large numbers of working families. Ernst May, head of Frankfurt's municipal building programme, called for new techniques to make best use of limited space and provide an 'apartment for minimum living standards'. Schütte-Lihotzky's response was a kitchen worked out with laboratory precision to rationalize housework and reduce the housewife's burden. The social imperative behind Modernism and Functionalism was paralleled by a growing interest in 'scientific management' in the home. Ideas readily adopted from America insisted that if kitchens were exclusively for preparing food they could be smaller, less wasteful spaces. Schütte-Lihotzky drew on these influences by creating a room that effectively separated domestic work from relaxation, whereas people then commonly used kitchens for dining, bathing and even sleeping, reserving the living room for special occasions. Inspired by confined but productive railway dining car kitchens, the Frankfurt Kitchen measured just 1.9 by 3.4 m (6.2 × 11.2 ft), its narrow shape determined by a time and motion study of kitchen tasks. Along one wall were a stove and sliding door to the living room and along the other were the sink, cabinets and labelled storage bins. Below the end wall's window was a work-space with sliding garbage drawer. There were also continuous work surfaces and a swivel stool giving access to the sink, chopping board and storage. Doors and cupboards were painted blue, which research showed to be the least attractive colour to flies. The success of the kitchen was clear as over 10,000 kitchens were installed in housing estates in Frankfurt through the late 1920s.

Margarete 'Grete' Schütte-Lihotzky

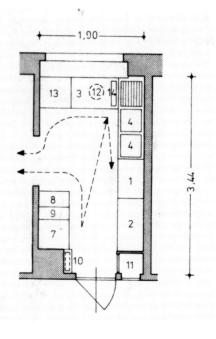

During the Editor's recent Continental tour he was deeply impressed by the ready-fitted kitchen standardised in all the hundreds of houses now being built by the municipality of Frankfurt. The following article has been specially written for " Feminine Life " by the woman architect who designed it. The photographs were kindly loaned by the chief architect of the Frankfurt Council.

THE New Frankfurt Kitchen

by Grete Lihotzky

(of the Architectural Staff, Frankfurt-on-Main City Council)

FOR some considerable time attempts have been made to adapt the household to the changing needs of our time. Architectural circles as well as their individual members have been trying by means of articles in the press, lectures, exhibitions, and model houses, to reform household furniture. Their special sphere of action is the small household. A small home is not to be regarded in the same way as a large household reduced to pocket handkerchief size; the ideal small house has its own rules.

Many more people are immensely interested in this problem. The *Hausrathilfebewegung*, a movement in Germany for advocating the use of modern furniture, has taken the lead in bringing before the public, machine-made furniture free from all additional ornamentation of traditional styles.

The success of this important work is still

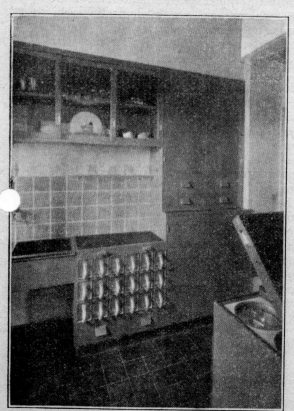

extremely small, firstly, because of the resistance to everything unconventional, and further to the lack of agreement among the promoters, how far the transformation is to go; one party cannot renounce profiles and curves for cosiness, even where their production and cleaning take more time and cost more money; others want the simplest furniture, which it is quite apparent is machine-made.

Apart from this problem, is the reform of the kitchen. Here there is only one opinion—what is most useful, is best. There are no obstacles to the fundamental reform of the kitchen.

In connection with the general scheme of housekeeping, we find it has grown out of all proportion to its importance. Kitchens are generally much too large, and a lot of time is wasted in walking about and fetching things. The remedy is diminution of size, and suitable arrangement of the furniture, as in the restaurant-car kitchen of a train, which is the perfect example.

The chief way of saving time and space, is to have furniture

built into the walls. This arrangement generally saves 35% to 40% of space; that is to say, the kitchen can be 35% to 40% smaller and this space utilised otherwise. Empty corners no longer exist, as in ordinary kitchens, with isolated furniture. The saving is in the whole room. Built-in furniture gives clear space for sweeping, as the method of not only in ground space, but construction makes cleaning easy. Built-in furniture is placed so that one can lay one's hand on everything without effort and in the least space of time.

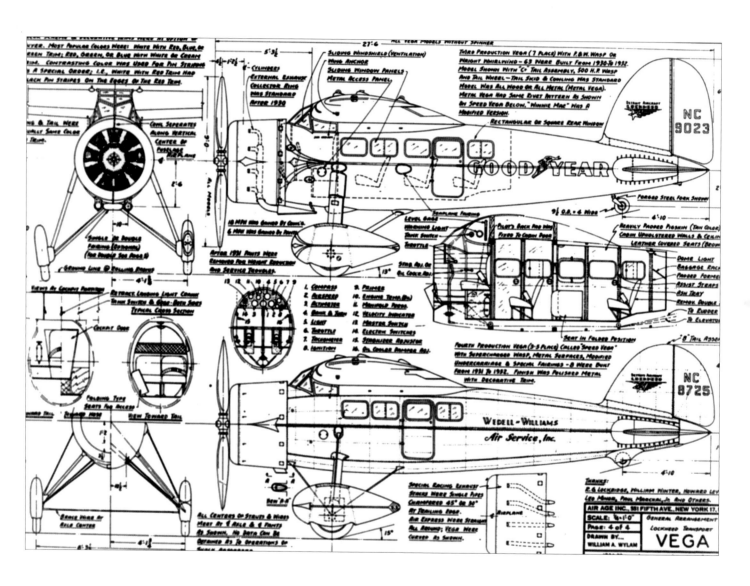

VEGA

With a monocoque fuselage, cantilever wings, a 12.5 m (41 ft) wingspan and at 8 m (26 ft) long, the first Lockheed Vega, called *Golden Eagle*, flew on 4 July 1927. The plane demonstrated its top speed of 217 kph (135 mph) at the 1928 National Air Races of Cleveland, then the fastest time yet recorded. The structure of the Vega, designed by Jack Northrop, marked the limits of wooden design. The monocoque was made of two halves of moulded plywood glued together; there were no struts or wires and no bracings on the cantilever wings to break the streamlined beauty of this monoplane. Shortly after the release of the Vega 1, Lockheed released the Vega 5 with improvements in the basic design now accommodating six passengers rather than four and with a new 450 hp air-cooled engine that allowed a cruising speed of 266 kph (165 mph). Although conceived as an airline aircraft, the Vega found its niche as an executive plane famous for its record-setting. One-eyed Wiley Post is probably the most famous Vega pilot, not only breaking the around-the-world record twice in his *Winnie Mae* but also flying at such unprecedented heights up to 17,040 m (50,000 ft), when today's jet planes fly at an average height of 9,150 m (30,000 ft) that he discovered the jet stream – the fast moving wind currents that flow in a westerly direction and allow greater fuel efficiency and speed. Because he was unable to pressurize *Winnie Mae's* cabin, he had to adapt a deep-sea diver's suit in order to fly at such heights. But the Vega is most closely associated with Amelia Earhart, the first woman to fly solo, non-stop, across the Atlantic in 1928. Her life is subject of numerous books as she was a widely-known celebrity during her lifetime and because her death is surrounded by mystery: she disappeared over the Pacific Ocean in 1937 while she was attempting to fly around the world with co-pilot Fred Noonan. This story has sparked the imagination of many writers as theories of what happened after the last radio contacts range from a tragic plunge into the ocean to an abduction of the two pilots by the Japanese or by Unidentified Flying Objects. Today Lockheed Martin, renamed after Lockheed's merger with Martin Marietta in 1995, specializes in information technology and space systems alongside its traditional expertise in aeronautics.

Ludwig Wittgenstein

What is now known as the Wittgenstein House, on Kundmandgasse 19, Vienna (1926–8), is a unique chapter in the remarkable life of Ludwig Wittgenstein, the enigmatic philosopher. The construction of the house (commissioned by Wittgenstein's sister, Margarethe Stonborough) is recognized by many as a pivotal event that led to his return to philosophy, after having moved away from it shortly following the publication of *Tractacus Logico-Philosophicus* (1922). Stonborough had originally assigned the house to another architect, however, her brother's ideas became more interesting to her as Wittgenstein strove to achieve a consistent sense of space, in order to convey rationality throughout – from the façade to the smallest interior detail. The exact spaces of the rooms, with tall, thin doors, influenced the design of the door handles so that their shape would not disturb the overall harmony of the architecture. Wittgenstein's handle, for the metal and glass doors, shows an excellent understanding of mechanics (from his initial training as an engineer) and a sensitive use of proportion and scale, while simultaneously solving the problem of making handles for narrow-framed doors. The door handles in the hall were mounted at a height of 154.5 cm (61 in) – nearly reaching the height of the shoulders of an average adult. The two main elements, inserted through the doorframe without a mount, are held together by a screw and washer, and are cast in brass, which was a Viennese standard at the time. This reduces the handle to four components, and leads to a seamless transition between handle and door. What is unique about this door handle is that it is not symmetrical on each side. The handle is formed from a cylindrical metal bar, curved at a right angle and ending in a square rod that protrudes through the doorframe, on the side of the door which opens outward. On the other side of the door, the handle looks completely different. It is again formed from a cylindrical metal bar, but this time, its shape is double curved: the cylindrical socket that holds it to the square rod passes through the doorframe. A screw countersunk connects the handles on the cover ring, and while the solution is simple, the manufacturing is not. Each of the handles were unique productions, and were lost when the house was abandoned between 1972–5, after which the house was sold to become the Cultural Institute of the Bulgarian Embassy. The handles were replaced by slightly altered versions, and today Tecnoline is producing a handle which is based upon the original, though greatly reworked using polished nickel plate, yet it is the brass-casted handle that established its own legacy.

Mme Scholefield née Perriand,
MM. Jeanner et (C.-E.) dit le Corbusier et Jeanneret (A.-P.)

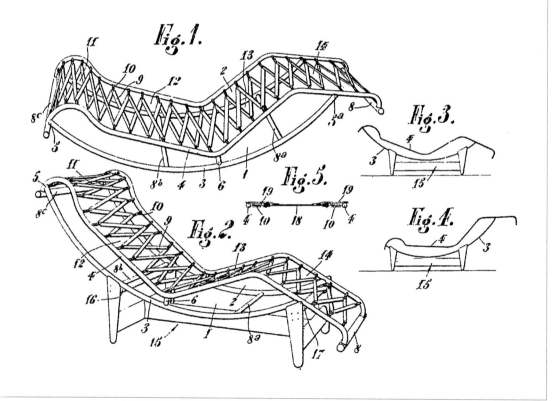

171

LC4 Chaise Longue (1928)
Le Corbusier (1887–1965)
Pierre Jeanneret (1896–1967)
Charlotte Perriand (1903–99)
Gebrüder Thonet 1930 to 1932
Heidi Weber 1959 to 1964
Cassina 1965 to present

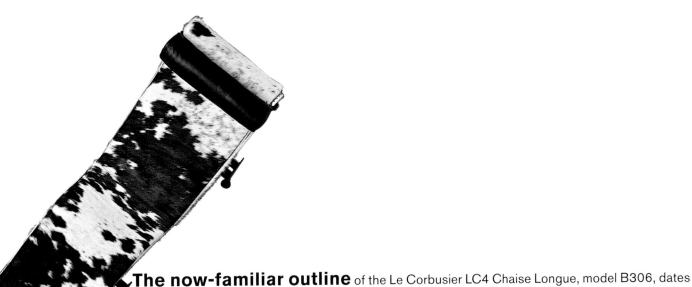

The now-familiar outline of the Le Corbusier LC4 Chaise Longue, model B306, dates from 1928. The H-shaped base and separate seating element, with hide upholstery and head cushion, are inherently linked with high-design interiors and architecture from the last seventy years. The Chaise Longue originated from Le Corbusier's concept of functional furniture as equipment for the home, that was itself a 'machine for living'. Le Corbusier revered the machine and its social and progressive associations. The Chaise incorporates flexibility of movement with the rocking, adjustable seat, while the base borrows its outline from the wings of aeroplanes. The design pays strong attention to ergonomics, with its adjustable neck roll and the free positioning of the chaise seat on its frame. Despite Le Corbusier's intention that designs be suitable for mass production, the LC4 was a relatively complicated design solution. A variety of steel profiles are used through the frame and base, while the upholstery was labour intensive in comparison to the planes of *Eisengarn* (iron cloth) favoured by other modernists of the period. Nonetheless, the LC4 offered comfort, flexibility and an original and progressive aesthetic that immediately found favour in the international high-design market. There is some controversy over who within Le Corbusier's atelier was responsible for the important furniture designs created for his buildings and interiors. Le Corbusier worked with his cousin Pierre Jeanneret and young designer Charlotte Perriand on the tubular steel designs that included the LC4, the LC1 Basculant Chair and the LC2 Grand Confort Chair, which defined aesthetic purity and characterized the International style. The LC4 Chaise Longue has undergone several design changes and different producers throughout its life, although Cassina, current producers of the licensed product, used Perriand as a consultant for their version. Its unmistakable outline has meant it has been widely copied and made available by a host of producers, to varying degrees of quality. It is perhaps one of the most familiar icons of twentieth-century furniture design, to the extent that it is known affectionately in certain circles of the design community as the 'Corb chaise'.

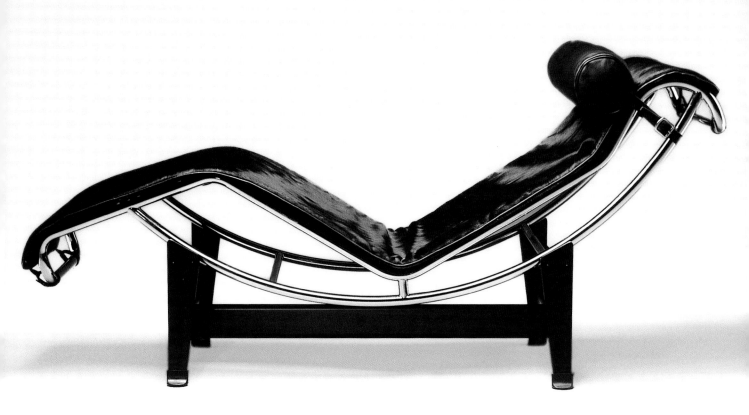

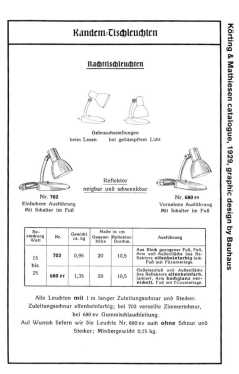

Körting & Mathiesen catalogue, 1929, graphic design by Bauhaus

Within the image:

Kandem-Tischleuchten

Nachttischleuchten

Gebrauchsstellungen
beim Lesen   bei gedämpftem Licht

Reflektor
neigbar und schwenkbar

Nr. 702
Einfachere Ausführung
Mit Schalter im Fuß

Nr. 680 ev
Vornehme Ausführung
Mit Schalter im Fuß

Be-steckung Watt	Nr.	Gewicht ca. kg	Maße in cm		Ausführung
			Gesamt-höhe	Reflektor-Durchm.	
15 bis 25	702	0,95	20	10,5	Aus Blech gezogener Fuß, Fuß, Arm und Außenfläche des Reflektors elfenbeinfarbig lack. Fuß mit Filzunterlage.
	680 ev	1,35	20	10,5	Gußeisenfuß und Außenfläche des Reflektors elfenbeinfarb. lackiert, Arm hochglanz vernickelt. Fuß mit Filzunterlage.

Alle Leuchten mit 1 m langer Zuleitungsschnur und Stecker.
Zuleitungsschnur elfenbeinfarbig; bei 702 verseilte Zimmerschnur,
bei 680 ev Gummischlauchleitung.
Auf Wunsch liefern wir die Leuchte Nr. 680 ev auch ohne Schnur und
Stecker; Mindergewicht 0,15 kg.

The Kandem Table Lamp was made from aluminium, with an adjustable stem and head connected by a ball-and-socket joint, and a push-button switch in the base. The lamp was the result of a collaboration between Bauhaus tutor Marianne Brandt and student Hin Bredendieck, and the Leipzig-based lighting firm of Körting & Mathiesen, or Kandem. There were a number of Bauhaus designs that were originally produced by lamp manufacturer Schwintzer and Gräff, with whom a contract was made and terminated in 1930, and subsequently passed to Körting & Mathiesen. General contact with this industry brought with it a greater awareness of manufacturing and marketing considerations, something which the designers approached with enthusiasm. Under the direction of László Moholy-Nagy, the metals workshop became focused in the late 1920s on industrial collaboration, chiefly in the field of lighting, which brought the Bauhaus remarkable industrial success. In 1928 Brandt herself established contact with Körting & Mathiesen, and a contract was set up for the design of standard lamps. This lamp, the first project, was a redesign of the desk lamp. Brandt became avidly interested in task-lighting after having worked on several ceiling designs. Both Brandt and Bredendieck experimented with making table and bedside lamps, with a shade shaped like a bell in order to provide an equal dispersal of light. They also produced a bedside lamp to a similar design, with a longer adjustable stem attached to the modified base. Both lamps were made in aluminium, an unusual material for the production of domestic electrical goods at the time. The lamps were usually painted white, as well as rare examples of lacquered green, because the material was not hugely popular in its raw state. As Brandt said, 'People in those days thought aluminium was dreadful and we therefore sometimes painted the shades. They were designed for everywhere, for living rooms, restaurants, workshops.' The lamp continued to be in production until 1945, with little modification, even after the 1933 closure of the Bauhaus. Its simple form has been copied by many other manufacturers, and this continues even today, although the original version is no longer in production.

In 1928–30, Mies van der Rohe designed a modernist villa for Grete Weiss Löw-Beer and Fritz Tugendhat on the slope of a hill in Brno, Czechoslovakia. The villa and its interior were designed with the intention of creating spaces that easily flowed from one to another. The Tugendhat Coffee Table, often mistakenly called the Barcelona Table, was originally intended for the entrance hall of the villa. This low table has a similar design concept to the famous Barcelona Chair, using an X-shaped frame. In the Barcelona Chair this X-shape is restricted to the side view and has an elegant, almost female line. The Tugendhat Coffee Table uses the X-shape both as a decorative element and as an essential structural solution. The table's hand-polished strips of steel are used vertically to give more stability, and refer to architectural solutions for a strong technical skeleton. The design of the table is spacious, dominantly linear and uncompromising. The use of the X-shaped frame in combination with a glass tabletop, 18 mm (0.75 in) thick, and 100 cm (40 in) square, with bevelled edges, emphasizes a new concept of assembling legs, as a unified base, and top to create a solid, symmetrical structure. The table was first produced by Berliner Metallgewerbe Joseph Müller and named as "Dessau Table". In 1931, a tall version was produced by Bamberg Metallwerkstätten, Berlin, in nickel-plated steel. Tops were available in clear and black glass and rosewood. Knoll took over the production in 1952. From 1964 Knoll produced the table in stainless steel with a glass top, and referred to it as the 'Barcelona Table'. The table has received awards from both the Museum of Modern Art in New York, and the Design Centre in Stuttgart, in 1977 and 1978 respectively, many years after its initial production.

Barcelona™ (Tugendhat) Table (1928)
Ludwig Mies van der Rohe (1886–1969)
Berliner Metallgewerbe Joseph Müller 1927
to 1931
Bamberg Metallwerkstätten 1931
Knoll 1952 to present

Thonet No.8751, c.1928

Tric Chair, Achille & Pier Giacomo Castiglioni, 1965

17-4

Thonet No. 8751 (c.1928)
Gebrüder Thonet Design Team
Gebrüder Thonet 1928

Tric Chair (1965)
Achille Castiglioni (1918–2002)
Pier Giacomo Castiglioni (1913–68)
Bernini 1965 to 1975
BBB Bonacina 1975 to present

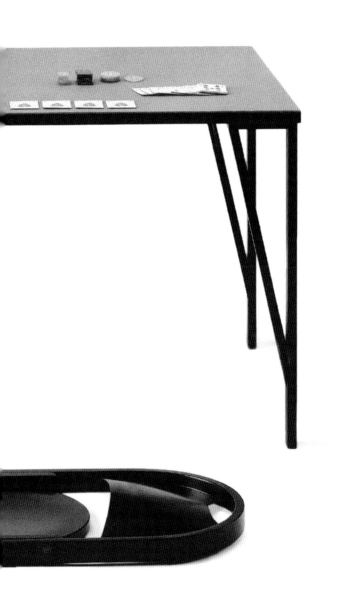

As well as producing close to 150 original designs, every-thing from light switches to vacuum cleaners, Achille Castiglioni also championed the 'ready-mades' – furniture constructed from found objects. A third line of work was concerned with 'redesigning'. This saw Castiglioni update existing designs to suit technological developments and the needs of modern life. The Tric Chair from 1965 was one such redesign, which tooks its influence from a simple beechwood folding chair designed by Thonet in 1928 but was no longer in production. Castiglioni took the basic model and made two changes: he raised the back for better support and he made a model with red felt covering the backrest and seat for increased comfort. Folded, the chair is only 4 cm (1.6 in) deep. Despite its status as a reworked piece, the Tric Chair is most commonly credited to Castiglioni. In an interview released in 1988 Castiglioni spoke of 'reinterpreting' the Thonet Chair: 'Sometimes the manufacturer asks the designer to restyle an old object. The designer can just reinvent the object or choose to limit the intervention to a new interpretation of the old object. This is what happened when I redesigned the Thonet chair ... But even this choice needs to be made after doing some research; it can't be just a restyling for aesthetical purposes. Research is extremely important for a good designer. One could research forever. But at some point you have to stop.' Originally produced by Bernini in 1965, the Tric Chair has been manufactured since 1975 by BBB Bonacina. The Tric Chair was included in a display of a modern dining room in the '*Prima mostra biennale degli interni d'oggi*' (First Biennial Exhibition of Today's Interior Design) in Florence in 1965. All the objects featured in the exhibition were industrially produced and included two further examples of Castiglioni's 'redesigns' of old and well-known pieces in cutlery and glassware. In 1975 the collaboration with BBB Bonacina was resumed for the design of the Trac Table. Built with the same materials as the Tric, the Trac is as easy to fold and store as its sister chair. Yet, it must be acknowledged that the Thonet No. 8751 set a standard for the evolution of folding chairs, remaining as one of the first, most uncomplicated designs for this type of seating.

The ubiquitous Corkscrew with twin arms and central screw may appear as an uncelebrated design. It is, however, a design that since being patented in the United States in 1930 has been little altered, bar minor cosmetic changes such as the addition of the cap opener at the top. Its practicality has never been improved upon. Anyone who has opened a bottle of wine will without doubt have used a Double-Lever Corkscrew, and variations on the Rosati design can be purchased virtually anywhere, from supermarkets to specialist wine merchants. The patent drawings lodged by Dominick Rosati on 29 October 1928 show two arms cut with cogs to lift the central 'Archimedean worm' topped with a turning key. The key facilitates easy entry of the 'worm' into the cork, with minor damage to the cork's internal structure. When the raised arms are lowered, the cork is smoothly drawn into the central cavity of the corkscrew. While the design is by no means the earliest patented corkscrew, it is certainly the most influential. The original version has seen many adaptations, from whimsical to decorative to functional. Collectors seek designs fashioned into the erotic outline of the female form or small production runs where the top screw is cast as a duck's head or similar peculiarity. A common and functional reworking of the original again relies on the adaptation of Rosati's top screw through the addition of a bottle opener. Wine storage in corked bottles is a relatively recent phenomenon. Animal skins, earthenware jars and wooden barrels were used originally, though once these were opened the quality of the wine deteriorated rapidly without an airtight seal. While the ancient Greeks and Romans used cork stoppers in terracotta amphorae, the knowledge of cork was apparently lost after the collapse of the Roman Empire. By the seventeenth century glass-blowing techniques were sufficiently advanced to create robust bottles with narrow necks. The use of cork to provide an airtight seal offered a long-term solution, cementing this now common marriage of materials. By the 1880s the straight-sided cork was being used and from this point on the race was on to provide designs for instruments to ease the removal of the cork. Between this time and that of Rosati's design over 300 corkscrew patents were registered, but it is Rosati's design that remains the most readily copied.

April 1, 1930.   D. ROSATI   1,753,026

CORK EXTRACTOR

Filed Oct. 29, 1928

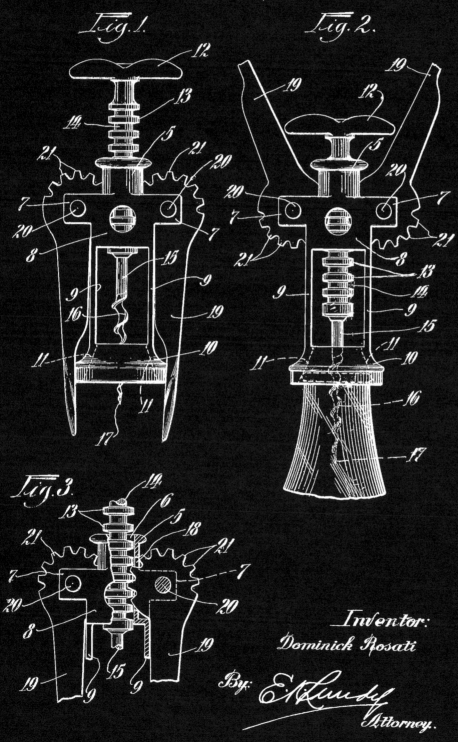

Fig. 1.   *Fig. 2.*   *Fig. 3.*

Inventor:

Dominick Rosati

By: E. N. Lundy
Attorney.

The LC1 Basculant Chair by architect Charles Édouard Jeanneret, better known as Le Corbusier, Pierre Jeanneret, and Charlotte Perriand, is an early exercise in tubular steel and calf hide. Its pivoting backrest allows for easy adjustment, a feature reprised in Le Corbusier's later chairs. The reclining back provides continuous comfort and support in different working positions. The arms, two solid leather straps, can rotate freely around the upper ends of the uprights, as shown in the sketch below by Perriand. The modulated, cubic form enveloping the form and the upright pommels are consistent with Le Corbusier's architectural forms. As a reminder of the colonial

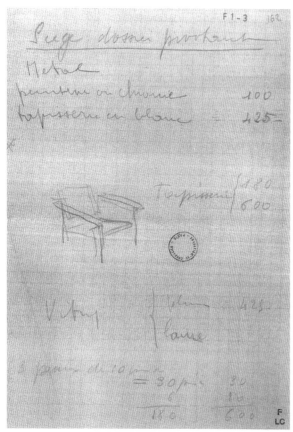

mentality of the 1920s, the chair is also called the Safari Chair, since its shape, the mobility of its back and the presence of straps were inspired by the traditional folding chairs used by British colonial officers during expeditions throughout India. Le Corbusier had previously used such chairs in his interiors, most noticeably in his pavilion at the 1925 Paris Exhibition. The pavilion, named L'Esprit Nouveau after the magazine Le Corbusier had founded in 1920, was a showcase for his work and those of his contemporaries. During this period Le Corbusier turned his attention to furniture, approaching it as part of 'home equipment'. In 1929, he presented a series of furniture designs in collaboration with Jeanneret and Perriand at the Paris Salon d'Automne, which were later produced by Thonet. All the exhibited items, such as the LC4 Chaise Longue, are still extremely popular as furnishings for public and domestic use.

176

LC1 Basculant Chair (1928)
Le Corbusier (1887–1965)
Pierre Jeanneret (1896–1967)
Charlotte Perriand (1903–99)
Gebrüder Thonet 1930 to 1932
Heidi Weber 1959 to 1964
Cassina 1965 to present

Wilhelm Wagenfeld designed the Door Handle WD in 1928 and it was put into production by S A Loevy in Berlin that same year. After only a few years it disappeared from the market, but then became well known after the architect Erich Mendelsohn used it throughout the Columbus-Haus Building, Berlin, built between 1930 and 1932. This building, once located in Potsdamer Platz and then torn down following World War II, was originally built to be a department store, but was used as an administrative office. It is believed that over 1,000 of the door handles were used in this building and also in many of Mendelsohn's commissions for private houses. In 1984 the German company Tecnolumen (known as Tecnoline from 2002) reissued the door handle on an exclusive basis. The handle is manufactured today using a traditional die-casting technique, which requires labour-intensive sanding and polishing by hand in order to achieve the desired quality. The fact that this

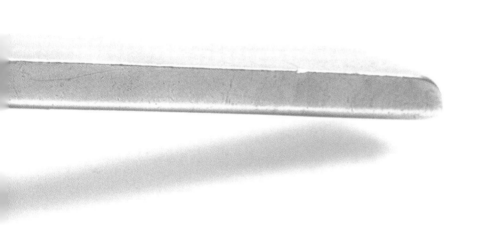

door handle is still available is because of the high production standards and the use of expensive materials such as brass. Even imitations could not detract from the value of the original and Wagenfeld's product has been able to survive, despite mediocre copies. It is a wonderful example of a semi-industrial icon, and its revival demonstrates high production values and a continued desire on the part of the consumer. Wilhelm Wagenfeld was one of the first heroes of industrial design in Germany who saw the connection between good design and industry. In this way he not only created successful products, but also provoked discussions with manufacturers. Today Wagenfeld could be regarded as one of the first minimalist designers who avoided any deference to the fashionable or ephemeral. His Door Handle WD is a timeless example of elegance.

The LC2 Grand Confort Armchair was designed by Le Corbusier in association with his cousin Pierre Jeanneret and Charlotte Perriand. It was part of a short-lived but fruitful collaboration that also produced the LC1 Basculant Chair and the LC4 Chaise Longue. It is constructed from a welded chromium-plated steel frame into which five upholstered leather components are held. This sets it apart from other armchairs of the period, whose traditional internally framed forms opposed the logic of Le Corbusier's radical architectural philosophy. Here, the construction is reduced to the bare minimum and exposed for all to see. The welded components are comprised of a mitred tubular top frame and legs, a thinner solid retaining bar and thinner-still L-section bottom frame, which supports the unfixed cushions with tensile straps. Once in place, the leather cushions complete a compact cube shape, with corresponding compact space for sitting. This novel design was first shown at the 1929 Salon d'Automne in Paris. A production of the LC2, along with the other concepts, was to be by the Peugeot factory because of its expertise in working with tubular steel. Following a favourable public reception, however, production was taken up by the Thonet furniture company. There have been various incarnations of the Grand Confort Armchair, with and without the ball foot, as a sofa and as a wider 'female' version (the LC3), which compromised the original cube form but allowed the sitter to cross their legs. Since 1965 it has been produced by Cassina in Italy, who also make a two- and three-seater sofa in the same style. Through his writing, Le Corbusier expounded his belief in the 'universal object' or ideal type-form. Along with many of his contemporaries he believed that for certain things there were universal platonic ideals that, through refinement, utility and economy could establish themselves as basic, anonymous and permanent typologies. It is fitting, then, that his Grand Confort Armchair should have become so ubiquitous in the lobbies and receptions of wealthy hotels and corporations the world over. This model has become a byword for respectability and gravity in these institutions and as such remains in huge demand.

178

LC2 Grand Confort Armchair (1928)
Le Corbusier (1887–1965)
Pierre Jeanneret (1896–1967)
Charlotte Perriand (1903–99)
Thonet Frères 1928 to 1929
Heidi Weber 1959 to 1964
Cassina 1965 to present

Le Corbusier, photograph by René Burri

Although he is best known as an architect and planner, Le Corbusier was also active in the fields of theory, painting and furniture design. The Swiss designer's LC7 Revolving Armchair and LC8 Stool were first unveiled at the 1929 Salon d'Automne in Paris, as part of a display called 'Equipment for the Home', which he had designed in collaboration with his cousin Pierre Jeanneret and Charlotte Perriand. It is based on a traditional typist's chair, and is intended to be used with a desk. The chair's design is in keeping with Le Corbusier's notion that buildings should be functional above all else, that they were to be 'machines for living' as he famously termed it. The four chrome tubular legs, which are produced as polished chrome, either shiny or matt, bend at right angles and meet in the centre under the seat, from where the seat revolves. The only concession to ornament in the LC7's design is the fact that its leather or fabric upholstery is available in a variety of colours today. As with the majority of Le Corbusier's work in both architectural and furniture design, the LC7's elegance and beauty are a result of the lines generated by its structure, in this case the chrome-plated steel tubing which composes the frame. Because the metal tubing used in the chair was similar to that used in the manufacture of bicycles, Le Corbusier had originally attempted to persuade Peugeot to manufacture his furniture. In the end they declined and Thonet Frères who had manufactured the bentwood furniture Le Corbusier had used to dress his interiors before he started creating his own pieces stepped in. In 1964, the Italian manufacturer Cassina acquired exclusive rights to Le Corbusier's furniture designs, and continues to produce them, with rights given by Le Corbusier himself. They are stamped with the official Corbusier logo and numbered to ensure their authenticity to this day. A version with five legs is also available, but purely by commission.

LC7 Revolving Armchair (1928)
Le Corbusier (1887–1965)
Pierre Jeanneret (1896–1967)
Charlotte Perriand (1903–99)
Gebrüder Thonet 1930 to c.1932
Cassina 1978 to present

THE FAMOUS

Sunbeam

MIXMASTER

It is fun to cook
and bake if you
have the
MIXMASTER

Endorsed by Good Housekeeping Institute and
other home service laboratories as well as domestic
science experts and cooking authorities everywhere

ATTACHMENTS FOR MIXMASTER ARE SHOWN ON OTHER PAGES

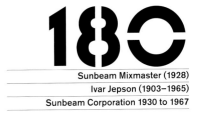

The Sunbeam Mixmaster is a model of 1930s domestic appliance design. From the moment it was awarded a patent in 1929, the Mixmaster swept on to confirm itself as a cornerstone of millions of American households, and became the flagship appliance of the Sunbeam Corporation. In 2003, as a further measure of its enduring appeal, the Mixmaster defied its seventy-plus years by being relaunched to a modern generation of homemakers increasingly looking towards the comforting brand values of this time-proven design. The mechanical arm-over-bowl format of the Mixmaster created a blueprint to which today's electrical mixers still remain loyal. The amply proportioned bowl takes its place on a flat one-piece base unit. This foundation tapers inwards before sweeping up and around the back of the bowl, to attach to a motorized tilting arm that clicks into place, perpendicular to the bowl below. The two metal whisks attach to the front part of the motor and drop down into the bowl where they remain, suspended. A gently arching handle travels back to emphasize further what is already a remarkably streamlined design. Mixmaster can largely be credited with mechanizing a generation of American kitchens. Where hand-powered kneading and beating of ingredients had once held sway, cooks across the country were quick to take up on the efficiency offered by an electrical alternative. Mechanical mixers, in particular milkshake makers, were in existence before the arrival of Ivar Jepson's design. Indeed, Sunbeam had been responsible for patenting the first ever electric mixer in 1911. However, no design lived up to the task with such fluency or with a marketing game plan as well considered as Sunbeam's. To an American market deep in the throws of the Depression, the reasonably priced, mass-produced Mixmaster proved a revelation to home-based entertaining, the most popular venue in a time of recession. Where America led, the rest of the world followed and before long the Mixmaster formula was influencing rival brands quick to chase a growing international market. But nothing was to equal the Sunbeam patent and, in 1998, Mixmaster was awarded its own stamp by the American Postal Service having been chosen as 'an icon of household convenience'. Original Sunbeam Mixmasters are now one of the most sought after vintage appliances for a global network of collectors.

ASTER SAVES HARD WORK

NYTHING   SHARPENS KNIVES   OPENS CANS

The
Powerful, sturdy,
mixer

Does more things
better **than any**
other mixer

Pays for itself
Quick

MIXMASTER
is one of

Sunbeam
THE BEST ELECTRIC APPLIANCES MADE

WITH EVERY MEAL—EVERY DAY

Sandow's developer poster, c.1898

IMP. CHARLE VERNEAU – 114, Rue Oberkampf – PARIS

René Herbst's Sandows Chair, first displayed at the Paris Salon d'Automne in 1929, has never been produced in any great quantity, but it has become an important touchstone for contemporary furniture design. Born in Paris, Herbst studied in London and Frankfurt before establishing his studio and workshop in Paris in the early 1920s. He was known as the 'iron man' not only because of the extensive use he made of steel tube in his furniture designs, but also because of his forceful character. In addition to his early adoption of steel tube as a furniture material, he was also a pioneer in the use of springs to form the seat and back of his chairs. The inspiration for this came from observation of the spring exercise devices used by body builders. The Sandows Chair, named after the famous body builder Eugen Sandows (1867–1925), was produced by Herbst's own furniture company in limited numbers from 1929 to 1932. It was produced in three styles, as a side chair, a chair with arms and a lounge chair. Constructed from nickel-plated or black-lacquered steel tubing, the simple linear forms of the two steel parts are joined together where they cross. The elegant outlines of the legs are animal-like and beautifully proportioned. Within the frames, rows of tensioned springs –'Sandow' straps or cotton-covered elastic cord – provide a comfortable place to rest. This is an object full of potent energy, a chair that offers both relaxation and movement. The influence of this chair can still be observed in many contemporary works. Herbst designed little other furniture and his latter career was mostly concerned with interior, retail and film set design.

Fritz Heidecke

The idea of a twin-lens reflex camera had been explored by camera designers from the 1860s and was reasonably popular by the 1890s. Although its popularity waned as new smaller and more portable cameras were produced, the design persisted in a horizontal format, with stereoscopic cameras with a pair of taking lenses and a central coupled-viewing lens. Franke and Heidecke's Heidoscop of 1922 and roll film Rolleidoscop of 1926 are examples of the design. Heidecke used the knowledge acquired in producing stereoscopic cameras by turning the basic stereo design around by ninety degrees and producing a twin lens reflex for taking single pictures while retaining the coupled viewing lens. The original Rolleiflex made use of 117 roll film, producing negatives 6 cm (2.36 in) square. The viewing and taking lenses were on the same front panel so that focusing was accurate, although parallax (the difference between the view of the two separated lenses) meant that at close distances some manual adjustment had to be made. That aside, the camera was small compared to previous twin lens reflexes and immediately found success. By the end of 1932, 30,000 Rollei cameras had been sold, increasing to 300,000 by 1938 and one million by 1956. Within a short time imitators were producing similar TLR cameras, ranging from those that were little more than box cameras with fixed focus to high-quality models such as Zeiss Ikon's Ikoflex range. Heidecke developed the design further. A smaller camera taking 127 roll film, the Baby Rolleiflex, was introduced in 1931; the Rolleiflex Standard, taking more readily available 120 roll film, appeared in 1932 and in 1933 the cheaper Rolleicord range appeared. The 1950s and 1960s were the camera's heyday, when it was the design of choice for press photographers. Later models incorporated f/2.8 wide-aperture lenses, built-in exposure meters and a range of accessories to extend the versatility of the camera. Wide-angle and telephoto models were produced to alleviate the lack of interchangeable lenses. Competition from the single-lens reflex in both 35- and 120-roll film sizes effectively meant that twin-lens reflex design was a photographic dead-end, and by the 1970s it had no advantage over its competitors. The Rollei company moved into 35 mm and developed its medium-format range of cameras. The Rolleiflex 2.8GX was introduced in 1987 with through-the-lens metering and flash metering and limited edition models targeting collectors.

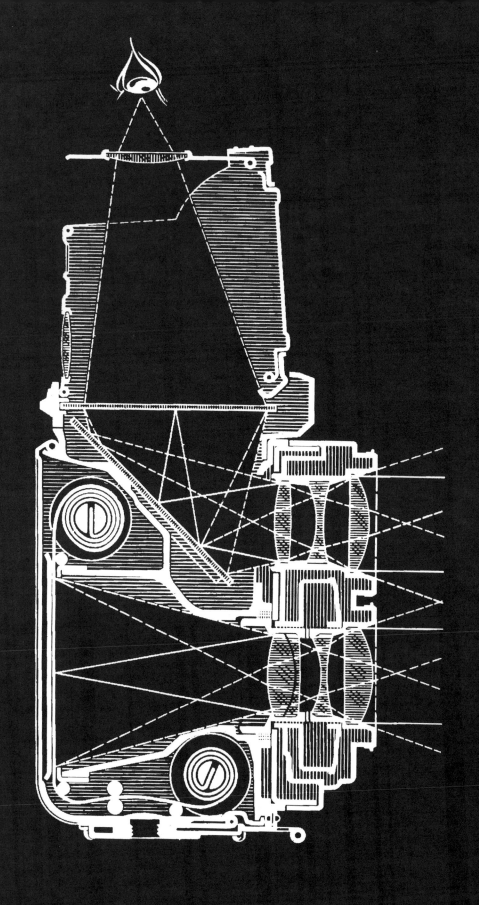

Advertisement, c.1929

183

LC6 Table (1928)
Le Corbusier (1887–1965)
Pierre Jeanneret (1896–1967)
Charlotte Perriand (1903–99)
Gebrüder Thonet 1930 to 1932
Cassina 1974 to present

The Swiss architect Le Corbusier was passionate about aircraft, both as examples of functional design and as symbols of the modern world. His interest is evident in the design of this table. The frame is made of oval-profiled steel tubing that recalls the aerodynamic profile of aeroplane wings. The massiveness of the frame, a pair of simple inverted U-shapes joined by a beam, is contrasted by the lightness and transparency of the glass top. The analogy of flight is continued, as the glass top appears to float above the frame, supported at four points by adjustable risers. Le Corbusier often contrasted lightness with weight, and mass with invisibility. Le Corbusier designed the table in collaboration with his cousin Pierre Jeanneret and Charlotte Perriand. The three designers were responsible for most of the furniture we now know simply as Le Corbusier's. The table was first shown in the Paris Salon d'Automne of 1929, in an arrangement organized by Perriand with examples of their tubular steel and leather chairs. Photographs of this exhibition show a gold-coloured glass top supported on a metallic grey-lacquered base. Thonet sponsored the display and added the table to its range of bent metal furniture. It was, however, only ever made in limited quantities. Le Corbusier was interested in balance and proportion, and in the interplay of mass and voids, but an awareness of human proportions may also be why the height of the table top can be adjusted by 5 cm (2 in) to suit different users. Since 1974 the Italian furniture manufacturer Cassina has produced the table under the name LC6, with both glass and wooden options for the top. It is part of a series of Le Corbusier furniture designs manufactured commercially by Cassina many years after the first examples were exhibited. That his furniture designs have taken decades to reach a mass audience, and still appear contemporary, is testament to how groundbreaking they were in the 1920s.

Arch. Marcel Breuer

**B 32
Thonet**

18-4

B32 'Cesca' Chair (1928)
Marcel Breuer (1902–81)
Gebrüder Thonet 1929 to present
Gavina/Knoll 1962 to present

Marcel Breuer

The Cesca may be considered a familiar and even unworthy seating form. It does, however, mark a revolution in design. The Wassily Chair of 1925 illustrated Breuer's understanding of new typographies for seating design and further, marked the starting point of an ongoing design process to invent truly important ideas in the history of modernist seating. Breuer did not suffer any traditionalist perspectives on design; he was one of the most youthful architects and designers of the prewar period, completing his studies at the Weimar Bauhaus in 1924 at the age of twenty-two. He was educated and trained within a modernist vacuum and did not rely on the perceived 'modern' forms of the past. The B32 remains an important cornerstone because of the design's definition as a cantilever chair. Unlike traditional precedents made of both timber and tubular steel that relied on support at both front and back, the Cesca allowed the sitter to 'rest on air'. The originator of this concept remains a contentious issue and Dutch architect Mart Stam is believed to have been the first to execute the concept of the cantilever, utilising pipes and pipe fittings. Stam's designs of 1926 were shown at the 'Die Wohnung' ('The Dwelling') exhibition in 1927, although Mies van der Rohe also exhibited a graceful cantilevered design at the same exhibition. It would appear that all the feuding designers were enjoying a share of 'collective art' and hundreds of designers soon took to designing chairs with two legs. It is, however, elements beyond the core principle of the cantilever that mark the B32 as an elegant design. After the immediate consideration of two legs or four, the design of the B32 is a sensitive understanding of comfort, resilience and appreciation of materials. The B32 shows understanding of historical precedents through its use of a bentwood frame for the seat and back, a mature treatment of proportion and geometry and an unsurpassed demonstration of elegance that would endure for decades to come. The design illustrates sophistication and is unique in its mixture of modernist shining steel, wood and cane. These materials soften and offer a humane warmth to the B32 that many other hard-edged and clinical modernist designs could not attain. The armchair version, the B64, enjoyed similar success and when both designs were re-launched by Knoll International in the early 1960s they were renamed 'Cesca' after Breuer's daughter. The host of clear imitations of this graceful cantilever design are a credit to Marcel Breuer's perceptive balance of form and materials.

185

Cité Armchair (1929–30)
Jean Prouvé (1901–84)
Ateliers Jean Prouvé 1930
Tecta 1990 to 2000
Vitra 2002 to present

Jean Prouvé's Cité Armchair

is a remarkable seating design. The chair bears little resemblance to any predecessor, is difficult to date and few designs since have dared pay homage to its unique form. It is a design that quietly encapsulates many of Prouvé's theories and processes. The mixture of materials provides for a wholly functional design. The profile of the seat dictates its use, providing depth where the structure requires, reducing the high back and the front edge of the seat to a fine outline. The upholstery is simplified to a canvas 'stocking' stretched over a tubular frame. The steel sled base suggests engineered machine parts that give the seat a foundation and support the sitter through a strong upstanding cross-brace. To fulfil the matrix of materials and naturalize the design, leather straps are drawn through the side profiles and fastened with buckles to create taut armrests. It is a design that makes reference to the engineered as well as to found objects, and is dynamic while remaining austere. Its design qualities and engineering and manufacturing credentials make it a reference point for important seating designs. Originally a competition entry for the Cité Universitaire in Nancy, France, for use in student dormitories, the Cité is an early work by Prouvé and establishes a design vocabulary for his later works. Prouvé began his illustrious career as a *ferronier d'art* (art metalworker) in Nancy in 1923. Based on a practical understanding of materials and processes, many of which were developed through experimentation, Prouvé's designs were soon recognized through awards at important exhibitions. He pursued creative solutions for an enormous

range of designs, from door furniture to lighting, seating, tables and storage, through to architectural facades and prefabricated building designs. Prouvé's work was admired by many of his contemporaries, including Le Corbusier, and his furniture designs have always maintained a cult following among enthusiasts and collectors. While his output was prolific, many designs were for institutional use or were site-specific and few original designs exist. However, Vitra recognized a growing enthusiasm and market for Prouvé's designs and in 2002 relaunched the Cité as part of a wider collection of his work.

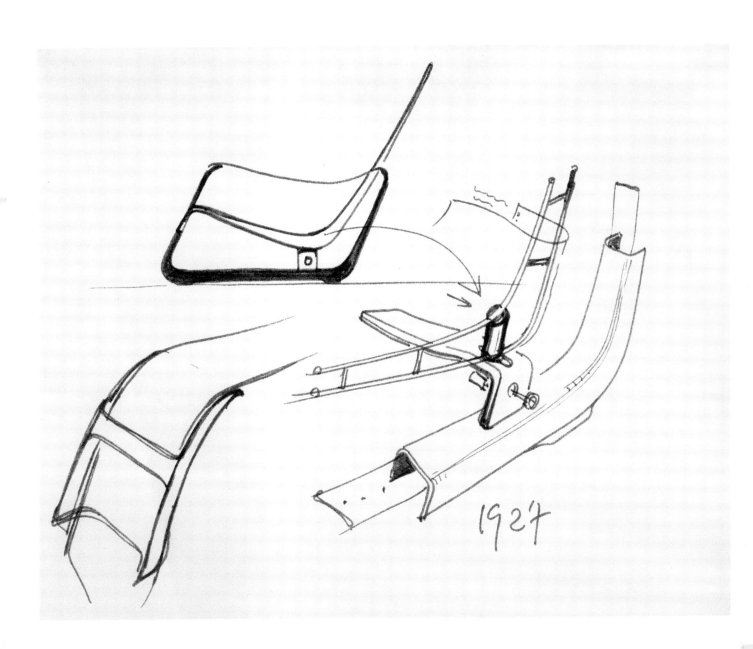

1927

The sinuous profile of the ST14 Chair suggests a design more recent than 1929. The sweeping arc of the cantilevered frame is echoed and balanced by the moulded plywood sheets, which offer support through the seat and back. The seat itself seems to float in mid-air with minimal structural support. The chair design evolved from an exercise in the rational use of new materials and standardized forms. After the destruction of World War I many progressive designers sought to minimize the use of expensive materials and married this with new technologies and ideologies. The ST14 Chair met several of these ideals. Its aesthetic was adventurous and remains so to this day. The acceptance of modernist principles of reduction and function are wholly realized. The frame is uncomplicated and the support does not rely on upholstery for comfort: the plywood supporting elements meet the contours of the user, without the need to offer soft, relatively short-lived fabrics or upholstery. The Luckhardt brothers successfully practised architecture and were active theorists as part of the Novembergruppe. They worked together in Berlin from 1921, gaining a strong reputation as leading architectural exponents of Expressionism. Their designs, such as the Hygiene Museum in Dresden, illustrated individualistic flair. However, when this style proved unforgiving in a post-war period of shortages, poverty and escalating inflation, they adopted a more sensitive and democratic approach in their designs. This change of ideology was evident in their terraced housing schemes, the re-planning of Alexanderplatz and in the remarkable ST14 Chair, which embraces the demands of mass production. The design is still in production today resissued as S36, testament that, in an evolving market-place, the qualities of good design remain constant.

186

ST14 Chair (1929)
Hans Luckhardt (1890–1954)
Wassili Luckhardt (1889–1972)
Desta 1930 to 1932
Gebrüder Thonet 1932 to 1940,
Gebrüder Thonet Germany 2003 to present

Hans Luckhardt

Jean Prouvé trained first as a blacksmith and then as an engineer, and that combination of craftsmanship and a structural understanding of materials defined both his furniture and his architecture. Collaborating with such architects as Charlotte Perriand, Prouvé would go on to pioneer the use of sheet metal in construction and eventually in prefabrication. Prouvé's early furniture was innovative in its use of sheet steel, a radical departure from the tubular steel furniture made so ubiquitous by the Bauhaus, which he personally found unsatisfactory. Instead, using industrial materials, Prouvé's chairs required a degree of handcrafting and were the product of a workshop rather than a factory. The Folding Chair, with a lifting seat, was one of Prouvé's earliest pieces of furniture. It is possible to trace the origin of this design as Prouvé gave the first six prototypes to one of his sisters as a wedding present in 1929. Although these chairs could not fold they are otherwise identical to the later model. Made of flattened steel tubes and folded sheet steel, with canvas stretched across the back and seat, its hollow-body structure was relatively light and yet, extremely solid.

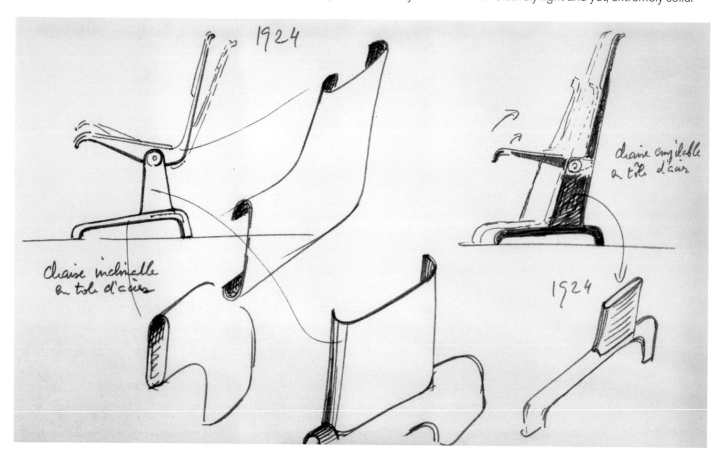

Prouvé used diagonals to maximize the chair's structural capacity, directing the sitter's weight into the angled legs. With the seats folded up, the chairs stack one behind the other. While the shaping of the tubes was done by hand, the materials and the use of sheet metal presses and electric welders gave the chair a stark industrial look. Prouvé said, 'I used to think of furniture as being on a par with the seating of heavy-duty machinery. I therefore took the same care over construction and applied the same tensile standards to the materials, indeed using the very same materials.' The chair is structurally confident, practical and efficient, with a technical delight in its one moving part. Rather than self-consciously styled, its striking design relies on an integral understanding of its materials. Increasingly influenced by the methods of automobile and aircraft construction, Prouvé would go on to use such methods to transform building construction.

187

Folding Chair (1929)
Jean Prouvé (1901–84)
Ateliers Jean Prouvé 1929
Tecta 1984 to 2000

The Viennese company Lobmeyr has been successfully building on its international reputation for glass-making since Josef Lobmeyr founded the business in 1823. Today the company can boast nearly 300 different drinking sets, including this bar set designed by the Austrian architect Adolf Loos in 1929. Loos was commissioned by company director Stefan Rath, who embraced the skills of several other prominent architects and artists when he took over the reins from his uncle, Ludwig Lobmeyr, at the turn of the century. From 1897 Loos worked as an independent architect in Vienna. As his Café Museum Chair of 1899 illustrates, he introduced a more rational and often geometric style to his designs, away from the abstracted, nature-inspired forms of the Vienna Secession group of artists and architects. As well as designing, Loos also voiced his opinions on broad cultural issues in influential essays that were published in *Das Andere*, a periodical that he established in 1903. In one essay titled 'Ornament und Verbrechen' ('Ornament and Crime') of 1908, Loos challenged the value of decoration, claiming it was a waste of energy and represented cultural degeneracy. Subsequently, his ongoing design work embodied these forward-thinking principles. Indeed, this drinking set for Lobmeyr captures a refined, sturdy sophistication that is free from period-specific patterning or ornamentation. Today the glasses are hand-blown from lead-free crystal, made in Germany to Austrian specifications. Each glass is then cut and engraved by a copper wheel, creating the simple, geometric grid. It could be argued that the grid-like engraving on the solid bases of the tumbler and decanter as well as on the decanter stopper is uncharacteristic decoration. One suspects that Loos would insist it is a practical feature, adding friction to aid grip on surfaces and to prevent polished glass from slipping out of one's hands. Whatever the answer, the set, including a Finger Bowl, Beer Glass, Water Pitcher, White Wine Glass and Liqueur Glass, has sustained successful market positioning for the specialist glass-maker and retains a timeless appeal for customers today.

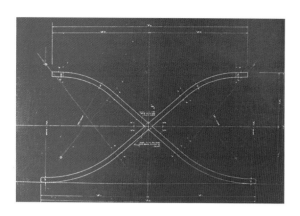

The design for this graceful chair arose from the commission for the German Pavilion (1928–9) for the Barcelona International Exhibition in 1929. Ludwig Mies van der Rohe designed a building that has been pronounced as the epitome of modernist architecture, and created a poetic structure of horizontal and vertical planes built of marble and onyx walls, tinted glass, and chrome-plated columns. (The pavilion was demolished in 1930 and rebuilt by the Fundació Mies van der Rohe to original specifications, 1983–6). There was no existing furniture that he envisioned could be used in this open and uninterrupted space; he then designed the Barcelona chair so it would not appear too solid nor affect the flow of space, in order to complement the pavilion. The King and Queen of Spain were to be received there, and Mies was determined to produce a chair that was 'important, elegant, monumental'. Using a scissor-frame – with two flawless, curving, chrome-plated steel legs like slashes of Chinese calligraphy – each side was joined by a cross-bar with bolts, and the entire frame was welded and hand-filed. The flat steel was an exclusive material at that time, and leather straps, which were stretched over the frame, cleverly concealed the bolts. While the original chairs were laborious to manufacture, not to mention expensive, Knoll began to produce the chair but decided to create an entirely singular-welded frame. This solution reduced the necessity for intensive polishing and sanding, and in 1964, the thin chrome-plated steel was replaced with polished stainless steel. The frame however, has always displayed its construction; the cantilever principle is seen by the floating seat. The chair was refined by Mies in the 1950s, to put more spring in the seat, and said that, 'the chair was to open up for its occupant under the weight of the body. The back was to go back, the seat was to go down.' In the German Pavilion, Mies used white glacé leather cushions (each with forty panels joined by hand-sewn welts), and used only two chairs placing them next to a honey-coloured onyx wall, lending the room breath. By doing this, Mies gave the chairs an instant air of authority. The Barcelona Chair was never intended for mass production, but became a cult object because of its designer, who began using it in the formal or reception areas of his influential buildings – which explains why it is particularly seen in the lobbies of today's office buildings.

Barcelona™ Chair (1929)
Ludwig Mies van der Rohe (1886–1969)
Berliner Metallgewerbe Joseph Müller
1929 to 1931
Bamberg Metallwerkstätten 1931
Knoll 1948 to present

Elegance, speed and technical innovation were the starting points for Johan Anker's Dragon, one of the most popular 9-metre racing boats in the world. The original design had two berths and was ideally suited for cruising in Anker's home waters of Norway. It quickly attracted buyers and within ten years had been sold across Europe. In 1937 the Clyde Yacht Club Association organized the first Gold Cup, a race which quickly became one of the principal championships for the 9-metre class and a prestigious trophy in the world of competitive yachting. Initially the Dragons were made by Anker's yard, Anker & Jensen, as a cheap skerry cruiser for novice sailors. When the design was submitted to the International Race Yacht Union, someone translated Anker's name into the Norwegian word 'draggen'. Someone else changed this to 'dragon', assuming it was a misspelling of the English word. And the name stuck. While the original Dragon's long keel and elegant 9 metre boat lines remain unchanged, today's Dragons are made from fibreglass, which is both durable and easy to maintain, rather than wood. Both the new and the old wooden boats regularly win major competitions, however, and both look beautiful afloat. Exotic materials are banned throughout the boat, and strict rules are applied to all areas of construction to avoid sacrificing value for a fractional increase in speed. The key to the Dragon's enduring appeal lies in the careful development of its rig. Its well balanced sail plan makes boat handling easy for lightweights, while a controlled process of development has produced one of the most flexible and controllable rigs of any racing boat. More than seventy Dragons from nearly as many countries recently took part in the seventy-fifth anniversary race in Monaco, confirming its longevity.

190

Dragon (1929)
Johan Anker (1871–1940)
Anker & Jensen 1929 to c.1949
Various 1940s to present

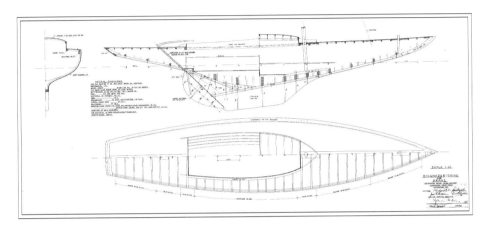

191

Brno Chair (1929–30)
Ludwig Mies van der Rohe (1886–1969)
Berliner Metallgewerbe Josef Müller
1929 to 1930
Bamberg Metallwerkstätten 1931
Knoll 1960 to present

In 1928, Ludwig Mies van der Rohe designed the Tugendhat Villa, situated in Brno in the Czech Republic, for Grete Weiss Löw-Beer and Fritz Tugendhat. He designed both the exterior and interior, and some of the furniture designs he created for the Tugendhat have far exceeded the fame of the building. The Brno Chair is one such example. For the dining room, Mies van der Rohe initially intended to use his MR20 Chair with elbow rests, designed for the Weissenhof Siedlung Exhibition in 1927 in Frankfurt. It turned out that it did not fit into the space defined by a built-in table and a circular separation wall, and a less spacious alternative was therefore needed. His adapted version, the Brno Chair, was based on intuition rather than mathematics and is one of his most elegant chair designs. The Brno contrasts the elegantly tensed line of the frame and the angularity of the back and seat; frame and seat seem to be fixed invisibly to the frame, which gives a light, luxurious and mythical dimension to the chair. The first Brno Chairs were made in nickel-plated tubular steel, and were produced in 1929 by Josef Müller in Berlin. In 1931, a variation called the MR50 was introduced, available nickel- or chrome-plated, or painted red, blue or yellow, and produced by Bamberg Metallwerkstätten, also in Berlin. The chair could additionally be ordered with textile or leather upholstery. The American company Knoll reintroduced the Brno Chair in 1960 in chrome-plated tubular steel and then from 1977 in flat steel bands. Both the tubular steel and flat steel band versions were used throughout the Tugendhat Villa, in either red or white leather.

Tugendhat House, Brno, Czech Republic, 1930

Ladislav Sutnar's spherical tableware design was the winning entry in a competition organized by Krásná jizba Design Studio in 1928 to encourage modern porcelain tableware design and production in Czechoslovakia. The design did not immediately go into production due to a lack of investment and a suitable manufacturer, but due to Sutnar´s managerial skills, the production of the Porcelain Tea Service was eventually financed by subscription among the massive membership of the progressive publishing house Drustevní práce (DP). The development of the prototype and its production continued for three years, and it was finally put on the market in 1932, being promoted as the first Czech porcelain tableware. The Epiag factory in West Bohemia was responsible for the thin, translucent and light-reflecting porcelain of the highest standard. During the 1930s the basic tea and coffee sets were completed, along with the production of forty-seven pieces in total. Sutnar's Porcelain Service was exceptional in its consistent geometry of the extreme simplicity of a sphere, either whole or half, and represents the most significant and typical functionalist porcelain tableware of the period. His use of the sphere was endlessly adaptable and resulted in a rich variety of pieces, including a Soup Tureen, Sugar Bowl and Jam Pot, as well as dishes and plates. Handles on lids are created from cone shapes, giving the set a distinctive silhouette. The basic model of the Porcelain set was in pure white, but the most popular model was in white with a red rim. The rim was not simply decorative, but served to articulate and stress the geometrical purity, and distinguish the body from the lid, or the cup from the saucer. By 1932 the set was being produced in several variations in order to satisfy consumer demands: ivory with a green rim, which was purchased for the staterooms of the first Czech president, ivory with a platinum rim, and also in solid red, terracotta, yellow and blue. In 1936 more than 10,000 sets had been sold, particularly among the highly educated and progressively orientated middle class who accepted the tenets of Functionalism without hesitation. Sutnar also initiated new flexible methods of selling the Porcelain sets: customers could buy parts or single pieces according to their needs. During World War II, while Sutnar was in exile in the United States, Krásná jizba tried to sell off all its stock, including spoiled and faultily executed sets. Without Sutnar's knowledge, additional decoration was added to mask imperfections, including a blue textile-like design and floral patterns. These sets also sold out, but the decoration completely opposed Sutnar´s functionalist ethos. The production of Sutnar's Porcelain Tea Service was disrupted by Nazi occupation of Sudetenland in 1938 and was never renewed because sadly, the moulds were destroyed during World War II.

Advertisement, 1929–33, photograph by Josef Sudek

Ferdinand Graf von Zeppelin

The LZ 129 Hindenburg went into service in 1936. It was only operational for a year, during which time it undertook 60 voyages, becoming legendary when it exploded at its mooring mast on 6 May 1937. The use of highly explosive hydrogen as the buoyancy gas was forced upon Zeppelin, due to the fact that the non-flammable helium gas was only manufactured in the United States at the time, which had banned its export because of rising diplomatic tensions and fear of impending war. Zeppelin had invented the rigid airship in 1900, developing the concept of a spindle-shaped optimum aerodynamic form through a series of designs that culminated in the *Hindenburg*, the largest airship in history. The remarkable shape honed by extensive wind tunnel testing marked the pinnacle of aerodynamic research at the time. It used an aspect ratio of 6:1 (length to width) optimal for lowering the coefficient of drag, and was constructed from longitudinal fabric strips over a metal frame to further reduce drag and create an utterly functional yet hugely iconic form. The airship had a structural volume of about 250,000 m³ and weighed 80 tons empty, 140 tons with a full load of fuel and approached 200 tons fully laden. Unlike a blimp, the rigid airship was not constructed from a dirigible balloon, but rather carried interior gas tanks within the outer skin that provided buoyancy. Powered by four diesel engines producing a total of 4,400 hp, the Zeppelin could travel at speeds up to 135 kph (83.9 mph). This was limited aerodynamically by the enormous surface area and surface friction associated with it. Passengers were housed in a suspended 2-floored gondola of over 400 m². The interior design of the passenger section was carried out by the successful Berlin Architect, Fritz August Brehaus-De Groot. While the Nazi government had rejected the modernism of the Bauhaus, the need for lightweight furnishings led the regime to allow the prestigious interior to feature metal-framed furniture and a specially designed lightweight metal piano! The destruction of the *Hindenburg* marked the end of commercial transatlantic airship flight, until the recent emergence of blimps for promotional use and leisure flights.

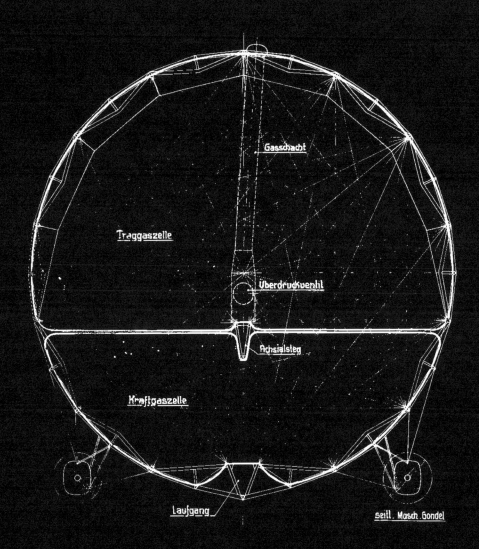

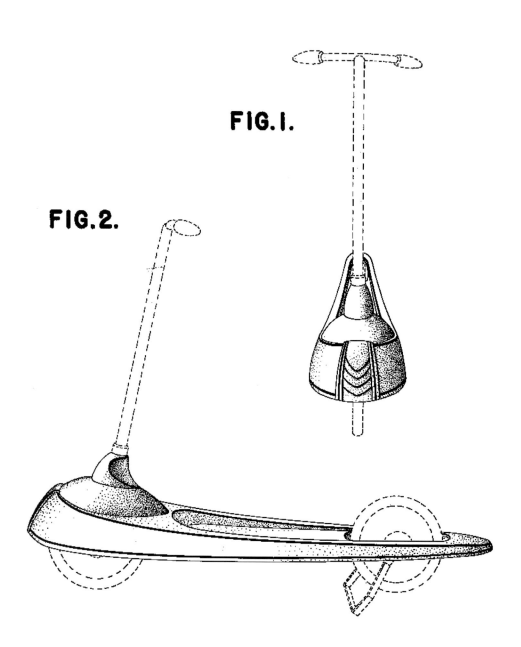

FIG. I.

FIG. 2.

INVENTORS
HAROLD L. VAN DOREN
JOHN G. RIDEOUT

BY

Whittemore, Hulbert, Whittemore & Belknap

ATTORNEYS

Wee-Wheelers Scooter (c.1930)
Harold van Doren (1895–1957)
John Gordon Rideout (1898–1951)
United Specialities Company c.1930 to nd

Made from steel with a footplate, a couple of wheels, an elongated axle and handlebars, the scooter has been a popular children's toy for eighty years. One of the first producers, when the product hit the market in the late-1920s, was Wee-Wheelers – part of The United Specialities Company. The reason for the Wee-Wheelers Scooter's popularity is easy to understand. At the height of the American recession after the Wall Street Crash of 1929, here was a product that was reasonably priced – costing around $2.10 plus extras such as brakes and a bell – and was remarkably tough. According to the original Wee-Wheelers advertising, it was also 'a great muscle developer for children between 4 to 15 years of age' as they could 'cover from 14 to 18 feet on good pavement with no more effort than an ordinary step'. And like a Ferrari, although the scooter came in many shades, its classic colour was red. Curiously though, the fascination with the toy carries on into adulthood and there are a slew of motorized variations on the classic scooter for an older age group. One of the early derivatives was the 'off the highway cycle' called the Tote-Goat designed by Ralph Bonham in 1958, which put a motor and a seat over a rougher, tougher scooter-like frame. More recently, in 1985, Steve Patmont launched a motorized version called the Go Ped that has found a whole new, mature market. Radio Flyer, founded in 1923 by Antonio Pasin and producer of the famous No.18 Classic Red Wagon toy, has also recently launched an award-winning retro-styled 'classic' scooter for the new millennium that features chrome fenders and 'steel wheels with real rubber tyres'.

The Stacking Chair by Robert Mallet-Stevens symbolizes a philosophical shift from the leading style movements of its time. The successful Parisian exhibitions of the early twentieth century showcased the elaborate, highly decorative furniture and objects of the Société des Artistes Décorateurs that formed the Art Déco movement, a predominant European influence of the time. In strong opposition to what he referred to as the prevalent 'arbitrary' nature of decoration, Mallet-Stevens's precepts emulated more closely the principles of functionality and simplicity at the core of French avant-garde architecture of the late 1920s and early 1930s. His primary practice was architecture and he helped to form, and became president of, the Union des Artistes Modernes (UAM), a group of designers working in the modernist style who emphasized geometric form, pleasing proportions, economy of manufacture and the absence of ornament. The Stacking Chair, constructed of tubular and sheet steel, originally lacquered or nickel-plated, exemplifies the principles that informed Mallet-Stevens's ideology. The chair began to appear in the interiors designed by Mallet-Stevens, most prevalently in the kitchen of the Villa Cavrois, Croix, and the offices of the Barillet house, Paris. It was also used widely throughout the Exposition Coloniale in 1931 in Paris. His metal chairs were particularly suited to mass production and this, combined with the efficiency of stacking, as well as the availability of the seat in either metal or upholstery, created an economical chair that suited many environments. The dominant plane created by the back and rear legs suggests a minimal 'wall' of sorts from which the seat and front legs are suspended, adding implied visual strength to this diminutive chair. Mallet-Stevens was influenced by many pre-eminent European designers of the time, notably Josef Hoffmann, a member of the Wiener Werkstätte (Vienna Workshop). Interestingly, some controversy exists about the design origins of this chair, as it is somewhat different from other furniture designs by Mallet-Stevens and he was known to include the works of other designers in his interiors. Still, most historians attribute this chair to Mallet-Stevens. Tubor, the original manufacturer, holds the patent, but the firm of De Causse manufactured the seat in various colours, which Mallet-Stevens used for the restaurant Salon des Ménageres, from 1935 to 1939. The chair has been reissued by Écart International, and is available in white, black, blue, hammered grey and aluminium.

195

Stacking Chair (1930)
Robert Mallet-Stevens (1886–1945)
Tubor 1930s
De Causse c.1935 to 1939
Écart International 1980 to present

Nº 717.660   Société Anonyme Tubor   Pl. unique

Fig.5

Fig.6.

Fig.3

Fig.4

Fig.1

Fig.2

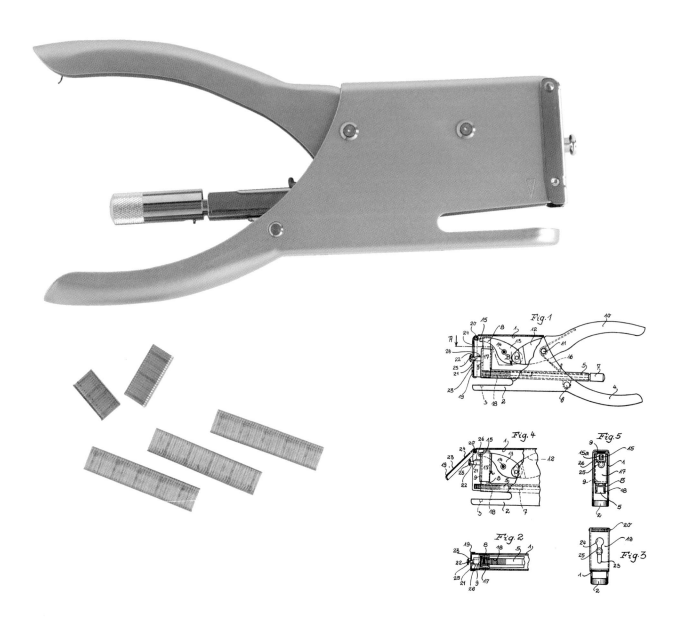

196

Juwel Grip Stapler (1930s)
Elastic Design Team
Elastic 1930s to 1986
Gutenberg 1986 to 2002
Isaberg Rapid 2002 to present

Within the context of the twenty-first-century office, bearing all that bristles by way of technological wizardry, the Juwel Grip Stapler appears defiantly sober by contrast. This manually operated device is devoid of any of the technical advances lauded by today's automated office workers; nevertheless, it remains all the more attractive for it. Branding is understated to the point of passiveness and superfluous detail is non-existent. And yet, in the absence of these contemporary characteristics, this unassuming design and Elastic, the Mainz-based manufacturer that originally produced it, have proven successful to the point of becoming icons within their field. The Juwel Grip Stapler was designed in the 1930s and takes its name from the spring-loaded handle ergonomically shaped to provide greater control. The slab-sided, nickel-plated, rectangular metal body fits the hand as would a pair of pliers. The mouthpiece is left agape, ready for paper to be inserted, and the staples are dispensed from a rear-loaded magazine. The design is both tough-looking and timeless and it is acknowledged as being one of the most reliable staplers on the market today, rarely jamming and delivering staples with a precise, firmly closed grip. The Juwel Grip is indicative of the rigours of German office administration where emphasis was placed on thoroughness and accuracy, rather than on speed. The design remains in its original format, unchanged by time and unthreatened by a disposable contemporary culture and the propensity for cheap mass-produced gadgetry. The Juwel Grip instead succeeds in fulfilling a brief for a routine product, built to endure a lifetime of use. It remains in production today, although the Elastic brand and the rights to its production were recently acquired by Rapid, the Swedish office equipment manufacturer. The quality of its design and its consequent longevity means the Juwel Grip Stapler is yet to be superseded by novel devices incorporating modern, lightweight materials.

Many of the world's classic chairs have been designed by people who came to them through architecture, but Renzo Frau, founder of Poltrona Frau, learned about chair design and construction through the traditional artisanal route of upholstery in early twentieth-century Milan and Turin. It was in the latter that he set up the manufacturing company Poltrona Frau, staffed by skilled craftsmen who had previously been car-leather workers. Using the traditional tools and skills of the artisan to achieve a level of craftsmanship of the highest quality, Frau set them to work on strikingly modern designs of divans and armchairs, with none more so than the Vanity Fair. In this armchair, Poltrona Frau instilled not just quality, but star quality. Originally conceived around 1910 by Renzo Frau as the Model 904 Chair, it was not until the 1930s that the chair finally saw the light of day. It was a timely entrance, for the early part of the decade was synonymous with glamour, particularly in transport, where ocean liners, trains and aeroplanes were like mobile palaces replete with luxurious fixtures and fittings. Thus it was appropriate that the Vanity Fair graced the Italian navy's flagship transatlantic liner the Rex, a ship for which Poltrona Frau had been commissioned to design the interior furnishings. With its bulbous, plump leather form stuffed with goose down and padded with horsehair, all balanced solidly but gracefully on seasoned beechwood glides and famously finished with leather piping and a long, graceful row of leather-covered nails on the back of the seat, the Vanity Fair offered a louche, languid and graceful seating experience that was a perfect metaphor for the era. The chair was discontinued in 1940, but was reintroduced in 1982 as Vanity Fair and made available in its now trademark bright red leather, since which time it has been carving out a niche in another glamour industry, the movies, starring in *The Last Emperor*, as Vittorio Gassman's armchair in *La Famiglia* (The Family) and alongside Whitney Houston in *The Bodyguard*.

Kaare Klint, who founded the school of furniture design at the Royal Danish Academy of Fine Arts in 1924, is an important figure in the development of the Danish furniture industry. Many well-known designers of the postwar period were trained by him or in his methods and held him in high regard. Klint stood against some of the excesses of Modernism and instead advocated that important lessons could be learned from studying often anonymous furniture models from the past, especially those that he called 'timeless types' that had survived use through several generations. He thought that designers should work via a process of the modification of existing designs, disregarding style, and that they should be encouraged to study human proportions. The anonymous, 'timeless type' of furniture that Klint adapted for his Propeller Folding Stool of 1930 was the standard, military-issue folding stool with a fabric seat; a type favoured by the British army. From Klint's perspective, this was clearly a useful piece of furniture that had proved its worth but which, as a design, could still be improved. He saw that the stool could be made to fold up more neatly if each pair of legs was thought of as being made from a single cylinder of wood cut in a vertical helix that twisted evenly through 180 degrees. That way, subject to achieving a narrow and perfectly clean cut, the pair of legs, if pivoted about the centre, could be completely closed or opened and could be given neat slots at one end to hold the seat rails. It is a solution noteworthy for being so simple and yet so ingenious, and also for representing so clearly Klint's working methods.

In 1930, the lighting manufacturer, Best & Lloyd, took a gamble on their latest design. Inspired by the Bauhaus philosophy, Robert Dudley Best created a plain, black lamp which harkened back to his studies in industrial design at the Dusseldorf School and the Interior Design Atelier in Paris. The design was not well received, as it stood in stark contrast with the highly decorative trend the company had been pursuing to great success. Indeed, its initial appeal was industrial, and it became indispensable in car mechanic shops and aircraft hangars during World War II. An inexpensive addition to the Best & Lloyd collection, it only came to the attention of the design world when its use in architects' studios made it the lamp of choice for new, cutting-edge buildings. Most notably, it became a favourite of Winston Churchill, who gave the lamp pride of place on his desk at Whitehall, and, it is rumoured, insisted on its being taken with him when he travelled. Temporarily forgotten after the War, as the company concentrated on new machinery, the BestLite was rediscovered by chance by Danish designer Gubi Olsen. Having spotted the lamp in a shoe shop in Copenhagen, he set about obtaining the distribution rights for Denmark and the rest of Scandinavia. The sales of the BestLite for domestic and business use have increased steadily since 1989 and in 2004, GUBI took over full responsibility of the production and worldwide marketing of the BestLite collection. Today, in addition to the original table lamp, the collection comprises floor lamps, pendants and wall fixtures, available in black, chrome and cream finishes. The collection is still in development. Few lamps have been in continuous production for seventy-five years, but the BestLite, characterized by its simple, elegant design and versatility has proved to be a timeless focal point in any setting. Robert Dudley Best is now widely recognized as one of the pre-eminent British designers of the twentieth century, and his hugely popular BestLite is displayed in London's Design Museum.

BestLite (1930)
Robert Dudley Best (1892–1984)
Best & Lloyd 1930 to 2004
GUBI 2004 to present

Advertisement, 1935

Household Balances

THE "POPULAR" BALANCE.

A **Well Made Balance** of Cheaper Type, but far superior to the usual cheap Domestic Scale. Cellulose Finished All Gold.

Fitted with White Enamelled Pan 5/6
Fitted with Oblong Tin Pan ....   5/-   Weights extra
Fitted with Round Tin Pan 4/3

Cellulose Finished All White.

Fitted with White Enamelled Pan **7/-**

Flat Drill-Adjusted Weights. Silver Finished.

In sets .... 1lb.—¼oz.   2lb.—¼oz.   4lb.—¼oz.
       1/3   1/9   3/-

NOTE.—Special quotations for quantities of 1 dozen and upwards.

The gushing handwritten letters of thanks that arrive regularly at the North London offices of H Fereday & Sons set the Weylux Queen Kitchen Scales firmly in the Victorian context of their ancestors. The rough, cast iron version of balance scales adapted for domestic use in the late nineteenth century may have put the focus firmly on function rather than aesthetic appeal, but by the 1930s, when Fereday introduced its three domestic versions, the scales had become a prestige kitchen product as a result of their simplicity of design, weighing accuracy and longevity. The Queen, Rex and Princess were not, however, without problems: the rough iron castings negatively affected the smooth flow of the mechanism and weighing accuracy, and created a look that was clunky and unwieldy. The Weylux Queen, developed by David Fereday a century after his grandfather, Henry, founded the company in 1862, addressed these problems by refining the scales in a number of ways. Firstly, the iron bearings and beam edges were replaced with modern alloys to allow smoother movement and therefore greater accuracy on lower weights, then a wider metal pan was introduced, in either brass or stainless steel, and a range of colours were added to the cast-iron body. A choice of metric and imperial weights were then offered in a range of different designs. The resulting scales are a rare success: an old-fashioned mechanical piece of engineering that sits well in a contemporary space. The low-slung, fluid lines of the platform and dish are in keeping with the clean lines of contemporary urban spaces but also stand out for their obvious pre-machine age aesthetics, and the transparency and simplicity of their mechanism appeals to a consumer society increasingly disconnected from the workings of everyday objects. So confident are Fereday of the Queen's durability that they offer a lifetime guarantee on it.

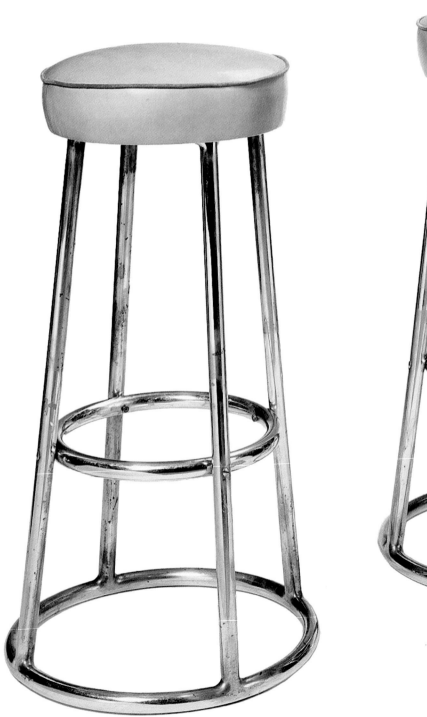

Parisian designer and architect Louis Sognot was renowned in his day. He designed a number of variations on the bar stool, a design that has since become both the archetype and prototype for most chrome-framed stools. In the 1930s designers became increasingly preoccupied with the idea that design should embrace notions of rationalization and standardization. These concepts were brought to life in the form of storage systems and furniture designs that used new materials and technologies and in turn defined the interior spaces in which they were used. Set against the retro-spective, historical approach still adopted in the late 1920s for mass-market design, the burgeoning modernist design politics of the day were represented by the Union des Artistes Modernes (UAM), which sought 'balance, logic and purity' in design. Louis Sognot was a founding member of this group and his work illustrates its ideologies, with his Bar Stool symbolic of this period in design. It made use of the latest developments in material technology: tubular steel, which combined lightness with strength; chrome plating, which allied the design aesthetically with the emerging modernist style; vinyl seat upholstery, which was practical, cheaper than leather and gave the traditional covering style a contemporary twist. The form is sleek and minimal, yet the proportions are generous. While many of the designs that appeared during this period, were largely restricted to the affluent tastes of a metro-politan elite, despite the utopian ideals of the designers, Sognot's Stool found a home in popular public bars and, although it had a limited production, it became a standard for bars in both Europe and the United States.

202

Form 1382 (1931)
Dr Hermann Gretsch (1895–1950)
Arzberg 1931 to present

Form 1382 was not the first modern porcelain collection – there were more avant-garde designs in the decade before it – but it was the most influential and was produced by the German porcelain manufacturer Arzberg in 1931. Weimar Germany was in a dire recession and Arzberg needed to produce a dinner service that was modern yet affordable. For the design, the company turned to Dr Hermann Gretsch. Gretsch, an architect and designer who went on to become head of the Deutscher Werkbund, created a simple, elegant and eminently functional dinner service that is still in production and has been much imitated. According to a probably apocryphal story, Gretsch could not find a soup tureen that could be emptied with a ladle. Form 1382 includes one, and the entire dinner service, along with the accompanying tea and coffee sets, is informed by the same prominent practicality. Influenced by the Bauhaus, Gretsch was determined 'to create shapes that meet real daily needs.' The dimensions of his teapot, for example, are generous enough for a family. Its globe shape is geometrical but not severe and the handle is broad enough to be easily grasped. It is spare in its detailing but thoroughly unselfconscious. The entire sixteen-piece dinner service is similarly plain and yet possesses a lyrical quality in the curve of a handle or plate rim, or in the barely discernible lip of a teacup. Form 1382 was perhaps most revolutionary in being the first dinner service available to purchase by the piece, which meant that less well-to-do families could start to assemble a modest collection and complete it over time. Originally produced in white, it had a thoroughly democratic lack of ornamentation. There were subtle variations, though, with a platinum-coloured set and one with a blue rim and handles. Today, there is a much broader range of decorations to choose from. Arzberg updated the collection in 1954 with Form 2000, which was rimless and more biomorphic in design, and which is still used today by Germany's Federal Chancellery for entertaining dignitaries.

Arzberg 1382
seit 50 Jahren
zeitgemäß = zeitbeständig

Um diesen besonderen Wert aber geht es, wenn Arzberg es für der Mühe wert erachtet, das 50-jährige Bestehen seiner Geschirrform 1382 zum Gegenstand einer Jubelfeier zu machen. Darüber muß gesprochen werden. Das Besondere von 1382 ist im Laufe der Zeit immer wieder gewürdigt worden. Man hat versucht, diese Form in den historischen Ablauf des Stilwandels einzufügen und sie mit dem zur Zeit ihrer Entstehung aufgekommenen Geschmack zu begründen. Das ist ein legitimes Verfahren, das man auf jedes Kunst- und Gebrauchsobjekt anwenden kann. Den Kommentatoren war auch durchaus bewußt, daß der Form Arzberg 1382 eine Sonderrolle zukommt. Nicht eindeutig genug aber haben sie herausgestellt, daß mit diesem Entwurf etwas radikal Neues beginnt und das Neue an ihr eine Kampfansage an die bisherige Methode, Neuheiten von Industrieprodukten zu schaffen, bedeutet.

Arzberg 1382 und der VW Käfer in den
30er Jahren

Arzberg 1382 und der VW Käfer in den
40er Jahren

Arzberg 1382 und der VW Käfer in den
50er Jahren

Arzberg 1382 und der VW Käfer in den
60er Jahren

Arzberg 1382 und der VW Käfer in den
70er Jahren

Fig.9.

Fig.11.

Fig.12.

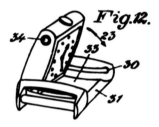

Fig.13.

Fig.14.

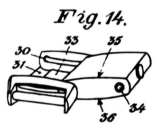

Fig.15.

Once the wristwatch

came of age in the interwar period, it started to be worn while out driving or playing sport. However, few dress wristwatches (and especially their glass crystals) could genuinely withstand the rigours of such sports as polo, skiing or car racing. The watch house of Jaeger-LeCoultre thus introduced the Reverso in 1931, with polo-playing British officers of the Indian army particularly in mind. It was an immediate success with the public. The Reverso was designed by César de Trey, Jacques-David LeCoultre and René Alfred Chauvot with the rectangular movement and dial within a self-contained case, which was itself mounted in a robust oblong carriage so that it could be turned over to protect the glass and dial. It was the first wristwatch to use the back of the case to protect these easily damaged parts. Its sleek lines, the easy sliding and rotating action of the reversible case, and its durability meant that the Reverso caught on immediately and was never successfully imitated. It has never gone out of production and has maintained its reputable status ever since its introduction. The original concept was so well engineered that it remained completely unchanged for over fifty years. Technical advances in watchcase-making resulted in the introduction of an improved version in 1985. Thus, while this modification of the unadorned, original Art Deco model (with over fifty individual components) remains the mainstay of production today, many elaborations have also been introduced. These include setting the case with jewels or enamel decoration, and pocket or handbag versions. The original model was confined to a simple timepiece but variations have recently been offered with, for example, dual-faced versions showing different time zones, or models with perpetual calendars allowing for leap years. Another development has been the intro-duction of three sizes: women's, men's and the large-sized 'grande taille', while most models come with a choice of precious metals or stainless steel. All in all, the Reverso remains one of the world's most enduring wristwatch models.

203

Reverso (1931)
César de Trey (1876–1934)
Jacques-David LeCoultre (1875–1948)
René Alfred Chauvot (nd)
Jaeger-LeCoultre 1931 to present

It was at the 'Neues Wohnen' ('New Living') exhibition in 1931 that Wilhelm Wagenfeld first met the head of Schott & Gen Jena, Dr Erich Schott. Wagenfeld commented that the existing range of household glassware lacked the aesthetic sensibilities provided by designers, as scientists were the driving force behind the product styling. With gentle persuasion, Schott agreed to embark on an experiment with Wagenfeld that would later change the face of his company in Jena, which has changed its name a number of times since then. Schott & Gen (now known as Schott Jenear Glas) was working with borosilicate glass, a new oven-proof alternative to conventional glass. While the heat-resistant properties would inevitably prove a big hit with consumers, Wagenfeld needed to push the boat out if the collection was to withstand subsequent market imitation. Previously assisting in the metal workshop at the Staatliche Bauhochschule Weimar (successor to the Bauhaus), Wagenfeld had to quickly learn the fundamental differences of manipulating glass with the close cooperation of the company's scientific team. He studied the material tensions of various glass bowls, which in turn inspired him to develop a largely tension-free household range. The glass teapot is characterized by its thin-walled, bubble-like body, a form normally equated with the fragility of art glass, not the industrial processes employed by the Schott & Gen factory. The teapot's light, organic appearance is heightened by the avoidance of a base ring, usually found on ceramic counter-parts. The conical tea-holder that hangs suspended within the pot cavity provides the central focus for tea-brewing activity. Indeed, the transparent housing of the teapot exposes the functional process and progression of tea leaf infusion. Rather unexpectedly, the teapot rose to prominence after appearing in a production of Oscar Wilde's *Lady Windermere's Fan* in Berlin. It caused a frenzy among audiences, who promptly rushed out to buy their own. Needless to say, bulk sales in the German capital contributed to the subsequent success of the product, which was in production until 2005.

Of all Alvar Aalto's furniture designs, this is probably his most famous, recognized for its structural ingenuity and novel use of materials in a combination of almost spare perfection. Along with several other furniture models also made from laminated wood, it was originally intended for use at the Paimio Tuberculosis Sanatorium in western Finland, the building that brought Aalto's architectural work to an international audience. Shortly after the building's completion, the Armchair 41 or Paimio was marketed as part of a range of plywood furniture envisaged as standard designs suitable for all human needs. While there were other chairs for dining, relaxing, for use at a desk and for 'dressing', the Paimio made a virtue of its rather hard seat, and the consequent alertness of the sitter meant it was an ideal chair for reading in. Aalto began experimenting with wooden laminates in collaboration with the furniture manufacturer Otto Korhonen in the late 1920s. By the early 1930s the company had formulated the major part of their range, solving on the way a number of significant technical problems. Aalto was especially concerned to keep the cost of the furniture as low as possible, and this was one of his main reasons for investigating the use of wooden laminates. But he also felt that wood had a number of advantages over tubular steel: it conducted heat less well, it did not reflect glare and it tended to absorb rather than propagate sound. The success of Aalto's furniture abroad followed on almost immediately from the launch of the range in London in 1933. Subsequent appearances at the Milan Triennale of 1936 and notably at The Museum of Modern Art, New York in 1938 presented the range of furniture to a larger audience and confirmed its popularity. While other Aalto furniture designs were notable for demonstrating to designers, including Gerald Summers and Marcel Breuer, the structural potential of wood laminates for supporting architectural devices such as the cantilever, the Paimio indicated most clearly the apparently simple but widely unrecognized potential of plywood, as used in the seat, to be bent permanently into shapes of considerable resilience, strength and beauty.

Paolo Venini was a lawyer from Milan until 1921, when his career changed quite suddenly. Entering into partnership with Giacomo Cappellin, the owner of a Milanese antique shop, he acquired a glassworks on the Venetian island of Murano. Although nothing in Venini's background suggested a career in glass-making, he would make a significant contribution to the revitalization of the Venetian glass industry. Before forming the partnership with Venini, Cappellin had been working with a glass-blower, Andrea Rioda, to produce a range of Renaissance-inspired pieces to sell in his gallery. Rioda died before he could begin working for the new venture, so Cappellin and Venini employed the painter Vittorio Zecchin as artistic director of their newly formed company, Cappellin Venini & C. However, from 1932 onwards Paolo Venini became more involved with the artistic direction of the company and worked with some key figures of the architecture and design world. It was from one such collaboration with the famous Venetian architect Carlo Scarpa that the Esagonali were created. This new work was in stark and refined contrast to the old Venetian style and made use of thinly blown glass and translucent colours. Such a delicate and understated treatment of material allowed for a much greater visual priority to the shape of the beakers, demonstrating clearly the technical virtuosity of their manufacture. This also allowed his subtle modernization of form, a hexagonal flattening of sides and a vertical elongation, to be seen more clearly. The partnership of Cappellin Venini & C lasted only five years, but during this time they created a revival in glass production. The work continued after Paolo Venini's death in 1959, and the company, now called just Venini, is part of the Royal Scandinavia group.

In 1932, the Pressed Glass 4644 manufacturing firm of Karhula – which later merged with its sister company iittala - held a competition to generate publicity and new designs for affordable utility glass. Today, the design that won the first prize is largely forgotten. However, the design that came second, by Aino Aalto, is now represented in museum collections throughout the world and has proved enduringly popular in its home market where it is viewed with nostalgic affection. Indeed, it prefigured the remarkable international profile of Finnish design of the 1950s and 1960s. The success of this design, which won a gold medal at the 1936 Milan Triennale, lies in the way Aino Aalto managed to produce such an integrated and apparently simple solution to a complex set of practical and aesthetic considerations. To keep the cost down – essential for achieving Karhula's aim of developing a large market and for satisfying Aalto's social concerns – all the different pieces of the set have a smooth interior/upper surface with a simple ribbed exterior that allows them to be produced easily from moulds in a mechanized pressing process using relatively cheap glass. At the same time, the underlying forms of the pieces and the corresponding annular ribbed bands satisfy a set of modern movement aesthetic preferences for straight lines and simple geometric shapes. Furthermore, the annular banding fulfils both decorative and structural functions. From a decorative perspective it helps to give a static and balanced appearance to each piece and, overall, to unify the set. Fortunately for Modernists opposed to decoration for its own sake, the ribbed bands can also be justified on a structural level because they provide a grip for the tumblers and give strength and rigidity to all of the pieces, making them robust enough for family use, whilst keeping down the weight of material used in manufacture. If one had to use one word to sum up what was important about this design, it would be economy.

Aino and Alvar Aalto

2O7

Pressed Glass 4644 (1932)
Aino Aalto (1894–1949)
Karhula 1932 to 1982
Riihimäki 1988 to 1993
iittala 1994 to present

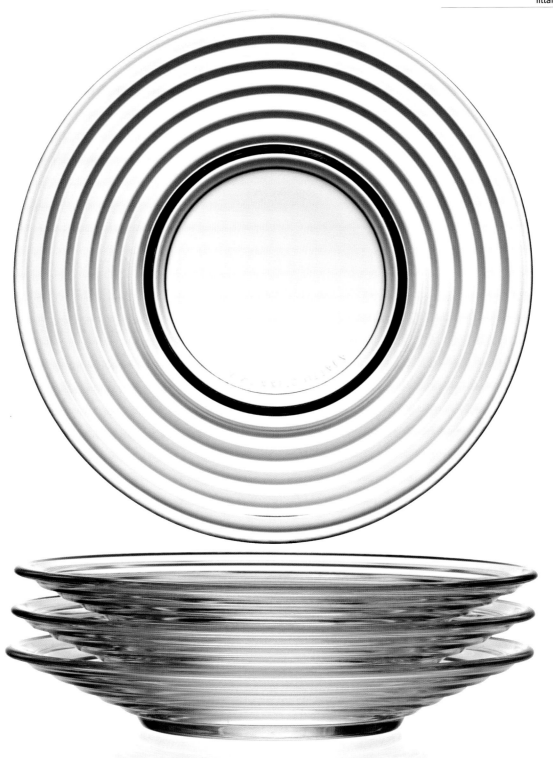

Aalto's simple stacking stool is one of his most straightforward pieces of furniture comprising a simple circular seat supported by three bent, L-shaped, part-laminated birch legs. Since its release onto the world market in 1933, Stool 60 has been one of his bestselling designs and is still in production today. Artek, the Helsinki-based producers of all Aalto's furniture, say that well in excess of one million examples have been sold. In the 1930s most European purchasers were attracted by the space-saving practicality of the stacked stools and their remarkably low cost. They might also have been attracted by the striking spirals created by the legs of the stools when set on top of one another, a device that Aalto was keen to exploit in exhibitions and promotional photographs of his work. Perhaps surprisingly for something that looks so inconsequential, especially in comparison with some of his other developments in the field, the L-shaped leg was regarded by Aalto as his most significant and original contribution to furniture design. What Aalto realized was that producing a sufficiently strong and resilient joint between the horizontal and vertical elements of a construction is a central problem in the manufacture of weight-bearing furniture. His solution was to cut staggered vertical slots in the end of a straight section of birch to allow glued sections of veneer to be inserted. The dampened result was then bent under stress while the glue set, leaving a permanently fixed right-angle, which he called the 'bent-knee'. The result was both innovative and successful, and all the more remarkable for being so unobtrusive. The stool is still being produced in birch veneer, as well as linoleum, laminate and upholstered versions.

208
Stool 60 (1932-3)
Alvar Aalto (1898-1976)
Artek 1933 to present

Viipuri Munipical Library, Russia, 1993–5

Glass has always played an important role in the work of Italian furniture and lighting company FontanaArte, and nowhere is this better illustrated than in Pietro Chiesa's Fontana glass table of 1932. In the same year the company had been founded as the artistic division of the Luigi Fontana company by Gio Ponti and Luigi Fontana, and merged with the Bottega di Pietro Chiesa company. Fontana was at the time a leader in glass design, much of its fame baed on the stained-glass work that still decorates world-renowned churches, including Milan's cathedral. As artistic director of the company, Pietro Chiesa was fascinated by the properties of this fluid, versatile material and the possibilities it offered the designer for domestic interior use, and he utilized a number of techniques, including cutting, moulding and grinding, to design a range of furniture, lamps and objects in which glass was one of the distinctive

features. The clay-moulded Fontana table is one of the earliest of these, and is typical of Chiesa's constant desire to experiment with the property of materials and find innovative ways to work with them. Purely on an aesthetic level, the curved float-glass table is an object of subtle and understated beauty, displaying perfect proportions in its shape and luminescent line, but its most staggering feature is that it is constructed of one continuous sheet of crystal, 15 mm (0.59 in). Bending such a sheet was – and remains – an extraordinary engineering and manufacturing feat, particularly when the largest table available in the series of four is 1.4 m (55 in) long and 70 cm (28 in) wide. Since its debut at the 1934 Bari Fair, which hosted an exhibition devoted to the model of a house, the Fontana table has remained an elegant piece of minimalist glass that has never been improved upon, nor will it lose its sense of timelessness.

The provenance of this unpretentious little drawing pin is quickly established: 'Swiss Made' reads the engraving stamped into the top of the thumbnail-sized pinhead, the centre of which has been punched out to leave a neat hole. The head sits atop three sharp pins cut with one edge straight and one slanted, which come to meet at a sharp point. Each pin is spaced equally, one from the other, around the underside edge of the pinhead. The effect is both precise and convincing, leading one to assume that, despite its size, this is a tool for professional use. Traditionally trained architects have indeed been using Omega Pins since the late 1940s. They remain in production and are even now sold in large quantities, mainly in Switzerland, a nation with an acute eye for quality. The design has remained unchanged since it was first patented by A Schild SA of Grenchen, Switzerland in 1932 as the 'ASSA' pin, and its longevity adds credence to this classic piece of equipment. Lüdi Swiss AG, which established itself in the 1930s as a supplier of paper clips and expanded further into the office equipment market during the 1940s, first manufactured the pin as 'Omega' in 1947. The Omega design was marketed as a precision implement for professional draughtsmen who required their drawings to be held firmly in place. The Omega Drawing Pin, in fact, has several advantages over the more commonly found single pin design. Firstly, the three-pointed version enables the pin to pierce the paper and backboard with ease, securing it with less effort than a single pin allows. Then, the increased surface area of the head permits more paper to be secured, enhancing the firmness of grip. And thirdly, whereas paper can be pulled and torn around a single point, this is less likely to occur when three separate tips are fastening it down. Once secured, the pin's grip is so effective that a specially designed lever device is needed for extraction; this instrument is included with each box sold. Despite the prevailing proliferation of computer-aided design, a market remains for the Omega Drawing Pin, ensuring that the family-owned company is likely to prosper beyond the third generation who currently administer the brand.

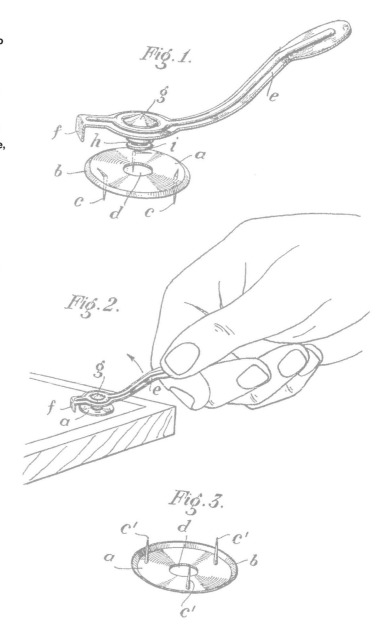

In the field of furniture design, the Danish architect Mogens Koch was strongly influenced by the work of Kaare Klint. Like Klint, he was careful to avoid superficial tricks, preferring a sober approach often based on the improvement of already existing furniture types and the use of traditional materials. Koch's MK Folding Chair, like Klint's, is modelled on military campaign furniture, but also has similarities to the director's chair. In this chair, despite such an historicist approach, Koch managed to develop an elegant and novel solution to the design of folding, and thus space-saving, furniture. Although based on campaign furniture, the starting point for Koch's innovative chair design was actually the folding stool with a canvas seat, the same type that formed the basis for Klint's Propeller Stool (1930). This stool element forms the central section of the chair and is enclosed by four poles, two of which, slightly longer than the other two, have canvas between them to provide a backrest. In order to hold everything together, metal rings that loop around each of the four poles are fixed into the stool section just below the seat. These allow the chair to be folded up, but restrict the seat from collapsing under weight when in use. Originally Koch's chair was designed in 1932 for a competition to provide church furniture. However, it was not put into production at the time due to the lack of a suitable manufacturer. It was not made in any quantity until the model was released by the firm Interna in 1960, along with matching large and small tables, and marketed for outdoor use. The additional pieces were also collapsible and cleverly designed to fit together, further minimizing storage space when folded up. Together, the pieces formed the world's only set of camping furniture designed for use by aesthetes.

211

MK Folding Chair (1932)
Mogens Koch (1898–1992)
Interna 1960 to 1971
Cadovius 1971 to 1981
Rud Rasmussen 1981 to present

The cone-shaped Campari Soda bottle was designed by the Italian artist Fortunato Depero in 1932, and has gone on to become the symbol of the brand. Looking like a cross between a light bulb and a miniature volcano, the design is utterly novel and notably distinct from the traditional bottle shape, which was used to house Campari's main line of herbal spirits (as well as most other spirits on the market). It is also evidence of Depero's characteristic use of bold geometry and striking colour, in this case, the ruby-red colour of the drink. Indeed, Depero's clear-glass bottle uses its contents as if it were paint and consequently fulfils every marketing executive's dream by quite literally placing the product at the heart of the design. Ultimately, it is Campari red that is responsible for highlighting the distinctive shape of the bottle on a crowded shelf. Depero was a member of the Italian Futurist movement and, to a greater extent than any of his colleagues, succeeded in achieving one of the group's primary goals, the breakdown of the traditional divisions between the arts. He was active as a painter, a poet, a designer and a graphic artist. Yet, despite his many talents, the

success of his Campari design is due in part to the marketing genius of Davide Campari, who commissioned artists such as Depero to create posters advertising his company's drinks (such as the above image of 1971). The only rules were that the posters should display the brand name, use uncomplicated colour and incorporate the brand into their picture as naturally as possible. In most respects, this is a brief that Depero's bottle follows as well. Campari's marketing campaigns may originally have been responsible for making Depero's packaging an instantly recognizable and iconic design, but the bottle itself continues to be an inspirational object. In 2002 Raffaele Celentano created a light shade consisting of ten individual Campari Soda Bottles strung together in a circular fan, for Ingo Maurer. Intriguingly, his design is based on the same principles that are at the heart of Depero's original product: a strong geometric shape, the fan evolves as a result of the bottle's sloping sides, and a strong colour, achieved by uniting Campari red and a light bulb.

By the 1920s Patek Philippe had established its reputation as the world's finest watchmaker, for both pocket and wristwatches. But the 1929 Wall Street Crash and ensuing world depression brought a liquidity crisis at Patek's, forcing its sale in 1932 to new owners who could inject the necessary capital into the business. The purchasers were the Stern brothers, whose company was already Patek's exclusive suppliers of watch dials. The Sterns installed Jean Pfister as company president. Pfister's immediate introduction of a new wristwatch model, the Calatrava, has more than stood the test of time. The name is derived from the fortress of Calatrava, in Spain, which was successfully defended against the Moors by a religious order in 1138. The order's symbol of a cross formed from four *fleurs-de-lis* had already been adopted in the late nineteenth century by Patek Philippe as its trademark and today emblazons all its watch movements, but the name has also become associated with the characteristic flat-rim bezel of this watch model. The model is unquestionably Art Deco in inspiration, but its circular shape was unusual among watches of that era, when rectangular or square cases, often with indented corners, were in vogue. Shape apart, the sense of recession embodied in the flat-rim bezel set back from the ring holding the crystal in place over the dial is classically Art Deco. The gentleman's model became an instant success, with its sleek masculine lines, and has endured as Patek's most long-standing model still in production. The Model 96 featured here was introduced in 1946. The range has been extended to include hobnail-cut or diamond-set examples, in white, yellow or rose gold. The rarest of all are in steel; very few of these have been made as the company has tended to concentrate on examples made in precious metal.

With the Zig-Zag, Gerrit Rietveld successfully broke with the conventional geometry of the chair by supporting the horizontal plane of the seat diagonally instead of vertically. This was a device repeated by the Danish designer Verner Panton, taking advantage of the new materials and technologies available some thirty years later. The Zig-Zag is angular and rigid, consisting of just four flat rectangular planes of wood of identical width and thickness: back, seat, support and base, each essential to the construction and function of the chair. Committed to economical design for mass production, Rietveld had been experimenting since the late 1920s with designs for a chair that could be cut or punched from one piece of material and easily assembled, or 'pop out of a machine, just like that'. Early drawings suggest that he was thinking about a chair that could be bent to shape from a single steel plate. In 1938 a version of the Zig-Zag was produced that appears to be made from a single piece of moulded five-ply wood. However, it proved more practical to join together four separate planes of solid 2.5 cm (1 in) wood. With the profile of the chair being so clear, just one single line, the eye is drawn to its construction methods. The dovetail joints between seat and back and the triangular wedges fitted to reinforce the forty-five degree angles become a recognizable feature of the design. Rietveld found that the basic structure was well suited to adaptation. Versions were produced with six round per-forations in the back and with short and long armrests, including a child's version in which the armrests extended to form a tray. First made in Holland by Van de Groenekan and also put into production by the Dutch manufacturers Metz & Co in 1935, the Zig-Zag established itself as a historical point in terms of its design.

21-4

Zig-Zag Chair (1932–3)
Gerrit Rietveld (1888–1964)
Van de Groenekan 1934 to 1973
Meltz & Co 1935 to c.1955
Cassina 1973 to present

In the early 1930s the average radio looked more like a piece of household furniture than state-of-the-art technology. The typical radio was large, heavy and expensive. The EKCO AD65, designed by modernist architect Wells Coates in 1932–3, changed that. The dark brown radio was lightweight, cheap and portable. Coates did away with the stately wood cladding of the past and replaced it with the modern material of the day: Bakelite. Although the new plastic had been invented in 1908, it was not widely used in domestic products until radio manufacturer EK Cole popularized the material with its series of radios with Coates in the 1930s. The new material freed Coates to design a form that moulded itself around the electrical components inside the radio. The circular shape was actually dictated by the large round speaker housed behind the Bakelite fascia. The shape was also economical as it meant the radio used less material than the traditional wooden box. The radio was hugely popular, largely because of its unusual shape and relatively low price tag, and helped EK Cole increase its turnover from £200,000 in 1930 to £1.25 million in 1935. It stands as a landmark in modern product design. The EKCO AD65 established an independent design style for household electrical equipment that stood distinct from furniture design. The Coates radio was one of the first products to be designed on its own terms rather than trying to blend in with the furniture of the average interwar living room. It established a vital grammar for electrical goods that would continue to be developed through the 1940s and 1950s. The curving shape could even be seen as an early precursor to the Wurlitzer jukebox of 1950s America.

The unobtrusive outline of the Hermes Baby typewriter looks instantly familiar, a seemingly obvious solution to the design of the portable typewriter. It is, however, the predecessor of the portable typewriter and came to be the model for many other designs that followed. It was the first truly portable typewriter to be put on the market and was small, very lightweight and inexpensive. Its success was further marked by becoming a favourite with journalists and reporters. Designed by Giuseppe Prezioso for the Swiss firm Ernest Paillard, and named after the Greek god of travel and commerce, it was conceived to fit in a briefcase. The austere housing, angular form and arrangement of the components reflect the honesty of the design and its requirement to meet the objectives of size and functionality. The design was an exercise in reduction. The actual casing of the typewriter was devised to strengthen the frame, and the roller and carriage were raised when capital letters were printed. Both features helped to eliminate additional housings, volume and components. The keys were identical in size and shape to reduce component machining, while maintaining a keyboard and operation technique, standard to other typewriters. The first commercial typewriter was manufactured in 1873 by Remington and was designed by Christopher Latham Sholes, who was also responsible for the qwerty keyboard, developed to reduce jamming of the type-bars. The evolution of typewriter design from this date was predominantly one of miniaturization and portability. The Hermes Baby successfully resolved this problem, and the quest in typewriter design predominantly became one of case styling and price.

In a March 1935 headline from *The New York Times Magazine*, journalist L H Robbins calls attention to the animated character Mickey Mouse's impact on the Depression, writing 'Mickey Mouse Emerges as Economist: Citizen of the World, Unexplained Phenomenon, He Wins Victories in the Field of Businessman and Banker.' More than just a mouse, Mickey had become a money-making phenomenon for his creator Walt Disney's company, which just two years before had been on the verge of bankruptcy. Born eight years earlier as the decidedly less appealing Mortimer, the cartoon mouse had taken hold of the popular imagination due to his humour, mischief and his 'Everyman' personality, a salve to Depression-era Americans who saw hope and distraction in the carefree character. When Disney hired the New York-based advertising man Herman 'Kay' Kamen in 1932 to field and manage merchandising requests, an onslaught of products resulted, from Mickey dolls to Mickey milk. The most popular manifestation, however, was the official Ingersoll Mickey Mouse Wristwatch, produced in 1933, a silver-toned metal-link watchband with a large, round watch face bearing a trademark smiling face, three-quarter profile and yellow-gloved hands that rotated to tell time. In addition, beneath the mouse's rotund red mid-section was a rotating plate showing three mini-Mickeys chasing each other. The watch proved to be so popular that its royalties saved Disney from receivership. After the success of its first watch, Ingersoll continued to make Mickey Mouse timepieces, including a twenty-year anniversary set of watches complete with glow-in-the-dark dials; an alarm clock made of Celcon plastic; an Ingersoll-Timex collaborative watch, which the Apollo astronauts took with them on their mission into space in 1968; and a neon wall clock that depicted Mickey's body somersaulting with every tick. More than childhood innocence, however, the original watch came to represent countercultural sentiment in the 1960s and 1970s. Young people scoured thrift shops and junk stores in search of the distinctive watch, whose mouse mascot took on the subversive qualities of the hippy movement. This was ironic given the fact that Disney had long ago split off Mickey's more trouble-making traits and given them to such subsidiary characters as Donald Duck in response to the heated request of American mothers.

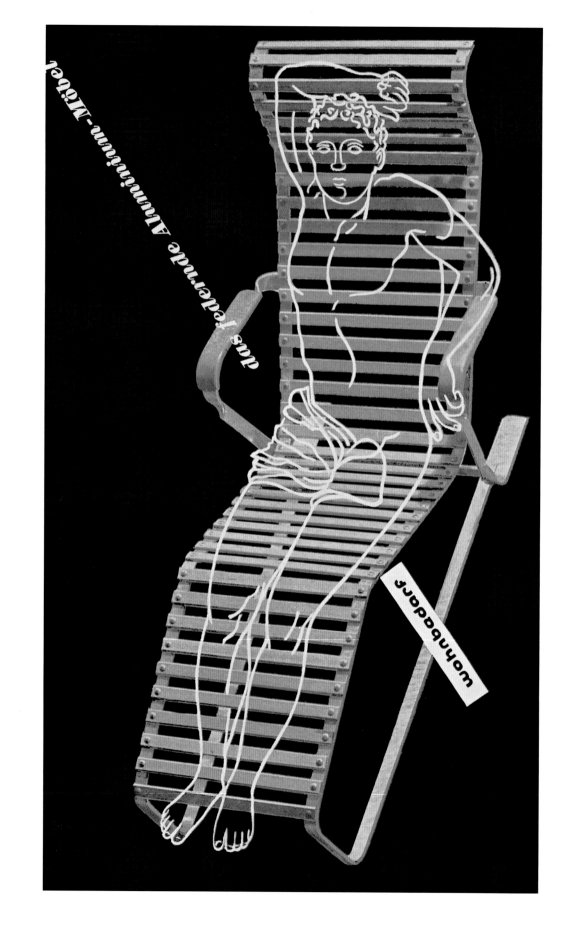

The curve of the legs and pronounced backward lean of the Chaise Longue are witness to Breuer's continued interest in the cantilevered forms he had so successfully achieved in tubular steel while working at the Bauhaus in the late 1920s. The Chaise Longue was part of a complete program of chairs and fauteuils and was first produced by Embru-Werke in Zurich, the city to which Breuer first emigrated from Germany. Seeking new ways of achieving low-cost mass production, Breuer and Embru began to experiment with aluminium, a material that was weaker than tubular steel but much cheaper. By cutting it lengthwise, Breuer was able to form both the front and back supports of the Chaise Longue from a single strip of aluminium. He had won a competition with CIAM in 1933 for this series in aluminium, and Embru put it into production the following year. The original name given by Embru was Model 1097 and Model 1096 for the steel version, but it has often been referred to as 'Chaise Longue 313' simply because the retail shop Wohnbedarf in Zurich, numbered it as such. In 1934 Breuer moved to London, finding work at the recently formed Isokon Furniture Company alongside Walther Gropius, his former director at the Bauhaus. Isokon's founder, Jack Pritchard, was committed to modern functional design, but his background was in the manufacture of plywood. This was therefore the material to which Breuer was asked to apply his thinking. Adapting the Chaise Longue to plywood provided an excellent starting point: where the aluminium model had used multiple slats for the seat and back, these could now be formed from a single sheet of plywood. Manufactured in Estonia, the sheets arrived in London packed in cases made from wooden laths, which Pritchard and Breuer discovered to be ideal for making the chair's laminated frame, the 'arms' and 'legs' between which the moulded plywood sheet was suspended. The prototypes lacked stability and tended to rock from side to side. At Gropius's suggestion a 'fin' was added behind each arm to give the required lateral stability. The Chaise Longue provides an unusual example of the successful translation of a chair design from one family of materials into another very different one. Using production methods almost identical to the original, the Chaise Longue is today manufactured by Isokon Plus only in wood even though Breuer provided Isokon with a licence for the aluminium lounge. The original metal version, using wooden slats and a flat steel-band, is still being manufactured by Embru.

The Zippo Lighter is legendary, managing to retain its credibility since its origins in 1933. Rarely is there a dramatic pause in film noir classics without the cool click of a Zippo as the rugged hero regards his nemesis through half-closed eyes. Other style accessories have gone in and out of fashion, but the Zippo's sleek silver case has always given the impression of its user as being cool, calm and dangerous, remaining virtually unchanged except for a rounding-off of the lid and the hinge mechanism being brought inside the casing. The Zippo made its reputation in World War II when the entire production of Zippo Lighters was ordered by the US government for army and navy issue. Its mythical status lives on in stories where it reportedly deflected potentially fatal bullets, acted as a signalling device in rescue operations and even heated soup in upturned helmets. Its designer, George Blaisdell, was a former oil company executive who was offended by a friend's blasé attitude to style. His friend was using a clumsy-looking Austrian lighter and when Blaisdell asked why he did not get a better one, the friend replied, 'Well, George, it works.' So Blaisdell purchased the US distribution rights to the Austrian lighter and when it proved to be as clumsy as it looked, he embarked on a redesign. First, he streamlined the chrome-plated brass case, fashioning a smooth, rectangular shape that fitted comfortably in the hand. Then he used a spring-loaded hinge enabling users to flick open the top. Finally, he surrounded the wick with a perforated screen to shield it from gusts of wind, yet still allow sufficient air flow for the spark to take. It works by using a piece of absorbent material inside the case to soak up the fuel and place it in contact with the wick. A striking wheel spins against a tiny piece of flint to create a spark that ignites the wick. In a clever piece of marketing, Blaisdell offered a lifetime warranty and free repair for any defects, a bold policy that still holds good today.

March 3, 1936.   G. GIMERA ET AL   2,032,695

POCKET LIGHTER

Filed May 17, 1934

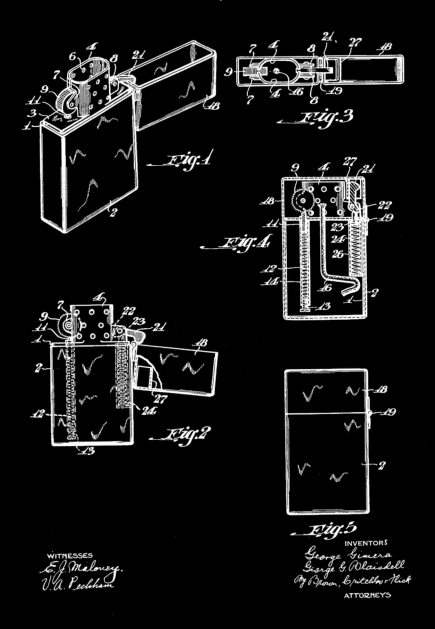

Fig.1

Fig.3

Fig.4

Fig.2

Fig.5

WITNESSES
E. J. Maloney.
V. A. Peckham

INVENTORS
George Gimera
George G. Blaisdell
By Brown, Critchlow Rich
ATTORNEYS

The Bialetti Moka Express is, according to its manufacturers, the only industrial object that has remained unchanged since its first appearance in 1933. The stove-top coffee maker is one of the simplest household objects and yet one of the most stylish. It echoes a traditional tall coffee pot in its basic form, yet has a distinctive Art Deco styling. Its octagonal shape is cinched in at the middle to form a kind of waist, before tilting outwards in eight facets of shiny metal, giving it, when first launched, an expensive, avant-garde aura. The pot consists of three metal parts, the base boiler compartment, the filter section which holds the coffee and an upper compartment with an integral spout. The pot unscrews in the middle, water is placed in the base and ground coffee in the centre compartment. It is then heated until the boiling water and superheated steam are forced up through the coffee grounds to form freshly made coffee which collects in the top compartment. Its smart looks gives it the added advantage of being transferable directly from cooker to table. Alfonso Bialetti, grandfather of the famous Italian designer and manufacturer, Alberto Alessi, was responsible for the design. He trained as a metalworker in Paris, learning aluminium casting techniques before opening a small metalworking shop in 1918 in the Italian town of Crusinallo. From making small metal products for the home, Bialetti graduated to experiments with coffee pot design and eventually developed his *pièce de résistance*, the Moka Express. It is said that he was inspired by early washing machines consisting of a boiler base and tub above. He used aluminium for the body because it both retains and transmits heat well, and because its porosity allows it to absorb the flavour of the coffee – intensifying the flavour with each subsequent brew. The knob of the lid and the handle were designed in heat-resistant Bakelite to prevent burnt hands, and just recently in 2004 the lid, lid knob, handle and valve have been slightly restyled. An impressive 200 million Moka Express coffee makers have been sold since 1933.

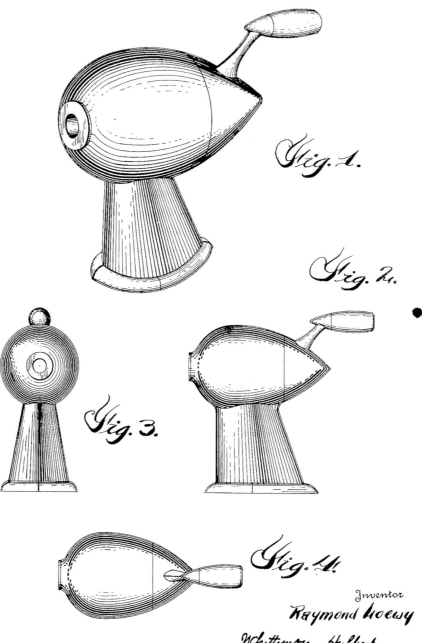

Fig. 1.

Fig. 2.

Fig. 3.

Fig. 4.

Inventor

Raymond Loewy

By   Whittemore Hulbert
          Whittemore + Belknap

Attorneys

It has been estimated that at the peak of Raymond Loewy's career, over 75 per cent of Americans came into contact with one or more of his products, every single day. This statistic may be overstating the case, or perhaps it is drawing on the popular but spurious myth that links Loewy with the Coke bottle, but as one of the country's pioneer designers, he was extremely prolific. And while Americans may have been riding in a Greyhound bus, a Studebaker car, an S1 or T4 locomotive, opening a Coldspot refrigerator, or enjoying a Lucky Strike cigarette, alas, they were unlikely to have been using a Loewy pencil sharpener. Despite surviving as one of the most striking icons of the streamlined age, this famous object only ever existed as a prototype. Loewy trained as an engineer in Paris, but found wealth and fame in New York first as an illustrator, then as an industrial designer. Following the founding of his company and his first

commission for Gestetner in 1929, his flair for self-promotion, as well as design, meant that he remained in the industry spotlight for the next fifty years. In common with many of his projects, the pencil sharpener does not represent any advance from a technical point of view: the planetary cylinders, which create the cutting motion, had been employed in mechanical pencil sharpeners since 1915. The significance of Loewy's model was its sophisticated styling. It had more in common with the chromium-plated flourishes of vehicle design of the time than with the stationery with which it might have shared a desk. It has come to symbolize one of the enduring debates surrounding the nature and ethics of industrial design. Loewy clearly understood design in relation to industrialization, mass consumption and progress. Many of his designs have been criticized as nothing more than restyling in an effort to stimulate sales. While this may have been true, he did a great deal to capture the spirit of an age of optimism, when technology and industry pointed towards a utopian future.

221

Pencil Sharpener (1933)
Raymond Loewy (1893–1986)
Raymond Loewy 1933

222

Bent Plywood Armchair (1933)
Gerald Summers (1899–1967)
Makers of Simple Furniture 1934 to 1939
Alivar 1984 to present

For design commentators of the 1930s, the excitement that accompanied the design of the bent plywood chair by Gerald Summers, transformed the introduction of a simple piece of furniture into a seminal moment in the history of modern furniture design. Produced from a single piece of plywood, bent and held in place without the use of screws, bolts and joints, it made a bold and provocative statement that questioned the essence of the traditional manufacturing techniques that preceded it. The Bent Plywood Armchair is one of the earliest examples of single unit construction – a technique that would not be achieved in metal or plastic design for several decades to come. Commercially it became a hot topic as well, triggering debate as to how this new technique could be implemented elsewhere in the industry. Even to those with only a passing interest in design, the chair's unique organic profile is easy to appreciate. To a world familiar with chairs made to a linear format of straight lines, square angles and flat surfaces, the undulating landscape of smooth curves, rounded silhouettes and sweeping surfaces offered by Summers, presented a profound contrast. Sitting closer to the floor in a low-slung, almost laid-back manner, Summers' chair is a degree more casual in appearance than conventional designs and it beckons the passer-by to take a seat. If you are looking for an early test bed for ergonomics, then this is possibly it. The chair was manufactured under Summers' own Makers of Simple Furniture brand, and it was most likely to have been designed for use in the tropics, where humidity would otherwise have caused fabric and wooden joints to rot. What was an ingeniously simple manufacturing process became an exciting blueprint for low cost mass-production furniture of the future. Although the design offered inspiration to an optimistic 1930s design scene, commercially its success was to be cut short. The glitch in Summers' vision arose when the British government imposed restrictions on the importing of plywood into the UK. As a result, 'Makers of Simple Furniture Ltd' was forced to close in 1939 having produced only 120 chairs. As such, original examples have become highly collectable.

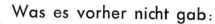

223

Egg Coddler (1933)
Wilhelm Wagenfeld (1900–90)
Schott & Gen Jena 1933 to 1963
Schott Jenaer Glas 1997 to 2004

The Egg Coddler by Wilhelm Wagenfeld is a curious design classic, primarily by virtue of its ascribed function; the necessity for coddling an egg does not feature highly, if at all, in many lives. Yet, the design becomes more understandable when seen as a storage container for preserves or other foods. Made from durable, heat-resistant Pyrex glass, the lid is forcibly held in place by the sinuous form of the sprung clamp, while the chamber beneath swells to create maximum volume, its apex barely lifted, but the whole form firmly grounded by the four flared feet. The outline of the design is quite individual, with little reference to other domestic products or stylistic movements. It is a design with personality, though with an acute functional treatment. The Egg Coddler typifies Wagenfeld's skilled approach to the design of glassware and ceramics, through an attuned understanding of materials, process and function. The uncomplicated simplicity and adherence to functionalism reflect his training, and later teaching, at the Bauhaus. Although he was tutored by László Moholy-Nagy as a metalworker at the Bauhaus, he readily accepted a cross-fertilization of materials and his glass MT 8 Table Lamp of 1923 was one of the few designs put into short production by the Bauhaus. On leaving the Bauhaus, Wagenfeld pursued a wide range of activities, creating functional designs in metal and glass for both the domestic and architectural markets. It was through his work for Schott & Gen Jena that his thoughtfully restrained and functional designs met the mass market. He redesigned their domestic glassware range and developed historically important designs with his Kubus storage containers, Sintrax Coffee Maker and now much-copied glass tea service. In 1954 Wagenfeld set up his own design office in Stuttgart, while he was a professor at the Hochschule für Bildende Künste in Berlin. He received the Grand Prix at the Milan Triennale in 1957 and the Bundespreis Gute Form in 1969 and 1982.

The only Dymaxion Car in existence (the second of three prototypes), one of the most original motor vehicles ever built, stands today in the National Auto Museum in Reno, Nevada, USA. This was not part of Buckminster Fuller's vision when he designed his fantastically innovative and eco-friendly vehicle in the early 1930s. The three-wheeled 6 m (20 ft) streamlined, capsular car carried eleven passengers at 192 kph (120 mph) with a 90 hp engine. A short promotional film from the period declared the vehicle could 'turn on a dime' and showed the teardrop-shaped Dymaxion performing a U-turn in its own length around a policeman in a busy urban setting. The car was designed with the intention that it would evolve into a jump-jet-style flying vehicle when the suitable alloys and engines became available. This ingenious design was one of the many ground-breaking ideas produced by the prolific practical philosopher Buckminster Fuller, as part of what he called his 'Comprehensive Anticipatory Design Science' and which he demonstrated through ideas and inventions that he called 'artifacts'. Albert Einstein said when he met him, 'Young man, you amaze me!' The three Dymaxion prototypes, designed by Fuller as director and chief engineer of 4D Company and built by the naval architect, Starling Burgess, with the aid of a crew of expert sheet-metal workers, were well on their way to making a substantial leap into the future. Attracting vast public attention and featuring in exhibitions such as the 1934 'Wings of a Century', the Dymaxion reflected the American public's intense infatuation with aerodynamics and economical product proposals. Weighing not much more the a VW Beetle, it did 12 km per litre (30 miles per gallon), and claimed that fuel consumption was 30 per cent less than a conventional car at 48 kph (30 mph) and 50 per cent less at 80 kph (50 mph). This was achieved by locating small motors in the wheels. In the second version each wheel could be steered independently, to allow for sharp city curves and sideways parking. The steering was to become a key issue due to a tragic accident that killed the driver and injured the passenger, a British auto enthusiast who was leading a group of investors. Development was brought to a halt and, in spite of an investigation exonerating the Dymaxion Car (it was recognized to be the fault of the other car), newspapers dubbed the vehicle the 'Freak car'. It may well have been a freak, as it was a design based on performance, not style or trend, and was informed by necessity and by radical ideas about what a car is and how it works. Automobile history since then has shown it to be one of the most influential breakthroughs in motor vehicle design.

The Dymaxion Car (1933)
Richard Buckminster Fuller (1895–1983)
Not produced

Starling Burgess and Buckminster Fuller with Dymaxion Car no. 1, 1933

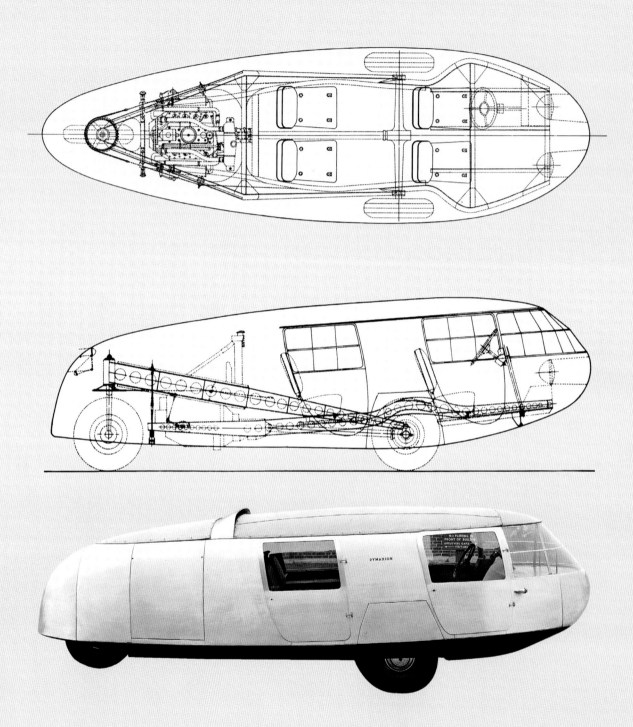

Wooden frame, covered with aluminium, 5.8 m in length

The 4699 Deck Chair epitomizes Kaare Klint's highly influential approach to modernity. His reinterpretation of a nineteenth-century design demonstrates his study of human proportion aligned with meticulous detailing and high-quality construction. The teak frame reveals the form of the structure while being dynamic in profile. The brass fixings are carefully detailed and exposed to illustrate their relevance in the construction of the chair. The elegantly arched profile of the folding seat and back is inlaid with cane to support the user, and a further concession to comfort appears in the full-length removable canvas upholstery pad with head-cushion. The 4699 Deck Chair reveals Klint's preoccupation with updating historical designs to suit contemporary requirements. This design was not reworked in response to transient tastes but rather as an improvement on a traditional design. This ideology had enormous impact on future generations of Danish and international designers. Trained as a painter and architect, Klint established his own office in 1920 and was commissioned to design furniture and fixtures for Danish museums, including Copenhagen's Thorvaldsens Museum. His furniture designs were internationally exhibited as early as 1929 in Barcelona, and were shown at the 1937 Paris exhibition. These designs provided the basis for an era of international dominance by Danish designers, such as Hans Wegner, Ole Wanscher and Børge Mogensen. Klint's theories on the marriage between traditional furniture types and the requirements of twentieth-century lifestyles were to provide designs of lasting importance: 'A

designer can learn to construct an item of furniture, section by section, on the basis of these dry facts, but at the same time give it the changing artistic form that suits him and his time.' His studies in anthropometrics were highly respected and influential in the development of furniture designs suited to the human form. Additionally, his studies into the science of storage provided templates for the standardization of dimensions for shelves and drawers. In a time when 'retro-design' finds favour with style magazines and media, the work of Kaare Klint should be used as the measure against which such stylistic re-workings are judged.

4699 Deck Chair (1933)
Kaare Klint (1888–1954)
Rud Rasmussen 1933 to present

Lampada da terra a luce indiretta in ottone verniciato grigio "Nextel". Lampadina I alogena 500W 220 V. Completa di dimmer
Pepso lordo kg 15
Pesso netto kg 10
Imballo in cartone
volume dm³ 338.7

0556M
Idem in ottone verniciato marrone "Nextel".

0556N
Idem in ottone nichelato

Lampadare à lumière indirecte, en laiton verm gris "Nextel". Ampoule I halogène 500 W 220 V Reglage d'intensè avec dimmer
Poids brut kg 15
Poids net kg 10
Emballage en carton
Volume dm³ 338.7

Idem en laiton vernibran "Nextel".

Ditto en laitas nickelé

Floor lamp with indirect lamp, varnished brown "Nextel" brass. Bulb: 1 halogen 500 W 220 V. dimmer included
Gross weight kg 15
Net weight kg 10
Packing cardboard
Volume 338.7 dm³

Ditto, varnished brass brown "Nextel".

Ditto, in nickeplated brass

Stehlampe mit indirektern Lichtaus gran lackiertem Messing (Nextel), Beleuchtung: 1 Halogenbierne 500 W 220 V
Dimmerregulierung
Bruttogewicht kg 15
Nettogewicht kg 10
Verpackung in Karton
Rauminhalt dm³ 338.7

Desgleichen. Messing braun lackiert "Nextel".

Ditto, vernickeltes Messing.

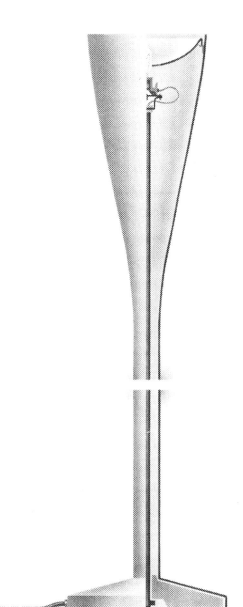

Ø cm 22 h 190

The name Luminator is probably most famously associated with Achille and Pier Giacomo Castiglioni, who designed their version of the uplighter in 1954. The duo named their lamp as a tribute to a version by Pietro Chiesa that was designed more than twenty years earlier – and an even earlier version exists, designed by Luciano Baldessari in 1929 and used at the 1929 Barcelona World Expo. The word was a generic term in the 1930s for uplighters, but it is Chiesa's domestic version that hindsight has shown to be the most innovative. Pietro Chiesa studied as an architect and worked principally on glasswork and *novecento* style furniture before merging his workshop, the Bottega di Pietro Chiesa, with Gio Ponti and Luigi Fontana's newly established design manufacturer FontanaArte in 1933. As artistic director, Chiesa was responsible for around 1,500 prototypes in all areas of design, and his Luminator floor lamp is a great example of a product whose simplicity results in a grand expression of form. It was also a design landmark: the first domestic uplighter or standard lamp. Chiesa took the idea of indirect lighting from the studio equipment of photographers, realizing that projecting light directly onto the ceiling, from where it could indirectly bounce back into the room, could produce a gentle, softly diffused light that could beautifully illuminate a room punctuated by task lighting. He housed it in an elegant and simple brass tube, fixed to a base that flared out like a funnel or champagne flute at its top, and in so doing successfully created a subtle and astonishingly simple piece of elegant minimalism that was determined by functional and structural demands. The honesty of its form belies the time during which it was designed, proving to be an enduring influence.

S Olufsen & P Bang

This freestanding radio, with its tubular steel base and frame, reflects the influence of the cantilevered furniture of Marcel Breuer. Because of its tubular steel legs and wood cabinet, the radio asserts its role as a piece of furniture, rather than as an accessory. In the history of radio design the Hyperbo Radio represents a remarkable departure in both style and function. Produced in 1934–5 by the Danish company Bang & Olufsen (which had only been established nine years earlier) the Hyperbo reflects in its appearance much of the spirit of early twentieth-century Scandinavian design. The emphasis on diligent and elementary characteristics dominated much of Northern Europe, particularly Denmark. Having become industrialized later than the rest of Western Europe, Scandinavian countries embraced the new style of Modernism. Like many furniture designs from the Bauhaus, the Bang & Olufsen radio is lifted from the ground by its chrome legs. Cantilevered off the floor, the upright position gives the unit a lightness of form and allows for easy cleaning underneath. The choice of ebonized wood over the more traditional walnut further modernizes its appearance. In addition to this German influence, the Hyperbo also displays the influence of the Swedish Functionalist movement, which reached its peak in 1930. Led by Gregor Paulsson and Gunnar Asplund, Functionalism embraced the new machine aesthetic and the radio, in its simple, geometric façade, created a new domestic machine. Steel, glass and concrete, and simple geometric forms were adopted, along with socialist political ideas, with the aim of producing a new social and domestic model for Europe. This radio set the way forward for the highest dedication to utilizing new technologies, and while it also functioned as a piece of furniture, it is considered as the precursor to today's music centre, as it combined radio, loudspeaker and a turntable into one unit. The turntable was similar to the modern CD player, as the record was slotted into a drawer, representing itself as a machine that would influence future designs.

Launched at Chicago's 'Century of Progress' exhibition in 1934, Chrysler's Airflow automobile was one of the first mass produced cars to exhibit the aesthetic of 'streamlining'. The science of aerodynamics was inspired by air transportation and resulted in car bodies exhibiting rounded edges, smooth surfaces and low horizontal profiles. Carl Breer, a graduate in engineering from Stanford University and Chrysler's head of research from 1925, consulted Orville Wright about ways of integrating aerodynamics into automotive design. Wright suggested the use of wind-tunnel testing and a new body shape in which passengers were moved nearer to the front of the car. The result was a radical shift in car body styling. The Airflow had an integrated body with a sloping windscreen and a continuous curving line, which united the front with the rear. Chrome strips were used to enhance its horizontality and the lines around the windows, as well as those joining the wheel arches at the rear to those in the front, were curved to accentuate the automobile's organic appearance. This was not a superficial style statement, however, but rather a significant engineering achievement: it depended upon a new approach to car body manufacturing which used single stressed-steel assembly thereby eliminating the need for a wooden frame. Nor was the interior ignored: tubular steel was used for the seats and marbled rubber mats for the floor creating a novel interior look for this radical car. The Airflow's large, rounded nose and heavily chromed radiator grille were considered ugly by the public, however, and the car did not sell in large numbers in spite of a number of face-lifts by the stylist, Ray Dietrich. Production of the car was, sadly, discontinued in 1937.

★ *Airflow* IMPERIAL
CHASSIS AND FRAME

Airflow design has made it possible to provide the most rigid chassis and frame ever built. . . . Notice the steel girders surrounding and protecting the occupants and absorbing shocks. In actual construction many of the body frame members shown above are integral with the body panels—the one reinforcing the other.

COLDSPOT
REG. U.S. PAT. OFF.
"Super Six"

Lovely Modern Design
Super-powered "Package Unit"
Full 6-cubic foot size
About half usual price

A NEW COLDSPOT for 1935 and a NEW Standard of Value in electric Refrigerators. By Value we don't mean just a lower price. You will never appreciate the Value offered in this COLDSPOT merely by looking at its price. Here is all we ask: Forget the price for the moment and consider this COLDSPOT purely in terms of Quality. Study its Beauty. Check its features. Analyze it strictly in terms of what it offers you. Then compare it with any other refrigerator of similar size, selling in the $250 to $350 class. We say that you will find the COLDSPOT actually a *Better* refrigerator, *In spite of the Fact That It Costs Only About Half as Much.*

USE YOUR CREDIT. You don't have to pay cash. See Easy Payments Prices and Terms on page at right.

All Prices for Mail Orders Only.

$5 DOWN

VEGETABLE FRESHENER

Large, covered, porcelain enamel vegetable freshener for keeping lettuce, celery, tomatoes, etc. in a fresh, crisp condition. Easy to keep clean and sanitary. Slides in and out exactly like a drawer.

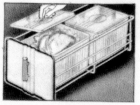

STORAGE BASKET

Large wire basket, containing two over-size covered glass dishes to keep butter, salads or left-overs from absorbing the taste of other foods in the box. These dishes can be removed for kitchen use if desired.

STORAGE BASKET

An open wire basket for holding coarse vegetables, fruits, etc. to eliminate breakage. (This container and the 2 shown at left suspend from lower shelf like drawers.)

WATER COOLER

Covered glass water cooler with swing down faucet. Holds about a gallon of liquid. Can be used for iced tea lemonade or other beverages. Especially valuable during the hot months.

Herman Price, engineer, and Raymond Loewy

At a time when manufacturers were desperate to boost sales in the aftermath of the Wall Street Crash, Sears Roebuck, one of the largest American mail-order companies, invited Raymond Loewy to redesign its Coldspot Refrigerator. Finding the existing model unattractive and lumpen ('an ill-proportioned vertical shoebox...perched on spindly legs'), Loewy determined to replace it with a design that would speak of 'quality and simplicity'. Though he moved the position of the main motor and pump and reduced their loud buzz to a 'comforting hum', the basic machine remained the same. Loewy's principal achievement was the remodelling of the casing. He gave it curved corners and rolled edges and subtly altered its proportions, running three fluted lines down the centre to emphasize the vertical. A single uninterrupted door was created by moving the handle and hinges to a return at the side. The long 'feather touch' handle was designed so that 'a housewife with both hands full could still open the refrigerator by pressing slightly with her elbow'. With perforated, rust-free aluminium shelves and a gleaming white, easy-to-clean finish, the new Coldspot Super Six appeared fresh, efficient, sleek and modern. In later models the wasted space beneath the fridge was occupied by a storage drawer, the returns either side of the door were eliminated and the hinges hidden to present a smooth, unified face, interrupted only by the brand name and door handle, each modified to run horizontally. Despite its six cubic foot capacity it was remarkably low priced. Backed by a strong advertising campaign that urged potential buyers to 'study its beauty', annual sales of the Coldspot rocketed from 60,000 to 275,000, more than 300 per cent, over the course of a year from its initial launch. Never one to miss an opportunity to champion his own achievements, Loewy later wrote that the redesign of the Coldspot marked the introduction to product design of the (soon to be universally adopted) technique of clay modelling over a wooden frame or 'buck'. Thick layers of modelling clay coating the buck gave a malleable surface that could be sculpted until the desired lines were achieved, thus adding 'flair and spontaneity' to the design process. The Coldspot made Loewy's reputation and it has often been argued, particularly by Loewy himself, that its launch marked the beginning of the profession of industrial designer in America.

LES MEUBLES
DES ATELIERS
JEAN PROUVÉ

Concessionnaire exclusif :
Steph SIMON
52, Av. des Champs-Elysées
Paris-8ᵉ / ÉLY. 45-78

230

Standard Chair (1934)
Jean Prouvé (1901–84)
Ateliers Jean Prouvé 1934 to 1956
Galerie Steph Simon 1956 to 1965
Vitra 2002 to present

Jean Prouvé's Standard Chair, with its solid structure and simple aesthetics, is an understated design. It evolved from Prouvé's work for a furniture competition run by the University of Nancy in France, in which he focused on designs combining metal and wood. For the Standard Chair, Prouvé used a combination of sheet and tubular steel with rubber feet for the base. Prouvé conceived the chair for mass production and during the war created a version that could be dismantled. Although he started as a blacksmith, Prouvé expanded into the realms of architecture, design and engineering. Today, he is regarded as a pioneer in developing series production furniture, and influential in his search to find modern solutions to daily living. The Standard was conceived for the institutional and contract markets, although today, its logical form and strong functionality make it a versatile chair that can be used in domestic environments as well as public areas such as restaurants, cafes and offices. It was to become a highly desirable object in itself and reflected Prouvé's belief that design should be a populist form of modern Functionalism. Proof of the design's longevity came in 2002, when Vitra reissued the Standard Chair almost seventy years after its initial conception. Vitra already had a collection of original Prouvé pieces, including the Standard Chair, in its Design Museum Collection, so it made sense for the manufacturer to produce what it regarded as a design icon. Prior to Vitra's production, Prouvé's designs were not widely known outside design collectors' circles. Vitra's endorsement, however, places the chair on a par with designs by the Eameses and George Nelson.

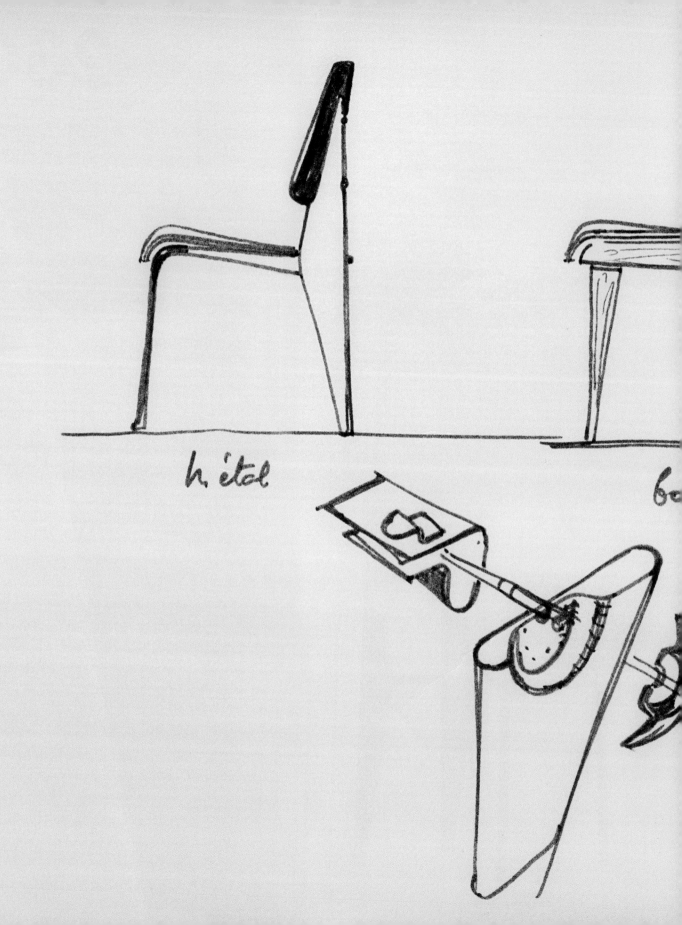

métal

bo

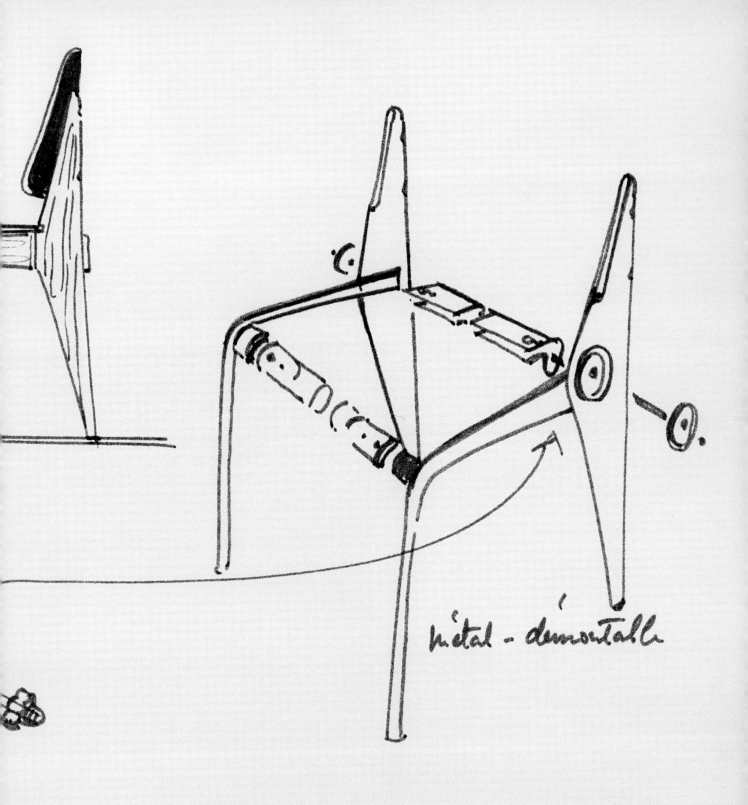

métal - démontable

It almost defies belief, but by 1939, only four years after it first flew in 1935, ninety per cent of the world's airline traffic was being carried by DC-3s. It was an auspicious beginning, for even in the post-war period and the advent of the jet age, the little DC-3, or Dakota as it was also known, continued its dominance of the short- and medium-haul airline business. Today, over 1,000 DC-3s are still thought to be in active service, even though production lasted only a scant twelve years. Ironically, the first hint of a future boom in airline travel came in the 1930s when the world's economies were struggling to recover from the Depression. In the United States, all passenger airline travel was heavily subsidized by government mail contracts, and the first airlines barely made a profit. Part of the problem was the lack of a passenger plane that could pay its way, with sufficient range and payload, and enough comfort to attract transcontinental passengers. But there was sufficient interest to encourage the airlines and manufacturers to find an aeroplane that could take passenger flying into new and profitable territory. Douglas had done reasonably well with its DC-1 and DC-2, both of which were reliable mail carriers. The newly designed DC-3 fit the passenger role perfectly. Powered by two Wright Cyclone radial engines, the DC-3 was first used by American Airlines in an overnight

231

Douglas DC-3 (1934)
Douglas Aircraft Design Team
American Airlines Design Team
American Airlines 1934 to 1946
Mitsui & Company (Japan) 1934 to 1946
Amtorg (USSR) 1934 to 1946

'sleeper' service between New York and Chicago. Day routes were quickly added and the DC-3 carried fourteen sleeper passengers, or twenty-eight 'day' passengers. The success of the DC-3 allowed the airline industry not only to become profitable, but to shed its reliance on government mail contracts, and with them, political interference and insecurity. The outbreak of World War II saw a huge demand for small, rugged and practical transport planes, and it was with the military that the DC-3 (C47 in military language) really came into its own. Capable of being flown in and out of rough airfields, the C47 became a ubiquitous image of the Allied air forces. At the height of the war, the

Douglas Aircraft Company, based in Santa Monica, California, was producing over 500 aeroplanes a month, an astonishing figure even by today's standards. After the war's end, there was a huge over-supply of DC-3s and C47s. In 1946, with the onset of the jet age, during which Douglas would become Boeing's most significant competitor, the company stopped production of the DC-3, having produced over 10,000 aeroplanes in twelve years.

PREIS LISTE 67/68

 LOLA-Werke Gebr. Schmidt

A staple addition to any German worktop, the LOLA Brush is one of those generic design items that people just seem to take to their hearts. The LOLA has become an icon of German domestic lifestyle, as coveted now for its familiar form as it is for its function of washing dishes. The brush's natural fibre bristles are secured into a circular wooden head and a slender arm is connected to the head by a metal clasp; this not only allows for a certain freedom of movement but also means that the head of the brush can be easily detached. The brush is efficient, agile and hard-wearing. A steady, basic price has no doubt helped to ensure the brush's longevity. What is unique about the LOLA Washing-Up Brush is that its design has required no updating or renovation: the brush available to buy today is manufactured using the same blueprint of seventy years ago. The product still bears the original logo, which in itself is a great example of iconic German

graphic design. Schmidt, the manufacturer of the brush, was originally based in Krempe, then later moved to Itzehoe, West Germany. The factory has specialized in brush manufacture since its inception and has been in the hands of the Schmidt family since 1929. The LOLA was first produced in 1934 at the new Schmidt factory in Itzehoe, which is where the brush received its unusual name; LOLA was an abbreviation for the 'Lockstedter Lager' where the brushes were stored before transportation across Germany. This simple, functional, everyday object is one of Germany's most celebrated and democratic design items.

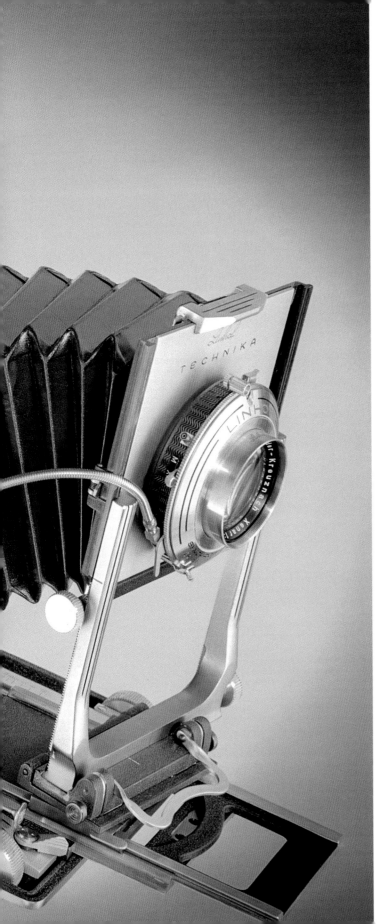

Linhof Technika (1934)
Nikolaus Karpf (1912–80)
Linhof Präzisions-Systemtechnik
1936 to 1957

The Linhof company, founded in 1887 by Valentin Linhof, started by producing metal photographic shutters. Linhof's first all-metal camera appeared in 1889 and was noteworthy for being square in shape, with a rotating back that allowed horizontal or vertical pictures to be taken. Linhof was a competent German camera manufacturer producing good-quality cameras, but it was the Technika range of cameras, introduced in 1936, which established the company's name among professional photographers and helped ensure its reputation as manufacturer of a well-designed and constructed cameras. It quickly gained a reputation for being suitable for the rigours of studio and location photography. After Linhof's death in 1929 his workshop continued with the production of all-metal cameras and shutters. The workshop was joined by Nikolaus Karpf, who later took over the company and introduced a number of innovations, including the swing-and-tilt standard. The first camera to incorporate the swing-and-tilt standard became known as the proto-Technika and was produced in 1934. Following further refinement, commercial production began in 1936. Over 60,000 Technika cameras have been produced to date and in 1959 and 1960 Linhof won eight iF Design Excellence awards for its various products. The Linhof design continued to evolve into its current form as the Master Technika, although the basic design of the camera has stayed constant. The swing-and-tilt controls could be applied to both the front standard holding the camera lens and the back standard carrying the sensitized material, allowing the photographer to make corrections to optical distortions. Karpf's design allowed these controls to be applied to a hand camera. When closed, the main body protects all the parts of the camera, making it very compact so it could be used outside the studio. The design allows a range of lenses to be fitted, from the ultra wide-angle 65 mm to the 500 mm telephoto. The versatile design means that the camera can also be used for specialized applications such as photomicrography and copying. Since its heyday during the 1950s and 1960s there have been many imitators, including the American Graphic and British MPP Technical range of cameras. But because of its superb quality of construction and finish, complemented by a range of matched lenses from Schneider, none ever reached the popularity of the Linhof Technika.

In the 1920s the Americans wanted to race bigger boats in the America's Cup and so they introduced the Universal Rule in 1929, which allowed increased waterline length, without restricting sail area. Yachts with a waterline length of between 22.8 and 26.5 metres (75 and 87 feet) could now race in what was called the J-Class. Only ten J-Class craft were built and they raced for just eight seasons between 1930 and 1937. Among them, and one of only three British boats, was the Endeavour. Keen sailor and aeronautics designer Thomas Sopwith commissioned Camper & Nicholsons to design a J-class boat that could win the America's Cup. They had already built two J-class boats, the Shamrock in 1930 and the Velsheda in 1933, and they used their experience to get the Endeavour in the water in just four months, ready to challenge for the 1934 Cup. Sopwith drew on his aeronautics background to organize the rig of the boat. The sails were designed by Ratsey & Lapthorne of Cowes and offered immense sail area and power, and are still used in J-Class yacht racing today. The hull of the boat is constructed of steel panels and the deck is made of Canadian pine. A lifting keel slides into the main keel, a system that gives the skipper greater flexibility during navigation. Did it win? The Endeavour gave Britain its best chance to grab the America's Cup but the defending American boat, the Rainbow, fought off the challenge with highly skilled sailing. Over the next forty-six years, the Endeavour passed through many hands, its fate often hanging by a thread. In the early 1980s, the boat was sitting in an abandoned seaplane base in southern England, a complete wreck, rusting and forlorn. Then in 1984, American yachtswoman Elizabeth Meyer rescued the ailing yacht and undertook a five-year rebuild. Since the hull was too fragile to be moved and was a long way from any boatyard, Meyer had a building constructed over the boat and hired welders to restore the hull in situ. The newly seaworthy hull was towed to the Royal Huisman Shipyard in Holland, where the mast, boom and rigging were rebuilt, the engine, generator and mechanical systems reinstalled and the interior joinery refurbished. Hard work, love and agony went into the restoration, and were repaid when the Endeavour sailed again in 1989, for the first time in over fifty years.

As was common among architects before the rise of a distinct design industry, Giuseppe Terragni did not separate his plans for the Scagno from any of the other elements of design and architecture for his enduring masterpiece, Casa del Fascio, in Como. Each were designed not to co-exist, but rather together as a single, unified whole. Unfortunately, installation of the Scagno chair was never completed and remained only as a series of sketches during Giuseppe Terragni's lifetime. Nearly four decades passed before this chair was first produced and the initial limited production of numbered editions of a few hundred in 1971 by Zanotta, was followed in 1983 by the production model still available today, and poorly renamed 'Follia', meaning madness. Giuseppe Terragni's short life had a tremendous impact on architecture which continues to resonate today. As one of the earliest proponents of rationalism, Terragni was a leading participant in the birth of Italian modernism and remains its most important architect. The Casa del Fascio, married the more rigid modernist dogma that Modernism is most commonly associated with a uniquely Italian expression that blended abstraction and constructivism with even the occasional historical reference. Terragni himself noted, '[an element] can assume the importance of a decorative or architectural event without thereby losing its functionality or honesty'. Unlike the other chairs designed for the Casa del Fascio with their tubular steel frames and padded seats, the Scagno chair avoids these soft curves in favour of the sculptural and architectural. The black lacquered beachwood base in isolation would give no hint of purpose; it isstriking in its rejection of expressive intention. The seat of the Scagno instead creates a heavy plane that joins four similarly imposing pillars or legs at each corner. The space occupied by this cube becomes structural. It highlights both the solid and the void and draws the viewer's eyes as much downward as upward. Offset against this base, the cantilevered supports, joining the seat to the backrest, are striking both in contrast and in construct. Originally designed with a chrome plated metal finish, but manufactured in 18/8 chrome-plated stainless steel, these twin sprung supports are both abstract and functional. Suspended at the end of each semicircular arc and spanning the distance between, a backrest, only modestly curved, is the only evidence of the Scagno's clearly obvious intended use as a chair. The Scagno is a testament to Terragni's perfectionism and fruitful rejection of orthodoxy, playing with symmetry, rotation and subtraction, and is one of the very few early examples of a uniquely Italian modernism.

In addition to its innovative, streamlined looks, the Bugatti Type 57 played a crucial role in the history of one of the great car manufacturers. Until 1934 Bugatti had made a different chassis for virtually every body type, making it an extremely expensive way to build cars. However, this all changed with the Type 57. For the first time, the company took a more contemporary, industrialized approach, creating a chassis that would fit with various different body styles. Bugatti's previous models, such as the Type 41 Royale and the Type 46/50 range, had not sold well as they were too expensive for the average consumer. Founder Ettore Bugatti was determined that his new car would not suffer the same fate. Placing his son Jean, aged only twenty-three, in charge of the project, the Type 57 reached the market in 1934. It had a smaller engine than its immediate predecessor, but made up for this with twin overhead camshafts, 90-degree inclined valves and central spark plugs. Importantly, it also came in four body types: the popular two-door Ventoux, the four-door

Galibier, the two-door Stelvio convertible and the sportier, exclusive two-door Atalante. However, arguably the most beautiful model was launched a year later. The Atlantic was an experimental, sportier offspring of the Atalante. Reminiscent of a raindrop with bulbous wheel arches, it featured a pair of oval doors and kidney-shaped windows, as well as a ridge that ran down the middle of the car from front to back, which was handy for bolstering the frame as the Atlantic could hit a top speed of 200 kph (125 mph). Although initially conceived as a road-going car, Bugatti could not resist the lure of the track, winning the famous Le Mans 24-hour race in 1937 and 1939. Sadly, just a few weeks later, its creator Jean Bugatti was killed when testing the victorious Type 57C. Production of the Type 57 lasted until the outbreak of World War II, and in total 546 Type 57s and ninety-six 57Cs were built. Certainly ahead of its time, the car combined a sleek aesthetic with raw speed – something every car manu-facturer aspires to.

BUGATTI

COUPÉ "ATALANTE"

237

Supermarine Spitfire (1934–6)
Reginald Joseph Mitchell (1895–1937)
Supermarine Aviation Works Vickers 1936
to 1938
Vickers-Armstrongs 1938 to 1948

The Supermarine Spitfire is one of the most exceptional fighter planes produced in the history and development of aircraft design. It originally came into production as a result of Britain's need for a fighter plane to respond to the threat of the Luftwaffe in the 1930s. Reginald Joseph Mitchell, chief designer at Supermarine Aviation Works, and designer of the winning Schneider Trophy Seaplanes, was invited by the British Air Ministry to design a new single seat monoplane to replace existing biplanes. After his first proposal (the Type 224 was a precursor to the Spitfire Type 330 Mk1), Mitchell modified his initial designs to incorporate revolutionary techniques in airframe construction. The first Spitfire F37/34 prototype flew at Eastleigh Airfield, Southampton, in March 1936. Although Mitchell saw the Spitfire

prototype produced, he did not see the Spitfire in full production during the war, or realize the contribution his work made to British aviation history, as he died in June 1937 from abdominal cancer, aged forty-two. The following year, the Spitfire entered Royal Air Force service at Duxford in Cambridgeshire, and when Britain went to war in 1939, a total of 2,160 Spitfires had been ordered. Structurally the Spitfire had a simple and efficient design, with a light alloy fuselage and a single spar wing with stressed-skin covering and fabric-covered control surfaces. The design added gear retraction, an enclosed cockpit and oxygen equipment. Elliptical wings gave the Spitfire a distinctive shape and allowed for eight fitted Browning machine guns. The thin curved wing cross-section made the design more streamlined, lessening drag. The Spitfire weighed 2,600 kg

(5,720 lb) and had a maximum speed of 580 kph (362 mph), with a maximum diving speed of 720 kph (450 mph). Rolls Royce produced a twelve cylinder 'Merlin' engine, which at nearly 1000 hp, gave the Spitfire substantial acceleration and power. The Spitfire outweighed the Hawker Hurricane and its cockpit visibility, speed and manoeuvrability made it an indispensable weapon in the dogfights against its German opponent, the Messerschmitt Bf 109E. More than 20,300 Spitfires were built in over twenty-nine variants, some remaining in service into the 1950s. Although many planes remain airworthy today, the Supermarine Spitfire is primarily maintained by aircraft museums and the RAF for air displays and memorial events.

The Radio Flyer No.18 Classic Red Wagon design - a shallow-sided steel tray painted fire-engine red, a set of four robust, black rubber wheels, a pull handle and accompanying scrolling logo - is so simple it belies the huge commercial achievements to which it lays claim. Considered in context, few if any of the American toys to have been manufactured during the first half of the twentieth century have proven as iconic as the No.18 Classic Red Wagon. Indeed, the wagon has traded so successfully under the moniker of being 'The Original Little Red Wagon' that it has become as embedded in America's suburban psyche as cream sodas and the sleepover. Not bad for a plaything born of nothing more than a basic design format and the wholesale adoption of the American way of life by the Italian immigrant who created it. Antonio Pasin was a young designer enthralled with the burgeoning radio and aircraft industries of the 1920s, from which the wagon's name took inspiration. He utilized the stamped-metal production technique adopted by the fledgling car industry as a blueprint for his first wagon design; indeed, later in his career he would be nicknamed 'Little Ford' in recognition of the mass-production methods that he employed. It was during the Depression of the 1930s that the wagon established itself by offering a wholesome form of entertainment for American children. Pasin's design was one of the safest toys of the period, with a controlled turning radius to stop the wagon tipping over and no-pinch ball joints to keep children's fingers safe. He marketed it as a toy 'for every boy, for every girl' and offered discounts when the purchase was accompanied by a grocery punch card. The mass-produced design struck a chord in everyday family life and with the children to which the design would form a backdrop to many an adventure, real or imagined. Now a trademarked toy, the wagon's seventy years of continuous production have set an American toy industry record, establishing an unparalleled benchmark for both quality and integrity. Without it, the quintessential American suburb would not be complete.

The Anglepoise 1227 lamp is all about function. It is task-lighting in its purest form – a supreme piece of British rational design that, unusually, is still manufactured by the same British company as when it was launched. Originally manufactured in lacquered metal with a solid Bakelite base, it has the shiny industrial aesthetic of the burgeoning 1930s machine age during which it was designed. However, that's not to say the lamp is without beauty. There is elegance in its long, narrow, angular body and the bonnet-like shade gives it a strangely

George Cawardine

touching, human posture, like a mother stooping to tend to her children. Neither of these observations is surprising when the background and inspirations of its designer, George Carwardine, are considered. Carwardine was chief designer at the Horstman Car Company before setting up his own business specializing in the design of vehicle suspension systems. As an engineer, the inadequacies of available lighting products were all too clear to Carwardine, prompting him to set about developing a frictionless mechanism that could balance and direct light to any position. Essentially, he wanted to create a lamp that was as versatile as a human arm – instant flexibility and, more elusively, the ability to hold the chosen position, all at the touch of a finger. The human arm was his inspiration for the action, but Carwardine took things a stage further by also basing the mechanics of the lamp on the tension principle of muscles in limbs. He used springs, instead of the more traditional counterweight method, to keep the arm in position, necessitating complex mathematical equations to create the optimum tension in the springs. The lamp was originally intended for commercial applications, but the market for home and office use soon became apparent.

239

Anglepoise® 1227 (1935)
George Carwardine (1887–1947)
Anglepoise® 1935 to present

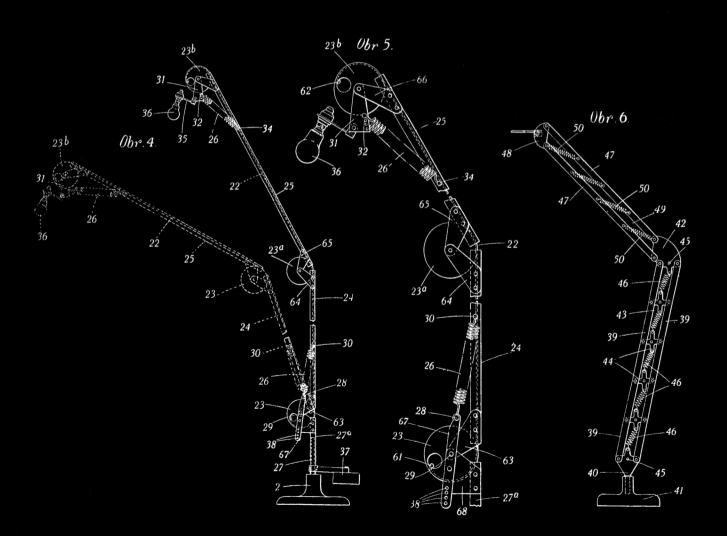

Obr. 4. Obr 5. Obr. 6.

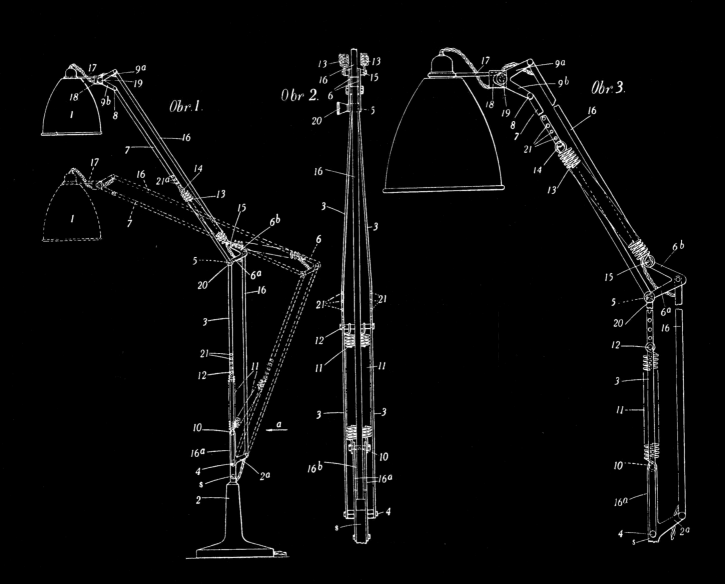

Obr. 1.

Obr 2.

Obr. 3.

Named after the French transatlantic steamship launched in 1935, the Normandie Pitcher, produced that same year, is a paragon of the 'streamlined decade'. Even household objects were taking on the glamour of speed epitomized by aerodynamic machines like the Chrysler Airflow of 1934 or the Normandie's own smoke stacks, which this water jug emulates. The jug was designed by German émigré Peter Müller-Munk for the Revere Copper and Brass Company of New York State. Although Müller-Munk had trained as a silversmith and specialized in hand-crafted metalwork, Normandie was designed to be mass-produced for the company's first foray into the household goods market. As elegant as any silverware, the chrome-plated jug was significantly cheaper and easier to clean. This was obviously an advantage as the Normandie was launched during the Depression, when the affluent were not only cutting back on silverware but also on the servants needed to polish it. The Normandie remained in production until 1941. Taking the classic teardrop profile of 1930s streamlining, Normandie is formed from a sheet of bent brass joined at the front. The slim strip concealing this join and the one around the base is its only marking. Tapering away from the mouth, the handle takes the jug's clean lines in the opposite direction of the sharp prow, accentuating the sense of motion that Müller-Munk was so keen to embody. Though often categorized as a piece of Art Deco design, Normandie has none of the superfluous trappings of that style. The use of chrome is practical rather than just a decorative affectation in homage to the automobile. Its stylistic drama and eminent functionality are inseparable, stemming from the same notion of aerodynamic efficiency. In a sense, Müller-Munk brought the simple act of pouring water into the machine age.

Normandie Pitcher (1935)
Peter Müller-Monk (1904–1967)
Rever Copper & Brass 1935 to 1941

The Zeroll Ice-Cream Scoop is a beautiful object in itself: elegant, shiny and sculptural. But its design is also perfect for the one very specific task it is intended for, and thus it has remained unchanged since it first appeared. Behind Sherman L Kelly's design is a straightforward task: serving ice-cream. In the 1930s ice-cream was changing from being a luxury product into being a widely available and affordable commodity thanks to industrial advances, notably the 'continuous process' in freezing technology. However, ice-cream fresh from the freezer is often very hard and difficult to gouge or scrape from its tub with a spoon. Kelly's innovation, which is literally at the heart of the Zeroll Scoop, is a hollow core that contains antifreeze. This antifreeze conducts the body heat from the scooper's hand and delivers it to the blade of the scoop, helping it to cut a path through the ice-cream. The handle of the scoop is intentionally thick, to leave room for the antifreeze chamber, but it also permits a far better grip than a spoon, which is a convenience when dealing with a slippery product in cold, finger-numbing conditions. Another advantage of the 18.5 cm (7.3 in) long Zeroll Scoop over the spoon is that it produces more standard portions. It is also much easier to clean and keep in good condition than its mechanical competitors, as it comprises a single piece with no moving parts. So the Zeroll Scoop was a great advance for the worker in the ice-cream parlours, but it has also embedded itself in the mind of the customer. It is uniquely associated with ice-cream, as that is all it is used for, and because it appeared when ice-cream was becoming a worldwide mass-market product. The Scoop amply lives up to those early expectations of ice-cream. Its shine gives it the look of a luxury item, more like a piece of jewellery than a kitchen utensil. Smooth, wonderful, and perpetually necessary, a timeless appeal may honour a nostaglic emotion towards this scoop.

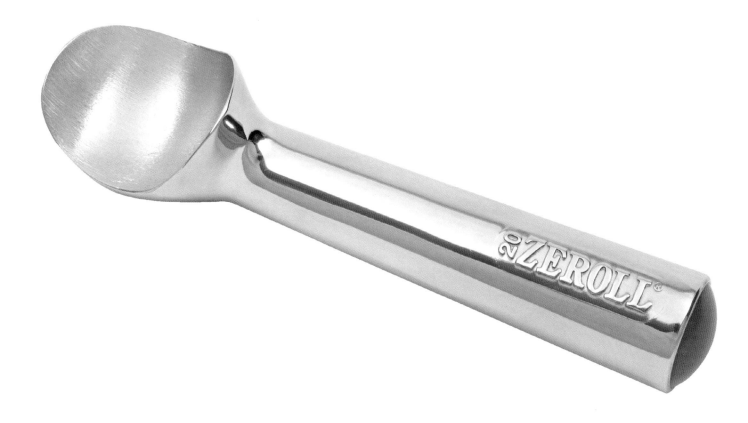

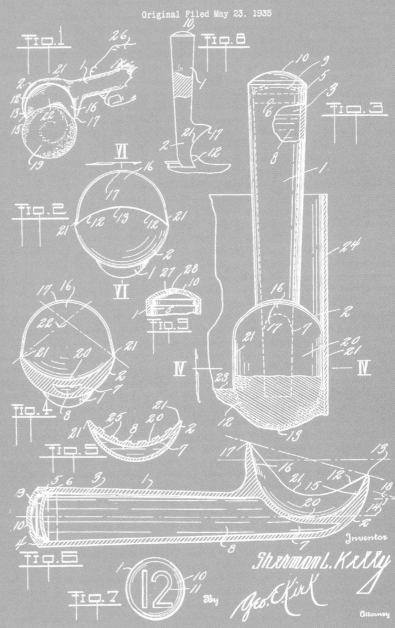

May 30, 1939.

S. L. KELLY

2,160,023

TOOL FOR HANDLING CONGEALED MATERIALS

Original Filed May 23, 1935

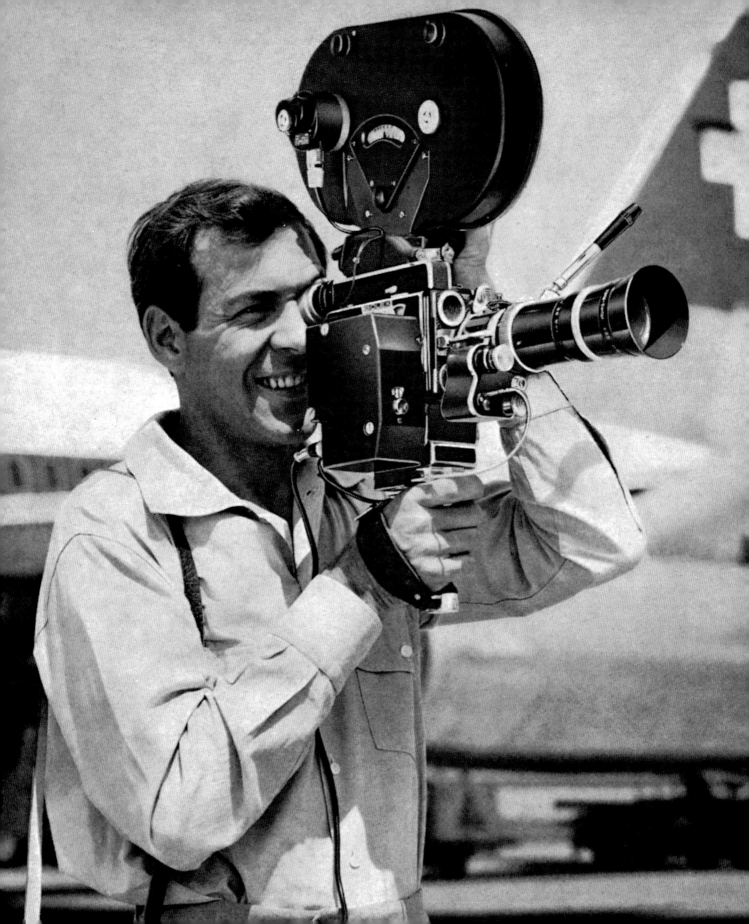

The Bolex H16 was designed by Jacques Bogopolsky, a Ukrainian engineer living in Geneva. He had a long-standing interest in movie cameras and in 1924 patented a design using 35 mm film. The camera was manufactured as the Bol Cinegraphe. Developments in film stock meant that new, smaller formats, such as 9.5 mm and 16 mm, were increasingly used for amateur cameras and Bogopolsky turned his attention to 16 mm film that was used by both amateurs and professionals. The result was the Auto Ciné, the first camera to be produced under the Bolex name. In 1930 the Paillard company purchased Bogopolsky's company, retaining him as an engineering consultant until he left in the early 1930s, creating a successful career in Switzerland and the United States designing still cameras, such as the Alpa and Bolsey ranges. Paillard continued to develop Bogopolsky's Auto Ciné, with the resulting Bolex H16 launched around 1935. The original Bolex camera was quickly improved and given a turret that was able to hold three lenses that could be quickly rotated into position as required. The design of black leather body panels and chrome metal trim remained for much of the camera's life. An 8 mm model was introduced in 1938. The original H16 viewing system was superseded in 1956 with a true reflex viewing system, which allowed continuous viewing through the camera's lens. Originally clockwork powered, an electric-motor-powered Bolex H16 was introduced in 1971 with the model EBM. Other refinements were made throughout the camera's history. The Paillard company was sold to the Austrian firm, Eumig, in 1970, although it continued to operate under the name Bolex International. The research and development functions of the two companies were merged and the models of the two companies were increasingly similar. This was compounded when there was a linkup with the Japanese Chinon company, who made some Bolex models. When Eumig hit financial problems in the early 1980s, its sold off the Bolex 16 mm business, which continues to operate independently. Since its introduction in 1935, the Bolex Ciné Camera has been adopted by the professional cinematographer who required a high-precision 16 mm movie camera. Suited for travelling with its quality of lenses, this camera been used for filming in difficult conditions such as time-lapse photography for wildlife programmes. Avante-garde film makers were drawn to it as it was relatively inexpensive but capable of producing high-quality results. Many of the older models remain in use, while more recent models are used in the film industry today, particularly for animation. Although it was launched as a serious amateur camera, it was quickly adopted by professional film makers and is a mainstay of film schools.

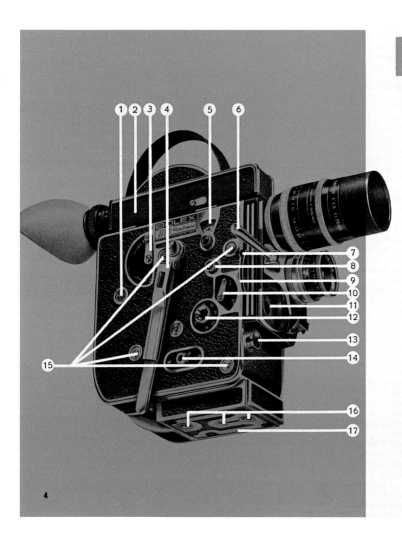

GET TO KNOW

1. Footage counter (p. 10)

2. Reflex viewfinder (p. 14)

3. Lever for disengaging spring motor (p. 12)

4. Spring motor winding handle (spring run: 37 secs. at 18 f.p.s.)

5. Frame counter (p. 10)

6. Turret lever (p. 17)

7. Variable shutter control lever (p. 34)

8. Coupling spindle for electric motor and hand cranking lever (p. 21)

9. Film plane (p. 29)

10. Exposure control lever for instantaneous (I) and time shots (T) (Single frame exposure) (p. 13)

11. Threaded hole for the turret locking screw (p. 47)

12. Speed control (p. 12)

13. Front release knob, for normal running (can be operated by cable) (p. 13)

14. Side release knob for normal running, continuous release (M) and single frame exposure (can be operated by cable) (p. 13)

15. Threaded holes for various accessories and motors (page 47)

16. Three threaded holes for a tripod or a hand grip (European = $^3/_8''$ and American = $^1/_4''$ threads) (p. 25)

17. Serial number of the camera (p. 1)

4

YOUR CAMERA

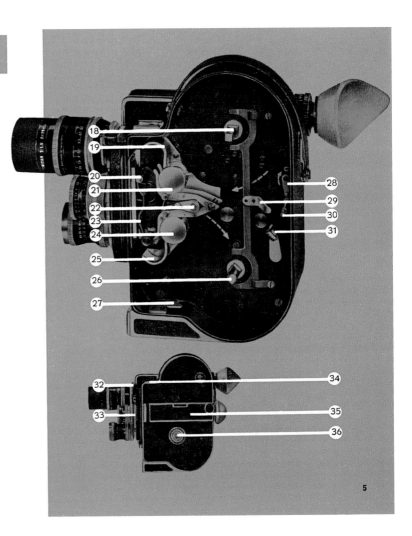

18. Upper spool shaft (for feed spool) (p. 8)
19. Upper loop former (p. 9)
20. Pressure pad locking pin (p. 8)
21. Upper sprocket (p. 9)
22. Loop former locking lever and opening control (p. 9)
23. Pressure pad (p. 8)
24. Lower sprocket (p. 9)
25. Lower loop former (p. 9)
26. Lower spool shaft (for take-up spool) (p. 9)
27. Film knife (p. 8)
28. Audible signal adjusting lever (p. 11)
29. Spool ejector (p. 8 and p. 22)
30. Footage counter pin (p. 10)
31. Retaining arm
32. Turret locking clamp (p. 17)
33. Filter holder (p. 18)
34. Shoe for attaching exposure meter (p. 28)
35. Auxiliary viewfinder (p. 15)
36. Lid lock (p. 8)

5

Among Alvar Aalto's designs for seating furniture, the Armchair 400 Tank Chair is relatively unusual. Many of the other models are notable for being pared down and light in weight. However, in this chair Aalto makes a much more robust statement, emphasizing mass and the appearance of solidity. By doing this Aalto made a much clearer statement about the range of physical possibilities that his laminated wooden furniture was capable of dealing with. In common with the majority of Aalto's furniture designs, the Armchair 400 makes use of laminated wood in its construction. In this model, thin sheets of birch veneer have been glued together and set around a mould or former to produce the wide, curved and cantilevered strips that provide the open frames either side of the mattress-type seat and back. These laminated strips are kept wider than in other models, partly to support the underlying bulky aesthetic of the piece, and partly to give added strength, needed because the centre of gravity of the chair is relatively low and far back. At the junction of the arm and the back, the downward-pointing terminals of the laminated strips help give an overall rigidity to the design by preventing excessive side-to-side flexing. This is one constructional detail in which the 400 differs from its close relative, the 406, where the laminated strip of the arm terminates in an upward curl. Although this is a small difference, it indicates the aesthetic function of such an element – which in the Armchair 400 helps to complete the picture of muscular, weight-bearing capacity – and how closely Aalto thought through the detail of his work.

In 1929, the Finnish architect Alvar Aalto submitted a number of prototype designs to a competition that the Berlin-based company Thonet was sponsoring to update its tradition-bound furniture line. Hoping that competition jurors Pierre Jeanneret (cousin of Le Corbusier), Josef Frank and Gerrit Rietveld would recognize the integrity and innovation of his furniture, Aalto sent a low-slung serving table that boasted three levels of surface space and curvilinear runners that were reminiscent of a sled. Although the illustrious judges did not see fit to award Aalto's design, the configuration was adapted over the following seven years to become the Tea Trolley 901, which was manufactured and marketed by Artek, the industrial arts collective and company Aalto set up with modernist colleagues in 1935. Replacing the sled runners with a curvilinear chassis that had planar wheels on one end, Aalto's birch, ceramic and rattan trolley is indicative of the Finnish designer's innovative but humane aesthetic, combining a gridded tile serving surface that is easy to clean with an adjacent basket to store silverware, napkins and the like. 'Moveable and foldable furniture enlarge a minimal dwelling,' wrote Aalto in a 1930 article for *Domus*, an indication that he had already begun considering the importance of putting furniture on wheels. Rather than create an object with wheels that referenced the speed and machined perfection of the industrial age, however, Aalto designed white laminate wheels with black rubber edges for his serving table that more resembled a child's Platonic vision of a circle. The trolley's birch structure is typically Aalto, created by the bentwood technique that the designer began experimenting with in the early 1930s and used in most pieces of furniture created thereafter. Although a linoleum-covered version with no basket was first displayed in the front window of Artek's showroom in 1936, Aalto's Tea Trolley 901 had its international debut at the Milan Triennale later that year. A second model called the Tea Trolley 900 was revealed at the 1937 Paris Expo in the Aalto-designed Finnish pavilion, and one year later appeared in a show at The Museum of Modern Art in New York. Thanks to its robust design, the continuing existence of Artek and special arrangements with Herman Miller, the Aalto Tea Trolley 901 and 900 models, are manufactured to this day.

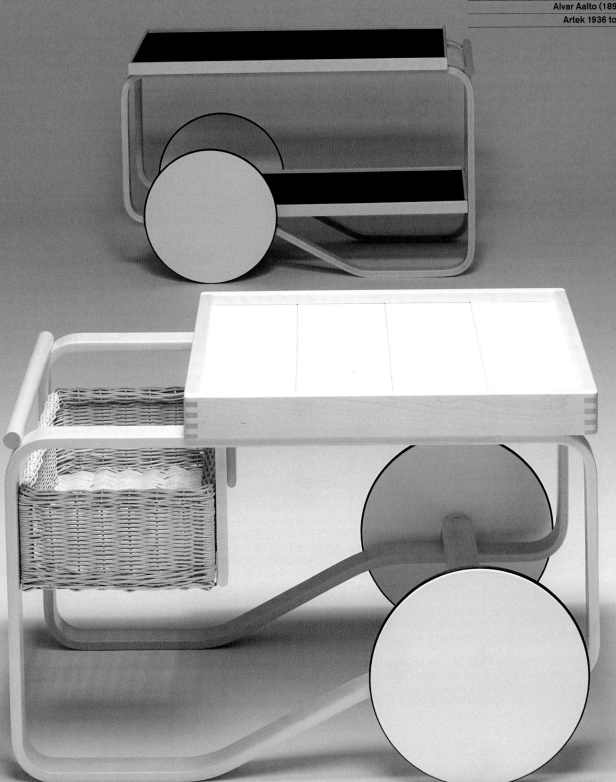

Fiestaware (1936)
Frederick Hurton Rhead (1880–1942)
Homer Laughlin China 1936 to 1973,
1986 to present

In 1936, when the Homer Laughlin China company released its Fiestaware range of ceramic tableware, America was still in the grip of the Depression and purchases by the average household were divided into the essential and the non-essential. Fiestaware made itself essential by appealing to middle-class notions of domestic propriety, and it was such a phenomenal success that it is still being produced today. Although the manufacturer was based in Ohio, Fiestaware was designed by an Englishman, Frederick Hurton Rhead. At a time when most popular dinnerware was still echoing Victorian and Art Nouveau china designs, Rhead introduced bold colours and simple Art Deco styling. It was a modern, informal take on the complete dinner service and, most importantly, it was within reach of moderate incomes. Families would save up to buy the complete set in their desire to realize the dream of a tasteful home and by the 1940s Fiestaware had become something of a status symbol. Rhead's design was solid rather than delicate or decorative and five concentric ridges serve as the only ornamentation. Colour was the keynote. Originally released in red, medium green, cobalt blue, yellow and ivory, Fiestaware (marketed as 'the dinnerware that turns your table into a celebration') helped transform the domestic interior long before Technicolor in the 1950s; the red range became somewhat notorious for being one of the most radioactive products on the market, because of the depleted uranium oxide used in the glaze. Fiestaware was discontinued in 1973 but then reissued in 1986 in a new range of colours to mark its fiftieth anniversary. The design of these plates, bowls and cups has changed little in seventy years except to reflect countless shifts in colour fashion. Even today, the release of a new colour is something of an event for collectors and aficionados.

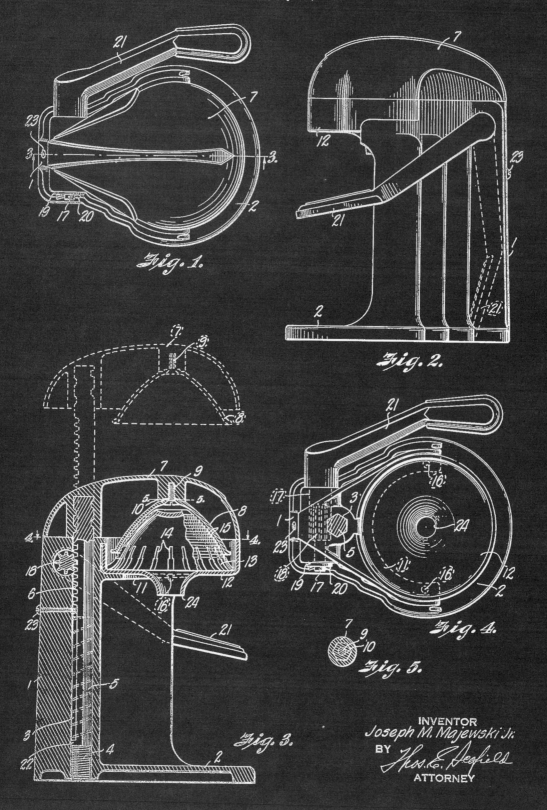

Fig. 1.

Fig. 2.

Fig. 3.

Fig. 4.

Fig. 5.

INVENTOR
Joseph M. Majewski Jr.
BY
Thos. E. Scofield
ATTORNEY

Gifts

Welcomed the World Over!

No Bitter Rind Oil!

Only Juice-O-Mat, the juicer women want most, has the patented Konvakone strainer... gives clear fresh juice without seeds, pulp or bitter rind oil! Single action handle tilts top back ...easier...handier...faster. Beautiful...all enclosed... streamlined. The perfect gift!

Gleaming chrome top and handle... bases in choice of four gay colors.
$7.98
In All-Chrome $10.95

*Trademark

TILT-TOP
Juice-O-Mat

Can-O-Mat* The Most Beautiful Can Opener Ever Made
In Chrome and Colors $4.98
Others to $6.95

ALAN LADD
STARRING IN
"BEYOND GLORY"
A Paramount Production

RIVAL MANUFACTURING COMPANY, Kansas City, Missouri

2-46

Juice-O-Mat (1936)
Rival Design Team
Rival 1936 to c.1960

The Juice-O-Mat is a quintessential American diner-style product, illustrative of the cult of the machine in the United States, which reached its apogee in 1939 with the New York World's Fair. This utilitarian object represents American values and the notion of home. During the 1930s and 1940s the drinking of freshly squeezed orange juice became widely popular as part of a healthy lifestyle, recognizing the benefits of Vitamin C. The expense and hence status of freshly squeezed orange juice contributed to the flood of Art Deco-inspired juicers into the commercial market. Domestic appliances such as these reflected the US reverence for technology and innovation, for the idea of machines for the home. The first Juice-O-Mat entered the market-place in 1936. The early models reflected the clean lines, glistening chrome and Art Deco style of the times. Many models can still be found with their baked enamel finishes intact, showing little sign of age. The first models were freestanding, but the company designed custom wall-mounts on many of its products, beginning in the late 1940s. The single-action juicer was made in cast iron and featured a powerful rack-and-pinion gear system, which leveraged up to 270 kg (600 lb) of pressure. The process was simple: the user placed a glass in the holder and half an orange in the strainer and pulled the handle down to release the juice. The Juice-O-Mat's smooth, one-stroke action (lifting the handle raised the top and flipped it back to allow access to the juicer; pulling down closed the top and squeezed the juice from the fruit) indirectly impacted the English language: as the forerunner of the later O-Mat and O-Matic kitchen appliances, Rival's product names contributed to a new English idiom that denotes ease and convenience. Production ceased in the mid-1960s, but the Juice-O-Mat is much copied today. Original examples are increasingly collectable and its popularity in Europe is a reflection of the enduring fascination with American retro designs.

As the Airstream literature reads, 'Wallace Merle Byam was practically born a traveller'. He was the founder of the Airstream Trailer Company and the designer of the Clipper. As a child he travelled with his grandfather, who led a mule train in Oregon, and later on moved around as a shepherd. Byam studied law at Stanford University, California, joined the merchant marines, and finally settled in Los Angeles where he owned his own advertising and publishing companies. Byam's first trailer was built as a response to complaints from his readers that the plans for building a travel trailer, which were published in one of his magazines, did not work. He found himself agreeing and set about designing an improved version of those plans. This initial design constituted a breakthrough that was to change the history of trailers. By simply introducing two basic changes, dropping the trailer's floor between the wheels and raising the height of the roof, so that a person could now easily stand straight inside it, he transformed the trailer into a mobile home. The story of the Clipper is one of continuous improvement. As Airstream proudly states, 'He never stopped building the better trailer.' After the first designs, Byam began to look at aircraft construction technology and aerodynamics to lessen wind resistance and improve the weight-to-strength ratio of the trailers. This culminated in 1936 with the design of the Clipper, which incorporated an innovative aluminium monocoque with an aerodynamic teardrop design, so light that it could be pulled by a man-powered bicycle. The interior design progressively became more important, and the Clipper was the first to incorporate an electrical system throughout. It carried its own water supply and even its own ice cooler air-conditioning system. This combination of technological advancement, performance and lifestyle elevated the Clipper to the status of American icon; so much so that the astronauts returning from the first landing on the moon were housed in one. With the start of World War II, aluminium became a strategic war material and its use restricted to aircraft construction, which led the company to its close. Wally Byam took his expertise in aluminium construction to Lockheed for the duration of the war. On its conclusion, Airstream reopened the factory and resumed the production of the Clipper. Even today, 60 per cent of all Airstreams ever built are still in use.

VOLETE DIVENTARE AUTOMOBILISTI?

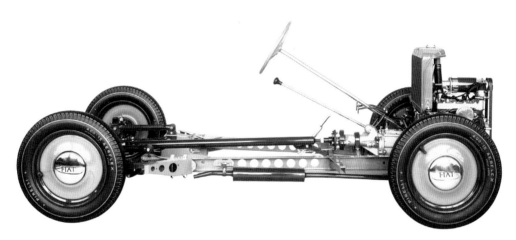

Of the many significant Italian car stylists who worked in the middle years of the twentieth century Dante Giacosa was among the most consistently radical and influential, especially in the context of mass-produced automobiles. Indeed, through his work for Fiat from 1928 onwards it could be argued that he was responsible for putting the mass of the Italian nation on wheels. Less flashy than the work of some of his contemporaries, the achievements of this engineer-designer were thorough exercises in rethinking the car from scratch. Giacosa graduated in engineering from the Polytechnic University in Turin and, in the early 1930s, in response to Fiat's desire to create an automobile for the masses, he proposed a water-cooled, rear-wheel-drive car which would compete with Britain's 'people's car', the Morris 8, and Germany's Volkswagen. The idea to create such a car had originally come from Giovanni Agnelli, Fiat's managing director, following the failure of a model designed by Oreste Lardone which had caught fire. Giacosa's version met with more success. It was essentially a one-man design from engine through to body-shell. This accounted for its highly unified appearance which reflected the vogue for streamlining and the integration of body components into a single shell. Only the headlights stood apart from the main body of the car. Unlike its more spacious, and luxurious, American predecessor, the Chrysler Airflow - from which it undoubtedly borrowed its rounded forms and curved radiator grille, this tiny two-seater presented a cute image to the public, earning it the nickname of 'Topolino' (Italy's name for the American cartoon character, 'Mickey Mouse'). The Fiat 500A proved a great success in the Italian marketplace: between 1936 and 1948 122,000 Topolinos rolled off Fiat's assembly lines.

Dante Giacosa

A Totally New Conception
of the
World's Greatest Cleaner

When we say "totally" we mean totally.

When we say "conception" we mean a basically new idea.

When we say "world's greatest cleaner" we mean the cleaner that has been just that for 29 years . . .

THE HOOVER

MADAM · HERE'S THE MOST HELPFUL CLEANER EVER BUILT

Women haven't had full service from their cleaning equipment . . . they haven't used their cleaning tools as consistently as their floor cleaners. So Hoover designed a Cleaning Ensemble so simple, so convenient, so fool-proof that women *would* use it.

Women wanted lightness—so Hoover adapted magnesium—the new airplane metal, one-third lighter than aluminum and just as strong.

Women are style conscious. So Hoover engaged Henry Dreyfuss to design this new Hoover. Its smooth flowing lines and its new non-marring finish will be instantly appreciated.

Women know a cleaner should be adjusted to rugs of varying thicknesses. Yet in the past they haven't been able, or haven't bothered, to do it. So Hoover developed the automatic Rug Adjustor. Simply press your toe on a pedal as you pass from rug to rug and the cleaner does the rest.

The new Hoover One Fifty Cleaning Ensemble, with these and many other new conveniences, is ready now. Remember, too, it is still the only cleaner with the patented, exclusive principle of Positive Agitation which saves rugs and keeps them bright.

See this new cleaner . . . try it on your own rugs, without obligation, through a trustworthy representative of your local Hoover dealer.

ALL THESE PATENTED OR EXCLUSIVE FEATURES

Agitator beats out

embedded grit

New Wonder-Metal, Magnesium
Plug-In Tool Connector
Automatic Rug Adjustor
Time-to-Empty Signal
Handy Cleaning Kit
Clip-On Plug
Easy-Empty Filtaire Bag
Instant Handle Positioner
Spring Cushioned Chassis
Comfort Handle Grip
Instant Bag Lock
Positive Agitation
Non-Marring Finish in stratosphere gray

Just slip connector in slot—you're ready instantly to clean furnishings. No stopping motor, turning over cleaner or disconnecting belt. Note Handy Cleaning Kit.

THE HOOVER *One Fifty* CLEANING ENSEMBLE $1 50 A WEEK PAYABLE MONTHLY

IT BEATS . . AS IT SWEEPS . . AS IT CLEANS

By the 1920s when vacuum cleaners were becoming more common, the dangers of allowing dust to accumulate in the home were well known. Anxieties focused around anything that might contain germs, and were promoted through education and reinforced in the advertising of companies who sold cleaning products. Thus, ever since James Spangler devised his motor-driven upright vacuum cleaner in 1907, from which William Henry Hoover developed the first commercial model in 1908, the principle selling point had been less to do with labour-saving benefits, than with healthy respiration and the expulsion of germs. This connection was never effectively achieved in the design of these early machines, though, and vacuum cleaners of all makes tended to look highly industrial, with no attempt made to hide their workings. Dreyfuss, who had started to work for Hoover in 1934, realized this lack in the design of the Model 150, and helped the company to capitalize on the widespread desire for a vacuum cleaner that reflected not only the optimism and technological advances of the age, but that also helped to deliver a message of health and hygiene. This model was easier to carry and manoeuvre than its predecessors, incorporating lighter magnesium alloy castings and a moulded Bakelite motor-housing. Its bold styling not only linked it to the prevailing Zeitgeist of streamlining and speed, but also seemed to suggest that the machine itself was clean, and impervious to dust. This strategy paid off handsomely at a time when Hoover was experiencing significant competition from other brands such as Electrolux, Singer and Montgomery Ward. While these companies were quick to update their own models, the Model 150 re-established Hoover as a market leader, a position that it enjoyed for many years.

During the 1930s, designer Bruno Mathsson began research into functions of sitting and lying down, or, as he termed it, 'the business of sitting', with the aim of creating new furniture forms that were customized to their function. Mathsson's Lounge Chair of 1936 was the result of this research, and remained an enduring legacy of his career. From 1933 he had designed pressed laminate chair frames with the seat and back forming one sweeping unit, which was clad with plaited strips of saddle girth. The Lounge Chair evolved from one of these earlier designs, the Grasshopper Chair of 1933. The Grasshopper had a woven, webbed seat stretched across a frame whose armrest and legs were made of one arched wooden piece, sculpted as a curvy interpretation of a grasshopper's legs. The Lounge was a more refined version of the Grasshopper and eventually evolved into a closely related series of webbed chairs, sofas and ottomans. The Lounge Chair is striking because of a lightness conveyed by its simple structure. Mathsson's characteristic use of woven canvas or leather for the seat gives the chair a sculptural form but also a dynamic tension. He based his designs on the actual physiology of sitting, with the need for support, activity and repose. He wrote that 'comfortable sitting is an "art" – it ought not to be. Instead, the making of chairs has to be done with such an "art" that the sitting will not be any "art".' Mathsson created furniture that repre-sents a perfect synthesis of thought and technology, function and form. Taking his cue from the Swedish craft tradition, he explored organic, even anthropomorphic shapes in his popular wooden furniture. He possessed a modernist openness towards emerging technologies, viewing them as an acceptable means to produce high-quality furnishings. His father Karl, whose furniture business in their hometown of Värnamo would later manufacture many of Bruno's designs, trained Mathsson as a cabinet-maker. In 1936 Bruno's work was shown in a one-man exhibition at the Röhsska Art and Craft Museum in Gothenburg; a year later he started to build an international reputation by showing his pieces at the Paris World's Fair. His work was shown at New York's Museum of Modern Art in 1939 and represented some of the first pieces of furniture ever exhibited by the museum. Mathsson's furniture designs combine beauty with form, and were seen as innovations both in their day, and at present.

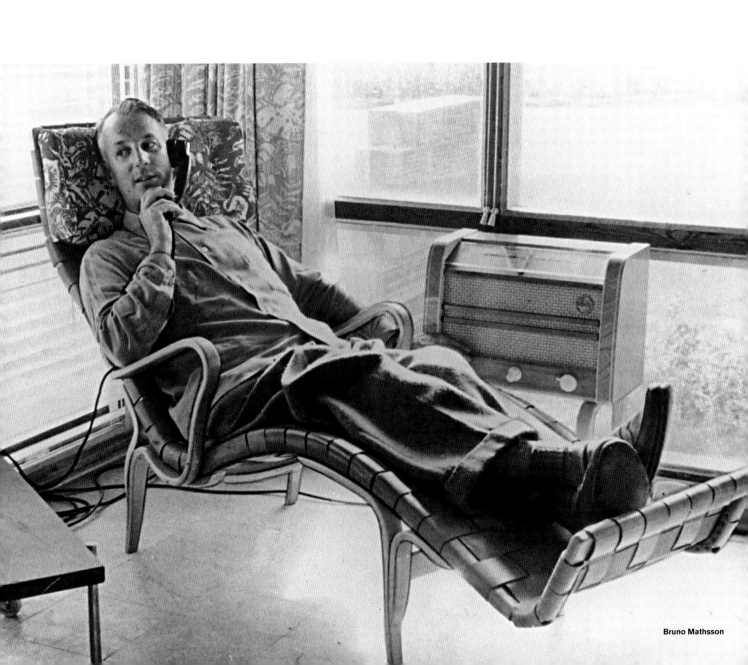

Bruno Mathsson

By the late 1930s, Gio Ponti was already widely known and respected, having founded the highly influential architecture and design publication *Domus* in the late 1920s, as well as being a participant in and promoter of the Italian Triennale exhibitions. Ponti did not limit himself in his evolving expression in architecture or interior design to any single material, technique or creative discipline, and the broad sweep of his attention to detail took in the smallest of scales, right down to the cutlery. The Flatware was designed in 1936 and its style set it apart from the conventional insistence of the time on decorated handles clearly delineated from the blades, bowls and prongs of each piece of cutlery. Ponti's softly undulating curves nearly disappear into the working ends of each piece, while these same curves sit naturally in the hand. Original production of the flatware was by Argenteria Krupp. It was manufactured in zama, an alloy using zinc rather than copper, which was in short supply during World War II. When production in stainless steel followed in 1942, it was one of the earliest examples of stainless steel cutlery. During the 1960s, the Sambonet family acquired the Krupp brand and continued to make Ponti Flatware until the early 1990s, when commercial production of the flatware ceased. It was not reintroduced until 2003. During the late 1980s, Sambonet also brought out a limited edition of 1,000 sets in a silver-plated alpaca, an alloy of copper, nickel and zinc, sometimes called 'new silver' or 'nickel silver'. Today the still contemporary, simple lines of this range are produced in both 18/10 stainless steel and mille silver electroplated stainless steel versions, each with either a mirror or satin finish. Ponti continued to design cutlery throughout his career, producing ranges for Reed & Barton, Sabattini, Christofle and Fraser as well as additional designs for Argenteria Krupp. Most of these later designs were more strikingly self-conscious and 'modern' than the early, simpler construction of the classic Ponti Flatware.

The Minox was the smallest production camera made at its launch in 1938. It was to become identified with spying in the 1950s, after having featured in several films, like *Calling Northside 777* (1948). When closed, the smooth stainless steel casing hid the lens and viewfinder, leaving just the focusing wheel, shutter-speed dial, shutter-release button and exposure counter visible on top. Opening the camera by pulling the two ends revealed the lens and viewfinder and also advanced the film ready for picture taking. The camera opened for loading by pressing the base plate so that a Minox film cartridge could be dropped in. Walter Zapp was a Latvian photographer with no formal training in engineering or optical design but an aptitude for technical work. He began work on a design for a camera that was to become the Minox in 1934, and patented the design in Britain in December 1936. The camera was introduced commercially in 1938 and shortly afterwards started to sell internationally. The camera was remarkable in producing fifty exposures on unperforated 9.5 mm film loaded into special Minox cartridges. Minox copying equipment, processing accessories and an enlarger were also produced to accompany the camera. The camera sold around 17,000 units before production was discontinued around 1943. During World War II the VEF factory was taken over by both Russian and German forces before it was re-established in West Germany in 1945 and production resumed in 1948. Minox cameras continue to be made today, with the current models clear descendants of the original.

James Stewart in *Calling Northside 777* (1948), directed by Henry Hathaway

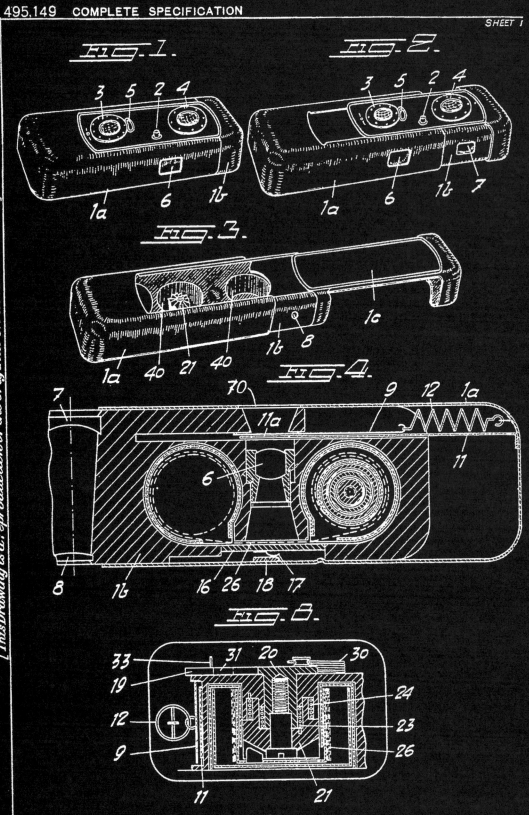

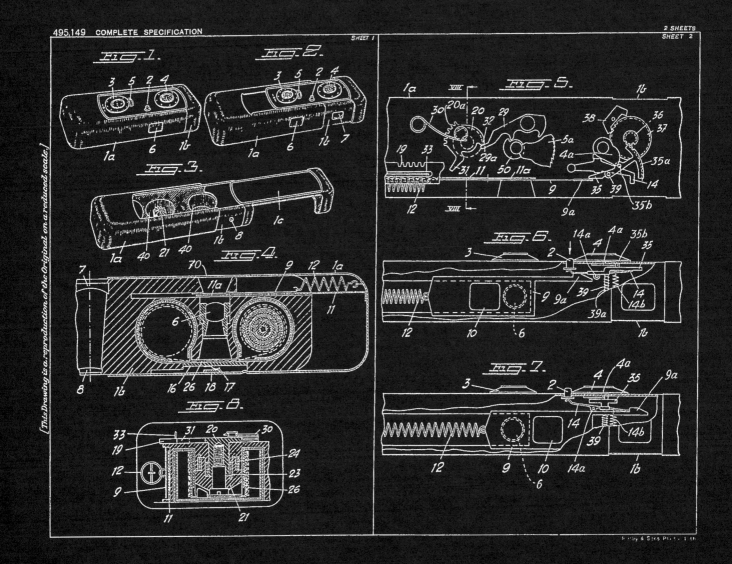

FIG.1.

FIG.2.

FIG.3.

FIG.4.

FIG.5.

FIG.6.

FIG.7.

FIG.8.

This steel and glass table was designed by Mario Asnago and Claudio Vender to update Bar Moka, a café located in Milan, Italy. The bar finally opened on 14 November 1939, and gained immediate popularity, but the table was actually displayed at the VI Milan Triennale the same year it was designed. The table is stripped down to its essence, and it is perhaps one of the purest and most enduring embodiments of Italian Rationalism, the short-lived design movement based on Modernism that flourished in Italy in the 1930s. Italian Rationalism emerged in 1926 with the founding of Gruppo 7, and developed into the Movimento Italiano per l'Architettura Razionale a few years later. Essentially, the movement was a response to International Modernism and to Italian Futurism, which had earlier celebrated the dynamism of the machine age. Although Italian Rationalism undoubtedly embraced a modernist programme, its *raison d'être* was also rooted in the classical tradition, resulting in an ordered, structured and undeniably elegant sensibility. While

other architects and designers of the period turned their attention to the nationalistic and monumental possibilities of Rationalism in order to promote the fascist cause (a close alignment that would eventually cause the rationalist movement to founder), architects Asnago and Vender stayed independent and true to their own vision, which is perhaps best exemplified in this table. The table is composed of a simple, 10 mm (0.4 in) rectangular tempered crystal top supported by a drawn steel-rod frame, intersected by two diagonal rods. This cross is the only embellishment, albeit a stark one, to the strict section, but this structural element also offers additional support. The design is precise in its proportions and its transparency, and minimal use of materials imbues the piece with lightness and grace. Asnago and Vender went on to apply their disciplined yet elegant rationalist principles to a series of architectural projects, yet it is their unique table design in which their legacy is encapsulated. Indeed, this is the most rational example of Rationalism remaining in production today.

The Benita chair, was designed by Giuseppe Terragni as an item of furniture created specifically for his most acclaimed building, the Casa del Fascio, in Como, Italy. The Benita was later re-named the Sant'Elia as a result of the unfortunate connection of its original name with that of the Italian dictator, Benito Mussolini. After the completion of the Casa del Fascio, characterized by its modernity and use of advanced materials, Terragni designed every element of its interior – windows, doors, lamps, tables, desks, shelves and chairs – with the same experimental attitude that he had used throughout the building. Conscious of creating a truly new and modern building, he was not satisfied with the materials that were available in Italy at that time and therefore created a number of pieces of furniture and fittings with the idea to develop them later, on an industrial scale. Terragni designed a cantilevered chair, named Lariana. This chair has a single, sinuous frame made from steel tubing, which supports either leather upholstery or a moulded wooden seat and back. For the formal atmosphere of the executive boardroom, he transformed the Lariana by extending the frame into an elegant armrest and called this chair the Benita. The various curves of both chairs' frames give the structure of the seat, back and armrest an unusual and comfortable flexibility, while also providing a strong gesture that combines beauty and function. Despite their being specially designed for the Casa del Fascio, the two chairs were also conceived as prototypes and it was intended that they would be mass produced by Columbus in Milan, who were starting to produce their own metal-tube furniture. Terragni, in his Kindergarten Sant'Elia, which he designed and built between 1936–7, used the two versions of the chairs again but they were never put into mass production. The designs were then overlooked, as a result of their connection with the fascist regime, until the 1970s, when Zanotta decided to re-edit both versions as part of their classic collection.

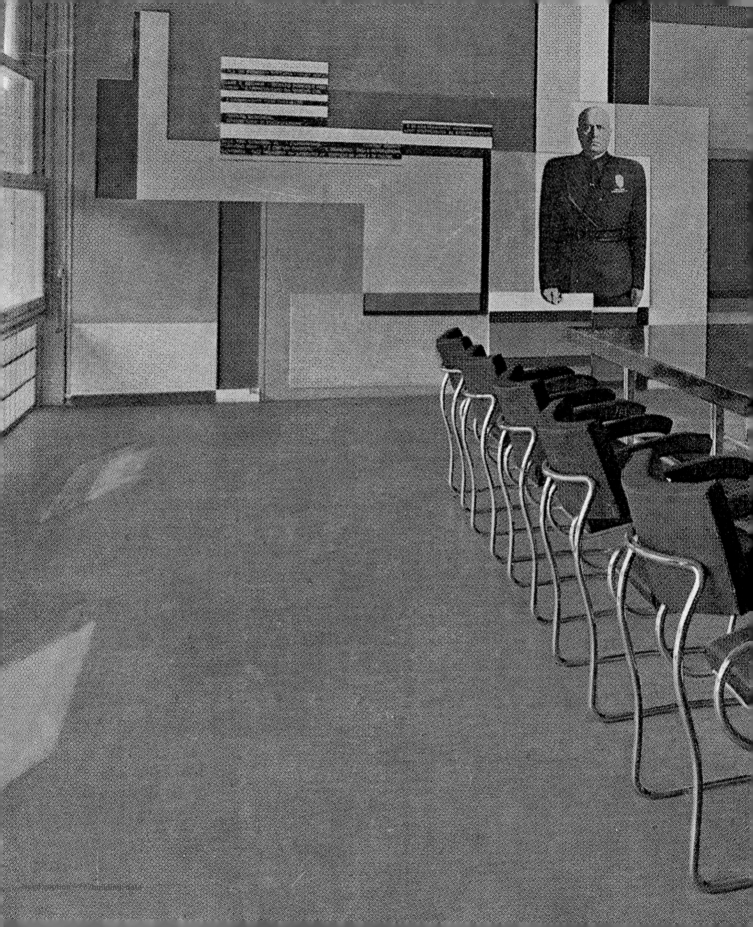

The Lancia Aprilia was one of the first commercially successful streamlined cars, and is considered the masterpiece of Vincenzo Lancia, who established the Turin-based company in 1906. Lancia, the son of a wealthy soup manufacturer, worked for Fiat before founding his own car manufacturer, although he continued to race cars for Fiat afterwards. His success began in 1922, with the Lambda, a car that integrated chassis and body, which brought his company much attention for the quality and performance of its cars. The Aprilia was presented to the public in 1937, just after the death of Lancia. The Aprilia was the first mass-produced car to use aerodynamic principles, and thus became the model for all future cars. The saloon body was a pillarless monocoque design with four doors, but its chief distinguishing feature was the V-shaped nose with its wind-cutting radiator grille. This pointed profile was designed to reduce air resistance, and set the precedent for a succession of Italian car bodies over the next few years. But the streamlined body was not the Aprilia's only virtue. It also had independent suspension on all four wheels, which was very rare for the time, a V-4 engine and hemispherical combustion chambers. Compact and relatively light, the car had a top speed of 128 kph (80 mph). The Aprilia proved more successful than earlier wind-tunnel designs such as the Chrysler Airflow of 1934, which, despite being radically innovative, failed to catch on, partly because of the economic climate of the early 1930s in the United States. A second series was developed and launched in 1939, which had a larger engine generating 48 bhp. Other variations were introduced, such as the instrument panel, but the specifications of the first series remained. The second series was produced until 1949, and 20,082 cars and 7,554 chassis were built at the factory in Turin. The combination of sophisticated machinery, tooling and design brought Aprilia acclaim, and allowed the company to survive through World War II.

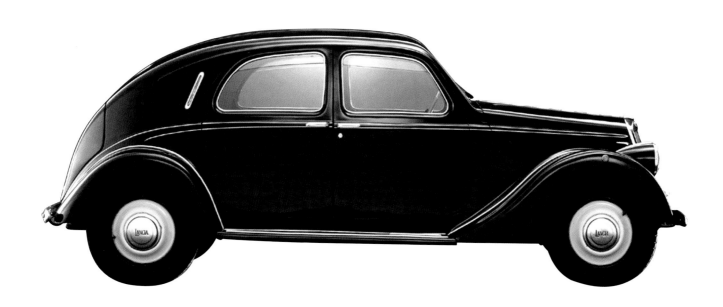

Often described as the 'mother of the modern motorcycle', the Harley-Davidson EL with its totally new engine, transmission and frame, was in many ways the prototype of all later Harley-Davidsons. At the height of the Depression in 1931, Harley-Davidson decided to stimulate the market by developing a completely new bike. When the EL model came out five years later, that decision proved to be one of the company's best, establishing Harley-Davidson as America's leading motorcycle producer. While its major rival of the time, the Indian Motor Company, opted to stay with the older side-valve motors, Harley-Davidson gave its EL a more modern overhead valve design that proved, in the long run, to be the engine of the future. The EL was characterized by bold styling changes and a unique look; the top of each rocker box resembled knuckles on a fist earning it the nickname 'Knucklehead'. In line with Harley-Davidson's reputation for evolutionary changes, the EL was introduced commercially with little publicity and minimal fanfare. The new bike was a sort of a prototype and underwent a variety of modifications in its first years. Apart from its valves, there were several notable features that would characterize future Harley-Davidson models: a separate U-shaped oil tank enclosing the battery so that oil was no longer carried in fuel tanks; a stronger, tubular-style front fork assembly instead of the earlier I-beam style; a smoother, more rounded fuel tank mounted with speedometer, oil pressure gauge, ammeter and ignition switch; and an improved oil circular system, in place of the total loss system used by previous models. Manufactured from 1936 to 1940 with a V-twin engine displacing 1000cc (about 61 cubic inches) supposedly producing 40 hp, the EL combined the light weight of smaller bikes with power rivalling that of 1200cc models. The results of this impressive engineering effort were demonstrated when racer Joe Petrali took an EL to a record 219 kph (136 mph), 294.5 kph (183 mph) at Daytona, and Fred Ham rode one for 2,937 kilometres (1,825 miles) in twenty-four hours.

Advertisement, 1936

Drawings of trailer, made
specifically to transport
and install the kiosk

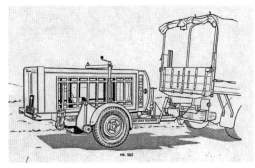

In 1924 Sir Giles Gilbert Scott won a three-way competition to design a mass-produced, standardized telephone kiosk for use throughout Britain. The K2, a classically proportioned steel and glass mini-building crowned with a saucer dome resting on segment-headed pediments, was mostly erected in towns and cities. Widely admired for its monumentality and dignity, it seemed to sit comfortably in an urban setting despite its unapologetic vibrant red paint. Eleven years later Scott was asked to modify his design to coincide with a major push to install a public telephone within relatively easy access of every home in the country. The result was the K6 or Jubilee phone box. Scott reduced the height of the kiosk to 2.5 m (8 ft 3 in) and cut its weight by half for ease of transport and installation. He increased the number of window rows from six to eight and moved the vertical glazing bars outwards, creating a wider central windowpane. These changes, coupled with the removal of the K2's Grecian fluting, reduced the kiosk's monumentality and gave the K6 a lighter aspect and a more modern look. As an architect Scott had an uncanny ability to make highly visible marks on the landscape. His buildings include the Anglican Cathedral that towers above the city of Liverpool, and three of London's most prominent buildings: Battersea Power Station (1929–55), Waterloo Bridge (1939–45) and Bankside Power Station (1955), now Tate Modern. The widespread distribution and the longevity of the K6's design (over 60,000 were erected between 1936 and 1968, when it was eventually replaced by Bruce Martin's toughened glass K8) meant that it, too, had a massive impact on the British architectural landscape. When it was first installed away from urban areas, the K6 met with considerable protest from those who found its appearance disturbing in a rural setting. It remains, however, one of the twentieth-century's most recognizable pieces of street furniture, and now that it is gradually disappearing from British streets and country lanes, it is more often mourned for than moaned about.

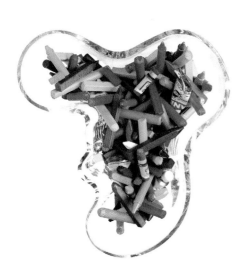  

Aalto's Savoy Vase, his best-known glass design, has provoked considerable speculation about the inspiration for its unusual amoebic shape. It has been suggested that the shape of the vase was influenced by the eccentric growth rings of trees or by the fluidity of water. The undulating outline is often said to have been inspired by Finland's many lakes. Although the vase has become so famous that it can now stand as a symbol for the whole of Finland, this suggestion, like all the rest, is ultimately fanciful, even if it does accord with a nationalism that was an important feature of much of Finnish design. For his part, Aalto remained tight-lipped about his sources. Even his original name for the Savoy Vase – he dubbed it 'An Eskimo Woman's Leather Breeches' (*Eskimoerindern Skinnbuxa*) – reveals more about his sense of humour than it does his inspiration. The vase, although ostensibly functional, represents one of the few occasions when Aalto came close to designing something ornamental for its own sake. Certainly, empty of flowers, it can stand alone as a piece of sculpture. But the shape also relates to the kinds of curves that Aalto was producing in his own laminated wooden furniture and marks a significant point in the development of his formal vocabulary, which was continued in his architecture. The vase was created for a competition for glass designs at the Paris World Fair of 1937, sponsored by the manufacturer Karhula (later iittala). It won first prize. But at more or less the same time several were ordered to complete Aalto's furnishing of the Savoy restaurant in Helsinki, which is where it its name comes from. Although the vase was originally blown into wooden moulds, a more durable cast-iron mould is now used. The vase has been in production, in a variety of colours and sizes, and in popular demand since its introduction.

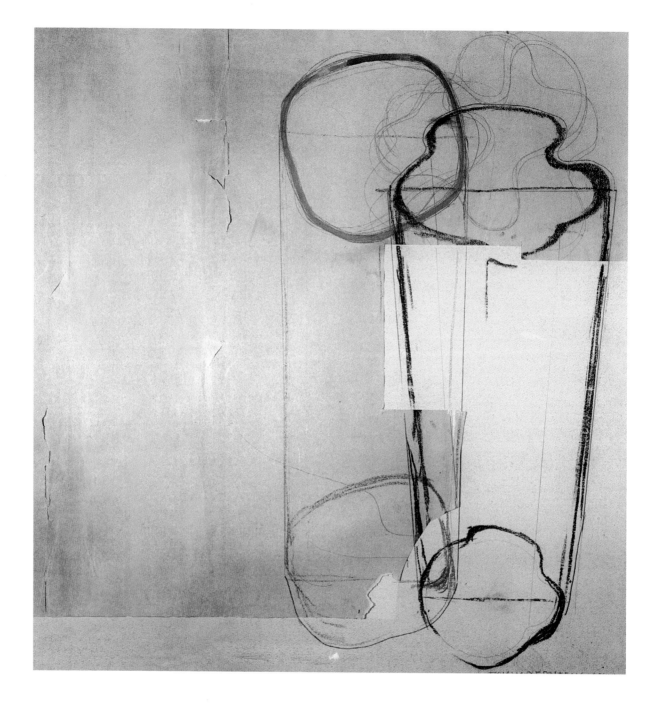

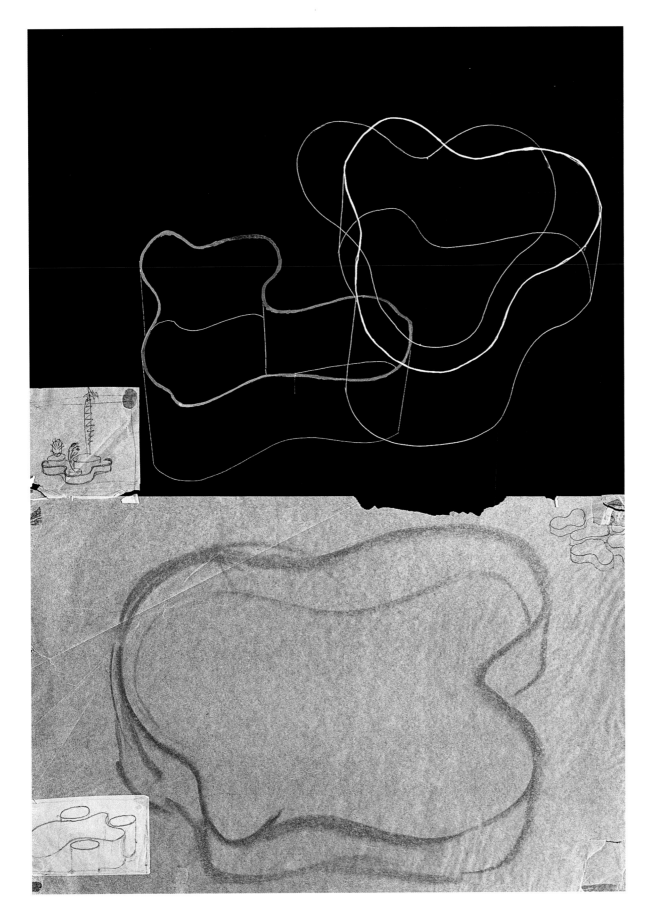

Sleek, streamlined and, when closed, fitting comfortably into the palm of the hand, the Bantam Special camera was a smart, stylish and well-made camera for the serious amateur. The cast aluminium body was painted high-gloss black, with raised exposed metal parallel tram lines and fittings. A small button released the sideways-opening baseboard to bring out the lens, which was connected to the back by bellows and lazy struts. The camera introduced the new 828 roll film to the public, essentially an unperforated paper-backed 35 mm, giving a negative size of 28 × 40 mm. The camera was particularly intended to appeal to photographers wanting to take colour photographs on the newly introduced Kodachrome slide film. Two versions of the camera were made. The first, from 1936 to 1940, had a Kodak Anastigmat Ektar f/2.0 lens in a German-made Compur shutter; the second, from 1941 to 1948, a Kodak Ektar f/2.0 lens in an American-made Supermatic No.0 shutter. A coupled-rangefinder for precise helical focusing and a direct vision optical finder were both incorporated into the raised camera top. Walter Dorwin Teague was already a well-known and established industrial designer by the time he was hired by the Eastman Kodak Company on the recommendation of Metropolitan Museum curators in 1928. Kodak was looking to modernize and update its range of cameras and Teague's work had been attracting increasing attention since he had established his own industrial design office in 1926. He maintained a working relationship with Kodak until his death in 1960. From the outset, Teague insisted on working closely with Kodak's engineers and was involved in the production process. Between 1928 and the early 1930s he designed a range of Art Deco-styled cameras, starting with the Vanity Kodak, Beau Brownies, Gift Kodak and Coquette. These had limited commercial success. Kodak launched its Bantam range of cameras in 1935. Intended for the amateur market and sold for upwards of $5.75. Most had streamlined moulded-plastic bodies. The Kodak Bantam Special was made to a higher standard than others in the range, and had a fast f/2 lens compared to the standard f/4.5 lens. Its high price of $110 (£28) precluded any mass market for it. The camera was deeply symbolic of the period and its design was characteristic of Teague's work for other companies. His later work for Kodak concentrated on styling affordable ranges of amateur cameras, including postwar Brownie cameras.

NEW....

KODAK BANTAM SPECIAL

1 Lightning-fast *f.*2 lens

2 1/500 Compur-Rapid shutter

3 Die-cast, machined aluminum body

4 Coupled range finder—built in

PRICE $110.00

YOU'VE never seen a miniature camera like this crack, new Eastman masterpiece—Kodak Bantam Special. It's altogether different in design, equipment, operation.

Beautifully streamlined, amazingly compact, its body is light-weight, high-strength, die-cast and machined aluminum. Closed, it gives complete protection to equipment and lens. Fittings are of modern stainless steel.

Eastman's new super lens, Kodak Anastigmat EKTAR *f.*2, places this remarkable little camera right up with the leaders in lens power. Its shutter is the 1/500 Compur-Rapid. Military-type, split-field range finder, coupled with focusing mount.

From pocket to picture takes but a moment with Kodak Bantam Special. It opens at the touch of a button...no fumbling with case or lens cap. It sets quickly, easily. Focuses in a jiffy. You can view as you focus.

Kodak Bantam Special takes 8 exposures per roll of Kodak Panatomic or Super X Film. It brings new convenience and economy to your picture taking. You can make your own enlargements from its needle sharp negatives, or you can have your photo finisher make up the standard, 2¾″ x 4″ pictures at low cost.

Be sure to see this latest—and finest—of Eastman miniatures at your dealer's. It's a real "buy" at $110.

Only Eastman Makes the Kodak

EASTMAN KODAK COMPANY ● Rochester, N. Y.

Terence Robsjohn-Gibbings & Mr Saridis

The Klismos Chair in walnut with woven leather thongs, like much of classical Greek art, presents a particular ideal of beauty and perfection that has inspired artists and designers for well over 2,000 years. The elegant strength of the joinery combined with the delicacy of the tapering curves and the obvious consideration of the human body make this the earliest historical example of a comfortable household chair. Although no wood chairs of this type have survived from antiquity, there are numerous representations of them in Greek painting and sculpture of the fourth and fifth centuries BC, usually associated with women and domestic scenes. Often the seat had a loose cushion on it. Considering its aesthetic, functional and political legacy, it remains one of the most important pieces in the history of furniture design. Long before ergonomics became the buzzword of the design world, the Klismos Chair stood out as seeming

to be in its essence an object based on its relationship to the body. Unlike other examples of ancient seating, which are either elaborate but rigid thrones not intended for comfort or relatively crude stools and chairs, the Klismos demonstrates an unprecedented level of sophistication. Terence Robsjohn-Gibbings, British-born interior and furniture designer, considered his designs of classical Greek furniture to be the greatest successes of his long career. In 1936 he opened his own showroom in New York to promote his vision of Modernism with historical references and in 1937, he designed this first Klismos Chair. This is a faithful reproduction drawn from ancient representations and it was so successful that he returned to it again and again. It is somewhat ironic that Robsjohn-Gibbings is best known for this chair because he was an ardent, if idiosyncratic, modernist. In his 1944 book *Goodbye, Mr*

Chippendale, he stated that 'the antique furniture cancer is a deeply rooted evil' and pressed the argument for Modernism. After a prolific period of work for Widdicomb in the 1940s and 1950s, where he produced many designs in his warm brand of modernist style, he turned again to ancient Greece for inspiration. In 1961, he designed the Klismos line of furniture in collaboration with Saridis in Athens, extending the collection to include reproductions of several types of furniture from classical Greece.

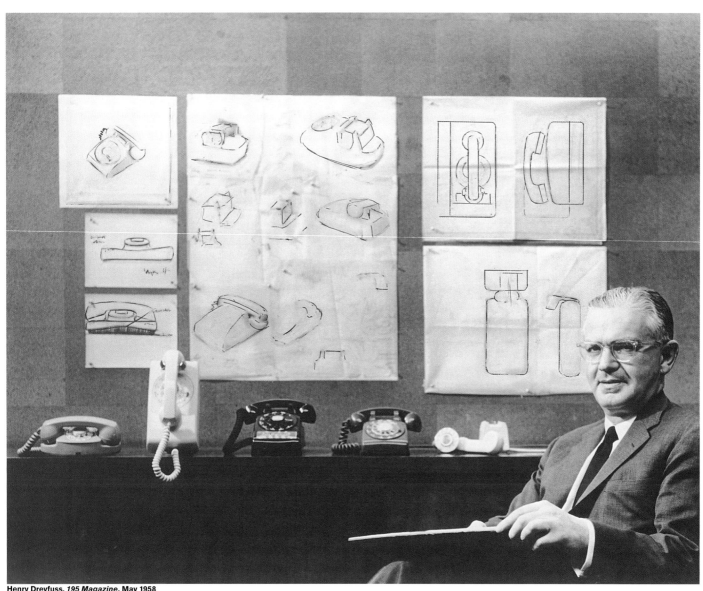

Henry Dreyfuss, *195 Magazine***, May 1958**

Dreyfuss, whilst part of the group who contributed so much to the 'streamlined' age, paid close attention to the ease of use of his products, and was concerned with user comfort from the outset. This informed his design work for such clients as Sears, Westclox, Hoover and John Deere. While much of this adheres to the dominant curvilinear aesthetic of the time, it can also be argued that they offered additional benefits through an appreciation of user interaction. So concerned with the notion that products should be designed 'from the inside out' was Dreyfuss that when he learned he would be unable to consult with the engineers responsible for the development of a new telephone, he refused an invitation to pitch for the job. This reluctance to compromise on his guiding principle paid off when the Bell Telephone Corporation offered him the job anyway. The result of this collaboration was the 'Type 300' handset, which remains an archetype to this day. Dreyfuss and his team developed the form through studies of hand and head sizes, as well as a consideration of the internal configuration and mechanics. They could not claim to be the first to combine mouthpiece and receiver in a single handset, as this had been seen on telephones since around 1930, but other innovations such as placing the numbers inside the finger holes added to the clarity of interface and ease of use. The model 300 was produced in black phenolic from 1937, and demonstrated its popularity and versatility by remaining in production until 1950. The ideas and processes developed through working on projects such as this helped to inform Dreyfuss' philosophy and approach to design. These would eventually culminate in his influential book of 1959 – *The Measure of Man*, which helped to establish methods for designers to incorporate anthropometric and ergonomic research into their work.

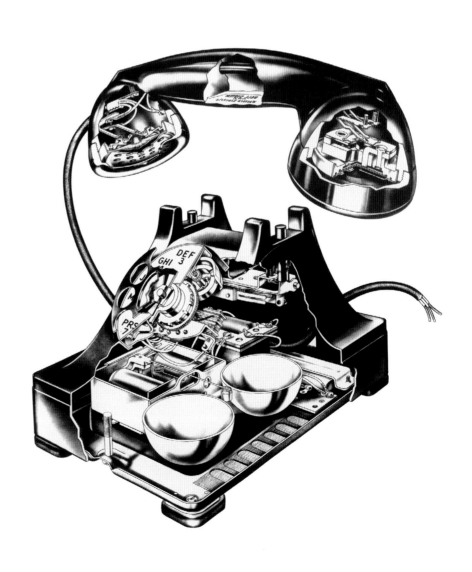

The Waring Blendor revolutionized the way we make drinks, as Fred Waring had predicted to a St Louis reporter at the time of the product's launch. Waring was a former architecture and engineering student who became the leader of the successful big band, The Pennsylvanians, and whose love of gadgetry had led him to become the dedicated promoter and financial backer of the blender that would eventually bear his name. He had been introduced to the blender by Fred Osius, the inventor, after a live radio broadcast of his show at the Vanderbilt Theater in New York City. And, although it was not the first of its kind (Stephen Poplawski had developed a precursor in 1922), Osius had made such significant improvements that the results were patented in 1933. In mid-1936, and $25,000 later, the design still needed technical improvements. During that period Osius sought financial support from Waring, who remained steadfast as development continued. The blender acquired its cloverleaf shape in 1937 and was introduced as the Miracle Mixer at the National Restaurant Show in Chicago. The blender retailed at $29.75. In 1938 the blender's name was changed to the Waring Blendor and the Miracle Mixer Corporation became the Waring Corporation. By 1954 one million of these popular kitchen appliances had been sold. Still manufactured by Waring and virtually unchanged since its introduction, the machine, with its round, gently undulating and tapered polished stainless-steel base, shows the influence of Art Deco. Coupled with its 40-oz clover-leaf glass bowl, the design is an icon of American pre-World War II design. With two speeds, its 360-watt motor crushes ice in ways that are more than adequate for almost any liquid food or beverage. Its handle, the splatter-proof opening in its top and its imperial and metric graduations provide additional features that all other blenders reference. Waring enthusiastically promoted the blender while on tour with his band, garnering press attention and demonstrating the blender's capabilities by giving out free samples of his concoctions. He also touted the device at hotels, restaurants and upscale department stores like B Altman's and Bloomingdales. Because of rationing, only a few blenders were made during World War II, for scientific purposes. The efficacy and reliability of the Waring Blendor made it the scientists' blender of choice, and it was used by Dr Jonas Salk while working on the polio vaccine.

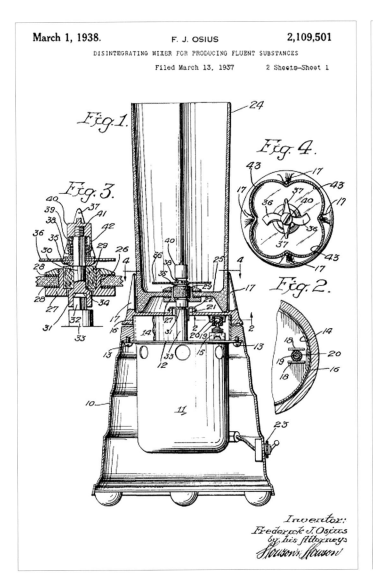

March 1, 1938.   F. J. OSIUS   2,109,501

DISINTEGRATING MIXER FOR PRODUCING FLUENT SUBSTANCES

Filed March 13, 1937   2 Sheets—Sheet 1

Inventor:
Frederick J. Osius
by his attorneys

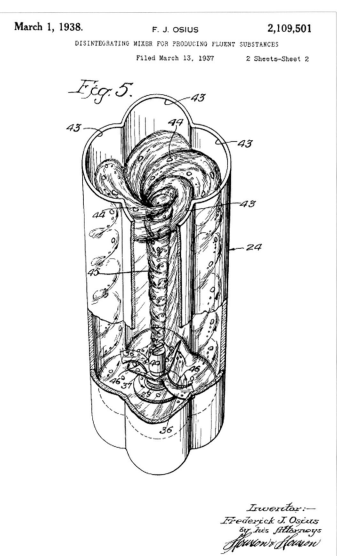

March 1, 1938.   F. J. OSIUS   2,109,501

DISINTEGRATING MIXER FOR PRODUCING FLUENT SUBSTANCES

Filed March 13, 1937   2 Sheets—Sheet 2

Inventor:—
Frederick J. Osius
by his attorneys

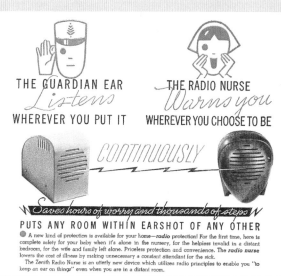

Brochure detail, c.1938

Radio Nurse (1937)
Isamu Noguchi (1904–88)
Zenith Radio 1937 to c.1941

As is frequently the case when a human tragedy captures the imagination of a country, the 1932 kidnapping of Charles Lindbergh's infant son inspired preventive strategies from laws to new technologies that sought to comfort the American public. In 1937, a year after the Lindbergh case came to a close, Zenith's production of the Radio Nurse and its accompanying Guardian Ear offered the concerned parent the chance to be in more than one place at a time. Hiring the thirty-three-year-old artist/designer Isamu Noguchi to develop his first piece of industrial design, Zenith provided a wireless intercom system consisting of Noguchi's Radio Nurse, a brown Bakelite receiver in a distinctly modernist casing reminiscent of the covered head of a nurse or a reductivist portrait by Brancusi, coupled with the Guardian Ear, a transmitter housed in a far clumsier curved metal box intended for installation in a child's room. In keeping with the rest of Noguchi's work, Radio Nurse gave an elegant, rarefied sculptural presence to a functional object and advanced the designer's exploration of a dialogue between biological and machined forms. His use of Bakelite also provided a potent alternative to the Art Deco idiom where the material's plasticity was most frequently employed. Oddly, despite the particularly privileged status of the Lindbergh baby, the crudeness of the boxed transmitter reveals notions about the social standing of children at the time and the diminished design standards that were applied to products for their environments. Housing the transmitter, the Ear was undistinguished, a plain enamelled case from which a microphone's output was amplified and modulated through a 300 kHz oscillator. Coupled to the AC power line, the signal was demodulated and amplified. In recognition of the designer hand in this product, Noguchi's name was stamped into the Nurse's casing. Ironically, despite its formal uniqueness, it was a social reality that sent the Nurse to the rubbish heap: after the Japanese attack on Pearl Harbor, the fact that the designer's name was Japanese, not technological obsolescence, resulted in the Nurse's disposal.

The Henry Dreyfuss designed-Model 'A' Tractor for John Deere was the first example of the application of industrial design to agricultural machinery. The design aimed to unify all of the previously disparate mechanical elements of tractor engineering within a homogeneous designed form, most notably in the combined hood and radiator cover for which Dreyfuss received a design patent. The firm of John Deere was founded in 1837 when John Deere fabricated the first steel plough, using steel from an old sawmill blade. John Deere's most popular tractor, the Model 'A', began production in 1934, spawning a popular line of two-cylinder tractors. Faced with the knowledge that their tractors were similar in performance to rival manufacturers due to a cooperative agreement to pool technical knowledge and patents, the vice-president of manufacturing, Charles Stone, realized that 'styling' offered the chance to distinguish their products from the competition. In 1937 he took the momentous decision to commission Dreyfuss to redesign their entire product range and, in conjunction with John Deere's own engineers, the brief was given to create a 'family resemblance' between the models. Dreyfuss and his associate Herb Barnhart produced a series of innovative designs based on the distinctive narrow hood and horizontal radiator louvres married to increased engine size and equipment levels. Featuring such technical innovations as an electric start, lighting, an ergonomically resolved 'armchair' seat and the casting of symbols into the major controls, the highly successful designs stayed in production until 1952, the trademark green and yellow liveried designs easily outselling their competitors and establishing a lasting brand image. In 1960 Dreyfuss reworked the entire range again to yet more critical and commercial success.

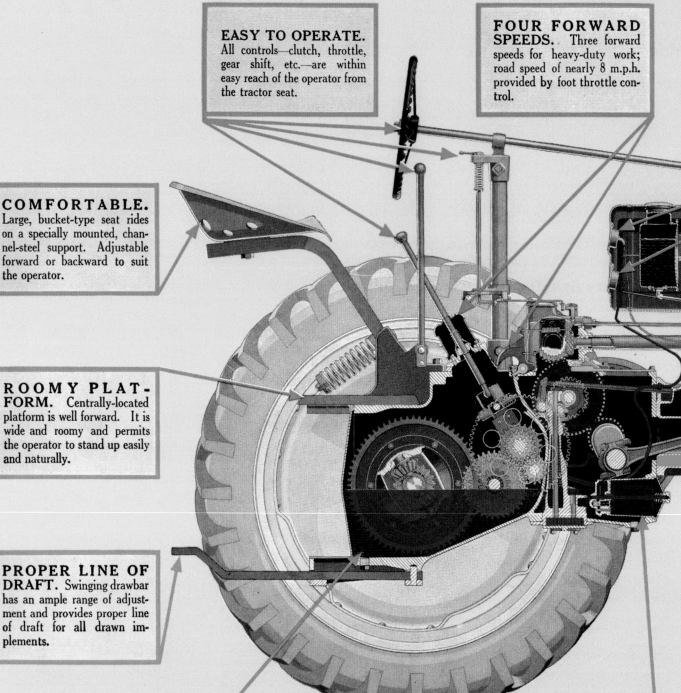

EASY TO OPERATE.
All controls—clutch, throttle, gear shift, etc.—are within easy reach of the operator from the tractor seat.

FOUR FORWARD SPEEDS. Three forward speeds for heavy-duty work; road speed of nearly 8 m.p.h. provided by foot throttle control.

COMFORTABLE. Large, bucket-type seat rides on a specially mounted, channel-steel support. Adjustable forward or backward to suit the operator.

ROOMY PLAT-FORM. Centrally-located platform is well forward. It is wide and roomy and permits the operator to stand up easily and naturally.

PROPER LINE OF DRAFT. Swinging drawbar has an ample range of adjustment and provides proper line of draft for all drawn implements.

AUTOMATIC LUBRICATION OF TRANSMISSION AND DIFFERENTIAL. Gears are fully enclosed and run **in a bath of clean** oil.

POSITIVE ENGINE LUBRICATION. Pump forces oil **under pressure** through filter to main and connecting rod bearings. Other parts automatically lubricated.

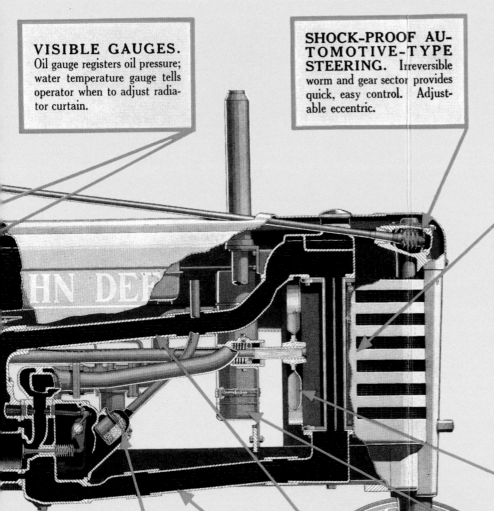

VISIBLE GAUGES. Oil gauge registers oil pressure; water temperature gauge tells operator when to adjust radiator curtain.

SHOCK-PROOF AUTOMOTIVE-TYPE STEERING. Irreversible worm and gear sector provides quick, easy control. Adjustable eccentric.

PROPER ENGINE TEMPERATURE. An adjustable curtain, allows you to regulate temperature for efficient operation. Radiator shutter, controlled from tractor seat, available as extra.

POSITIVE AIR FLOW THROUGH RADIATOR. Fan is gear-driven— no belt to slip, cause trouble, and require replacement.

CLEAN AIR TO ENGINE. Oil-wash air cleaner removes dust and dirt from the air that is drawn into the the engine. Easy to service.

VENTILATED CRANKCASE. Ventilator and breather maintain forced circulation of *clean* air throughout crankcase— remove gases and vapors.

AUTOMATIC TEMPERATURE CONTROL. John Deere thermosiphon system is fully effective under all loads and temperatures. Simple—no water pump or thermostat.

To many Germans the name Pelikan is likely to conjure up memories of the classroom where Pelikan ink pots were a fundamental desktop fixture. Today the company, is a manufacturer not just of ink, but also of pens, printing cartridges and artists' materials. Pelikan has become a global brand and icon not only of German industry, but of ink, that most noble of materials. This range of Pelikan packaging, designed in 1937, is indicative of the company's advanced understanding of the potential of packaging design as a branding medium. The fact that the designer was Wilhelm Wagenfeld, a famous Bauhaus exponent and celebrated German industrial designer, adds further to its allure. Made from glass, the ink bottles vary in shape and height, starting from the stout, traditional, square-shaped inkwell and expanding to include a set of taller bottles measuring up to 15 cm (6 in) high. Each vessel is topped off with a sage-green bottle top and ivory-coloured label displaying the famed Pelikan emblem. The effect is functional and understated: a classic example of 1930s German graphic design. Pelikan was founded as a colour and ink factory by German chemist Carl Hornemann in 1838. The company's grasp of the power of branding began early when in 1871 Günther Wagner, the new owner, registered the Pelikan emblem as its trademark. It was one of the first company trademarks to exist in Germany. With the introduction of the now world-famous 4001 ink series in 1901, Pelikan began producing beautifully designed packaging that served to underscore the artistic heritage on which the brand was founded. The ensuing bottles, and paper boxes in which they were sold, were so intricately designed that they were almost works of art in themselves. Indeed, the German Museum of Packaging features a range of Pelikan bottles dating from 1885 to 1965. The commission of Wagenfeld to design new bottles for the celebrated ink series coincided with the company's centenary. The involvement of an internationally celebrated designer lent an extra measure of cachet to the proceedings, and was a clear link back to Wagenfeld's early designs in glass. The bottles are collectable among today's packaging aficionados and serve as a timeless example of industrial graphic design from the period.

265

Pelikan Last Drop Bottle (1937)
Wilhelm Wagenfeld (1900–90)
Günther Wagner 1938 to 1968

266

Having been in production for over six decades, during which time over 25 million units have been sold, the multi-award-winning Luxo L-1 lamp is widely regarded as the forerunner of all self-balancing desk lamps. Yet despite this, the L-1 owes a large part of its success to an earlier lamp created by an automotive engineer whose main speciality was the design of vehicle suspension systems. In 1937 Jacob Jacobsen acquired the production rights to British designer George Carwadine's 1934 Anglepoise Lamp. Having trained as an engineer himself, Jacobsen recognized the potential of the Anglepoise's spring-based balancing system, derived from the constant tension principle of human limbs with the lamp's springs standing in for muscles, and which allows the light to be constantly repositioned and yet remain stable through every change. Consequently, Jacobsen's L-1 lamp uses a similar system (undeniably, both the L-1 and the Anglepoise look a lot like prosthetic limbs with a bulb attached), but harnesses it to a much more refined design, which is why the L-1 has become a definitive model. In particular, Jacobsen's design features a more elegant aluminium lampshade and is characterized by a formal harmony between shade, stand and the various articulated joints between them. Still manufactured today by Jacobsen's company, Luxo, the L-1 lamp comes in several versions, incorporating a selection of bases, mounts and shades. Despite many attempts to improve on it, it remains one of the world's leading task lights.

267

Shopping Trolley (1937)
Sylvan N Goldman (1898–1984)
Caddie 1937
Folding Basket Carrier Company
(later Unarco) 1937 to present

LIFE magazine, January 3, 1955

It is doubtful that any twentieth-century design object has ever received more magazine covers than the common shopping trolley, that steeled, wheeled chariot of the supermarket set. It was showcased on an archetypal *Saturday Evening Post* illustration from August 1940 calling the object 'the cart that changed the world', and again on *LIFE* magazine's January 1955 issue, sleek in profile with text heralding the '$73 billion market basket' splashed on the diagonal. The brainchild of a clever supermarket-chain owner in Oklahoma named Sylvan N Goldman, the classic shopping trolley was conceived in a single entrepreneurial moment as a means of increasing the amount of groceries customers could buy at one time. Addressing arm-weary housewives who lugged around wicker or wire baskets, Goldman's invention had its origins in the shapes of two ordinary folding chairs; he envisioned a cart made from a folding metal frame with holders for two parallel shopping baskets. Working with a handyman employee Fred Young to fashion the cart, Goldman produced a prototype that was first rejected by his largely female customers as too reminiscent of a baby carriage, and scoffed at by men whose masculinity was seemingly put into question. With an uncanny sensibility for marketing technique, Goldman secretly planted men and women in his Oklahoma City stores to walk around with the trolley, showing how convenient it was. The regional phenomenon soon spread across the country thanks to a display at a Super Market Institute event later that year where merchants were convinced that adapting the cart would lead to increased profits. It did, and Goldman iterated the model many times over the years through his Folding Basket Carrier Company, resulting in an outsized single-basket cart, of the sort ubiquitous today, that was designed specifically to nest in a long conga-line of trolleys. Seeing that women would put their toddlers in the basket while shopping, he added a built-in child's seat, and even a junior version that helped occupy older kids while their mothers shopped for ever-increasing numbers of groceries.

Fig.1.

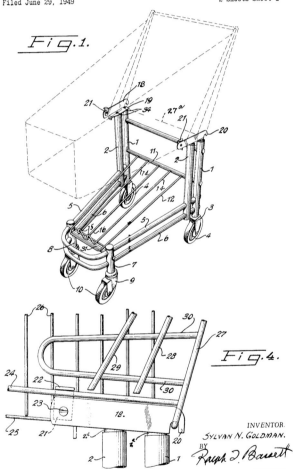

Fig.4.

INVENTOR·
SYLVAN N. GOLDMAN.
BY
Ralph J. Barrett
ATTORNEY

Fig.2.

Fig.3.

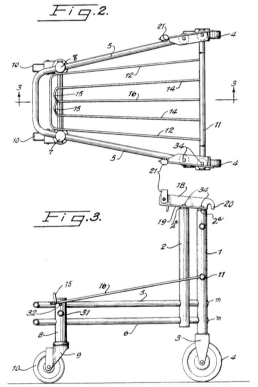

INVENTOR·
SYLVAN N. GOLDMAN.
BY
Ralph J. Barrett
ATTORNEY

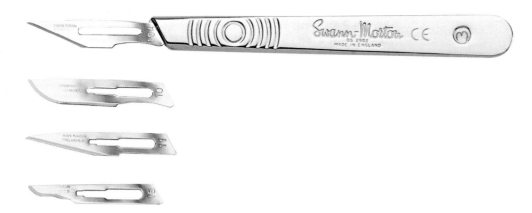

Walter Swann

Swann-Morton, based in the renowned steel-manufacturing town of Sheffield, England, first produced the sterilized surgical scalpel during the late 1930s. Mr W R Swann, Mr J A Morton and Miss D Fairweather founded the business in August 1932 to produce razor blades, adopting a socially inclusive management approach that continues to this day. In 1937 the company's emphasis shifted to the burgeoning market for sterilized surgical blades when the original US patent filed by the company Bard Parker expired. The design's innovative bayonet fitting enables sterilized blades to be simply attached to the stainless steel handle. The disposable blades are wrapped in a foil packet, which protects the blade, and maintains the requisite degree of hygiene for modern surgery procedures. The blades are attached to the handle by utilizing their material properties, and are flexed onto the slotted handle. Removal is a straight-forward process, and the design's intuitive qualities have helped establish the Swann-Morton Surgical Scalpel as the industry-defining product. The product has evolved into its current range of over sixty blade shapes and sizes, with twenty-seven different handle designs. There are specific products for surgeons, dentists, chiropodists and veterinary surgeons, as well as specialist scalpels for use in art, craft and design studios. In the 1960s, realizing the potential for innovation, Swann-Morton developed, with the expertise of UKAE at Wantage, Oxfordshire, a commercial fail-safe sterilization process using Cobalt 60 gamma radiation. The joint initiative led to the creation of one of the first commercial plants of its kind in the world and enabled Swann-Morton to be completely self-sufficient for all of its sterilization requirements. Swann-Morton now offers its irradiation and microbiological facilities to other healthcare manufacturers under contract. It continues to dominate the global market for surgical blades, producing 1.5 million surgical and craft blades each day, which are supplied to more than one hundred countries.

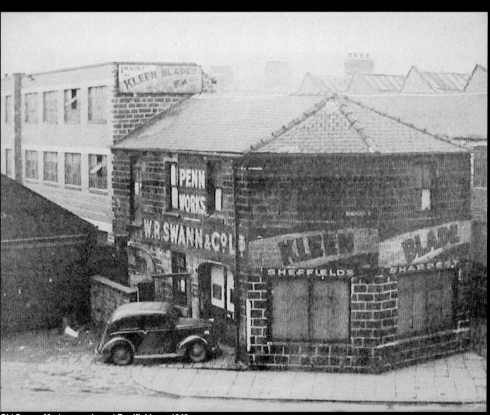

Old Swann-Morton premises at Bradfield, pre-1940s

When coffee was first introduced to

Europeans in the thirteenth century it was labelled the devil's drink. By the end of the twentieth century its energizing properties had made it one of the world's most important industries. Despite its popularity, counteracting the brew's characteristic bitterness became a preoccupation for many of its drinkers. While many remarkable and handsome contraptions were devised for this purpose, few had any impact on the drink's taste until 1908, when Melitta Bentz, an enterprising housewife from Dresden, Germany, came up with an idea. Believing that grounds and unwanted residues were the cause of coffee's bitterness, she thought that paper might make an effective filter. With this in mind, she made a hole in the bottom of a brass pot and lined it with blotting paper taken from the her eldest son's notebook. This simple invention changed the experience of coffee forever, removing both its grounds and bitter taste. Recognizing the potential value of her discovery, Bentz registered her filter with the Patent Office in Berlin in 1908 and, by the end of the year, had established the Melitta Bentz Company. In 1925 the now familiar red and green package was first used and Melitta became the brand name for an updated, round-bottomed filter. In the 1930s the brass pot was tapered into a cone shape that had a larger filtration area. By this time the cone was made of white porcelain with a cup-like handle and was flattened, with its interior surface ribbed to further enhance the brewing process. To complete Melitta's drip coffee system, a new filter was designed and patented that fitted into the porcelain holder and added still more brewing drip surface, thus requiring less coffee. Since that time new materials have been employed and production processes have been tailored to meet contemporary standards of environmental sustainability, but the design of each component has remained essentially unchanged. Melitta Bentz's company, however, has diversified and now produces vacuum bags, humidifiers, air cleaners, foils, wraps and cleaning products, and has evolved into the privately owned Melitta Group of Minden, Germany.

Melitta Cone Filter (1937)
Melitta Design Team
Melitta Group 1937 to 1940

The Jerry Can is a perfect example of innovation prompted by warfare. Although it is thought that the Italians first used it in Africa (possibly for the invasion of Abyssinia), it was the German army that would first use it on a large scale and to telling effect early in World War II. It is for this reason that British troops, who would first have seen it while on the run from Hitler's armies in Belgium and France, dubbed it the Jerry Can. The name stuck, though not surprisingly the Germans used another term: *Wehrmachtskanister*. Until its invention, the business of on-board fuel transportation was surprisingly hazardous. The British used a two-gallon pressed-steel container and a larger tin plate version. The first was rugged but expensive while the second was cheap but flimsy and easily punctured, particularly in rough terrain such as that encountered in the North Africa campaign. The transition from largely static warfare to the speedy movement of mechanized forces seen in World War II clearly called for a more reliable alternative. The five-gallon Jerry Can had several advantages that would aid the Germans' *Blitzkrieg* tactics, which were based on the rapid movement of tanks and infantry. Its three handles made it easy to carry, and the indentations in the sides allowed the contents to expand. An air pocket meant the can floated even when full, and its cam lever release mechanism worked better than the old screw caps. The can's design was considered so important that German units were ordered to destroy their fuel containers if in real danger of being captured. But despite this, by 1942 the British were able to copy the design after the Eighth Army captured Jerry Cans from the Afrika Korps. The design has remained virtually unchanged since, though it is now made in plastic as well as pressed steel and also carries water.

Jerry Can (c.1937)
Designer Unknown
Various 1937 to present

Think small.

Our little car isn't so much of a novelty any more.

A couple of dozen college kids don't try to squeeze inside it.

The guy at the gas station doesn't ask where the gas goes.

Nobody even stares at our shape.

In fact, some people who drive our little flivver don't even think 32 miles to the gallon is going any great guns.

Or using five pints of oil instead of five quarts.

Or never needing anti-freeze.

Or racking up 40,000 miles on a set of tires.

That's because once you get used to some of our economies, you don't even think about them any more.

Except when you squeeze into a small parking spot. Or renew your small insurance. Or pay a small repair bill. Or trade in your old VW for a new one.

Think it over.

Few cars have achieved the popular success of Volkwagen's little Beetle. It is one of the very few cars to have succeeded in transforming its image through its lifetime and to have had a distinctive appeal for subsequent generations. This was made possible by its simple, utilitarian character. In the 1930s Volkswagen's 'people's car' was part of Adolf Hitler's project to mobilize the German nation and to galvanize German manufacturing. Prior to Hitler's interest in a small, streamlined car its designer, the Austrian engineer Ferdinand Porsche had already been experimenting with the concept. His 1930 Kleinwagen, followed in 1932 by his Kleinauto Type 32, styled by Erwin Komenda, led the way to the development of the cheap, air-cooled, aerodynamic little family car that Hitler eventually made his own. In 1939 the German leader opened a factory in KdF Stadt (Work through Joy Town) dedicated to its production. Only two hundred cars were produced before the outbreak of war, however, and the real success of the Beetle belonged to the years following 1945, especially after 1949 when it was introduced into the USA. Throughout the 1950s and 1960s its rounded forms, defining rear window and air vents, sloping rear, strong personality and low price drew an audience of young American motorists who wanted to combine fun with efficiency. The Beetle soon acquired an iconic presence on American and European roads and became one of the most successful small cars of all time. Its popularity even inspired the feature film, Herbie, in which its toy-like quality was exploited to the full. Production of the VW Beetle ceased in Europe in 1974, when the company launched the Golf. However, production of the original model continued in Brazil until 1986, and in Mexico until 2003. The iconic VW Beetle was replaced by the 'new Beetle', first sold in 1998, which evoked its essential character without emulating it exactly, proving the public's fondness for this car has lasted into the early years of the twenty-first century.

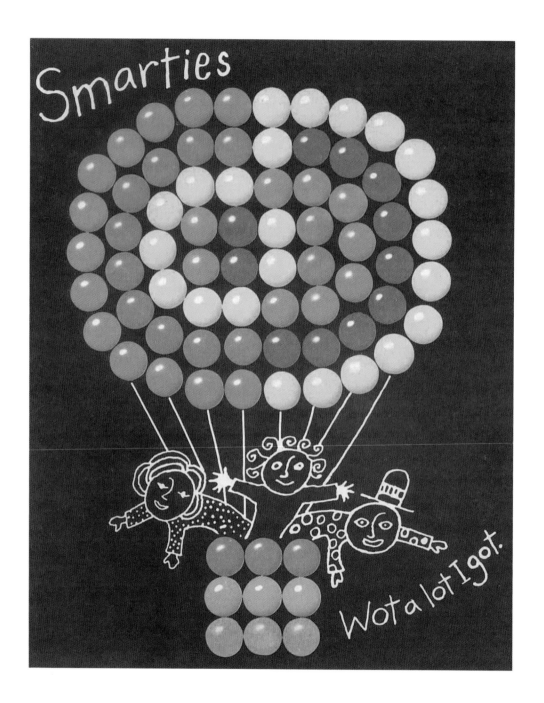

In 1937 Rowntree of York launched a new sweet in the UK called Chocolate Beans, following a successful test marketing exercise in Scotland. A year later Chocolate Beans were renamed Smarties and packed in their famous cylindrical tube. Smarties became one of the UK's bestselling children's confectionery brands with sales reaching £56 million in 2001. Smarties were directly inspired by *dragées*, a French confectionery item traditionally given out to guests at christenings by the godmother. *Dragées* were originally almonds covered in a shell of hardened sugar; later variations included hazelnut and chocolate centres and white, pink and blue sugar coats. The eight original Smartie colours – red, yellow, orange, green, mauve, pink, light brown and brown – remained unchanged throughout their production history, until the arrival of the blue Smartie with much razzmatazz in 1989 and the demise of the dreary light brown smartie. But research shows that orange is the favourite colour of Smartie-eaters. Past experiments with flavour variation have included a coffee-flavoured light brown Smartie and a plain chocolate dark brown Smartie. When production was resumed after World War II, Smarties had to be made with plain chocolate because of the shortage of milk. The classic cylindrical Smarties tube is an icon of packaging design, and the coloured plastic caps, each featuring one embossed letter of the alphabet, have proved perennially popular spelling aids. A slight modification was made to the packaging in 2002 with 'Smarties in a can', an attempt to capture the way children often 'drink' their Smarties. But more controversially, current manufacturers Nestlé revamped the famous tube and launched a six-sided Hexatube in February 2005, the first change to the traditional Smarties tube since the product hit the shops in 1938.

Caccia Cutlery (1938)
Luigi Caccia Dominioni (1913–)
Livio Castiglioni (1911–79)
Pier Giacomo Castiglioni (1913–68)
R Miracoli & Figlio 1938
Alessi 1990 to present

The Caccia Cutlery pattern, which takes its name from one of its designers, was first created in 1938 as a collaborative project by a group of highly influential Italian designers: Livio and Pier Giacomo Castiglioni and Luigi Caccia Dominioni. They all trained as architects in Italy and worked together on a broad range of projects over many years, designing interiors, exhibition installations, furniture and products.
The Caccia design was shown at the Milan Triennale in 1940, and was described by fellow Italian designer and commentator Gio Ponti in his publication *Domus* as 'the most beautiful cutlery in existence.' Ponti's opinion was widely shared, and such was the success of the design that Caccia is still manufactured and used in many Italian homes to this day.
The Caccia pattern represents a milestone in the history of cutlery design. In its day the set was a consummate example of how crafts-manship was embracing the industrial future of house wares. The profile is sleek and curved, while retaining an elegant and slender form, and there is a superb play on the thickness of the elements within the pieces. The Caccia is modern, yet retains the essence of classicism and its success in the eyes of the user is reflected in its enduring popularity. When originally launched, the Caccia Cutlery range was available in sterling silver only. However, over half a century later, Alessi saw the mass-market potential of the design and relaunched it in 1990 using stainless steel. Luigi Caccia Dominioni completed the set using the original design drawings from the 1930s, with the addition of a four-pronged fork, as the original three-pronged design had been thought by many to be too unusual.

The simple, but brilliant Landi Chair has remained a model of technical innovation, efficiency and understated elegance for over sixty years. The perforated seat and back section, made from one piece of stamped and rolled aluminium sheet, is suspended between the bent aluminium legs by minimal stretchers establishing a logical balance and proportion. The bending of the thin aluminium sheet stock adds stiffness and, along with heat treatment, makes possible a sturdy yet lightweight stacking chair weighing only 3 kg (7 lb). Originally intended for the garden, the chair's finish is accomplished by anodizing the aluminium, creating a surface quality suitable for outdoor use but also appropriate for common indoor use. The name Landi is an abbreviation of Landesausstellung, from the German word for National Exhibition and this is a significant aspect of the popularity of the chair. The Landi Chair was designed in 1938 by Hans Coray and introduced at the important Swiss National Exhibition of 1939, becoming forever associated with it. Coray began his career as a student of Romance languages and ended it in the world of traditional fine arts, but along the way his work as a designer represents his most notable productions, chief among them the Landi Chair. Designed in response to a competition for garden chairs, the Landi Chair quickly became a ubiquitous and popular symbol of the 1939 Swiss National Exhibition, which was organized to a great degree in defence of Swiss culture and national sovereignty. Surrounded by Nazism and Fascism, Switzerland was an isolated nation with good production capacities but hampered by a paucity of natural resources, with the notable exception of bauxite, the principle component of aluminium. In addition to being a beautiful, lightweight chair in the spirit of Modernism, the Landi Chair became a symbol of Swiss production, determination and national independence. It remains very popular and continues to represent the best in Swiss design. Its iconic status was recently reinforced when the government issued a postage stamp in 2004 with the image of the Landi Chair on it.

Eine der beglückenden Überraschungen der Schweizerischen Landesausstellung 1939 war der «Landistuhl». Seine rühmlichen Eigenschaften, die ihn vom ersten Tag an beliebt gemacht haben, sind die gleichen geblieben. Dank seiner einfachen, zweckmäßigen Form findet er immer neue Begeisterte. Er hat inzwischen in ungezählten Heimen, in der Schweiz und im Ausland, seinen Platz gefunden, im Freien, in Sonne, Regen und Schnee, aber auch im Innern des Hauses. Unverwüstlich – nach Jahren glänzend wie am ersten Tag. Seine Form verleidet nicht, er ist vielseitig brauchbar: im Garten, in Pärken, auf dem Balkon, im Spital, im Strandbad, Gartenrestaurant, in Empfangs- und Verkaufsräumen, Wohlfahrtshäusern usw. Beweis seiner stets «guten Form»: die Beachtung und Auszeichnungen, die er immer wieder an Ausstellungen findet.

Landi ein MEWA Produkt

Der Landistuhl wird geliefert in der silbrigen Urfarbe der Edelmetall-Legierung, der Sitz auf Wunsch in Rot, Grün, Gelb und Schwarz anodisch oxydiert, mit weißen oder schwarzen Gummifüßen.

100 HELVETIA

PERRON/MOEHRLE   2004   ENSCHEDÉ

A PRIORITY
PRIORITAIRE

275

Kubus Stacking Containers (1938)
Wilhelm Wagenfeld (1900–90)
Vereinigte Lausitzer Glaswerke
1940 to c.1943
VEB Ankerglas 1945 to c.1960

These modular containers, soft stackable bricks in moulded glass, were a high-quality everyday product in every facet of use and design. They are good for keeping food: transparent and hygienic so as to minimize waste and spoilage; compact, to maximize storage in the minimum space; and easily transportable. But not only that, they are beautiful enough to put on the table. Designer Wilhelm Wagenfeld's intention was to 'redefine the weight of things'. A student at the Bauhaus during 1923–5, Wagenfeld's Kubus Glass Containers were his greatest commercial success. Wagenfeld was one of those who most embodied the Bauhaus belief, admirably combining the emphasis on geometry with functionality; in production the containers are an even tighter square than on the original drawings. He stuck to these principles throughout his career, in which he concentrated on improving the quality of mass production. In fact, Walter Gropius later wrote to him, 'I appreciate your work and the path you have unwaveringly followed in your co-operation with industry in order to influence its production. Your work follows our first experiments at the Bauhaus to the letter.' Wagenfeld's work at the VLG was a landmark in the history of industrial design. As artistic manager he took a fairly ordinary company and brought it to the fore of the glass industry. His approach was holistic. Although design quality was paramount he was no believer in the designer ego; for him design was a collaboration. To this end he installed an artistic laboratory at the factory and hired several contemporary design figures to work as part of it. He also played a significant role in the marketing of the company's products, as well as improving the working conditions and education of his workers in order to instil pride in what was considered a semi-skilled profession. Wagenfeld worked first on the Rautenmarke (Diamond brand), then applied these principles of quality to pressed glass, previously the poor relation in the glass industry. The Kubus Stacking Containers embody the modern dream. Aside from its manifold visual and production qualities it also encapsulated a new attitude to tableware (i.e. kitchen to tableware) more successfully than many of its successors, as well as anticipating the modular forms of plastic storage.

Aug. 15, 1939.

H. DREYFUSS

Des. 116,180

LOCOMOTIVE

Filed Sept. 28, 1938

2 Sheets—Sheet 1

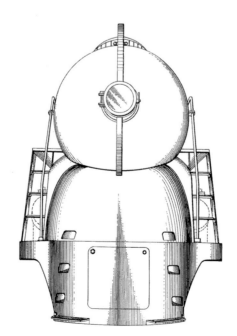

INVENTOR.
BY
ATTORNEY.

Aug. 15, 1939.

H. DREYFUSS

Des. 116,180

LOCOMOTIVE

Filed Sept. 28, 1938

2 Sheets—Sheet 2

INVENTOR.
Henry Dreyfuss
BY
ATTORNEY.

Dreyfuss's design for the Hudson J-3a locomotive engine to pull the famous 'Twentieth Century Limited' railway train was to become a technological and stylistic symbol. His aerodynamic redesign of 1938 was capable of reaching 166 kph (103 mph), a leap of 21 kph (13 mph) over the standard un-streamlined Hudson locomotive, although still some way short of LNER's record breaking Mallard which achieved 203 kph (126 mph) in the same year. The design featured a finned bullet nose resembling an ancient warrior's helmet that signified the style of the modern age. Rather than obscure the locomotive's shape with a shroud as had been done by contemporaries like Raymond Loewy, he instead exposed the running gear for easier maintenance, while creating an aerodynamic cowling that struck a wonderful aesthetic balance. Dreyfuss specified lights above the drive wheels to enable night-time servicing. Left on all night, these added to the sense of power and motion, as did the smooth half sphere of the engine's boiler. Not content with redesigning the locomotive, Dreyfuss created the first streamlined train to be designed in its totality. He unified the separate carriages by covering the spaces between them, creating vestibules that enhanced the sense of visual continuity. The interiors were a model of tasteful restraint, with everything from the furnishings to the tableware displaying the same motifs and colour palette, to create a total branded environment. Speakers were concealed behind paintings, while the formal seating layout of previous trains was replaced by more informal groupings, enabling passengers to relax in comfort and luxury. Entering service in 1938, the streamlined Hudson pulled the famed 'Twentieth Century Limited', which sped passengers between New York and Chicago, the fastest service of its time. The trains were to lose their iconic cowlings in 1945, and cease service in the mid-1950s as steam was finally phased out by the introduction of diesel-powered locomotives. A pioneer of industrial design, Henry Dreyfuss was responsible for the successful restyling of many American products, while also founding the Society of Industrial Design, and becoming the first president of the Industrial Designers Society of America. Perhaps his greatest contribution to design was his highly influential book entitled *The Measure of Man* published in 1960, which helped establish the industry wide application of anthropometric and ergonomic data.

This chair looks superficially
similar to the timber-framed Tripolina
Chair, yet, beyond its similar lines, the
Butterfly Chair is a very different
animal, with a rigid, welded-steel frame
instead of the Tripolina's folding timber
one. The framework is a fantastically
economical solution and its spare,
linear structure is reminiscent of the
trajectory of an asteroid. This is
achieved with wonderful simplicity
using just two loops of a very cheap
and readily available material – steel
rod – welded together to form a
seemingly continuous frame. The
frame is painted or plated, and a
leather 'glove' simply hangs over the
four 'fingers' of the frame, providing
part of the structure combined with
the seat and back. It was designed by
three Argentinian architects, who had
all previously worked together for
Le Corbusier, working under the name
Grupo Austral. The chair, originally
called Sillón BKF, was conceived for an
apartment in a building they designed
in Buenos Aires in 1938, Edificio
Charcas, and was first put into production by Artek-Pascoe. In 1947 it was
manufactured in much larger numbers
by Knoll in the United States, and sold
very widely, becoming an icon of a
certain style of 1950s furniture. The
chair's immediate popularity, combined
with simple material processing and
low investment tooling prompted many
copies, usually with canvas rather than
leather slings. There have also been a
number of hinged collapsible copies,
produced all over the world.

Butterfly Chair (1938)
Jorge Ferrari-Hardoy (1914–77)
Juan Kurchan (1913–75)
Antonio Bonet (1913–89)
Artek-Pascoe 1938
Knoll 1947 to 1973

**As steelworkers** in the 1930s headed off each morning to build the bridges and buildings of the new cities in North America, a Dome-Top Lunchbox was frequently seen swinging from their hands. The lunchbox was used by workers who were unable to go home for a midday meal, like Karl Axel Westerberg, heading off to the Ford Motor Company near Cass Lake, Mighican (the photograph was taken in 1924 by Arther Rothstein for Farm Relief during the Depression). Workers relied on their toolbox-grade metal rectangular box, with its domed-top to store a thermos flask, securely held by a simple metal clip, and its lower section for storing food. Prior to this workers would carry a metal lunchpail with a thin handle which resembled a bucket. Ernest Worthington filed a patent in 1938 for the Dome-Top, which became the widespread model for lunchboxes. Nearly two decades later, Aladdin Industries, a company that sold red-and-white lunchboxes to workers, began to create boxes specifically for children. Originally Aladdin decorated its children's lunchboxes with decals of popular action heroes of the time. The licences for the characters of television shows were expensive, however, and to save costs Aladdin reintroduced the traditional Dome-Top Lunchbox in 1957 decorated with generic cartoons, which did not require a licence, and were produced in-house. The dome-shaped lunchboxes were an instant success, and Aladdin's biggest seller, the 'school bus' design, which was in production between 1961 and 1973, sold 9 million units. In today's world of fast-food chains and supermarkets, the lunchbox has become a collector's item rather than a necessity, while it was once a crucial part of the working man's equipment, providing a nutritious meal wherever it might be needed.

Until the end of its production run in 1947, by which time more than 15,000 Piper J-3 Cubs had rolled out of the factory in Lock Haven, Pennsylvania, you could have it in any colour you liked as long as it was yellow. The Taylor brothers, Gilbert and Gordon, began in 1927 to develop a high-wing monoplane. They could not have chosen a worse time; American industry was in the grip of the Depression and their efforts stumbled and failed. Their first design, produced in 1930, was powered by a Brownbach engine and earned the nickname 'Tiger Kitten'

because it had about as much power as a kitten; if the engine was a kitten, then the plane was a cub, and so one of the great names in aviation was born. The design still needed work, but their company failed. With faith in the product and believing there was a market for an easy-to-operate, low-cost private aeroplane, oilman William T Piper bought up the company in 1931. By the mid-1930s, Gordon had been killed in an air crash and Gilbert had abandoned his partners to set up on his own, leaving Piper, with the help of the young designer Walter Jamouneau

(the 'J' in J-3) to develop the design. In bright yellow with black trim and with its distinctive snub-nosed shape, the two-seater J-3 Cub was launched in 1938. Easy and fun to fly at only 6.5 m (22 ft 2 in) long and with a wingspan of 10.7 m (35 ft 2 in), it quickly became the standard for light, affordable, tailwheel trainers. Its power increased from 40 hp when it was first made in 1938 to 65 hp by 1940; it was able to achieve a maximum speed of 137 kph (85 mph) and a maximum height of 2834 m (9,300 ft). The war sealed the Cub's reputation. In 1940 alone, over three

thousand Cubs were produced for military training. During the war itself, the Cub was used for reconnaissance, transporting supplies and medical evacuation, among other support roles, and it came to be known as the Grasshopper. Although the Piper Super Cub replaced the J-3 in 1947 and continued the Cub line almost to the end of the century, it was the J-3 that embodied the charm, personality and spirit of the great mid-century era of American light aviation design between 1938 and the 1960s.

The Depression of the 1930s hit the American motor industry hard. The bottom fell out of the luxury car industry and forced a number of manufacturers into a radical rethink. Cadillac responded to the harsh economic conditions by building a few cars that transformed its fortunes. First off the blocks was the Series 60 model, a mid-priced automobile that shared the General Motors B bodyshell with LaSalle, Oldsmobile and Buick. Its success allowed Cadillac to take a risk with the 1938 Sixty Special. This was the car that made the reputation of its twenty-three-year-old designer Bill Mitchell, who went on to succeed the legendary Harley Earl as head of design at General Motors. The Sixty Special marked such a departure for the marque, that its head of sales at the time Don Ahrens later commented, 'I do not need to remind automobile men that the Cadillac market is ultra-conservative. The bulk of our business is conducted with sound and substantial families. How would this

revolutionary car affect our position in the industry? Was it too startling for our price class? Was it too rakish for our reputation?' It turned out to be an enormous success. Mitchell, under the watchful eye of Earl, got rid of the traditional running boards, which allowed the body to be widened and the interior to have more space, and installed thin chrome windows that provided improved visibility. Importantly, he also used chrome sparingly, ensured all the doors were front-hinged, and integrated the boot into the overall style of the car. The Sixty Special was defiantly modern and the US consumer, in need of some good news after a decade of financial turmoil, lapped it up. In 1938 it outsold the Series 60 by three to one, despite the fact that it was significantly more expensive. Indeed, it could possibly be seen as a sign that the US was ready to re-emerge from its dark tunnel as a fully fledged global force.

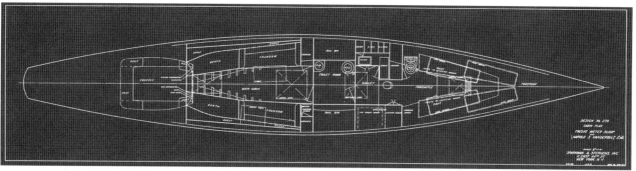

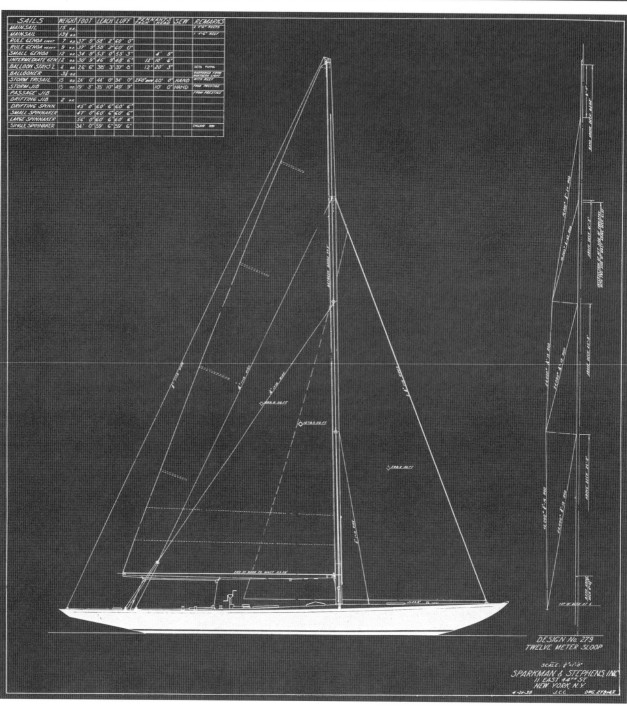

| SAILS | WEIGHT | FOOT | LEACH | LUFF | PENNANTS | | SEW | REMARKS |
					FOOT	HEAD		
MAINSAIL	15 oz.							4 4'6" REEFS
MAINSAIL	13½ oz.							1 4'6" REEF
RULE GENOA light	7 oz.	37' 9"	58' 2"	60' 0"				
RULE GENOA heavy	9 oz.	37' 9"	58' 2"	60' 0"				
SMALL GENOA	12 oz.	34' 9"	53' 0"	55' 3"		4'	9"	
INTERMEDIATE GENOA	18 oz.	30' 9"	46' 9"	48' 6"	11'	10'	6"	
BALLOON STAYS'L	4 oz.	26' 6"	36' 3"	37' 6"	12'	20'	3"	SETS FORM
BALLOONER	3½ oz.							RECOVERED FROM HEATHERS LIGHT WITH REEF
STORM TRISAIL	15 oz.	26' 0"	44' 0"	34' 0"	EXQ'nt	40' 0"	HAND	
STORM JIB	15 oz.	19' 3"	35' 10"	49' 9"		10' 0"	HAND	FROM PRESTIGE
PASSAGE JIB								FROM PRESTIGE
DRIFTING JIB	2 oz.							
DRIFTING SPINN.		45' 0"	60' 6"	60' 6"				
SMALL SPINNAKER		47' 0"	60' 6"	60' 6"				
LARGE SPINNAKER		56' 0"	60' 6"	60' 6"				
SINGLE SPINNAKER		34' 0"	59' 6"	59' 6"				ENGLAND 1939

DESIGN No. 279
TWELVE METER SLOOP

SCALE: ¼" = 1'-0"

SPARKMAN & STEPHENS, INC.
11 EAST 44TH ST.
NEW YORK, N.Y.

4-24-39   J.C.C.   DWG. 279-63

Most of the vintage yachts on show at today's regattas were originally designed to compete in the America's Cup, among them the Endeavour, the Ranger and VIM, now beautifully refitted by Beconcini of Italy. The story of the VIM began in 1938 when Harold S Vanderbilt commissioned Olin Stephens of Sparkman & Stephens to design a 12 metre class boat to win the America's Cup. The '12 metre Designs' were established as a collection of racing yachts specifically for the America's Cup. Sparkman & Stephens was the initiator of this, and had created a design for which everything was intended to produce a winning yacht. It took advantage of the Davidson Laboratory experimental towing tank, located along the Hudson River, New York City, to perform extensive performance trials. After being shipped to England in 1939, she was victoriously winning nineteen out of twenty-seven races, and became the standard for all other 12 metres built during the next twenty years. Innovations included the 'coffee grinder', which helped the crew during the jib-tack and to adjust the jib, and an aluminium mast, which proved much stronger than the traditional wooden mast. Interior design was kept simple to keep the boat as light and fast as possible. Materials included mahogany for the hull, steel for the frame floor and teak for the deck. At 14.21 m (46.5 ft) long, the VIM weighed 28.4 metric tons. VIM did not race again until 1958, by which time the faster Columbia had been developed. She then became a cruising yacht and was still sometimes used as a training boat for America's Cup sailors. Bought in 1991 by Italian publisher Alberto Rusconi, owner of two other 12 metre boats, the VIM underwent extensive refitting. However, it still retains most of its original rig, including the 1939 aluminium mast, and continues to compete successfully in famous boat races.

Seen in profile, the interlocking open curves of both the frame and seat of the Armchair 406 present one of Alvar Aalto's clearest and most elegant designs. In many ways, the 406 is similar to the 400. But whereas the Armchair 400 makes a forceful statement through its squat bulk, the Armchair 406 emphasizes qualities of slenderness. The 406 was the result of a slow process of refinement, being a variant of the Paimio Chair with a solid curving plywood seat, which was originally designed for the Paimio Sanatorium. The 406 retains the technically innovative cantilever frame of the plywood chair, but has a seat made from straps of webbing. The final version of the Armchair 406 was initially designed for the Villa Mairea, the home of Aalto's patron and business partner, Maire Gullichsen, but it is not clear whether she requested that the plywood seat of Model 41 be replaced by something softer and more comfortable. It is likely that the suggestion for the use of webbing came from Aalto's wife Aino. She had used it on a cantilevered reclining chair that was first shown at the Paris World Fair of 1937 and marketed as her husband's design. However, the use of plain exposed webbing as the main seat material in furniture was popularized in the 1930s in Sweden, where it began to be used by modernist designers such as G A Berg and Bruno Mathsson. For these designers, webbing was seen as an inexpensive and perfectly satisfactory material in its own right. For Aalto, webbing also had the advantage of being thin enough to prevent the lean profile of his design from being obscured, allowing the clearest possible expression of its structure.

Poster, 1971, designed by the painter André François, 1971

The simple, utilitarian forms and idiosyncratic character of Citroën's little 2CV or TPV (*toute petite voiture*) have made it one of the most lasting car designs and one for which large numbers of people continue to have a high level of affection. Founded in 1919, the Citroën company was a radical firm from the outset, pioneering mass production and embracing streamlined styling. Pierre Boulanger, who took over as managing director of Citroën's Paris factory in 1935, conceived it as a car for the French countryside. Indeed he specified the 2CV so that it would be capable of carrying two farmers and a bag of potatoes and of crossing a field without breaking the eggs that the farmers were transporting. Lightness being the chief priority, the original materials used for the components of the car – a magnesium alloy chassis, mica windows and a corrugated metal body and cloth and tubular steel seating – emphasized that this was a practical rather than an aesthetic car in the first instance. In the spirit of modernist design, and with the important contribution of the Italian sculptor, Flaminio Bertoni, however, 'functional' became 'beautiful' and, right up to its demise in 1990, the 2CV became one of the most appreciated and lasting designs of the twentieth century. The post-World War II version of the car was launched at the Paris Automobile Salon of 1948. Slightly modified for a more sophisticated, urban audience (the magnesium was replaced by steel, the mica by glass, and two headlights replaced the single one), the 'Tin Snail', as it came to be known, quickly acquired a large community of admirers beyond its original target consumers. Its appeal lay, without doubt, in the combination of its straightforward, useful character, its quirkiness and its essential 'French-ness.' Bertoni designed the Ami 6, another quirky little car, intended to replace the 2CV, but it failed to meet that challenge.

Prototype with single headlight

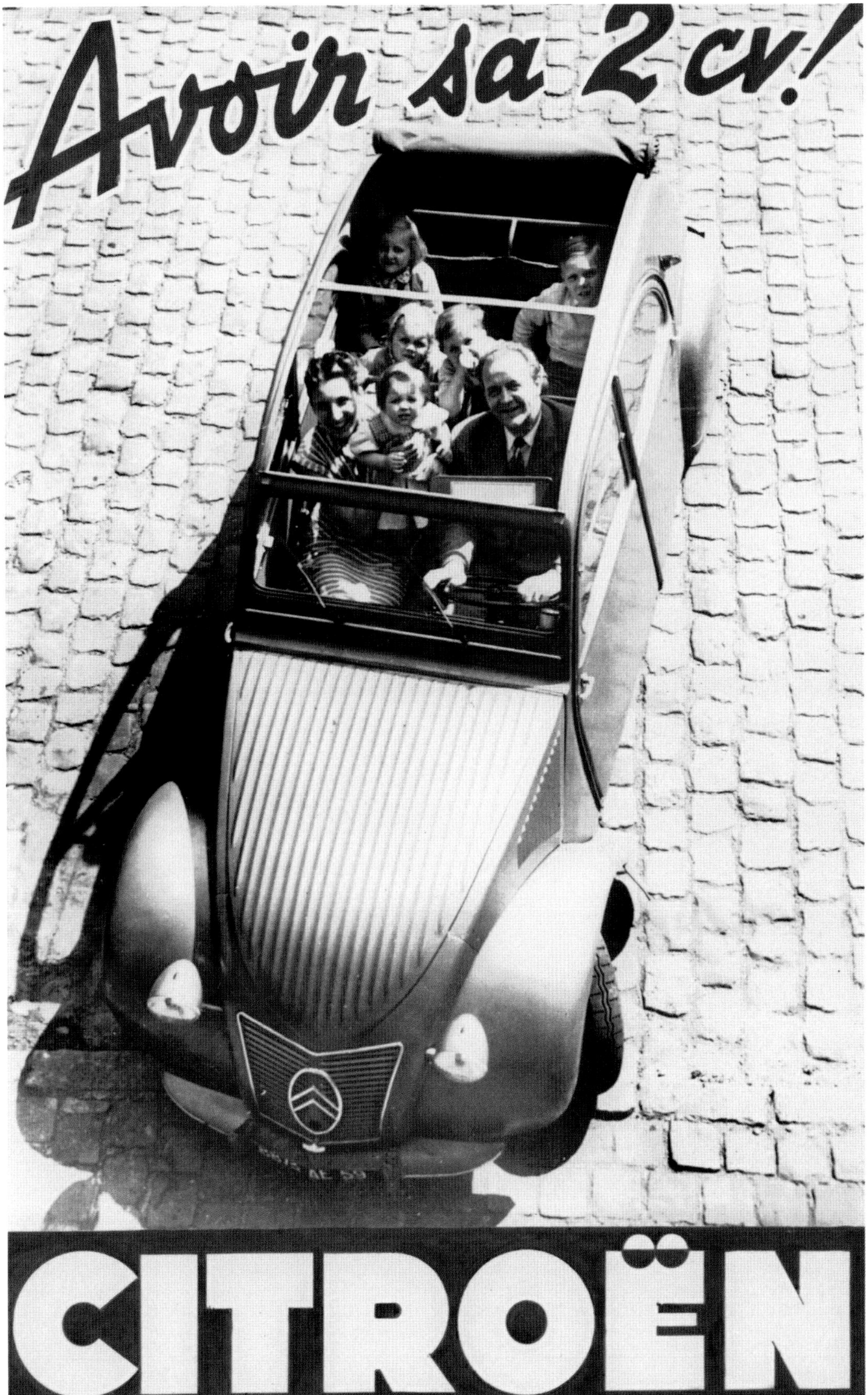

Advertisement, 1953

The Castiglionis and their colleague Caccia Dominioni turned heads at the VII Milan Triennale of 1940 with this design, the first to depart from the hitherto common Italian practice of housing radios in wooden cabinets. The all-Bakelite 547 Radio for Phonola, which won the Triennale's gold medal and was part of a whole exhibition of radios curated by the trio, exerted a powerful influence on the future design of radios. Taking its cue from typewriter and telephone design, it concealed the various components, by then reduced in number and becoming ever simpler, in a highly polished moulded case that had an almost organic appearance. The radio could be used either sitting on a table or hanging on a wall, because the speaker, push-button controls and tuning dial were placed at an angle to the base. Livio Castiglioni worked as a design consultant for Phonola from 1940 to 1960, alongside working in partnership with Pier Giacomo and their younger brother Achille on a variety of projects, including town planning, architecture, industrial design and exhibitions, until 1952. The brothers' partnership with Dominioni was short-lived, with their studio closing in 1940 after only two years, though the 547 and a selection of other Phonola models were a notable and influential result. The 547 exemplifies Livio's aim to create objects with such a unity of form that no one detail was obtrusive. The form itself was determined by the components, but at the same time it represented more than their sum. The influence of this harmonious detail, and the radio's flowing lines, has been observed by fellow Italian Toni del Renzio in designs including radios, televisions and telephones by Marco Zanuso and Richard Sapper, and Mario Bellini and Sylvio Pasqui's Logos 270 data processor of 1970 for Olivetti.

28-4

547 Radio (1939–40)
Livio Castiglioni (1911–79)
Pier Giacomo Castiglioni (1913–68)
Luigi Caccia Dominioni (1913–)
Phonola 1940

With its sweetly splayed lolly-stick legs, inwardly tilting shelves and centre slot perfect for newspapers and magazines, the Penguin Donkey is a laminated plywood bookshelf whose playful shape belies the serious technology and ideology that went into its making. Designed by Viennese immigrant Egon Riss with Jack Pritchard, for the latter's avant-garde furniture company Isokon (short for the appropriately rationalist Isometric Unit Construction), the Penguin Donkey is a classic example of British design's softened adaptation of continental Modernism. Rather than rely on traditional methods of bending wood, Pritchard pioneered ways to press plywood into moulds. Isokon was one of Britain's most successful proponents of progressive design thanks in large part to the steady stream of German and Austrian architects fleeing Europe's increasingly hostile atmosphere. With Walter Gropius as official controller of design, Pritchard worked with such luminaries as Marcel Breuer, as well as with lesser-known architects like Riss. In a remarkable instance of consumer co-evolution Pritchard and Riss's creation was greatly popularized by the marketing genius of Allen Lane, publisher of the recently released Penguin paperbacks that so happened to fit neatly into the unit's shelves. In a clever quid pro quo, Lane placed 100,000 Isokon leaflets in his paperbacks and Pritchard dubbed the bookshelf the Penguin Donkey. England's entry into World War II, however, disallowed widespread manufacturing of the unit. The hundred or so pieces that did hit the market soon became collector's items, though, and many years later Pritchard asked British furniture and textile designer Ernest Race to tweak the unit in a more rectilinear manner. Although Race's 1963 model sold reasonably well, the original Penguin Donkey was re-released in 1994 by the Isokon Plus brand, designed as Donkey3 by Shin and Tomoko Azumi.

285

Isokon Penguin Donkey (1939)
Egon Riss (1902–64)
Jack Pritchard (1899–1992)
Isokon 1939 to 1940
Isokon Plus 1994 to present

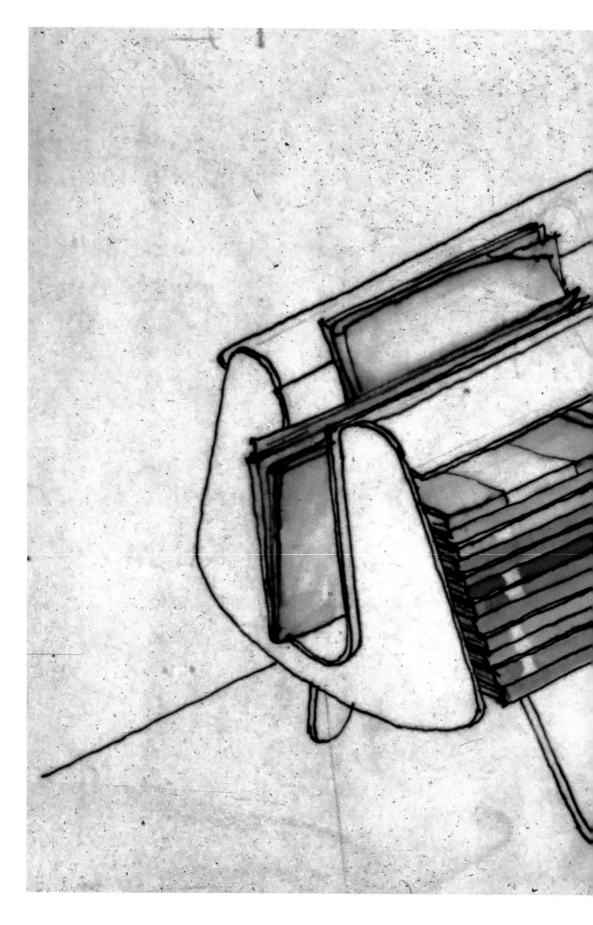

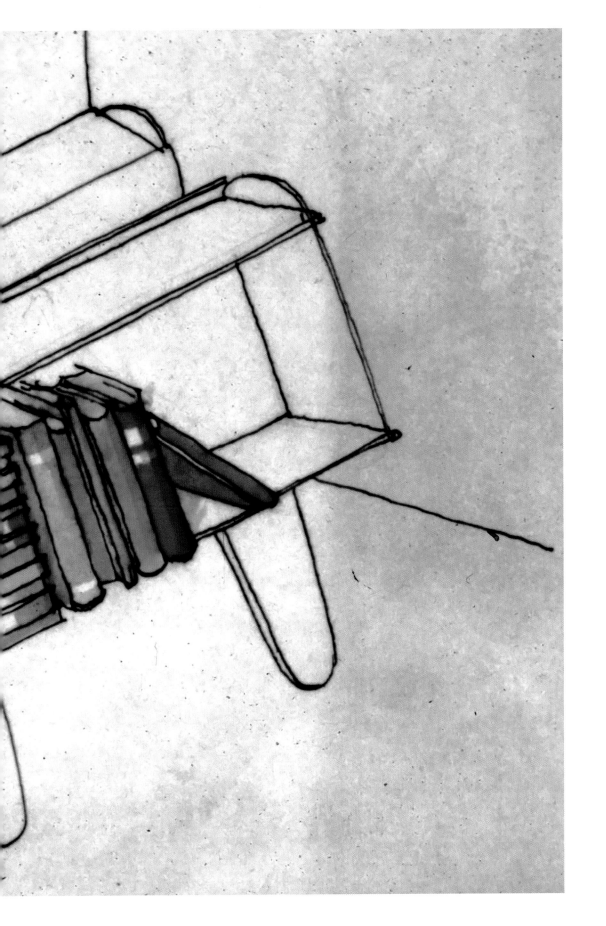

It used to be that children around the United States commuted to school on a motley assortment of vehicles, from trucks and buses to horse-drawn wagons. That is until Dr Frank W Cyr, a professor of rural education in Nebraska, got it into his head that there might be a way to apply the 1930s rage for standardization to the size, shape and colour of this daily means of transportation. In April 1939, equipped with a grant from the Rockefeller Foundation, Cyr proceeded to organize a week-long conference that gathered educators, transportation authorities and bus-related industries to brainstorm standards that would not only insure safer and more comfortable conveyance, but also enable manufacturers to streamline production on assembly lines. While most of the forty-four standards that were adopted during the meeting have changed over the years, the iconic yellow vehicle continues to be differentiated from other buses through design details that include high-back rounded seats that absorb jolts and bounces; lights, reflectors and swing-out stop signs that indicate loading and unloading; an array of mirrors that provide the driver with all-angle vision; and a specially constructed roof that resists crumpling in case of accidents. One of the companies with engineers present at the 1939 conference was the Blue Bird Corporation. Although they initially started making buses in 1927 they have become one of the most famous manufacturers of the yellow school bus and still produce it today. With 450,000 yellow school buses on the road carrying over a million students daily, and safety records that beat any other form of ground transportation, this American icon has even been marketed to the UK population since 2002. The hallmark orange-yellow hue of the school bus body has remained the same since Cyr's first convocation, although before the invention of standardized colour systems it was necessary to choose three shades of yellow since manufacturers separated by great distances could not guarantee exact matching. For Americans below the age of sixty, Cyr's yellow bus joins the Dixon lead pencil in evoking school days as readily as any Proustian madeleine.

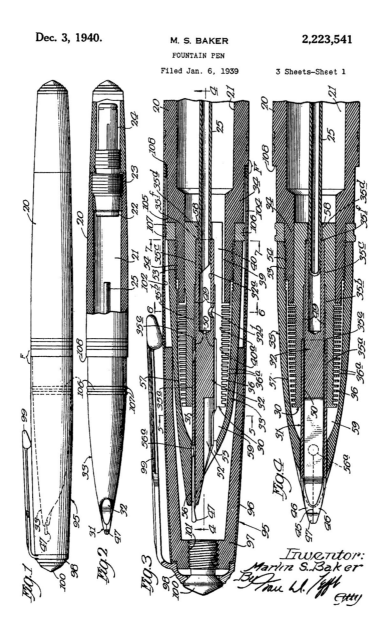

Inventor:
Marlin S. Baker
By Hau W. Tefft
Atty

Originally priced at $12.50, the Parker 51 Fountain Pen sold 6,236 units in 1941, the year it was launched, and became an immediate commercial success. According to legend the pen was designed by László Moholy-Nagy, but in fact it was the result of the ingenuity of Kenneth Parker, the entrepreneurial president of the Parker Pen Corporation, research engineer Marlin Baker and patent attorney Ivan Teft. The Parker 51 is the model that best reflects the company's policy for producing fast-turnover products in tune with the optimistic mood of postwar American consumerism. A chemist, Galen Sayler, who had been involved with the Parker Corporation since 1930 when he established a small laboratory at Parker headquarters, was also involved in the fountain pen project. Among his inventions was the self-cleaning ink Super Quink and a non-conventional instant-drying ink of alkali composition Superchrome. Because this new ink corroded the Pyralin material commonly used for pen barrels and caps, Sayler came up with a new opaque DuPont plastic he called Lucite. The Parker 51 was the first fountain pen

made of Lucite and employing Sayler's ink. Its advertising slogan was 'Write dry with wet ink'. Parker wanted the 51 Pen to be totally different from previous models. Baker created eight new patents for the model, including the design patents for the cap and barrel, the shell, the collector and the cap clutch. In terms of design, the 51 Pen is slim and sleek, with a very lightweight metal cap (made from gold, silver or stainless steel) that slips rather than screws onto the Lucite barrel. The gold nib and feed are hooded, with only the tip of the nib exposed. The pen's most unique feature, the clear Lucite collector that holds the excess ink when the filled pen is in the writing position, is never seen unless the pen is disassembled. The name '51' was coined because it was first researched in 1939, Parker's fifty-first anniversary, it was also a name that would easily translate into other languages, for marketing abroad. An alternative explanation, however, is that Kenneth Parker saw a highway sign beside the first Parker factory that said 'US 51', and felt it would denote an object that was ahead of its time.

Field Marshall Montgomery signing the Treaty of Germany's surrender in 1945

287

Parker 51 Fountain Pen (1939)
Marlin Baker (nd)
Kenneth Parker (1895–1979)
Parker Pen 1941 to 1978
Special Edition 2002

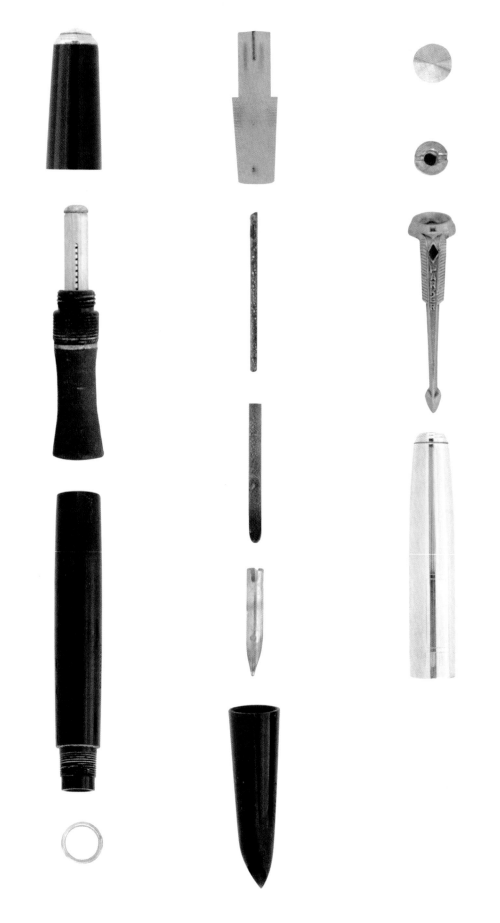

These famous P-51's have more than a name in common!

There's a world of kinship in these two—the P-51 Mustang, famed as one of the fastest fighters in existence, and the brilliant, streamlined Parker "51" fountain pen.

For, like a plane in flight, the Parker "51" responds smoothly, instantly to your touch. Its beauty is the beauty of flashing wings.

Your natural desire, of course, is to possess this finest of all writing instruments at once. Yet, you may have to wait for yours.

You see, production of *all* fountain pens has been curtailed by official government order.

Secondly, Parker craftsmen are today creating primers, fuzes, parts for aircraft engines (including that of the P-51 Mustang) and a long list of other vital war equipment.

All the Parker "51" pens we can produce are rationed to dealers. Still, if a new pen is essential for your war tasks—or to write letters of encouragement to someone in Service—place a reservation with your local dealer for a Parker "51".

The Parker "51" is the *only* pen of its kind—protected by U. S. Patents. It *alone* can use the new Parker "51" Ink—*world's fastest drying ink!*

Dries as you write! You need no blotter. Of course, you can use *any* ink with the Parker "51" if you so desire—but you won't "so desire".

Colors: Black, Blue-Cedar, Dove Gray, Cordovan Brown. $12.50; $15.00. Pencils, $5.00; $7.50. Parker Vacumatic pens, $8.75. Pencils, $4.00.

♦ *GUARANTEED BY LIFE CONTRACT! Parker's Blue Diamond on the pen is our contract unconditionally guaranteeing service for the owner's life, without cost other than 35¢ charge for postage, insurance, and handling, if pen is not intentionally damaged and is returned complete to: The Parker Pen Company, Janesville, Wisconsin.*

Make your dollars fight—BUY WAR BONDS NOW!

Parker "51"

"Writes dry with wet ink!"

COPR. 1944 THE PARKER PEN COMPANY

In the annals of tobacco collectables, few objects invoke such nostalgia as the Spinning Ashtray. Originally conceived in 1939 by a Stuttgart-based inventor named Georg Katz and later modified and popularized by the German company Erhard & Sohne, a purveyor of tobacco-related products, the Spinning Ashtray matches the modern obsession with mechanical moving parts with the need to mask a mess. Slick and shiny like the streamlined cars of the day, Katz's invention evokes a time when smoking was a sign of sophistication rather than addiction, when a flick of the wrist would send the less-than-elegant remains of a smoke out of sight and out of mind. With a central vertical tube topped by a hand-friendly plastic knob activating a ratchet wheel that sets the slightly sunken ashtray surface spinning and opening like a trap door, the Spinning Ashtray works with centrifugal force. Once effectively flung into the lower, covered receptacle, the ashes remain hidden until the owner empties them out after removing the top. Bearing some of the same mechanisms and visual intrigue as a toy top, the Spinning Ashtray blends innocence and experience in one shiny package. Erhard & Sohne's modification, in 1953, of Katz's original model further enhanced the smoking-and-ashing experience by adding a sound-dampening mechanism that lessened the clanging return of the ashtray's false bottom once the spinning action was complete – an added benefit for the user.

Sept. 3, 1940.   G. KATZ   2,213,915

RUBBISH RECEPTACLE

Original Filed March 6, 1939

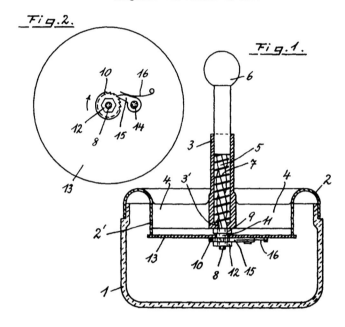

Fig.2.

Fig.1.

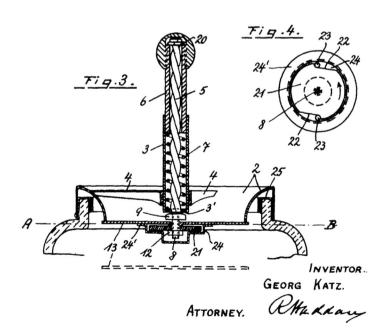

Fig.3.

Fig.4.

INVENTOR.

GEORG KATZ.

ATTORNEY.

CONVERSATION

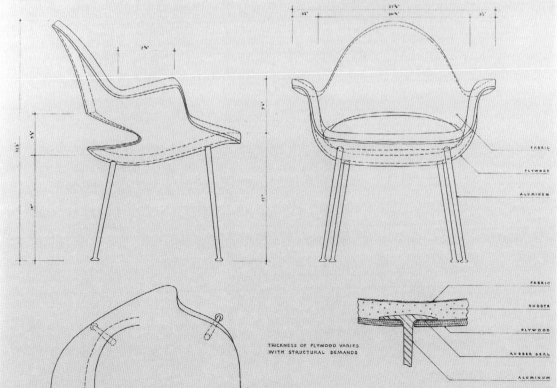

FABRIC

PLYWOOD

ALUMINUM

FABRIC

RUBBER

PLYWOOD

RUBBER SEAL

ALUMINUM

THICKNESS OF PLYWOOD VARIES
WITH STRUCTURAL DEMANDS

ONE QUARTER FULL SIZE

289

Organic Chair (1940)
Eero Saarinen (1910–61)
Charles Eames (1907–78)
Haskelite Corporation, Heywood-Wakefield,
and Marli Erhman 1940
Vitra 2005 to present

Though born in Finland, Eero Saarinen is considered to be one of several influential American modernist designers who were committed to redefining domestic and industrial design and space. Highly celebrated for his architecture, Saarinen is equally important for his furniture designs of the 1940s. These were crucial benchmarks for design innovations of the immediate postwar decades, wherein the approach to form, function and material took a dramatically new direction. The outstanding Organic Chair, part of a series of moulded plywood seating forms, represents the initial step towards the revolutionary furniture prototypes Saarinen designed over the next two decades. He collaborated with Charles Eames, both men being interested in exploring the structural and aesthetic possibilities of moulded plywood in combination with other, more traditional materials. Preliminary prototypes were successful – the two designers won the Museum of Modern Art's 'Organic Design in Home Furnishings' competition of 1941, the Organic Chair being a key component of their exhibition entry. Saarinen and Eames's progressive ideas were inspired by their interest in organic form, by the possible uses of plastics and plywood laminates and by the technological advance of 'cycle-welding', a process developed by the Chrysler Corporation that enabled wood to be joined to rubber, glass or metal. The Organic Chair's seat and back, made of a single three-dimensional piece of compound-moulded plywood, was conceptually ground-breaking; the exhibition plaster model, encasing a reinforced, wire-mesh body, had been fractured and reset until an appropriate human form seating shape was found. This structural shell, designed to support layers of glue and wood veneer, was nonetheless only possible through a hand-manufactured process; at this early developmental stage, it was difficult to conceive a way to mass-produce the design and only between ten and twelve prototypes were built. Despite being key to the Eameses' development of plywood furniture, the Organic Chair is a design that is fundamentally associated with Saarinen. It provided him with a seminal prototype, leading him directly towards the creation of his highly successful furniture designs for Knoll, most notably the No. 70 Womb Chair (1947–8), the Saarinen Collection of office seating (1951) and the Tulip Pedestal group of chairs and tables (1955–6).

The design of the milk bottle is not in itself remarkable, but the way it came to symbolize both its contents, and a particularly British way of life, is. The first milk bottles were produced in 1880 by the Express Dairy Company in London, and were gradually adopted in a variety of designs by dairies throughout the country. The bottles came in a number of sizes; indeed, until the advent of pasteurization in 1894; milkmen delivered small quantities of the product four times per day. The pint became the most common bottle size once domestic electric refrigerators became more commonplace in British households during the 1940s. Prior to the use of bottles, milkmen would fill customers' jugs from a churn and part of the bottle's success is, ironically, the way in which the new industrially produced container replaced a centuries-old farmyard vessel as a symbol of the freshness and naturalness of dairy products. Indeed, by the 1980s, when the dairy industry was marketing its product with the slogan 'Milk has Gotta Lotta Bottle' (as opposed to anything that mentioned cows), packaging and product seemed to have become one. While the consumption of milk was associated with good health (for which reason bottled milk was provided free in all schools until 1968), what the bottle itself appeared to advertise above all else was cleanliness. Unlike wooden or metal churns, the clear glass bottle gave customers a vision of the milk's impeccable whiteness (against which any dirt was sure to show up), while bottle-top technology, which graduated from porcelain stoppers held down by wire to cardboard tops and, finally, aluminium caps, was constantly evolving to achieve greater degrees of hygiene. The milkman's daily collection of empty bottles and delivery of full ones also allowed the milk bottle to symbolize a relationship of supply and demand between the countryside and the city, and the interconnectedness of rural and urban areas. In the process, the dairy industry was presented as a service, in the same category as water, gas and electricity provision, rather than as a manufacturing business. Today, the glass milk bottle along with the cheaper and more practical plastic and cardboard containers is still used throughout the United Kingdom, with electric milk floats still delivering fresh milk daily.

Pinta value!
-on your doorstep, rain or shine

HOW BIG IS THE FAMILY
IN THIS HOUSE ?
COUNT THE PINTAS !

May 20, 1941.   G. DESSONNAZ   2,242,458

PENCIL SHARPENER

Filed March 29, 1940

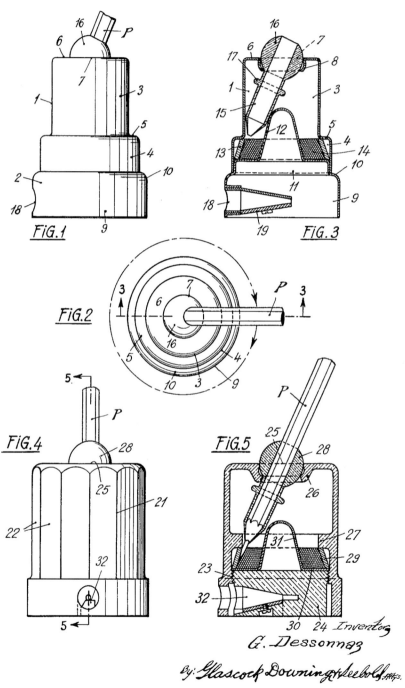

FiG.1

FiG.3

FiG.2

FiG.4

FiG.5

Inventor

G. Dessonnaz

By Glascock Downing Seebold Attys.

In 1941 Georges Dessonnaz patented his innovation for a pencil-lead sharpener that revolutionized the draughtsman's toolbox. Hand-held bladed sharpeners became available in the late nineteenth century. These were adapted for use by draughtsmen, who carefully positioned the blade to trim the pencil's wooden casing, leaving the lead uncut. The exposed lead would then be sharpened with sandpaper, a practice that had been in use before the introduction of mechanical sharpeners or bladed lead pointers to maintain the sharp point required for the accurate line weights demanded in the field of engineering design and drafting. While some draughtsmen used finger-held bladed blocks and mechanical crank-operated sharpeners, they were less than ideal. Such devices could force softer degree pencil leads to break, while the harder lead might not be suitably exposed. Dessonnaz's design solved these frustrating problems by ensuring the pencil was perfectly centred, thus reducing pressure on the delicate lead and ensuring a consistent level of abrasion, with a dramatically reduced breakage rate. Early versions of the design included a wood-case trimmer in the base to allay the fears of the conservative engineering community, but this feature was soon phased out as the primary mechanism proved so successful. The office-product firm Kuhn, based in Bassersdorf near Zurich, bought the rights and began large-scale manufacture and exports after World War II. The result was the GEDESS Lead Sharpener, which featured individually replaceable parts, and a novel, rotational case-hardened steel movement housed within a distinctive Bakelite shell. The GEDESS, usually complemented by a selection of Swiss Caran d'Ache drafting pencils, became a ubiquitous sight throughout drawing offices in postwar Europe. The widespread adoption of computer-aided design since the 1980s has largely led to the end of manual drafting and the lead sharpener to become a relic of a previous mechanical age.

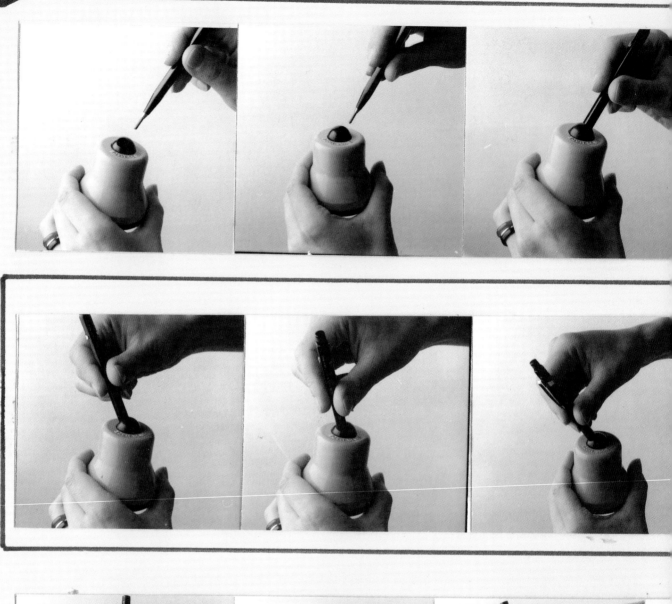
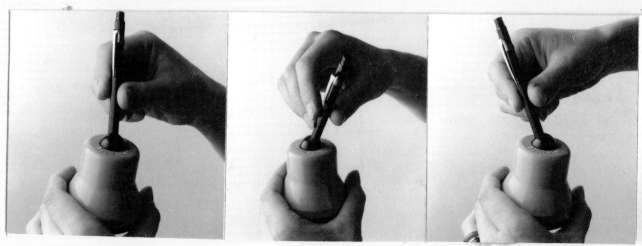

Twinings, purveyor of fine teas since the early 1700s, left its lidded tin virtually unchanged for more than four decades after the end of World War II. But far from indicating a brand in decline, this lack of variation was a deliberate symbol of unshakeable, reassuring British quality in an increasingly fast-changing world of post-imperial uncertainties. Although the tin's simplicity was a nod to the austerity of the times, the 'teamen to connoisseurs' legend on its side was a defiant signal that a touch of class in the form of a drop of Earl Grey was still within reach in ration-book Britain. Even in the mid- to late 1940s the Art Nouveau-like swirl of the tin's artwork must have seemed old-fashioned. In fact it hearkened back to the appearance, early in the century, of the first individually pre-packaged branded goods. For the first time customers were able to make their own choices rather than relying on their grocer to fill bags and cartons. Consequently, packaging that suggested freshness and quality was a must for manufacturers looking to stand out on the newly democratized shelves. The Twinings Tin was a perfect blend of form and function. Its lever-lid mechanism, usually opened with the help of a teaspoon, proved unbeatable at maintaining the tea's freshness. This made it the mainstay of Twinings' postwar drive to reclaim its export trade, which had previously rested on a mixture of packaging methods such as part-glued cartons and pre-manufactured paper bags. So successful did this method become that, to keep up with demand, the manufacturer Barnsley Canister Company had to switch from labelling plain tins to printing directly onto tin plate, coating the ink with eggshell varnish for protection. The only other change to the design was a move from square to round lids in the late 1960s, which allowed the lids to be applied by machine more efficiently. The plainness of the tins as objects made them a practical and aesthetically durable feature of kitchens, parlours and pantries through the decades. Despite the arrival of tea bags, a trend Twinings itself embraced, loose tea's appeal endured for the discerning drinker and the tin endured with it. But its demise eventually came in 1997, with Twinings now using a larger hinge-lid tin equally suitable for bags and loose tea, and reminiscent of a traditional caddy.

This little vehicle not only set the standard for all future off-roaders, but also became a world-renowned generic name for lightweight off-road vehicles. The idea of a small, purpose-built utility vehicle was first conceived by the US Army following World War I. They set the brief and invited bids to produce a vehicle with very particular characteristics: mainly that it should be as light and manoeuvrable as a small car, yet with the robustness and versatility of a truck. The very first prototypes were built by the Bantam Car Company, using components left over from when the same company was making Austins for the American market. These prototypes were then developed with some haste, involving two other manufacturers, Willys Overland and Ford. Because of this confused beginning, the authorship of the final design is still under dispute today. Production was finally ordered in 1941, from both Willys Overland and Ford to a standardized design, to supply the US Army in time for use in World War II. Following its successful introduction it was exported around the world with US troops, setting a global standard for lightweight, robust, four-wheel-drive vehicles. Perhaps the world's most purely utilitarian vehicle, which inspired, amongst others, the Land Rover, the Jeep has been owned, loved and documented by at least three of the twentieth century's most significant designers: English architects, Alison and Peter Smithson, and Japanese product designer, Sori Yanagi. The fact that this was the vehicle of choice by such seminal thinkers of the twentieth-century design world is testament to its rugged, honest beauty.

293

Willys Jeep (1941)
Karl K Probst (1883–1963)
Willys Overland/Kaiser
Jeep/Chrysler/DaimlerChrysler
1941 to present

The Round Thermostat was possibly the most ubiquitous domestic design of late-twentieth-century America, and represents a long and successful partnership between Henry Dreyfuss and the Honeywell Regulator Company. Its low price and ability to fit most situations has made the Round one of Dreyfuss's most successful designs ever. Conceived in the early 1940s from a simple circular sketch by Honeywell's president H W Sweatt, the Round was then developed by Dreyfuss and design engineer Carl Kronmiller. It went through a significant engineering development programme until finally making its debut in 1953, with an advertising launch featuring Dreyfuss himself. Although the project had been significantly delayed by World War II, it also benefited from new innovations developed during the war. A Bimetal coiled thermometer and a scaled mercury switch prevent dust settling, which ultimately contributed to the Round's continued success. Several versions have since followed, including units with air-conditioning control and digital display features. Visually, the Round not only represented a more appropriate, less technical aesthetic for the domestic setting, but its form had an in-built logic, too, as it could never be mounted crooked, unlike its rectangular competitors. The removable cap was even designed to be painted to match the interior decor. In postwar industrial America, Dreyfuss was often seen as representing the puritanical conscience of his profession, a designer who dutifully served industry and the people rather than himself. His designs were intended to last, as he reaffirmed in 1968 in an article in the *Wall Street Journal*: 'We say that a design expresses the excellence of its engineers and reflects the integrity of its manufacturer. That hardly suggests seasonal change. We [industrial designers] are not in the business of style or fashion. Ours is a basic approach; our designing must be generic by nature. If the most contemporary design can be called "classic," then call us classicists.' Indeed, over fifty years since its launch, the Round has sold over 85 million units and is still in production, representing Dreyfuss's ideal of a product that has successfully stood the test of time.

Ring snaps off for decorating

A modest pull is all it takes to remove
the cover of the Honeywell Round.
Long-life spring steel clips hold it firmly in
place when you snap it on again.

A new improved thermostat

It's easy to paint

In just a few minutes the silver-bronze plastic
cover can be easily painted to match your color
scheme. No special paints are required.

Actual size

New, more visible dial and temperature
indicators make settings easier. The Honeywell
Round is available through any heating dealer.

$12.80 *plus small
installation cost*

*A base plate (not shown) is also avail-
able at slight extra cost to cover any
hole left by old-fashioned installation.*

hat matches any color scheme—
the Honeywell Round

Here it is—the first really new idea in thermostats in years.

It's now available—through your heating dealer—to replace the old-fashioned thermostat on your living room wall.

Different from any thermostat you've ever seen, its pleasing round lines lend themselves to any decorating plan. The snap-off cover of the Honeywell Round makes it easy to paint the silver-bronze cover to match any decorating scheme. This means you can paint it to blend with any wall.

And there are real improvements *inside* the Honeywell Round— engineering improvements that give greater comfort by cutting down see-saw temperatures, an enclosed, dust-free mercury switch to lower maintenance costs.

What's it cost to replace your old-fashioned thermostat with the Honeywell Round? Only $12.80, plus installation cost.*

When's a good time to have the installation made? When you're decorating or having the furnace checked. But there's no need to wait for a special occasion. Your Honeywell Round can be installed any time in a few minutes, with no muss or fuss.

So why not call your heating dealer and have him show you the new Honeywell Round—the new, beautifully styled thermostat that's made all other standard thermostats obsolete!

Designed by
Henry Dreyfuss

Credit for the "new model" appearance of the Honeywell Round goes to designer Henry Dreyfuss. Known around the world for his work in design, Mr. Dreyfuss spent many months in research and design development for the new thermostat. The final result, as seen at left, was a thermostat wonderfully different, completely modern.

MINNEAPOLIS
Honeywell
 First in Controls

The Chemex Coffeemaker looks as if it belongs as much in the laboratory as in the kitchen. It was created by a chemist and every aspect of it, from its name to its design, is engineered to present a scientific approach to coffee brewing. The chemist was Dr Peter J Schlumbohm and his coffee maker started off as a simple chemistry set: an Erlenmeyer flask and a glass laboratory funnel. It never got much more complicated than that. That original flask and funnel combination is what gives the finished Chemex – made of a single piece of heatproof, laboratory-grade, borosilicate glass – its distinctive hourglass shape. All Schlumbohm did was to make some practical modifications, such as adding an air channel and a pouring spout, a small 'belly button' on the side of the flask to mark the half-full level, and a wood and leather collar so it can be picked up when it's hot. The simplicity of Schlumbohm's coffee maker has made it an enduring success. Not only is it in museum collections around the world, but it is also still in production and still a favourite with coffee aficionados today. Thanks to Schlumbohm, all the user of the Chemex has to do to get some of the purest coffee available is add grounds, hot water and Chemex filter paper, which is thicker than normal filter paper and consequently produces purer coffee. You control the variables and the Chemex takes care of the rest. Schlumbohm's economic use of materials was partly a result of the need to use non-priority materials at a time of war, but it also reflected the Bauhaus principles of simplicity and honesty in design that he had brought with him from Germany. Ultimately his coffee maker is the perfect fusion of science and art: it does what it looks like it does and it looks good as well. Hence the Chemex slogan: 'The best coffee in the world only comes in one shape.'

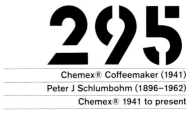

295

Chemex® Coffeemaker (1941)
Peter J Schlumbohm (1896–1962)
Chemex® 1941 to present

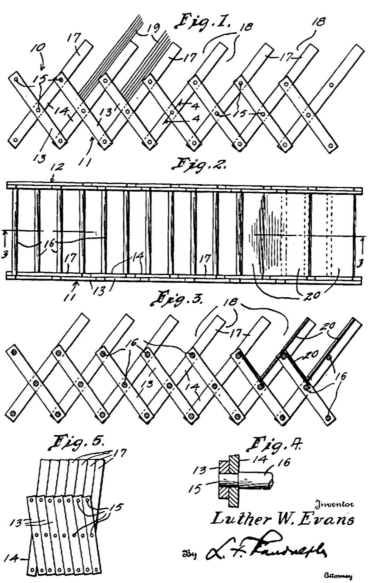

Fig.1.

Fig.2.

Fig.3.

Fig.5.

Fig.4.

Inventor

Luther W. Evans

By L. F. Landreth

Attorney

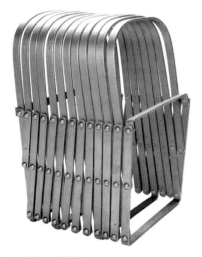

The FlexiFile portable filing, collating and sorting system is not only cleverly flexible in its function; in terms of design it is truly timeless. It has changed little from its original 'Adjustable Rack' patent model of 1941, which itself was based on a mechanism that has appeared throughout history, even in the manuscripts of Leonardo da Vinci. The beauty of the FlexiFile lies in the simplicity of this mechanism, which is widely known as the 'Lazy Tongs' system. It comprises a series of levers with simple rivet joints that are pivoted together like a pair of scissors, with the whole action creating a concertina effect. This mechanism first gained prominence with the Lazy Tongs corkscrew, designed by Marshall Wier, and which was awarded a patent in 1884. The FlexiFile's Lazy Tongs mechanism allows the file to expand quite extensively according to the needs of the user, and when not in use it can be folded into an extremely compact and easily stored unit. The system also lends itself to flexibility in terms of unit size: it is currently available in twelve, eighteen or twenty-four slots according to the scale of the job required. The file is remarkably accommodating, as each slot can hold up to a ream of paper. The patent for the original Adjustable Rack, designed in 1941 by Luther W Evans of Richmond, Virginia, described the functional flexibility of the product and its suitability as a freestanding desk unit, shelf unit or inside element for drawer files. It also described the variety of materials that could be used for the rack bars, including wood, plastics or metal. A version of the FlexiFile, currently produced and manufactured by Lee Products, has addressed twenty-first-century environmental concerns by using recycled aluminium in its construction, which succeeds in making the product durable and lightweight as well as ecologically friendly. The FlexiFile is a successful design because it uses a straightforward mechanism simply and ingeniously, and in so doing provides a complete all-in-one office organizer.

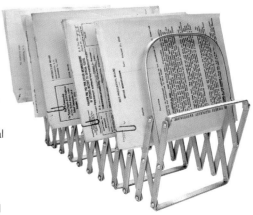

The simple wood and webbed construction of the 666 WSP Chair is the result of both the constraining circumstances of wartime and Jens Risom's Danish roots. Born and raised in Denmark, Risom attended the University of Copenhagen, studying under the important modernist figure Kaare Klint. Klint advocated the use of traditional forms with an emphasis on simple, straightforward construction. He also insisted that a chair be designed with human proportions as the primary guide and introduced the study of what he called 'anthropometrics' – an early form of ergonomics. In 1939 Risom emigrated to the United States and in 1941 he designed his first piece of furniture for the company headed by Hans Knoll. The 666 WSP Chair was first produced during World War II and as a result it could only be made of available, non-regulated

materials that were not necessary to the American war effort or made scarce as a consequence of it. Risom soon followed this design with a number of variations, all using the same army surplus webbing, a material Risom described as, 'very basic, very simple, inexpensive.' Easy to clean, easy to replace and comfortable to use, the webbing made a perfect material for these everyday household chairs. In addition, the light, airy structure afforded by the material gave the chair a less weighty appearance and an informal quality. Ultimately this was more consistent with the light-filled and flexible characteristics of the new, modern homes. The elegance and practicality of Risom's 666 WSP Chair has ensured its popularity since the early 1940s.

There is something undeniably toy-like about the big bubble canopy of the Bell Model 47 helicopter, and this, together with its technical brilliance, is what may have helped establish the little Bell as the very definition of a helicopter in the popular, postwar imagination. The Bell 47 is largely the work of Arthur Young, perhaps the pre-eminent helicopter designer of the mid-century. Before World War II, Young met with Larry Bell, owner of the Bell Aircraft Company, and demonstrated for him a small, remote-controlled rotary-winged craft. Helicopters had been in the making for some years, but the inherent instability of rotary

aircraft created an equally difficult problem of controllability. Unlike fixed-wing aircraft, which are relatively stable and easy to fly, helicopters by contrast present massive gyroscopic and aeronautical challenges for the average pilot. Bell was impressed by the stability of Young's design, and recognized Young's addition of a stabilizing bar underneath the rotary as a major innovation. He set Young up with a team of engineers at an old Chrysler dealership in Gardenville, New York, and the team got to work on what would ultimately become the Bell 47. It became the first commercially licensed helicopter when it was released in 1946.

The bubble canopy is instantly recognizable, and was typical of Young's inventive genius. His second test helicopter had no wind protection for the passengers, so Young, along with his assistant Bartram Kelley and pilot Floyd Carlson decided to inflate a piece of heated Plexiglass like a balloon. Thus was born the Bell Bubble, perhaps its most famous feature. The uncovered steel truss fuselage is another masterpiece of high-tech industrial production. Taken together, the space age aesthetic of the Bell 47 all but guaranteed its place in the design pantheon. It is a signature object in the industrial design collection of the Museum of Modern Art,

New York. In its almost half a century of production, the Bell 47 was seen in numerous different contexts, from the opening scenes of *La Dolce Vita*, carrying a statue of Jesus, to the transportation for heroes as diverse as Batman and James Bond. Young himself is worthy of celebration as one of the brilliant innovators of the twentieth century. Trained as a mathematician and philosopher, it was through his love of model-making that he set about solving the stability problems inherent in helicopter design. After his work at the Bell Aircraft Corporation, Young returned to philosophy, publishing several books and papers.

298

Bell Model 47 (1941–6)
Arthur M Young (1905–95)
Lawrence D Bell (1894–1956)
Bartram Kelley (1909–98)
Bell Aircraft Corporation 1946 to 1973
Agusta 1952 to 1976
Westland 1965 to 1968
Kawasaki 1952 to c.1975

Richard Neutra practised architecture as a catalyst for improving the human social experience. He developed the Boomerang Chair with his son Dion for the government-sponsored Channel Heights Housing Project in San Pedro, California in 1942. This garden community was designed to house a growing mass of shipyard workers employed for wartime industry and to illustrate an ideal community where children could walk to school without crossing a street. The use of low-cost materials and straightforward construction created a chair that these workers could assemble and perhaps even construct themselves for use in their compact residential units. The assertive yet softened raking lines of the chair create a striking and efficient structure, held together with simple pegged-through-tenons and webbing. The plywood side panels economically eliminate the need for separate back legs, and support the side dowels, which form the front legs. The resulting structure is thereby fashioned from two bold side profiles, two dowels, minimal cross rails and a webbed seat and back. Interestingly, despite

299

Boomerang Chair (1942)
Richard Neutra (1892–1970)
Prospettiva 1990 to 1992
House Industries & Otto Design Group
2002 to present

its name, it was not inspired by the Australian boomerang. The elegant boomerang shape that emerged as the chair's final form ordered the effectiveness of the structure. Viewed from the side, the chair suggests an abstract letter-form, coaxed into three dimensions. The unique proportions and forms of the overall object evidenced Neutra's belief that 'architects must have a razor sharp sense of individuality'. Dion Neutra licensed Prospettiva to manufacture the chair with subtle changes in 1990, creating an outdoor version for the patio. In 2002, with Otto Design Group, he again revisited the design and licensed House Industries to produce the chair in limited editions, still available today. The latest version introduced spacers that visually separate the dowels from the side panels, and allow the webbing to be serviced without disassembling the frame. The chair's continued popularity over a sixty-year span is evidence of its powerful and lasting appeal.

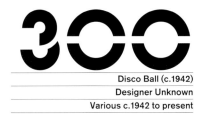

Disco Ball (c.1942)
Designer Unknown
Various c.1942 to present

John Travolta in *Saturday Night Fever* (1977), directed by John Badham

Whether it was the school dance, a wedding reception or a bar mitzvah, the crowning glory, suspended from the ceiling in all its high-tech radiance, was the disco ball. The epitome of nightclub chic, the mirror ball was the staple effect for any self-respecting disco, but it had graced the ceilings of dancehalls for many years and had even made a screen debut in the 1942 classic *Casablanca*. The 'disco' became the common name for the dancehall from the early 1960s, when people began dancing to recorded music on discs, rather than live bands. It was not until the 1970s, however, that the disco scene really found its identity. The cover poster for the film *Saturday Night Fever* provides an enduring image of the disco: John Travolta in his flared white suit striking a pose and basking in the glory of the disco ball. The design of the disco ball is relatively simple. Hundreds of small mirrors cover a sphere, motorized to rotate on a vertical axis. Any spotlights shining on the ball as it rotates are reflected off the mirrors at various angles, with each beam creating numerous soft beams. The many mirrored facets create random flashes as well as a constant dispersal of light playing on any surface it catches. Patterns of light cover the walls and ceilings, giving the impression of a starry night sky indoors. The idea of stars twinkling in the sky seems to have been an influence on the development of the disco ball. The imagery of a limitless universe of stars, or flashes of light like photographer's flashbulbs exploding, suggests the glamour of Hollywood and the sparkle of diamonds and precious jewels. Still visually stunning and essential to any dance floor, the disco ball was the forerunner to modern stage and nightclub lighting effects. Lighting effects began to play an ever more important part in nightclubs and theatres, and advances in engineering meant that lighting could be directly linked with the music it was enhancing or designed to generate specific and complicated patterns. It is an undisputed design icon and inspiration for countless new designs, from miniature disco ball earrings to NASA satellites.

Eva Zeisel entered the Budapest Royal Academy of Fine Arts in 1923 and went on to train for an apprenticeship in pottery and ceramics. By the early 1930s she had gained valuable experience in the modernization of the ceramic industry: she worked for the Imperial Porcelain Factory in Leningrad until she was appointed Artistic Director for the Porcelain and Glass Industries for the whole of Russia. On her arrival in America in the late 1930s, Zeisel taught ceramics at New York's Pratt Institute, where her curved and stylish designs gained recognition, establishing her as a leader in modern ceramic design. In 1941, The Museum of Modern Art's, 'Organic Design in Home Furnishings', exhibition was seen by the president of Castleton China, a ceramics company based in Pennsylvania. Although ceramics were not included in the exhibition, the company asked Eliot Noyes, then director of the Museum's design department, to recommend a designer who could create a modern dinner service. Noyes knew of Zeisel's work and suggested her to Castleton, who

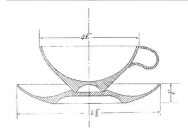

Eva Zeisel

immediately signed her up. The elegant and simple design of the Museum White table service was a departure from Zeisel's more geometric work of the 1930s, which had been influenced by the Bauhaus and the abstract shapes of Hans Arp. Its fluid lines are an achievement of Zeisel's quest for understated beauty through the understanding of history, materials, process and function; the service balances these issues perfectly by infusing the translucency of the porcelain with both a visual and structural weight. Zeisel's most recent

work includes designs for the Zsolnay Factory in Pecs, and Kispeter-Granit in Budapest. The Museum of Modern Art and the Metropolitan Museum in New York have both reissued new versions of some of her earlier designs in new glazes and colours, the production of which has been supervised by Zeisel. Considered to be one of the primary ceramics designers of the twentieth century, Zeisel continues to regularly design and produce porcelain, whilst originals of her early work have become collector's items.

One of the most intriguing designs of the twentieth century, now much sought after by design collectors and displayed as a piece of sculpture, had its origins in the field of medicine. This leg splint was designed to support a broken limb in a war situation. The lower, cage-like section protects the heel and the slots cut along its length allow bandages to pass through to secure the limb in position. In December 1941 Wendell G Scott, a doctor and an old friend of Charles Eames's, visited the Eameses's apartment, where he was shown their wood-moulding experiments. Scott explained the problems that the navy was encountering with its existing metal leg splints. They did not secure injured legs properly and were cutting off the circulation, leading to gangrene. In some circumstances the metal splint was 'so bad that it was actually contributing to deaths rather than helping anyone,' Ray recollects. Metal was also a scarce material at the time. The couple went ahead to develop a splint that would immobilize and support the injured limb in relative comfort. Other advantages included a very lightweight but strong structure that stacked easily for transportation. The shape was moulded from plaster on Charles's leg and then turned into a form that would suffice for either a right or left leg of any length. In 1942, after a second prototype had improved the heel protection, the navy accepted the design and production began for the first order of 5,000. The final design was constructed from ten pre-cut wooden laminates. This was the couple's first mass-produced product, and they set up their own company, Plyformed Wood Company, to fabricate it. The company also produced a plywood stretcher designed by the pair. The splint went on to be produced by the Evans Products Company from 1943 and by the end of World War II over 150,000 splints had been produced. Although it was not produced after the 1940s, the leg splint pushed moulded-wood technology to a new level, which has been unsurpassed to this day. The leg splint was designed purely for a functional purpose and its beauty is found in the strong visual language that is derived from the performance of its function.

3O2

Leg Splint (1942)
Charles Eames (1907–78)
Ray Eames (1912–88)
Plyformed Wood Company 1942
Evans Products 1943 to 1949

Now that air travel is a basic transport option accessible to millions every year, it is hard to remember a time when flight was the privilege of the few. Before jet planes took over at the end of the 1950s the Lockheed L-049 'Constellation', or 'Connie' as it was affectionately known, was a significant step towards more accessible and affordable commercial flight. The charismatic industrialist, filmmaker and aviator, Howard Hughes, as a major stakeholder in Transcontinental and Western Airlines (TWA), is often credited as being the dynamic force behind the Constellation's evolution. Lockheed's chief aerodynamicist Kelley Johnson and TWA president Jack Frye were also involved in working on the design programme that Hughes apparently insisted on keeping top secret. The result was the L-049. Originally christened the Excalibur, it was later changed to Constellation and took its maiden voyage in 1943. Although TWA and rival airline Pan Am had already placed orders, the Constellation was almost immediately pressed into service for the US Army Air Force and used throughout World War II as a transportation plane known as the C-69. At the end of hostilities Lockheed repurchased the planes and re-fitted them for civilian use. The plane could seat forty-four or carry twenty sleeping birth passengers and travelled at an impressive speed of 480 kph (300 mph). The elegant, tapering body with its distinctive triple rudder has long been considered one of the most beautiful in passenger flight history and made the Constellation unmistakeable in the air. In 1951 a larger version, the Super Constellation, was introduced, which could hold up to sixty-six passengers. This was followed in 1957 by the Starliner, which could carry as many as the Super Constellation yet was powered by more effective turbo-compound engines. The Starliner had the capability to reach any European capital without a stop from all major airports in the United States – a major development for the industry. Although these planes went out of service with the advent of the jet era, they are still much-loved icons of US aviation history and the few remaining air-worthy models continue to delight crowds at public air shows.

ELECTROLUX

The New Cleanness

Sweden was becoming

an industrialized nation during the 1930s, and although its rapid advance towards mass production was halted by World War II, industrialization progressed apace directly following the war. This was seen in the influential ideal home exhibition of 1955, 'H55', in which Swedish products were exhibited by the Swedish Society of Crafts and Design. This exhibition clearly displayed the new focus on products, fittings and equipment for the home, as the postwar environment was centred on improving the consumer's lifestyle. Women, in particular, were required to work out of the home, and therefore needed tools to assist them in accomplishing household chores with speed. Sixten Sason was one of the pioneers of Swedish industrial design, having had a wide and diverse training as a silversmith, graphic designer and illustrator, as well as a pilot. He was employed by Saab in the late 1930s, and later worked with Hasselblad and

Husqvarna, as well as Electrolux. The concept of 'industrial designer' as a profession became commonplace during this time, and a variety of industries brought their engineers together with designers to develop products. As the market grew for products to modernize the home, Sason, together with Swedish manufacturer Electrolux, created this new vacuum cleaner. Using his streamlined aesthetic for both appearance and perform-ance, the Electrolux Vacuum Cleaner was a low-lying, bullet-shaped cleaner with a variety of parts designed to get into every nook and cranny. The cleaner, with its red handle and echoing metal strips alongside, was portable and easy to use. Interestingly, it was designed with independent people living in small spaces in mind. This message was backed up by the company's advertising campaign, which featured a single person sitting happy and content alone in a bijou, but obviously very clean, flat. By 1943 the vacuum cleaner had come a long way from Ives McGaffey's

first official patent for a sweeping machine in 1869 to Hubert Cecil Booth's British patent for a petrol-driven contraption that was horse-drawn and had to be parked outside of the building it was supposed to be cleaning. Sixten Sason's vacuum cleaner was designed in 1943 during World War II, and the cleaner was not properly introduced onto the market until 1949.

Electrolux Vacuum Cleaner (1943)
Sixten Sason (1912–67)
Electrolux 1943 to 1958

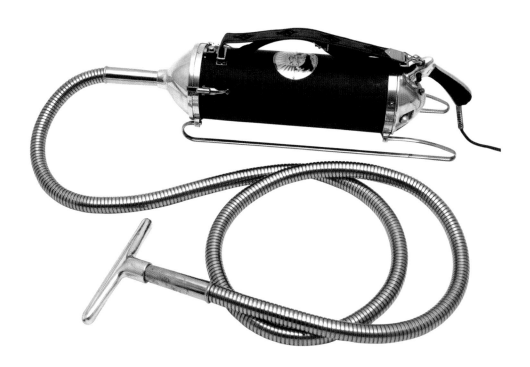

Argentina

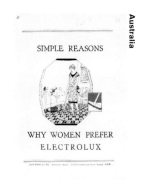

Australia

Austria

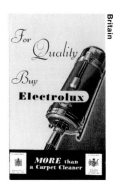

Britain

Britain

Czechoslovakia

France

France

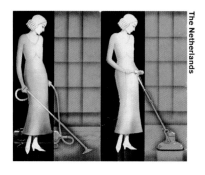

The Netherlands

France

Italy

Italy

Yugoslavia

Italy

Italy

Italy

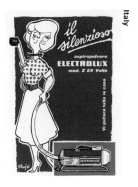

Italy

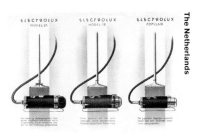

The Netherlands

The Netherlands

The Netherlands

Norway

Poland

Spain

Switzerland

Uruguay

Advertisements from various countries

Fruit Lantern (1943)
Kaare Klint (1888–1954)
Le Klint 1943 to present

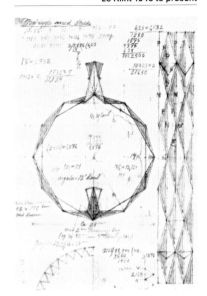

Kaare Klint's Fruit Lantern illustrates the grace and ingenuity of the best Danish design. The lanterns are made from paper, which makes them fragile, but also affordable. Indeed, since they first appeared on the market in 1943, Klint's Fruit Lanterns have sold in their millions. Kaare Klint first trained as a painter, and was always looking for ways to make design more democratic. He was an important and tireless theorist, who often looked overseas for inspiration. The influence of origami, a traditional Japanese discipline, can clearly be seen in the complex technique of paper-folding used in these lamps. Although he was emboldened by his knowledge of origami to attempt such an ambitious design, it was his father, PV Jensen Klint, who first introduced him to the idea of using folded paper in lighting design. Paper lanterns were something of an obsession within the Klint family; it is thought that the Fruit Lantern design was developed by Kaare Klint with the help of his son. Where PV Jensen Klint's experiments in folded paper were handmade in very small numbers, Kaare Klint insisted that his Fruit lamps should be available to everyone. Le Klint, a family company, soon went from being an artisanal industry to becoming a mechanized manufacturer. Fruit Lanterns were, and still are, made from sheets of paper scored by machine and assembled by hand. Kaare Klint is widely acknowledged as the father of modern Scandinavian design and echoes of his output can be seen in much of the work that followed him. Poul Henningsen's celebrated lighting designs for Louis Poulsen, in particular, owe a considerable debt to Klint's innovations, not only in their simple, geometric styling but also in their design-for-all agenda.

The Luminor Base wristwatch is the simplest of all Officine Panerai (Workshop Panerai) models. It was first produced in the early 1940s and has a modernist style that defies its military origins. In the early 1930s, Panerai established a close relationship with the Royal Italian Navy and began supplying it with precision pocket watches and aiming sights for torpedoes. The first Luminor appeared around 1943 using developments in the construction, design and performance of timekeeping instruments. The company Officine Panerai was established by Giovanni Panerai in 1860 in Florence, and has been dedicated to the production and development of professional timing instruments for over 140 years. Initially the company was committed to creating professional timepieces more than pocket watches, but later the company was able to capitalize on this experience to produce watches for the retail market, which became renowned for their accuracy and craftsmanship. The Luminor

Base has a hand-wind mechanism featuring only hour and minute hands. The watch face has a clear, modern styling, featuring over-sized sans serif numerals in keeping with the design aesthetic of the time and contributing to the watch's enduring popularity. With the addition of a device that protects the winding crown and keeps it in position, the watch could descend to a depth of 200 m (656 ft), an innovation that was a remarkable achievement for the time. Soon after, in 1949, the patent was approved for Luminor, a luminous substance based on tritium that replaced radiomir, both of which allowed the dial of the watch to be read in absolute darkness. Fifty years after the watch was developed exclusively for supply to the commandos of the Royal Italian Navy, the Luminor Base was reissued for limited edition retail, opening the market for this deft balance of Italian styling and Swiss technology.

307

Coffee Table IN50 (1944)
Isamu Noguchi (1904–88)
Herman Miller 1947 to 1973, 1984 to present
Vitra Design Museum 2001 to present

The Coffee Table IN50 consists of two identical asymmetrical shapes, one inverted and glued to the other. The relationship of the two is arranged to form a steady three-sided leg structure. Intriguingly Noguchi achieves this triangular structure without appearing to do so formally and explicitly. A glass top of a loosely triangular shape sits directly on this leg configuration. The result is a symmetrical structure with the appearance of a dynamic and asymmetrical form. Formal and material restraint is achieved with great eloquence and masterly control, generating a product that is simultaneously bold and graceful. The table was a striking example of the organic design being promoted in the United States in the early 1940s as a result of the highly influential exhibition in 1941, entitled 'Organic Design in Home Furnishings', at The Museum of Modern Art. Yet the use of formal asymmetry in this piece also shows Noguchi's Japanese cultural heritage; much of the Japanese tradition in painting, ceramics and garden design lays great emphasis on asymmetrical balance and the art of carefully considered naturalness. In 1949, 631 tables were produced. From 1962 to 1970 the table was given a plate glass top, and a base of solid walnut or ebony-finished poplar. According to the blueprint specifications, the glass was originally 2.2 cm (0.87 in) thick, but was reduced to 1.9 cm (0.75 in) after 1965, after which time there were also slight modifications to the base and height. But certain details remained the same, such as the dowel connecting the table base, which has always been metal. When it was first manufactured the clever use of two identical parts made this table easy to produce economically. A distinctive product at an accessible cost, the table proved to be very popular, and was quickly established as an enduring icon of the period. In 2003 Herman Miller added Isamu Noguchi's signature to the tables, because of the rapid increase of imitations.

Isamu Noguchi

Wilton C Dinges

The 1006 Navy chair's distinctive form and character directly arise from the wartime conditions surrounding its development. Emeco (The Electric Machine and Equipment Co) was founded in 1944 by Wilton C Dinges, a master tool-and-die maker with an engineering background. This chair resulted from his collaboration with the aluminium industry and naval engineers to create a chair that was seaworthy. In 1944 the US Navy was in the final stages of fighting World War II and was a major customer for industry. Aluminium was chosen for this chair because it offered very specific advantages for a seaworthy product. Firstly, it is light and strong, easy to transport, yet durable in heavy use. Aluminium is resistant to corrosion and lasts longer at sea than steel or wood. And unlike wood, it is non-flammable – an essential consideration on board ship. The most significant design concept of this chair is that it is entirely made of a single material. This ensured that the chair was sanitary and almost maintenance free, important qualities for use on a warship. The use of a single material predicts developments in moulded plastics some twenty years later. However, whereas today's plastic chairs can be made in single mouldings, up to seventy-seven processes are required to weld, shape and finish the Emeco Chair. Despite its appearance as a purely manufactured, uniform product, it is in fact the result of intensive craft skills and processes. The Emeco's appearance has sometimes been described as 'neutral'. This is because it arises purely as an engineered response to the need to make a durable seaworthy chair. But it is this neutrality that has ensured that the Emeco has become a classic piece of twentieth-century design. From the basic model 1006, Emeco has developed a whole family of high chairs, stools and chairs with swivel bases and even upholstery. In 2000 Emeco began production of the Hudson Chair designed by Philippe Starck, a homage to the original chair by one of the best contemporary designers.

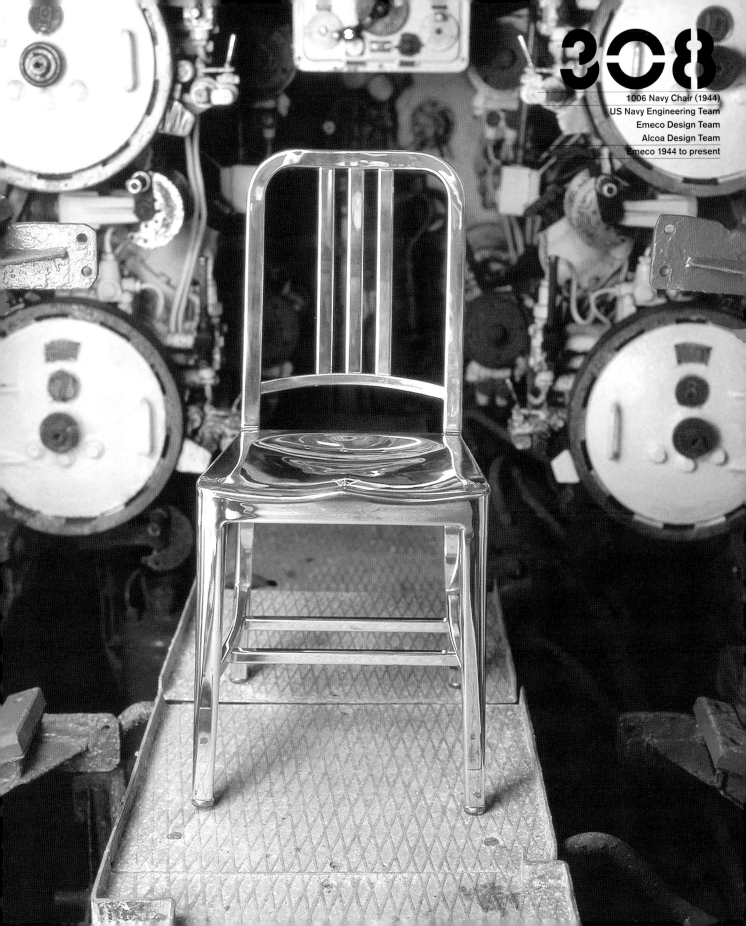

308

1006 Navy Chair (1944)
US Navy Engineering Team
Emeco Design Team
Alcoa Design Team
Emeco 1944 to present

Isamu Noguchi's artistic vision combined Japanese cultural traditions with a strong Western modernist idiom, and is evident in the many different examples of his work, from his large-scale sculpture and public works, including gardens, parks and playgrounds, to stage sets, domestic products and furniture. He moved fluidly between the worlds of fine art and design, exhibiting in top New York galleries and international museums, while also designing for prominent companies, such as Knoll and Herman Miller. An early Three-Legged Cylinder Lamp design for Knoll in the 1940s was the precursor to a series of lighted sculptures Noguchi called 'lunars'. He first conceived the notion of an illuminated sculpture in his Musical Weathervane of 1933, a mass-producible sculpture that would create musical sounds as it interacted with wind. Initially using magnesite, a material used in a fountain created for Ford, Noguchi moulded organic forms over electric light sources. These were eventually developed into a number of functional lighting fixtures. The first example of the Cylinder Lamp was a gift made for his sister. It was constructed from opaque aluminium, with metal legs, and had a paper shade wrapped around the cylinder. Knoll put the design into production in 1944, replacing the aluminium legs with cherrywood and the paper with translucent plastic. The use of three legs and organic forms runs through many of Noguchi's pieces, such as Coffee Table IN50 (1944) and the Prismatic Table of (1957). Knoll originally stopped production of the Cylinder Lamps because of the abundance of cheap imitations, a common occurrence with Noguchi's works. The Cylinder Lamp and Akari light sculptures were only recently reissued by Vitra Design Museum in 2001.

'Sembra una vespa!' ('It looks like a wasp!') This was
Enrico Piaggio's reaction when his ace designer Corradino D'Ascanio
showed him his new prototype motorcycle in 1945. The name stuck.
Interestingly, the Vespa was born out of near despair. The Piaggio
industrial giant had been decimated by the war; first by the Allies, and,
at the end, by the departing Germans, who bombed the factory, which
was nestled on the Serchio river, east of Pisa. Henry Ford and his ability
to mobilize large numbers of a poor and hungry population with a simple
and affordable car, inspired Enrico Piaggio. A car was out of the question,
but a motorcycle might just do the trick. The job was given to D'Ascanio,
one of Italy's foremost aeronautical designers, and the best designer at
Piaggio's disposal. Piaggio had his engineers create a basic motorcycle,
but D'Ascanio hated it and went back to the drawing board. He wanted
to create a bike that was simple to ride for men, women and even young
teenagers. He wanted to design a motorcycle that afforded some
protection from the weather, in a way that traditional motorcycles did
not. And he wanted to design a bike that was the antithesis of the
heavy, noisy, oily, macho machine of motorcycling tradition. D'Ascanio's

Gregory Peck and Audrey Hepburn in *Roman Holiday* (1953), directed by William Wyler

masterpiece came off the drawing board simply because he threw out all the preconceived notions of what a motorcycle should be and should look like. He created a 'step-through' chassis so women could ride it without having to wear trousers. The Vespa's leg shields were designed to protect the rider from the elements, whether it was sunny or raining. With its small, fully enclosed engine, the bike was easy to start and to ride. And the full bodywork was a perfect canvas for bright, attractive colour schemes. This first scooter was a design that would have a profound impact on the economy, the style and the popular culture of

Italy, and most parts of Europe for the second half of the twentieth century. Its impact did not stop there. It is no exaggeration to say that the Vespa started a trend of affordable, stylish transportation that continues to flourish into the twenty-first century. Its connection to Rome was sealed when the beautiful princess, played by Audrey Hepburn, and the dashing journalist, Gregory Peck, fall in love while touring around in *Roman Holiday*. The Vespa has been in continuous production since 1945 and has spawned a burgeoning host of clones and imitations. But there was, and is, only one Vespa.

LCW Chair (1945)
Charles Eames (1907–78)
Evans Products 1945 to 1946
Herman Miller 1946 to 1958

In 1941 New York's Museum of Modern Art hosted a design competition entitled 'Organic Design in Home Furnishings'. The competition called for new ideas aimed at improving domestic interiors. Charles Eames and Eero Saarinen jointly won two of the first prizes within the furniture category. Their designs explored three-dimensional moulding of plywood, which advanced the earlier two-dimensional lamination used by Alvar Aalto and others. Eames and Saarinen's prize-winning Organic Chair comprised a ply shell form, which integrated seat, back and side in a single continuous shape mounted on a separate leg structure. Although formally advanced it was technically difficult and expensive to produce. Eames, however, pursued the principle of three-dimensional moulded ply further because its successful resolution would combine material economy with contoured comfort. In the following few years he developed contour moulded ply leg splints for the US military but his single shell chair experiments refused to deliver a viable product. In the end, the solution resulted from a literal breaking down of the problem into simpler parts and generated the LCW design of 1945. LCW was a much simpler way of delivering cost-effective and comfortable support. The back and seat were made as separate components and held in the correct relationship to one another with a third laminated link element. This in turn was connected to laminated leg frames. The connection between each component was mediated through elastic rubber shock mounts providing resilience within the structure. Breaking the chair into discrete components offered other possibilities and generated LCM (Laminated Chair Metal) using the same LCW seat and back elements but, in this instance, mounted on to a welded steel frame. Here was a mid-century high point in furniture design, delivering organic, ergonomic comfort with visual lightness and economic viability. In this chair Eames combines the lyricism of Thonet's Chair No.14 with the floating detachment of Rietvelt's Red and Blue Armchair in a superlative synthesis.

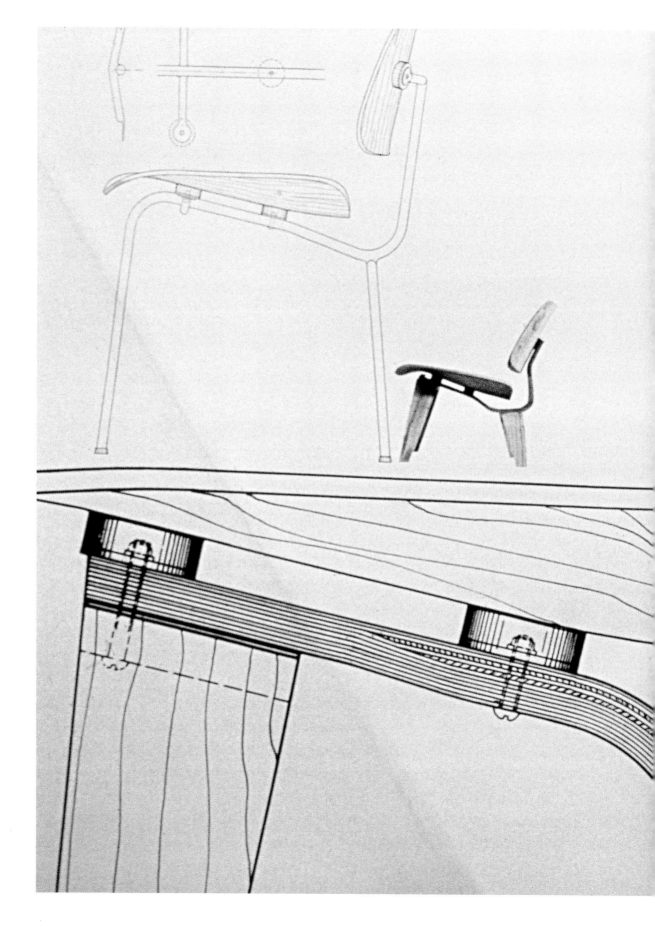

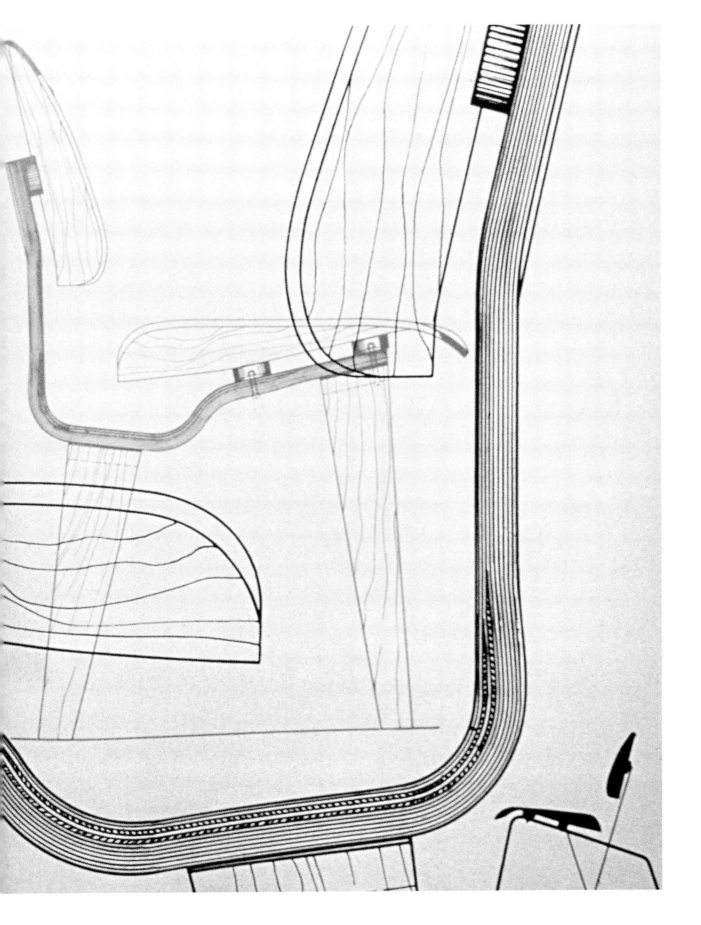

Earl Silas Tupper and Brownie Wise, co-founders of Tupperware

Tupperware boxes, those pastel-coloured, soft plastic containers, are seen in every kitchen around the world and revolutionized lunchbox culture. New Hampshire-born Earl Silas Tupper worked as a chemist for DuPont in the 1930s. In the early 1940s, he heard of a new thermoplastic, polyethylene, which the English were starting to use to protect electric wire. Most plastics at the time were hard, like Bakelite, which was used in place of more expensive materials like marble, but polyethylene was soft and flexible at room temperature. Tupper worked with his DuPont employers to produce a finer version of the plastic which he grandly called 'Poly T – Material of the Future'. He also developed a new injection moulding process in order to make products out of it. In 1945 as the American economy was beginning its postwar recovery, Tupper Plastics launched its range of food containers. Ingeniously, the patented lid rim formed an airtight seal – as the lid was pressed down, it caused negative air pressure inside the container and thus the external atmospheric pressure kept the seal tight. But the secret of Tupper's success lay not only in the fact that he was a great chemist and inventor, but also that he had the mind of a great salesman. In 1951 he came up with an audacious yet risky plan. He withdrew all Tupperware products from stores and began to sell them exclusively through gatherings held by an army of travelling saleswomen in customers' homes – the Tupperware party was born. They were a huge hit with housewives across the Western world and Tupper sold his company to the Rexall drug conglomerate in 1958. Tupper himself was able to retire to Costa Rica as a multi-millionaire.

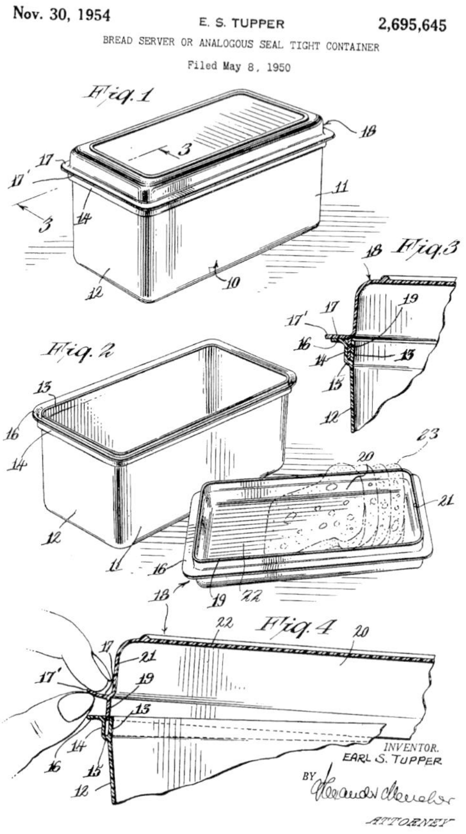

Nov. 30, 1954 E. S. TUPPER 2,695,645
BREAD SERVER OR ANALOGOUS SEAL TIGHT CONTAINER
Filed May 8, 1950

Fig. 1

Fig. 2

Fig. 3

Fig. 4

INVENTOR.
EARL S. TUPPER
BY
ATTORNEY

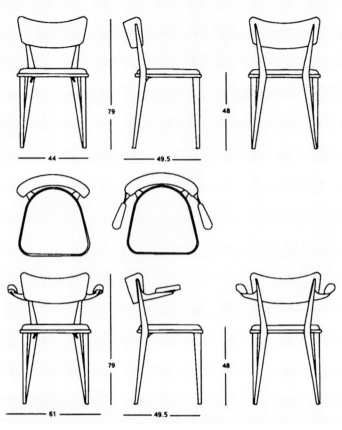

Ernest Race

The BA Chair occupies a unique place in British design of the late 1940s. Its innovation and style were symbolic of a new spirit in furniture design. The shortage of traditional furniture-making materials in postwar Britain motivated Ernest Race to design the BA Chair using the novel construction technique of cast recycled aluminium. Race had previously achieved some success before the war as a fabric designer. In 1945, after responding to an advertisement in *The Times* newspaper, Race established his company, Ernest Race Ltd, in collaboration with engineer JW Noel Jordan. The BA Chair was the company's first product, introduced later that year. It initially came to public attention at the Victoria and Albert Museum's 'Britain Can Make It' exhibition of 1946. Lightweight but strong, reasonably priced, and with a different aesthetic from the tubular steel furniture of the Modern movement, the BA Chair was an immediate success. Its construction allowed mass production without the need for traditional skilled labour. The chair is made from five cast aluminium components, with the addition of two aluminium sheets for the back and seat. The seat was initially finished with rubberized padding covered with a cotton duck fabric. The legs have a tapered T-section, giving them strength with minimal material use. Each leg is attached to the seat casting with three screws. Originally, the components were sand cast, but after 1946 a pressure die-cast technique was used; this change allowed a significant reduction in materials and cost. From the outset the chair was available both with and without arms, and after 1947, as wood became more plentiful, mahogany, birch and walnut veneer finishes were introduced. In 1954 Race was awarded the gold medal at the Milan Triennale for the BA Chair. Used in many public buildings throughout the 1950s, the chair is still in production, with in excess of 250,000 made to date.

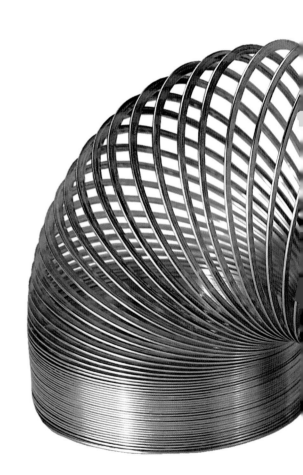

Slinky® (1945)
Richard James (1914–74)
Betty James (1918–)
James Industries 1945 to present

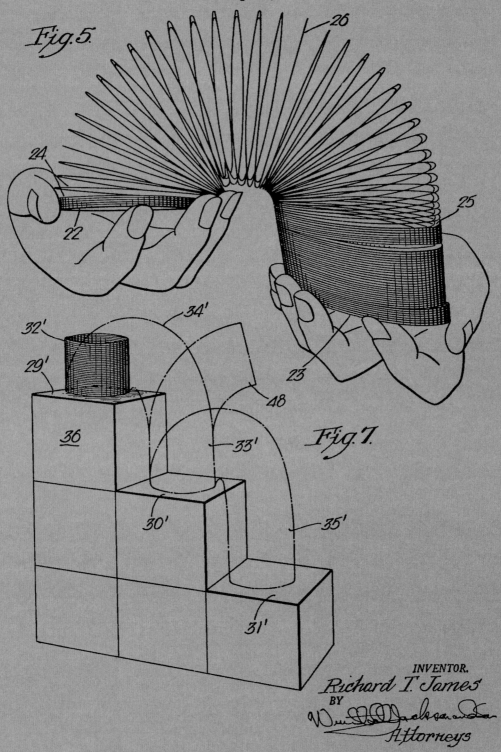

Fig.5.

Fig.7.

INVENTOR.

Richard T. James

BY

Attorneys

In an age filled with toys that require expensive digital equipment or bulky plastic carapaces, it is difficult to imagine that the Slinky became an overnight hit with nothing more going for it than a simple shape and a silly name. Indeed, Slinky is an example of a design that is hardly designed. Instead, the snaky steel coil seems to have sprung from the mind, or hand, of its creator, Richard James, fully formed. James was a designer based in Pennsylvania who spent much of 1943 developing a spring mechanism that would help stabilize war ships in the roughest of seas. Not counting on the roughness of his own movements, however, James one day accidentally knocked a single spring off a shelf and watched as it gracefully stepped down a series of surfaces. Dubbed 'Slinky' by James's wife Betty, the toy was perfected over a period of two years by the couple, who took their time researching the best materials, lengths and production methods for the bobbling coil, which they were sure would intrigue the public as much as it had them. The Slinky was instantly popular when it was first marketed to the public in 1945 by James Industries (later known as Poof-Slinky). The first time it appeared in a department store in Philadelphia, 400 units sold in less than two hours, a success that paved the way for the Jameses to establish a toy conglomerate called James Industries that continues to make the Slinky to this day. Using the machines that were developed by Richard James in 1945, the company has produced more than 250 million toys to date, with the same ingredients: 20 m (63 ft) of wire that is spun and coiled into the archetypal walking spring shape. Although James Industries proceeded to branch the Slinky's evolutionary tree into other species such as the Plastic Slinky, Slinky Jr and the much-loved Slinky Dog, the simple Slinky has remained such an enduring design icon that it was honoured with its own stamp in 1999.

The pure, stripped-down elegance of the Potence Lamp has made it one of Jean Prouvé's emblematic works and one of the best domestic lighting solutions of the twentieth century. The French architect originally designed it for his Maison Tropique, an experiment in prefabricated housing, and the final product has all the qualities such a project would require. Consisting of little more than a metal rod, which extends approximately 2.25 m (7 ft), a light bulb and a wall-mounted bracket, the lamp can be rotated via a wooden-ball-ended handle to cover a 180 degree arc. In addition to its simplicity and practicality, the lamp does not take up valuable floor space or require electrical wiring through the ceiling. Prouvé had originally trained and worked as a blacksmith, and the sensitivity he developed as a result of this is evident in the material elegance of his lamp. Regardless of its practical purpose as a lighting device, the perfect engineering in the lamp's bracket and wire support make this a sculptural object worth marvelling at. Prouvé's reputation was for a time overshadowed by that of Le Corbusier and his circle, but he returned to a more public prominence in 2002, when a number of his designs, including the Potence Lamp, were reissued by Vitra, and he became justly recognized as one of the great designers of the twentieth century. Prouvé has always been well known in France, but now his designs have become collectable internationally. This lamp is regarded by Vitra as being the purest of his designs, being both sparse and highly detailed.

315

Potence Lamp (c.1945)
Jean Prouvé (1901–84)
Ateliers Jean Prouvé c.1945 to 1956
Vitra 2002 to present

At the time that Captain Charles 'Chuck' Yeager set about breaking
the sound barrier in the cryptically named Bell X-1, the idea of a wall of
sound that human beings could not penetrate ran deep, both in the
scientific community and in the popular imagination. It is worth
remembering that just forty years earlier, popular belief held that
humans could not withstand speeds greater than 97 kph (60 mph).
The Bell X-1, only three of which were ever built, was the perfect, bullet-
shaped projectile to get through the sound barrier. Although it was
designed to take off from the ground, the project engineers at Bell
Aircraft Corporation considered a rocket-propelled launch too risky.
Instead, the Bell X-1 was slung under a Boeing B29 Superfortress and
dropped in mid-air, like a bomb, into flight. Once free of the mother ship,
Yeager fired up the 2,718 kg (6,000 lb) thrust engine and pointed the
nose skywards. Every stage of this endeavour was fraught with danger.
Yeager, the crusty World War II flying ace and test pilot, was chiselled out
of the right stuff. Construction of this extreme machine, high tech for its
time, included an adjustable horizontal stabilizer that made control at
trans-sonic speeds, and particularly the shock wave at Mach 1, easier.
Named 'Glamorous Glennis' after Yeager's wife and painted orange for
greater visibility, the Bell X-1 was a virtual flying laboratory, with a heavy
payload of test instruments. On 14 October 1947 Yeager piloted the craft
to an altitude of 14,654 m (43,000 ft) and reached a speed of Mach 1.06,
or 1,126 kph (700 mph). It was the first of many supersonic flights that
Yeager made in the X-1 before it was retired in 1951. A potent and very
tangible symbol of the space age, the X-1 now hangs on display at the
Smithsonian National Air and Space Museum in Washington DC.

Bell X-1 Rocket Plane (1945)
Lawrence Bell (1894–1956)
Bell Design Team
Bell Aircraft Corporation 1945 to 1951

Research pilot John Griffith leaning out of the hatch on the X-1, 1950

In many ways the Bombé Tea and Coffee Service can be seen as a symbol of the history of Alessi production. The service was designed by Carlo Alessi, who joined the company following studies as an industrial designer in Novara. He became general manager of the company in the 1930s and was responsible for designing most of the objects produced between the mid-1930s and 1945. In 1945 he launched his final project: the Bombé Tea and Coffee Service. This product, more than any other, helped to establish the company's reputation for producing modern and innovative products. The Alessi company, founded in 1921, initially advertised itself as a workshop and foundry specializing in working brass and nickel sheet. Its first products included coffee pots, serving dishes and trays for the hotel and catering trade. In 1932 the founder Giovanni's eldest son, Carlo Alessi, an industrial designer, joined the company and was appointed principal designer. The ensuing years saw the company make the transition away from craft-based methods to industrial production. In 1945, the year in which he also became general manager, Carlo

conceived the Bombé Service. The enduring design, produced in four different sizes, is an unashamedly industrial product. The Bombé Tea and Coffee Service displays a purity of form that pays homage to some of the great creative moments in modern design history. The service now forms part of Alessi's Archivi range, which draws on the creative ideals of schools such as the Bauhaus and the Weiner Werkstätte. Alessi first reissued a tea and coffee service designed by Bauhaus designer Marianne Brandt in 1924. The company then went on to reissue a large collection of pieces by the British designer Christopher Dresser. The Bombé Tea and Coffee Service has clearly been inspired by the simple geometric forms and lack of adornment that characterize works by earlier designers. It was originally made from silver-plated and chrome-plated brass and has been produced in stainless steel since 1965. At the time of its production it was unashamedly modern and now sits comfortably alongside new designs. It is still one of the most successful tea and coffee sets sold by Alessi.

Carlo Alessi

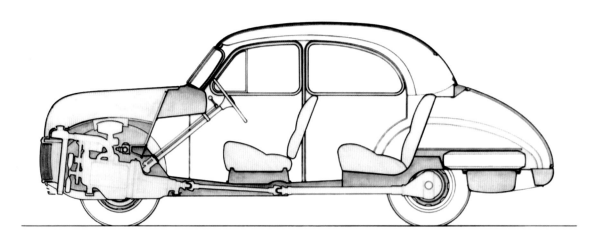

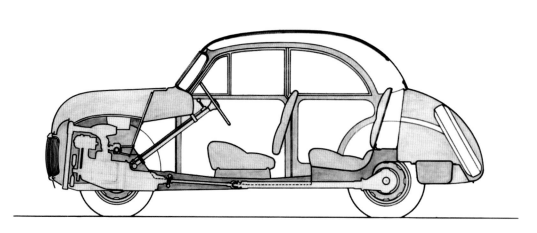

The Morris Minor, which was launched at the 1948 Earls Court Motor Show, set many milestones in car design, not least of which was being the first British car to reach a production of one million. Morris Minors are now considered classic cars by a worldwide network of collectors, who work hard to uphold the historical significance of the design and its enduring legacy. The Morris Minor is best known for its distinct rounded outline; indeed, straight lines feature little on this car. When it was unveiled, the Minor's ample curves proved to be a somewhat provocative departure from the more upright aesthetic of the time. The car's bulbous charm, however, quickly became a defining characteristic of the brand. The perfectly proportioned cabin, incorporating a tiny rear window, almost hovers over a set of slim 36 cm (14 in) wheels. Chromework appears on the bumpers, hubcaps, around the lights and as a decorative detail running from the front of the bonnet to the windscreen. A split windscreen and cheesegrater-style grille, both of which were updated in the 1954 MK II version, also marks out the original design. Code-named 'Mosquito', the car was designed by Alec Issigonis (who went on to design the Mini) and a team including Reg Job and Jack Daniels. They set out to establish a set of innovative features in car design including a monocoque design, rack and pinion steering, independent front suspension and smaller wheels. Costing £358 at launch, demand quickly outstripped supply, with the international market claiming over seventy-five per cent of the early series MM model. The car's popularity was kept afloat with a string of modifications including larger engines, more user-friendly gearboxes, indicators, a touring version, a convertible, and the introduction of vans for the commercial market. And on 22 December 1960, the millionth Minor rolled off the production line, an occasion marked by the limited release of 349 lilac-coloured cars. Ironically, it was Alec Issigonis's new design of the Morris 1100/1300 that threatened the Minor's popularity. Sales dropped throughout the 1960s to the point when production of saloons, and then Travellers, ceased in the early 1970s. Yet the original Morris Minor went on to outlive almost all its contemporaries, earning Alec Issigonis a knighthood and the car a place in motoring history.

Max Gort-Barten

The Dualit Vario Toaster, with its coolly functional modern styling, was the essential kitchen accessory in the 1980s. First designed in 1946, the Dualit Toaster has come to represent the fundamentally British attitude that it is the simple things in life that are the most rewarding. Since the 1980s the design has been harnessed to the cause of millennial minimalism and is a key player in the continuing fascination with retro home styling. The designer of the Dualit Toaster was primarily an engineer, which explains the innovative mode of function as well as the machine aesthetic of the exterior styling. In 1946, Max Gort-Barten produced the original Dualit Toaster from his workshop just off London's Old Kent Road. The first product Gort-Barten invented was the Dual-Light Fire, the manoeuvrable electric heater with a double element that gave the company its name. The Dualit brand has since become synonymous with solidly chic, hand-made kitchen products that until recently were all produced at the factory in South London. The key to the success of the toaster's design is the 'stay-warm' premise, the toast being cooked for a specified period by setting a time switch and then manually ejected by depressing a lever rather than being automatically 'popped'. This allows the toast to be kept warm inside the machine if left unejected, a concept that became widely accepted and hugely popular. Dualit responded to the surge in demand by keeping the clean-lined styling of its classic model but introducing chrome finishes and black ProHeat elements, which were coated in a membrane that made them unbreakable and incorporated the same heatproof material used in the space shuttle. It was this ProHeat innovation which won the company a 2000 millennium award. Still in production today, the Dualit Vario Toaster continues to top the majority of wedding gift lists. Each toaster is assembled by hand and includes the assembler's individual mark on the base plate. Enduring in style and popularity, the toaster is built without compromise.

Although the first electric typewriter was produced by Thomas Edison as early as 1871, the capacity of such machines to use mathematical symbols was developed much later. Commercially produced adding machines were not developed until after World War II. In Italy the Elettrosumma 14 was first introduced in 1946 and functioned as a ten-key electrical adding machine that aimed to revolutionize the mathematical language of calculation. Designed by the Italian design company Olivetti, Elettro ('electric') summa ('add') was superior in speed and form to earlier adding machines, which resembled more a modern supermarket till than a calculating machine. The thinking behind the Elettrosumma was that it was more than a mechanical device to process logical operations or express mathematical equations; it was an object of intuition and beauty designed to create a direct rapport between human and electronics. Its release marked the end of World War II and in turn a small victory for Olivetti, which had striven throughout this conflict to keep Italian industrial design alive. With a peaceful future ahead, Adriano Olivetti saw the opportunity to pursue his design objectives with the development of new technology. Pioneering the electronic revolution, he invested in two electronic research labs, one in the United States and one in Pisa. One of the first products to be developed was Elettrosumma's bigger brother, the 22-R. It was launched in 1957, its advertisement claiming 'With a speed of 210 cycles per minute the Elettrosumma 22 is the fastest adding/listing machine yet produced.' This larger offspring came inclusive of improved 'static memory' that allowed sums to be continually multiplied to reach a total. These developments in technology led to the realization of the Elea 9003, Italy's first electronic computer. In 1960 Olivetti died suddenly and the company fell into debt from which it never quite recovered. With the introduction of slimmer calculators and personal computers in the 1980s the electromechanical calculators were considered to be outdated and ungainly. Ultimately, Olivetti was sold to the Pirelli and Benetton groups, following mounting financial problems. Nevertheless, the Elettrosumma 14 remains a motivational gadget, recognized and beloved by those of technical talent. With its colourful plastic exterior, the product stands apart from its American IBM brethren and sums up the fun of Italian design. With a bold voice, this calculator states, 'I'm not just a simple adding machine but a way of operating and thinking.'

The strong architectural form of George Nelson's Platform Bench is a reflection of the immediate postwar ethos promoted by American creative endeavour. North American designers in the 1940s began to enthusiastically embrace the philosophical and aesthetic tenets of European Modernism, and uphold them as models for everyday, twentieth-century living. As a member of the Yale University architectural faculty, and later of the School of Architecture at Columbia University, New York, Nelson was crucially placed to help refine the vision of the next generation of designers in all aspects of the built environment. A writer, teacher and environmentalist, Nelson, like many architects of this period, was inspired by Bauhaus principles,

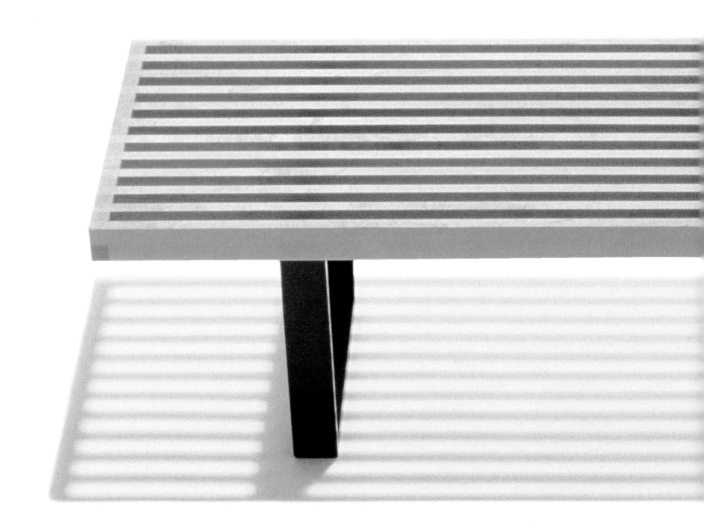

which promoted honest construction, clear functionality, and a design's ability to employ innovative use of materials and industrial processes, whilst supporting design as a viable business. Nelson joined Herman Miller in 1946 as director of design, and his Platform Bench was introduced in that same year. It was a flexible and useful piece of furniture, designed to accommodate both people and objects. Its purpose was not ambiguous, but rather, it was an example of a modernist design imperative aligning duality of function to form. Constructed in maple with metal levelling glides and strengthened by finger-jointed, ebonized legs, the rectilinear bench top is a plane of slats, purposely spaced to allow both light and air to pass through,

expressing a sense of both transparency and elegance. As part of Nelson's first collection for Herman Miller, it was described in the 1948 furniture catalogue as 'primarily a high base for deep and shallow cases, but it also serves as a low table for extra seating'. By 1955 it had proved to be one of Herman Miller's most flexible and useful pieces. Nelson enjoyed a twenty-five-year association with Herman Miller, both as director of design, and in collaboration with his own firm, George Nelson Associates. The bench was reintroduced in 1994, and its enduring legacy as an important piece of postwar furniture is a testament to the prophetic vision of its designer.

322

Eames Screen (1946)
Charles Eames (1907–78)
Ray Eames (1912–88)
Herman Miller 1946 to 1955, 1994 to present
Vitra 1990 to present

The folding Screen that Charles and Ray Eames designed for Herman Miller in 1946 was an adaptation of a similar screen designed in Finland in the late 1930s by Alvar Aalto, made of pine and marketed by Artek as Screen 100. Aalto's screen was constructed of flat strips of wood connected by canvas 'hinges'. The Eameses adapted Aalto's idea into something more practical, flexible and elegant. They widened the strips to 22.5 cm (9 in), used plywood moulded into a U-shape and then connected the strips of ply with full-length canvas hinges running from top to bottom of the screen. These innovations gave the screen much greater stability. The tape could not withstand regular folding and unfolding so this gave rise to the use of canvas hinges that were sandwiched into slots in the plywood. Once this detail was rectified, the screen could be folded up easily for efficient shipping, carriage and storage, with each U-shape acting as a receptacle for its neighbour. The tooling and the first units were produced at the 901 Washington Boulevard shop. Subsequently, production was transferred to the Evans Products plant in Grand Haven and then to Herman Miller. The production process to insert the canvas hinges involved a lot of hand labour and considerably reduced the product's potential for mass production. As a result, the manufacturing costs of the Screen became too high and went against the couple's mission to provide good design for a fair price. Production ceased in 1955, but the Screen was later reintroduced using a polypropylene mesh held securely by a new process to ensure a longer life without compromising the integrity of the 1946 design. The Screen was available in different heights and lengths as well as a variety of finishes. Its flexibility would have appealed greatly to the couple. Charles Eames spoke fondly of his time spent working as a set designer for MGM, when he often had to construct an entire film set overnight from a limited range of available props. The Screen is the perfect example of an unselfconscious piece of practical design that allows room for personal statement, fitting Charles and Ray Eames's belief that anyone and everyone could, and indeed, should be an architect or a designer.

molded plywood folding screens

THE MOLDED PLYWOOD FOLDING SCREEN designed by Charles Eames, offers an excellent solution for problems involving division of areas, screening off objects or activities, or providing backgrounds for furniture groupings. The molded elements fold into each other to form a compact unit when not in use. Their shape enables the screen to stand free open or closed. The plywood surface is decorative yet unobtrusive.

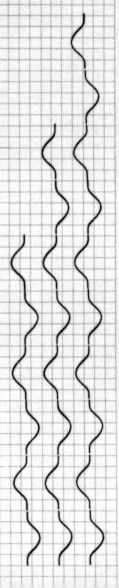

FSW 10

HT.	L.	WT.
5′8″	8′4″	45. lb.

34 FSW 10

HT.	L.	WT.
2′10″	8′4″	23 lb.

FSW 8

HT.	L.	WT.
5′8″	6′8″	36 lb.

34 FSW 8

HT.	L.	WT.
2′10″	6′8″	18 lb.

FSW 6

HT.	L.	WT.
5′8″	5″	27 lb.

34 FSW 6

HT.	L.	WT.
2′10″	5″	14 lb.

WOOD FINISHES Birch
Calico Ash
Oak

weights shown are net uncrated
scale plan views shown on 2″ grid

6 big reasons why you won't be happy unless you buy genuine

FLINT KITCHEN TOOLS

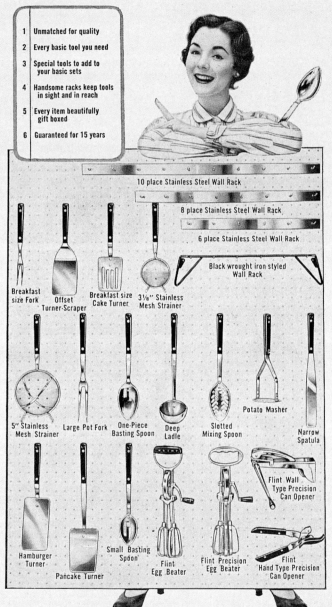

1. Unmatched for quality
2. Every basic tool you need
3. Special tools to add to your basic sets
4. Handsome racks keep tools in sight and in reach
5. Every item beautifully gift boxed
6. Guaranteed for 15 years

10 place Stainless Steel Wall Rack

8 place Stainless Steel Wall Rack

6 place Stainless Steel Wall Rack

Black wrought iron styled Wall Rack

Breakfast size Fork

Offset Turner-Scraper

Breakfast size Cake Turner

3⅛" Stainless Mesh Strainer

5" Stainless Mesh Strainer

Large Pot Fork

One-Piece Basting Spoon

Deep Ladle

Slotted Mixing Spoon

Potato Masher

Narrow Spatula

Hamburger Turner

Pancake Turner

Small Basting Spoon

Flint Egg Beater

Flint Precision Egg Beater

Flint Wall Type Precision Can Opener

Flint Hand Type Precision Can Opener

There's no doubt about the fact that gleaming vanadium stainless steel Flint Kitchen Tools are the most magnificent kitchen tools ever made. Everybody has tried to copy them! But *nobody* has ever matched them for quality! From their nickel silver rivets to their quintuple mirror polish and the fine temper of their steel, Flint Kitchen Tools—and *only* Flint—are so good they're guaranteed for 15 years! Available wherever fine housewares are sold in U. S. and Canada.

the greatest names in housewares!

Ekco Products Company, Chicago 39, Ill.

209

The innovation of EKCO's Flint 1900 cooking and kitchen utensils lies in its developments in manufacture and production, and in the aesthetics of its design. In fact, the Flint 1900 marks a point where a design and manufacturing standard was established that has not been surpassed. Prior to the Flint 1900, on the whole, kitchen tools were made of relatively cheap materials such as stamped metal, which had the disadvantage of rusting. The typical standard for handles was turned wood, which when repeatedly washed and exposed to moisture, cracked and split. The staff at the EKCO Products Company addressed this issue by introducing a range of kitchen utensils wrought from stainless steel, with the handles made of moulded plastic. The EKCO designers' primary concern was not to reinvent the basic forms of the utensils, but to make improvements to the design that would enhance their strength and durability and give quality and heftiness to the items. The use of double rivets together with polished steel presented the consumer with a set of kitchen tools that were more allied to quality knives and cutlery than the usual utensils on the market. EKCO further reinforced this association by using the name and trademark of Flint, which was already associated with their range of fine quality kitchen knives. The Flint 1900 range was available and marketed as a set, rather than as individual items, and came complete with a wall-mounted rack on to which they were hung and stored away. The set was comparatively expensive, but EKCO's quality was picked up by the consumer and the range was a huge success. The enduring legacy of these utensils is in EKCO's commitment to high-quality production and design for utilitarian items previously deemed outside the remit of product design.

323

Flint 1900 (1946)
EKCO Design Team
EKCO Products 1946 to c.1959

324

Freeform Sofa (1946)
Isamu Noguchi (1904–88)
Herman Miller 1949 to 1951
Vitra Design Museum 2002 to present

Japanese-American sculptor-designer Isamu Noguchi's predilection for the language of biomorphism is well represented in his 1946 Freeform Sofa. As with much of his design work, his sculptural background informs the fluid shape of the piece, which looks as though it is made from two large, flat stones yet has a dynamic, light appearance. The thin cushion and ottoman ensure comfort and also reinforce the piece's sculptural appearance. Freeform is upholstered in wool and supported by a beechwood frame with maple feet. In all his design work, Noguchi combined a knowledge of contemporary sculptural forms with a mastery of technical skills. An assistant of Constantin Brancusi in 1927 and an admirer of Alexander Calder, Noguchi drew on these influences in his later work. As a sculptor, Noguchi was interested in materials and shapes as well as their interaction with space itself. He believed that everyday objects should be perceived as sculptures with a functional value, or 'things for everyone's pleasure'. Noguchi adopted the Japanese design ethos, according to which there is no distinction between fine and applied art, and worked towards bridging the gap between crafts and fine art in a democratic and functional way. Throughout the 1940s and 1950s he designed chairs and tables for Herman Miller and Knoll, and his body of work was hugely influential on the organic design language of the 1950s. The Freeform design, radically different from his other works of the time, was only produced for a few years and in small quantities by manufacturer Herman Miller, making the original a highly collectable piece. Vitra, in collaboration with the Isamu Noguchi Foundation, reissued the Freeform Sofa along with other seminal pieces.

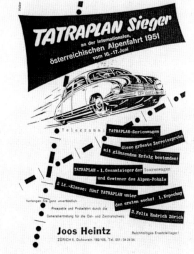

Advertisement, proclaiming the Tatra winner of the Austrian Alps rally, 16–17 June 1951

Created between 1946 and 1947, the Tatraplan, manufactured by the Czechoslovakian firm Tatra, broke the mould by bringing the notion of streamlining to the public. The car's story began in Nesseldorf in 1850 when wagon-maker, Ignaz Schustala, founded Schustala, a company manufacturing horse-drawn coaches. By 1897 Nesselsdorf automobiles were rolling out of its doors and twenty-three years later its products were re-badged with the Tatra logo. In 1933, director of the company's automobile division Hans Ledwinka, along with chief automotive engineer, Erich Uberlacker, launched the forerunner to the Tatraplan, the T77. The new car had a rear-mounted engine that aided aerodynamics and created a larger interior for passengers. It caused a sensation at the Berlin Autosalon in 1934, and the rear single fin immediately becoming a Tatra trademark. The company followed this up with a string of other models but it was not until after the World War II that the classic Tatraplan emerged. It had a difficult genesis. In 1945, with Czechoslovakia now under communist rule, Ledwinka was accused of collaborating with the Nazis and was jailed for six years. In a state of flux, the company – renamed Tatra – turned to its chief engineer Julius Mackerle for leadership. However, it was the company's director of body design, Frantisek Chalupa, who, after a long consultation with the incarcerated Ledwinka, came up with the idea for a steel monocoque that enclosed the wheels. The resultant car, which went into production in 1947, was arguably the first product to bring the principles of streamlining to the public. It was wide at the front, with a sloping split windscreen and tapered at the back into a virtually indistinguishable fin – essentially looking like a mobile teardrop. Vitally, the Tatraplan also had an impressive 0.32 drag coefficient. In 1951 production of the vehicle was moved to Skoda but by 1952 production halted completely. By the end of its life a total of 6,342 units were produced and exported to 17 countries.

When it was first produced, the Folle Classic Stapler so transcended the limits of its function that it was stocked by exclusive furniture stores as well as office-supply shops. Designed by a Dane, Folmer Christensen, it was first produced in 1946 by Folle, a company based in the town of Vanløse that Christensen founded in order to manufacture steel goods. Instead of articulating the crocodile-like snapping action of most desk staplers, the Folle, with its large polished steel button, has been designed to perform a simple downward action. It is direct and delicate and the presence of the button suggests that you should operate it with a single digit, and presents the stapler as something that requires only the minimum of human effort to operate, thereby being more a machine than a tool. And, unlike many more modern staplers, it is a true desk stapler, designed to be used while it sits on the desk rather than by being picked up in the hand. The Folle is constructed of sheet steel and beneath its deceptively simple exterior is a more complex design based around four spring mechanisms. The most obvious of these is coiled beneath the button, giving the latter an almost screw-like presence, further suggesting a degree of precision. Others allow the user to open the stapler head and select between settings that cause the staples to close either inwards or outwards. The classic 1946 Folle Classic Stapler is still manufactured using the original machines and tools, along with a number of variations, even including a long-arm version and a side stapler for binding magazines. They are so sturdy, with a weight of approximately 290 g (10.22 oz), many retailers boast that the groove at the stapler's base can be used as a bottle opener in order to prove the quality and thickness of the steel.

GREYHOUND

The Greyhound bus restyled by Raymond Loewy, has always been a symbol of freedom and adventure. If a character in an American novel or film is going through a life-changing experience, they will inevitably be seen waiting at the Greyhound depot to be rescued, or boarding the great silver tube itself, as with Cary Grant in the Hitchcock classic, *North by Northwest*. Its fluted sides suggest that the open road is its natural habitat and the windows slant backwards as if trailing with the speed of travel. The character will always give a rueful back-ward glance before entering the hissing doors and riding off to discover a new life in the vast expanse of opportunity that is America. Loewy was initially approached by Orville S Caeser, the chief executive at Greyhound, to redesign its logo in 1933. Not one to mince his words, Loewy had suggested to the chief executive at an earlier meeting that the company's logo was more 'fat mongrel' than elegant greyhound. The American Kennel Club sent Loewy an image of a thoroughbred greyhound, and his silhouetted, sleek version is still used today. The famous Scenicruiser model was the result of Greyhound's efforts to develop a modern coach after World War II. Loewy was com-missioned for the styling and employed his famous streamlining aesthetics not only to make the coach look more appealing and reflect the movement of the vehicle, but to enhance performance and efficiency too. Loewy rented an empty store on the corner of Park Avenue and 45th Street, in which the first double-decker was built on a General Motors chassis. He improved safety by reinforcing the lower part of the body in case of collision, and by placing a large white disk with a red arrow that would point down towards the stairs when the door was open. Loewy introduced practical innovations such as a seating textile with a small repeat pattern to disguise stains, showing that Modernism need not be all about impractical minimalism.

Cary Grant in *North by Northwest* (1959), directed by Alfred Hitchcock

Saab 92 (1946–9)
Sixten Sason (1912–67)
Saab 1950 to 1956

Sixten Sason

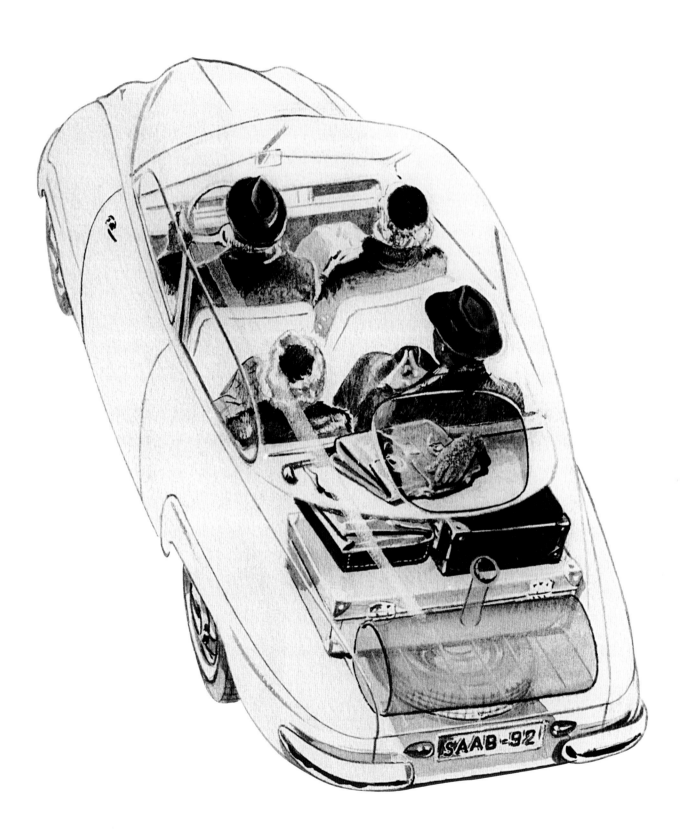

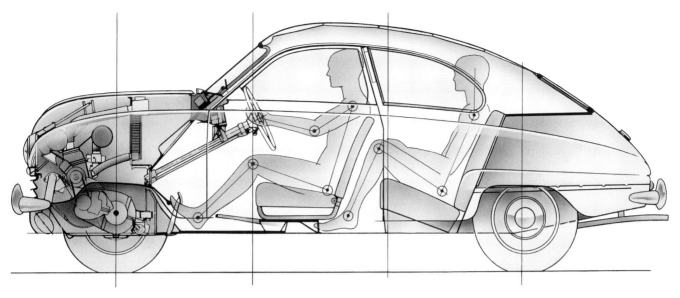

Sweden's contributions to car design have been less substantial than those of Italy and the USA but a few models have achieved classic status nonetheless. The work of Sixten Sason for the company, Saab, is significant, especially the model he created just after the World War II. At that time Saab had just turned to car manufacturing from an aeronautical background and its early postwar production was strongly influenced by this change of direction. Sason, a technical illustrator who worked for the company on a freelance basis, was brought in to create an appropriate aesthetic for the results of the company's experiments in aerodynamics. This marriage of aeronautical engineering and visualizing skills produced a remarkable car, the Saab 92. The first Saab 92 prototype was unveiled to the press on 10 June 1947, although regular production did not start until December 1949. Designed like an aircraft

wing its dramatically streamlined form was a result of both advanced aerodynamic experimentation and sophisticated form-giving. Like its American precedents, by such designers as Norman Bel Geddes, Sason eliminated fenders, wheel arches and all other potential protuberances to create a sleek body-shell. The body was now given a tapering rear, a curved front end and continuous lines which united the front with the back to create a single unit. Prototypes were created from 1946 onwards and the first production models appeared in a distinctive bottle-green colour. His collaboration with Saab lasted until 1969 when he was replaced by his younger collaborator, Björn Envall, who carried forward the company's tradition of combining aerodynamic precision with appropriate and appealing styling. The Saab 92 remains, however, one of the company's most radical and respected achievements.

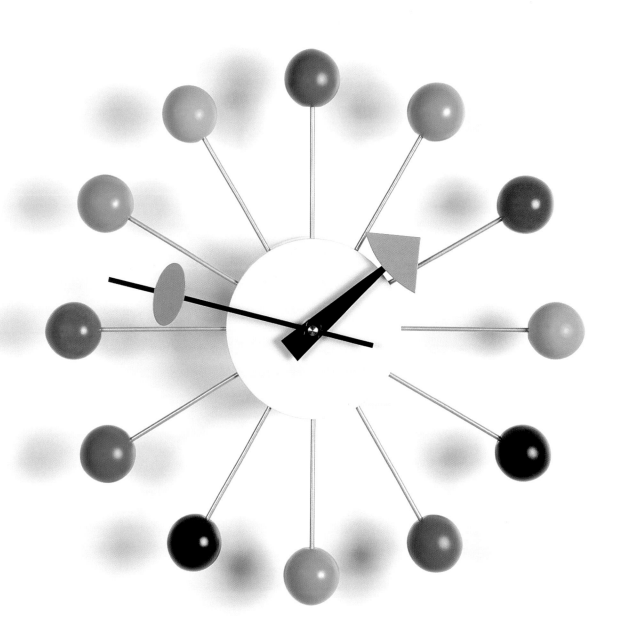

Ball Clock (1947)
Irving Harper (1917–)
George Nelson Associates
Howard Miller Clock Company 1948 to 1952
Vitra Design Museum 1999 to present

After

the devastating displays of nuclear power had
ushered in a new world, during World War II, a long shadow
was cast over modern design and consumerism in the United States.
The postwar generation was optimistic yet anxious, a fact George Nelson and
his design colleagues were to address, while at the same time acknowledging how the
public realm was being shaped by the cool hand of the International Style. The Atomic or Ball
Clock is a quintessential example of such an object. Designed in 1947 and produced by the
Howard Miller Clock Company, it became an icon of the 1950s before the American Dream had lost
its lustre. In its original version the Atomic Clock featured a brass central hub, painted red, from which
radiated twelve identical brass spokes terminated by red-painted wooden balls indicating the hours. Its
black hands are punctuated at their ends by geometric forms: a triangle for the hour, an ellipse for minutes.
The openness of its structure and the shadows it casts incorporate the background as a field determined by
the user and add complexity and variation to the clock's visual configuration. As such, over time this clock has
become both one of the most famous and most interpreted home accessories of the period. Its design has
been seen to represent an atom's molecular structure, as though it was an effort to pacify nuclear energy.
Lacking numbers or other conventional signs that indicate the time, it reflects a metaphysical state in which
time passes without reference. Whether this was the designer's intention when it was created is
questionable, as is whether Nelson even designed it. In his book, *The Design of Modern Design*, Nelson
denies that he or his associate, Irving Harper, designed the clock. He recalls that the design
appeared on a roll of paper covered with drawings by Harper, Buckminster Fuller, Isamu
Noguchi and himself, made during a night of too much drinking and a playful debate over
what would constitute a good clock. Nelson's contention is that the drawings bear
the signs of Noguchi's mind and hand alone, but the key attribution is given
to Irving Harper. Reissued by Vitra Design Museum, this clock
is available in a white, natural beech or multicoloured
versions.

Tapio Wirkkala's trumpet-shaped Kantarelli Vase, which gets its name and basic shape from a woodland fungii, was his entry for a competition to generate new designs for art glass organized by the Finnish glass-making firm of iittala. The original model, in clear glass, with a gently undulating and curled lip and carefully engraved on the outside with a series of splaying vertical lines, was produced only in two short series of about fifty models each. A modified design, with a more regular, less curled lip that could be wheel-engraved more easily, was conceived for serial production. It was not until early in the 1950s, when both versions were included in a series of worldwide travelling exhibitions of Finnish design, that the Kantarelli began to attract international recognition. The serially produced models were part of Wirkkala's contribution to the Finnish display at the Milan Triennale of 1951, for which he was awarded a grand prix, and, as general interest in post-war Finnish design accelerated, in 1954 the Victoria and Albert Museum acquired the more costly example. Since then Wirkkala's Kantarelli Vase has become one of the most frequently illustrated pieces of Finnish design, partly because of its visual presence and partly because it can be used to represent a starting point for the irresistible rise of Finland in the world of design after the end of World War II. From an aesthetic perspective, commentators have often remarked approvingly about the sculptural qualities of the piece, especially the flowing sense of balance achieved by Wirkkala between the undulating horizontal lip and the engraved vertical lines inspired by the gills of the fungus that enhance the waisted stem. In a more romantic vein, looking at the material, others have drawn comparison between the clarity of the glass and the frozen lakes of the Finnish winter. However, in Finland the popularity of the serial version of the Kantarelli has engendered an ambivalent and less nostalgic attitude, especially amongst a younger generation who recognize it as the kind of thing their parents were given as a wedding present.

330

Kantarelli Vase (1947)
Tapio Wirkkala (1915–85)
iittala 1947 to present

FROM THE COLLECTION OF MOLDED PLASTIC CHAIRS DESIGNED BY EERO SAARINEN ● KNOLL ASSOCIATES, INC., 575 MADISON AVENUE NEW YORK 22, N.Y.

The Womb Chair, launched onto the American market in the late 1948 and in more or less continuous production ever since, represents one of the most commercially successful and popular outcomes of Eero Saarinen's experiments with the use of organic shell-type seats in furniture design. These experiments were initially conducted with Charles Eames for the competition organized by New York's Museum of Modern Art, in 1941, 'Organic Design in Home Furnishings'. By the second half of the 1940s, Saarinen had begun to move away from the use of plywood, testing glass-fibre reinforced synthetic plastics instead as the basic seat material, as used in his final design for the Womb Chair. In order to keep the design as light as possible the shell seat was supported on a frame with thin metal rod legs and given a slim but sufficient layer of padding for comfort. Saarinen paid considerable attention to comfortable seating positions when working on his designs. He initially wanted to train as a sculptor, and this chair in particular shows his awareness and understanding of three-dimensional forms. He emphasized that people sat in many different ways, often in positions that would have been considered impolite in the past, and developed the form of his chair to allow people to draw their legs up on the seat, to slouch and to lounge. In this way the Womb Chair was created as a modern chair for a modern way of living. But it was also a chair with an enfolding, comforting and cloak-like seat that allowed the user a little space to withdraw and shelter themselves from the modern world.

The elegant sports car, created by the Italian car manufacturer and designer Battista Pininfarina and the Cisitalia company in the early post-World War II years, took the idea of an automobile being a piece of sculpture to the ultimate extreme. This sculptural definition was reinforced by the fact that Pininfarina's Cisitalia was selected by New York's Museum of Modern Art for inclusion in its 1951 'Eight Automobiles' exhibition and that its body shell is still exhibited in that museum's design section to this day. Pininfarina led the way in Italian design in the inter-war years, responsible for such classics as Lancia's dramatically streamlined Aprilia of 1936. The exquisite, abstact, curvilinear form of the 1947 Cisitalia undoubtedly

owed its origins to American aerodynamic styling but combined it in a unique way with the aesthetic restraint of the Italian approach to car design. Pininfarina had visited Detroit in the 1930s and was inspired by the all-metal pressings and mass production techniques he saw there. Avoiding the temptation to add American-style chrome detailing to his car, however, he relied instead on its form speaking for itself. To this end he left the vertical lines of the radiator grille unadorned and the sleek body form was left free from surface details and excrescences, everything being integrated into the shell. Seam lines and component joints were left exposed and no bulbous wheel arches were added. The minimalism of the design focused the eye upon all the necessary, functional details, the door handle and the air outlets among them. The exposed wheel spokes acted as a strong visual accent next to the unadorned body shell. The Cisitalia was extremely expensive to produce and was largely unsuccessful on the racetrack. However, these limitations have not prevented it becoming a classic object in the history of automobile design, even though it was only in production until 1952.

Cisitalia 202 (1947)
Battista Pininfarina (1893–66)
Cisitalia 1947 to 1952

Nathan G Horwitt wearing a prototype of the Museum Watch, c.1960

Nathan George Horwitt was a Russian immigrant who settled in New York City in the 1930s. Influenced by the design principles of the Bauhaus, he developed a range of products through his firm, Design Engineers, including radios, lamps, furniture, refrigerators and digital clocks. He called one of his products Cyclox and patented it in 1939. Cyclox was the initial inspiration for a watch face devoid of any articulation save a gold dot at the top of a circular field, signifying 12:00 and thin, linear minute and hour hands endlessly dividing the orb geometrically. The concept was radical in its simplicity, so much so that in 1956, it was first considered unworthy of a patent by virtue of its absence of defining features. Horwitt made the case that it was precisely the reduction of a timepiece to a circle, a dot and two lines that was truly revolutionary. As a result the design of the watch face was granted patent No. 183 488 in 1958. Horwitt considered the design as equal, in its essential nature, to the sundial. He had three prototypes made. One of these watches was presented to the Brooklyn Museum, another was accepted into the permanent collection of New York's Museum of Modern Art and the third Horwitt used to show to manufacturers. But these manufacturers remained unwilling to take on the production of Horwitt's watch until 1961, when the Swiss manufacturer Movado decided to produce the timepiece in limited editions and place them in a few New York shops. Exploiting its exhibition in The Museum of Modern Art, the watch was dubbed the 'Museum Watch'. Initially Horwitt's watch face was applied to Movado's standard programme and sold only in the United States, but it was eventually accepted into the company's Swiss programme and given a flat manually wound movement, Calibre 245/246, in keeping with Horwitt's concept of the watch casing. Ironically, the watch that took nearly two decades to make its way onto the market has defined Movado's reputation.

designers

1663
Household Scissors, Zhang Xiaoquan 001

1700s
Arare Teapot, Designer Unknown 002

1730
Sheep Shears, Designer Unknown 003

1760s
Sack-Back Windsor Chair, Designer Unknown 004

1766
Jigsaw Puzzle, John Spilsbury 005

1783
Hot Air Balloon, Joseph de Montgolfier, Etienne de
    Montgolfier 006

1796
Traditional White China, Josiah Wedgwood & Sons 007

1825
Garden Chair and Bench for Potsdam, Karl Friedrich
    Schinkel 008

c.1825
Le Parfait Jars, Designer Unknown 009

c.1830
Galvanized Metal Dustbin, Designer Unknown 010

1837
Gifts, Friedrich Froebel 011

1840
Hurricane Lantern, Designer Unknown 012

1842
Pocket Measuring Tape, James Chesterman 013

1849
Safety Pin, Walter Hunt 014

1850s
Jacks, Designer Unknown 015
Clothes Peg, Designer Unknown 016
Moleskine Notebook, Designer Unknown 017
Textile Garden Folding Chair, Designer Unknown 018
Scissors, Designer Unknown 019

c.1855
Tripolina, Joseph Beverly Fenby 020

1855
Colman's Mustard Tin, Colman's of Norwich 021

1856
Lobmeyr Crystal Drinking Set, Ludwig Lobmeyr 022

1859
Chair No. 14, Michael Thonet 023

1860s
Shaker Slat Back Chair, Brother Robert Wagan 024
Folding Ruler, Designer Unknown 025
English Park Bench, Designer Unknown 026

1861
Yale Cylinder Lock, Linus Yale Jr 027

1866
Key-Opening Can, J Osterhoudt 028
Damenstock, Michael Thonet 029

1868
Remington No. 1, Christopher Latham Sholes,
    Carlos Glidden 030
Tabasco Bottle, Edmund McIlhenny 031

1869
ABC Blocks, John Wesley Hyatt 032

1870s
Waribashi Chopsticks, Designer Unknown 033

c.1873
Sugar Bowl, Christopher Dresser 034

1874
Peugeot Pepper Mill, Jean-Frédéric Peugeot,
    Jean-Pierre Peugeot 035

1878
Toast Rack, Christopher Dresser 036

1879
National Standard Pillar Box, Post Office
    Engineering Department 037
Type Edison Lamp, Thomas Alva Edison 038

360-12, Rickenbacker Design Team **615**

Nesso Table Lamp, Giancarlo Mattioli
  (Gruppo Architetti Urbanistici Città Nuova) **616**

1964

Superellipse Table, Piet Hein, Bruno Mathsson **617**

Ford GT40, John Wyer, Ford Motor Company Design
  Team **618**

Model N. BA 1171 Chair, Helmut Bätzner **619**

Action Office 1, George Nelson, Robert Propst **620**

Falkland, Bruno Munari **621**

Perch Stool, George Nelson, Robert Propst **622**

Mikoyan MiG-23 Flogger, Mikoyan-Gurevich
  Design Team **623**

Sling Sofa, George Nelson **624**

Cesta, Miguel Milá **625**

Tavolo 64, A G Fronzoni **626**

Tokaido Shinkansen (Bullet Train), Hideo Shima **627**

Computer Mouse, Douglas Engelbart **628**

Max 1, Massimo Vignelli **629**

Lockheed SR-71 Blackbird Aircraft, Lockheed Design
  Team **630**

Model 40/4, David Rowland **631**

Algol, Marco Zanuso, Richard Sapper **632**

Segmented Table, Charles Eames, Ray Eames **633**

Asahi Pentax Spotmatic, Asahi Optical Company **634**

1965

Djinn Series, Olivier Mourgue **635**

Super Ball, Norman H Stingley **636**

Cifra 3, Gino Valle **637**

TS 502 Radio, Marco Zanuso, Richard Sapper **638**

Allunaggio, Achille Castiglioni, Pier Giacomo
  Castiglioni **639**

Super Erecta Shelving System, Slingsby Design Team
  640

Spider Lamp, Joe Colombo **641**

Spirograph, Denys Fisher **642**

Sedia Universale, Joe Colombo **643**

Baby Buggy, Owen Finlay Maclaren **644**

PK24 Chaise longue, Poul Kjærholm **645**

Thrift (1982 Café), David Mellor **646**

Center Line Set, Roberto Sambonet **647**

DSC Series, Giancarlo Piretti **648**

Eclisse, Vico Magistretti **649**

Snurfer, Sherman Poppen **650**

AG-7 Space Pen, Paul C Fisher **651**

Polaroid Swinger Model 20, Henry Dreyfuss **652**

Bultaco Sherpa T 244cc, Sammy Miller,
  Francisco Xavier Bultó **653**

Umbrella Stand, Gino Colombini **654**

Dondolo Rocking Chair, Cesare Leonardi,
  Franca Stagi **655**

1966

Grillo Telephone, Marco Zanuso, Richard Sapper **656**

1600 Duetto Spider, Pininfarina **657**

Egg Carton, J W Boyd **658**

Platner Chair and Ottoman, Warren Platner **659**

Cronotime, Pio Manzù **660**

780/783 Stacking Tables, Gianfranco Frattini **661**

Foglio Lamp, Afra Scarpa, Tobia Scarpa **662**

Dedalo Umbrella Stands, Emma Schweinberger **663**

Chicken Brick, Designer Unknown **664**

Bulb, Ingo Maurer **665**

Lamy 2000 Fountain Pen, Gerd Alfred Müller **666**

Timor Calendar, Enzo Mari **667**

Range Rover, Land Rover Design Team **668**

Swan 36, Sparkman & Stephens, Inc **669**

Tongue Chair, Pierre Paulin **670**

1967

KSM 1 Coffee Grinder, Reinhold Weiss **671**

Volkswagen Transporter T2, Ben Pon **672**

Cylinda-Line, Arne Jacobsen **673**

Hobie Cat 16, Hobie Alter **674**

Pastil Chair, Eero Aarnio **675**

Pastis Ricard Carafe, Paul Ricard **676**

Concorde, Sir Archibald E Russell, Pierre Satre,
  Bill Strang, Lucien Servanty **677**

Blow Chair, Gionatan De Pas, Donato D'Urbino,
  Paolo Lomazzi, Carla Scolari **678**

1968

Adal Fruit Bowl, Enzo Mari **679**

GA 45 Pop Record Player, Mario Bellini **680**

Sacco Piero Gatti, Cesare Paolini, Franco Teodoro **681**

Clam Ashtray, Alan Fletcher **682**

Olympus Trip 35, Yasuo Hattori **683**

T2 Cylindrical Cigarette Lighter, Dieter Rams **684**

Boeing 747, Joseph Sutter, Juan Trippe, Boeing Design
  Team **685**

Sling Chair, Charles Hollis Jones **686**

Pyramid Furniture, Shiro Kuramata **687**

Living Tower, Verner Panton **688**

VLM Switch Interruttore Rompitratta, Achille Castiglioni,
  Pier Giacomo Castiglioni **689**

Daruma, Sergio Asti **690**

Garden Egg Chair, Peter Ghyczy **691**

Tam Tam, Henry Massonnet **692**

Texts were written by the following (the numbers refer to the relevant product entries):

Simon Alderson 051, 056, 084, 109, 115, 121, 147, 175, 184, 185, 186, 198, 216 223, 399, 494, 515, 559, 587, 602, 604, 651, 708, 729, 807, 811, 858, 874, 876, 945

Ralph Ball 023, 157, 307, 311, 372, 408, 526, 509, 546, 608, 631, 844

Edward Barber 001, 025, 302, 342, 355, 398, 572

Lis Bogdan 289, 321, 352, 386, 572, 574, 710, 732, 746, 796

Annabelle Campbell 044, 065, 110, 122, 151, 159, 160, 201, 246, 273, 306, 319, 323, 382, 385, 390, 404, 463, 492, 495, 531, 536, 567, 589, 629, 646, 647, 656, 664, 671, 673, 687, 765, 777, 779, 790, 798, 805, 833, 849, 850, 884, 888, 892, 911, 924, 925, 949, 974, 984, 988, 991

Claire Catterall 454, 704, 722, 726, 736, 740, 750, 755, 773, 793, 799, 809, 821, 827, 830, 842, 857, 860, 866, 913, 920, 926, 959, 971

Daniel Charny / Roberto Feo 103, 108, 224, 247, 422, 559, 593, 599, 812, 864

Andrea Codrington 014, 015, 029, 069, 071, 088, 131, 217, 244, 247, 267, 285, 286, 288, 314, 341, 358, 402, 413, 481, 488, 506, 521, 553, 609, 658, 707, 723, 905

Louise-Anne Comeau / Geoffrey Monge 130, 235, 251, 347, 400, 586, 679, 689, 791, 827, 834, 887, 929, 962, 940, 951, 957, 975, 986, 989, 994, 997

Alberto Cossu 105, 190, 234, 281, 340, 407, 447, 669, 674, 739, 803, 931

Ilse Crawford 009, 048, 150, 154, 275, 375, 457, 469, 504, 563, 745, 895

Kevin Davies 061, 111, 198, 205, 206, 207, 208, 211, 243, 250, 282, 330, 331, 364, 378, 383, 420, 423, 438, 460, 483, 498, 500, 513, 519, 552, 561, 579, 612, 645, 694, 737, 743, 774, 786, 916

Jan Dekker 008, 046, 050, 076, 078, 080, 099, 141, 143, 168, 270, 284, 292, 353, 361, 377, 388, 426, 429, 432, 499, 518, 520, 524, 542, 575, 615, 713, 763, 886, 912, 955, 993

John Dunnigan 035, 254, 262, 274, 371, 418, 505, 534, 597, 881

Caroline Ednie 039, 040, 077, 086, 090, 112, 253, 272, 296, 363, 434, 449, 458, 459, 527, 548, 570, 573, 582, 594, 636, 659, 660, 666, 698, 715, 717, 758, 767, 771, 772, 783, 800, 802, 824, 825, 838, 845, 867, 872, 882, 891, 906, 935, 937, 953, 960, 983, 995

Aline Ferrari 010, 013, 019, 089, 169, 256, 335, 387, 442, 490, 868, 939, 998

Max Fraser 022, 072, 085, 142, 188, 204, 381, 405, 428, 444, 508, 555, 596, 626, 675, 709, 711, 738, 770, 788, 808, 847, 853, 863, 919, 958, 981

Richard Garnier 114, 162, 203, 213

Charles Gates 215, 351, 431, 516, 532, 535, 537, 640, 718, 795

Laura Giacalone 003, 446, 648

Grant Gibson 016, 047, 054, 060, 067, 117, 125, 129, 194, 236, 288, 304, 325, 354, 445, 594, 614, 618, 697, 730, 735, 756, 859, 873, 875, 883, 990, 933, 999

Anna Goodall 012, 028, 056, 095, 097, 158, 303, 412, 501, 502, 623, 630, 753, 820, 904

Katy Djunn 063, 140, 164, 189, 219, 220, 239, 312, 327, 585, 688, 841

Ultan Guilfoyle 092, 113, 133, 137, 231, 279, 298, 310, 316, 360, 410, 510, 493, 533, 547, 571, 569, 577, 591, 653, 677, 685, 701, 705, 761, 851, 880, 908, 932, 951, 985

Roo Gunzi 087, 237, 336, 368, 379, 389, 468, 889, 943

Bruce Hannah 011, 074, 278, 301, 411, 436, 451, 616, 780

Sam Hecht 479, 632, 637, 734, 969

Albert Hill 124, 305, 401, 409, 440, 453, 471, 475, 491, 525, 541, 556, 568, 617, 620, 633, 693, 869, 961

The following abbreviations have been used to locate the position of images in this book:

picture credits

Phaidon Press Limited
Regent's Wharf
All Saints Street
London N1 9PA

Phaidon Press Inc.
180 Varick Street
New York, NY 10014

www.phaidon.com

First published 2006
© 2006 Phaidon Press Limited

ISBN 0 7148 4399 7 (3-volume set)

A CIP catalogue record of this book is available from
the British Library.

Art Direction by Alan Fletcher
Design by Hoop Design

Printed in China

ACKNOWLEDGEMENTS
The publishers wish to thank the designers,
manufacturers, archives and museums that kindly
supplied the wide range of material included in this
book. Thanks are also due to the academics, critics,
historians, curators, journalists, designers and architects
who assisted in the selection of the 999 objects.